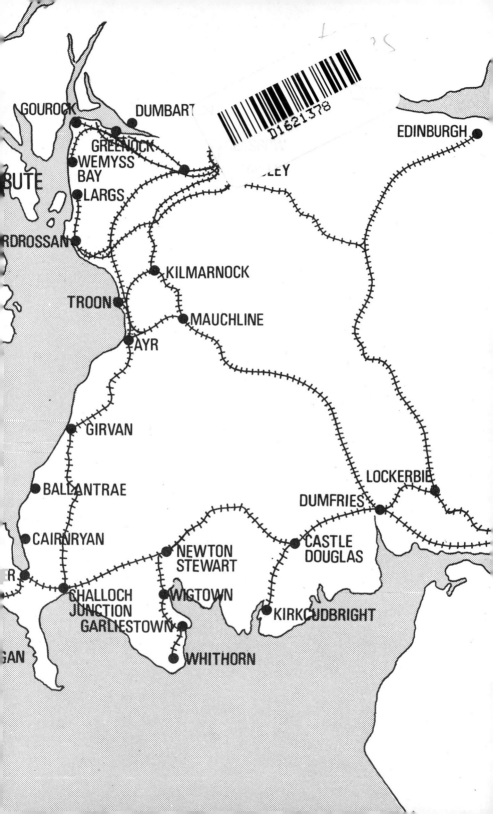

GOUROCK
DUMBART
EDINBURGH
GREENOCK
WEMYSS
BAY
BUTE
LARGS
RDROSSAN
KILMARNOCK
TROON
MAUCHLINE
AYR
GIRVAN
LOCKERBIE
BALLANTRAE
DUMFRIES
CAIRNRYAN
NEWTON
STEWART
CASTLE
DOUGLAS
CHALLOCH
JUNCTION
WIGTOWN
GARLIESTOWN
KIRKCUDBRIGHT
GAN
WHITHORN

THE SHORT SEA ROUTE

Frontispiece   *Princess Victoria* (1890) arriving at Stranraer

The Short Sea Route

PORTPATRICK — DONAGHADEE

STRANRAER — LARNE

CAIRNRYAN — LARNE

FRASER G. MacHAFFIE

19 75

T. STEPHENSON & SONS LTD · PRESCOT · MERSEYSIDE

First published 1975

© FRASER G. MACHAFFIE

ISBN 0 901314 16 1

Printed by
T. STEPHENSON & SONS LTD., PRESCOT, MERSEYSIDE

To Barbara

Contents

List of Illustrations

Third Section

Portpatrick Harbour c. 1819

1

Donaghadee Harbour *c.* 1834

To the left a mail packet is berthed at the south pier, while the original pier of Daniel Delacherois is seen in the centre of the drawing. To the right a temporary gangway connects the north pier to the shore.

2

Introduction

It is unusual to introduce the reader to a book with an admission of inaccuracy. But the title of this work should be in the plural, since we are considering three, not one, passenger routes between Scotland and Ireland which have claimed the epithet "Short Sea". These are Portpatrick–Donaghadee, Stranraer–Larne or Belfast, and Cairnryan–Larne.

For centuries Portpatrick and Donaghadee served as welcome havens for travellers between Scotland and Ireland, and this route is by far the shortest of the trio. But at the beginning of the nineteenth century demands for more efficient communications between the mainland of Britain and Ireland, together with the arrival of the steamboat, highlighted the limitations of the ports, especially Portpatrick. After two centuries as the route for the Royal Mail the crossing via Portpatrick was abandoned in 1849.

Towards the end of the period known as the "Railway Mania" plans were prepared with the object of overcoming the limitations stemming from the isolated situation of the terminals at Portpatrick and Donaghadee. The Government of the day guaranteed to render safe the harbours at Portpatrick and Donaghadee and to use the traditional route once again for the conveyance of mail if private enterprise constructed railway lines to Donaghadee and Portpatrick and established a packet service between the ports. Acting on the strength of this agreement of 1856, the railways were built to bring Donaghadee within easy reach of Dublin and Belfast and to link Portpatrick with Edinburgh, London and Glasgow, but the Government failed to carry out their side of the bargain and despite great expenditure of public money the harbour at Portpatrick was never made suitable for a mail service. Further, the Post Office indicated they had no interest in the re-establishment of the route as their mail between Ireland and Britain was already adequately served by the existing routes. In 1868, an attempt was made to operate a regular all-year-round service, but this quickly ceased and the subsequent traffic on the route was mostly of a summer excursion nature.

The railway to Portpatrick passed through Stranraer and a branch line was built to a new pier on the shores of Loch Ryan. While the mail was still passing through Portpatrick, Stranraer had seen the gradual increase of passenger and cargo trade to Belfast with ships of the Glasgow & Stranraer Steam Packet Co. and its predecessors. In 1862, the year that the railway reached the harbour at Stranraer, the small port of Larne on the shores of Larne Lough was linked with Belfast by rail, and it was to Larne from Stranraer that the first daily (except Sundays) service operated for the promoters of the two railways. This service of 1862 was the first fixed-schedule service between London and Belfast. This route was soon abandoned—prematurely it was later admitted—and after a gap another attempt was made to link Stranraer with Ireland. By now the Caledonian Railway, one of the railway giants, had stepped in and the destination was Belfast. This also failed.

After many months of negotiations, the Portpatrick Railway and the Belfast & Northern Counties Railway brought into being The Larne & Stranraer Steamboat Co. Ltd., with the former railway investing half the capital (mostly compensation from the Government following the breach of agreement at Portpatrick), while it was the directors and shareholders of the latter who raised the Irish money for the venture. On 1 July 1872, the company's first steamer reopened the regular service between Stranraer and Larne and, despite the pressures upon the crossing from within and without, we can trace a direct line from her to the "Sealink" ships sailing today on this route.

The success of the Stranraer–Larne route must be attributed partly to the natural advantage of the short sea crossing, where the slowest and most expensive part of the journey is minimised, but also to the reluctance of both the private and public sector to embrace the drive-on/drive-off revolution on other routes. As recently as 1956 and 1957 respectively, British Railways and Coast Lines Ltd. were content to take delivery of conventional passenger/cargo ships for main routes between Britain and Northern Ireland. It is indeed fortunate that persistence from Scotland overcame the inertia displayed by distant committees and brought about the commissioning of *Caledonian Princess* on the Stranraer crossing in 1961. During her ten year association with the Stranraer–Larne route, she wrote the success story of the sixties.

The Cairn in Loch Ryan had featured in several of the plans of the nineteenth century for linking Scotland and Ireland, but it required the emergency of the Second World War to bring about the development of the port of Cairnryan. Among the duties of the wartime port was the handling of the extensive milk traffic from Ireland *en route* to England. After years of doubt and speculation the potential of Cairnryan was brought to realisation by the opening in 1973 of a passenger and vehicle service to Larne. This is operated by the European Ferries Group of companies.

For a better understanding of each of the routes it is necessary to see them in the wider context of developing communications between the mainland of Britain and Ireland. A detailed consideration of all the services which have interacted with the routes linking Galloway with Down and Antrim is not possible, but appropriate mention is made of developments elsewhere where these have bearing on the short sea routes. From Scotland, reference is made in particular to the services of Burns & Laird Lines and their predecessors between Ardrossan, Glasgow, Greenock, Ayr and Larne and Belfast. From England the various railway-controlled routes to Belfast, direct and via Greenore, the Belfast Steamship Company's Liverpool service and the Preston-based operations of Atlantic Steam Navigation Co. Ltd. are introduced where this helps to sketch the background to the routes forming the main subject of the book. Brief mention is also made of the short-lived attempt by Silver City Airways to link Belfast and Stranraer with air car ferries.

The British Railways route between Heysham and Belfast, to which the Stranraer crossing was to be sacrificed in the 1950s, has now closed for passengers and accompanied vehicles. The Ardrossan–Belfast service of Coast Lines Ltd. is to be reduced, if not completely withdrawn, after the 1975 summer. Inevitably, part of the traffic diverted from these routes will cross by Stranraer or Cairnryan, thus continuing the growth pattern of the last fifteen years. In the summer of 1960 one conventional passenger/cargo steamer with the assistance of an adapted train ferry coped with the traffic, whereas in the summer of 1975, seven ships were plying between Ireland and the shores of Loch Ryan. All offer drive-on/drive-off facilities.

Much of the ground covered in this volume is new—especially the section concerning Portpatrick–Donaghadee—and as an aid to those wishing to pursue this area further, use has been made of footnotes. The employment of footnotes is not intended so much to give the pages the appearance of scholarship as to point to avenues which might be explored by the student of coastal shipping history. The average reader can safely ignore them without loss.

Since the research for this book was in the main carried out in Scotland, and as I am a Scot living in Scotland, there is an inevitable Scottish-bias built into the content of these pages. It is hoped this does not prove too irritating to those reading at the other end of the Short Sea Route.

Acknowledgments

Much of the research for this book has been conducted in various libraries, and I am indebted to the staffs of the National Library of Scotland, Edinburgh, the Mitchell Library, Glasgow, the Central Public Library, Edinburgh, Antrim County Libraries at Ballymena and Larne, the Wigtownshire County Library, Stranraer, the British Museum Newspaper Library, London, and the Public Record Office, London. The Librarian of the Shankhill Road Library, Belfast, has also assisted me. I have had access to records lodged with the Scottish Record Office and the National Maritime Museum and have received considerable assistance from the staff of both.

Various bodies have been approached with questions and all have replied with speed and courtesy—Lloyd's Register of Shipping, the Registrar General of Shipping and Seamen, Ministry of Defence (Naval Historical Library), Department of Trade and Industry (Marine Division), Atlantic Steam Navigation Co. Ltd., Ulster Folk Museum, Larne Harbour Ltd., Shun Tak Shipping Co. Ltd., the Blockade Runners Museum, Inc., and the offices of the Shipping and Port Managers at Stranraer and Holyhead.

Individuals who have made a contribution towards the finished book are the Misses Ruth Patterson, H. Joyce Taylor, Beverly A. Zink, Captain William Close and Messrs. Colin Campbell, W. Paul Clegg, John McCall, Don Patterson and Eric Schofield, Curator of the Clyde River Steamer Club. James Greer has done much valued searching in newspapers. My wife has found time in her busy schedule to prepare the chapter end drawings. Various individuals and bodies have assisted with photographs, and these are separately acknowledged.

Mr. Robin Boyd kindly undertook the reconstruction of the harbour plans for Portpatrick and Donaghadee and designed the map.

A record such as this book hopes to be would be impossible without the continual up-dating of information made possible by the dedicated editors of current and defunct periodicals over the years. My thanks go to the editors of the Clyde River Steamer Club's *Annual Review*, the Coastal Cruising Association's *Cruising Monthly*, the World Ship Society's *Marine News*, and to the former editors of the much-missed branch publications of the World Ship Society, *Ship Ahoy* and *Irish Shipping*. Over the past few years a valuable contribution has been made to the coastal shipping field by W. Paul Clegg in his monthly "Short Sea Survey" in *Sea Breezes*.

Over the years taken up in the researching of the book I have enjoyed the company of Mr. John S. Boyd, editor of the *Wigtownshire Free Press*, who, together with his staff, has given every assistance possible.

In the transfer from manuscript to book I have benefited from the professional expertise and personal interest of Mr. Leslie W. M. Stephenson.

Most of the typed draft of this book has been read by Messrs. James F. McEwan, Graham E. Langmuir, Geoffrey Grimshaw and Iain C. MacArthur. Each has brought considerable knowledge to bear and made helpful comments, factual and stylistic. Their encouragement and patience is greatly appreciated. Very occasionally I have put aside their suggestions and followed my own interpretation. Certainly the responsibility for the errors, explicit and implicit, inevitably contained within these covers rests with myself alone.

The finished article is dedicated to my wife, who has encouraged, searched, typed, victualled, and has been extremely tolerant during the years of gestation.

Abbreviations

A & M J R	Ayr & Maybole Junction Railway.
A & W R	Ayrshire & Wigtownshire Railway.
A S N	Atlantic Steam Navigation Co. Ltd.
B & C D R	Belfast & County Down Railway.
B & L R	Ballymena & Larne Railway.
B & N C R	Belfast & Northern Counties Railway.
B E A	British European Airways.
B R B	British Railways Board.
B T C	British Transport Commission.
B T S M (S)	British Transport Ship Management (Scotland) Ltd.
C	Compound.
C & C S Co	Clyde & Campbeltown Shipping Co. Ltd.
C & L R	Carrickfergus & Larne Railway.
C R	Caledonian Railway.
C (S) Co	Carpass (Shipping) Co. Ltd.
C S P	The Caledonian Steam Packet Co. Ltd.
C S P (I S)	Caledonian Steam Packet Co. (Irish Services) Ltd.
Cy	Cylinder.
D	Diagonal.
D & P S S S P Co	Donaghadee & Portpatrick Short Sea Steam Packet Co. Ltd.
G & P J R	Girvan & Portpatrick Joint Railway.
G & S S P Co.	Glasgow & Stranraer Steam Packet Co.
G & S W R	Glasgow & South Western Railway.
G S N	The General Steam Navigation Co. Ltd.
I o M S P	The Isle of Man Steam Packet Co. Ltd.
I T	Irish Time.
L & N W R	London & North Western Railway.
L & S S Co	Larne & Stranraer Steamboat Co. Ltd.
L & S S J C	Larne & Stranraer Steamship Joint Committee
L & S W R	London & South Western Railway
L M & S R	London Midland & Scottish Railway.
M o W T	Ministry of War Transport.
M R	Midland Railway.
N C C	Northern Counties Committee.
N E	New Engines.
N U S	National Union of Seamen.
O	Oscillating.
P & W J C	Portpatrick & Wigtownshire Joint Committee.
Parl Paper	Parliamentary Paper.
P R	Portpatrick Railway.
S A	Single Action.
S C A	Silver City Airways Ltd.
S C W S	Scottish Co-operative Wholesale Society.
S E & C R	South Eastern & Chatham Railway.
S R	Southern Railway.
S T O	Sea Transport Officer.
S T U C C	Transport Users Consultative Committee for Scotland.
T	Tandem.
T F S	Transport Ferry Service.
T H C	Transport Holding Co.
T T F	Townsend Thoresen Ferries.
W R	Wigtownshire Railway.

CHAPTER ONE

Betwixt Portpatrik and Dannachadie

FROM the early nineteenth century as far back as the written record goes, Portpatrick in the Rhinns of Galloway and Donaghadee in County Down served as the main ports for communication between Scotland and Ireland. Nature had provided each with a harbour between outcrops of rock running at right angles to the shore line. Each had an entrance some two hundred feet wide between the rocks, while Donaghadee had the added advantage of the shelter provided by the Copeland Islands. The Irish Sea narrows at its northern end and this constriction produced some powerful currents which when combined with the prevailing south-west wind could provide excellent conditions for sailing ships on the twenty-one mile crossing. It was often possible for ships to make across on one tack.

THE ULSTER PLANTATIONS

These small, natural harbours provided sufficient shelter for fishing boats and small coasting craft. These were flat-bottomed, referred to as "bottoms", and the method of landing was simple—pulling them up on the sandy beach. The shortness of the passage between Donaghadee and Portpatrick made for an attractive route in the days of sail and trade built up to the extent that larger ships came to be employed and these would anchor within the confines of the harbours and the "bottoms" would serve as tenders for cargo and passengers, while livestock swam ashore.

The traffic on the crossing increased greatly as a result of the establishment by King James VI & I of the Ulster Plantations. In 1607, most of the acreage of six of the nine Ulster counties was opened up for colonisation by loyal English and Scottish "undertakers". The idea was essentially one of "divide and rule". The undertakers were encouraged to bring over the bulk of their labour force from the mainland and these labourers were intended to have a civilising influence on the native Irish. On account of the proximity of Ulster to Scotland, a considerable number of lowland Scots found themselves in Ireland.

Alongside the Plantations there were associated developments in Antrim and Down. In 1605, Hugh Montgomerie from Ayrshire had managed, by a rather shady deal, to obtain ownership of a considerable expanse of land in north Down. While an "opportunist", Montgomerie proved a most able and energetic coloniser. The land he had taken over in Down was waste and depopulated, but under his authority it soon flourished and trade developed. Other Scots followed, and within a generation Antrim and Down were transformed, in population and way of life, into an extension of the Scottish lowlands.

The route between Donaghadee and Portpatrick had become popular for illegal as well as legal travellers, and in April 1615, Thomas Hamilton, Lord President of the Privy Council, wrote to James I indicating that the Council was to meet soon to discuss means of preventing this traffic. The Council was having trouble with disorder in Argyll and the Western Isles and some support for the islanders was coming from Ireland, though the Plantations scheme had reduced the opportunities of organised support in Ulster. The Council was now setting its mind to plans to restrict further any undesirable traffic between Scotland and Ireland.[1]

The Council's solution was to restrict the number of ports that could be used for crossing between Ireland and Scotland. The report to the Council indicated the findings of the Commissioners appointed to investigate the matter. The Commissioners declared "Donaghady to be the only fittest place, betweene the River of Strangford and the River of Knockfergus for the saftie of Boates, the good ease of Passage, and the abilities of the Towne for the entertainemente of Passengers". The person selected to put the Council's plan into action was Hugh Montgomerie, in whose lands lay the ports involved, Donaghadee and Portpatrick.

At Dublin on 16 July 1616 a Warrant was issued containing the duties and privileges attaching to Montgomerie. Montgomerie was to appoint a clerk at Donaghadee whose function was to keep a register of all passengers passing through the harbour, and he (Montgomerie) was to secure an oath of allegiance to the monarch from any passenger that aroused his suspicion. The Donaghadee—Portpatrick route was the only crossing permitted between Down and Galloway, and the traffic expected by the Commissioners is indicated by the recommendation that not less than sixteen boats of 8–10 tons would be required. The charges for the route were also contained in the Warrant, and we find that 8d (3⅓p) was the charge for a passenger on the crossing, while a man and his horse had to pay 2s 6d (12½p) in the summer and 3s (15p) in the winter. The sole use of one of the boats could be secured for 15s (75p) in the summer and £1 in the winter.[2]

THE DAY BEFORE YESTERDAY

A system of passports and customs would appear to have been in operation at Portpatrick prior to the appointment of Montgomerie in July 1616. In February 1616 the Privy Council meeting in Edinburgh considered a complaint from the Earl of Abercorn concerning treatment of a party of servants travelling from Ireland to Portpatrick. On 17 November 1615 they had arrived at Portpatrick and one Patrick Adair had demanded customs duty on their horses. This was refused on the grounds that the horses were not merchandise but the Earl's property for the use of his servants. But this did not satisfy Adair who "not onlie disdanefullie and churlischlie utterit mony proud, reprotchfull, and unreverend speitcheis aganis the said Erll and the haill noblemen of the countrey, saying that he 'comptit for no Lord nor Erll in Scotlande, he was in nane of thair commonis, and that thay sould all pay custome, nill thay wald thay, gif thay come athorte his way'," and then he "maisterfullie reft" the said horses from the Earl's servants and kept them all night. The Privy Council found that Adair had committed a great offence, and he was imprisoned in the Tolbooth of Edinburgh at his own expense during their pleasure.[3]

The arrangement of 1616 must therefore have been an attempt at tightening up a control system already in existence, but even this did not work very well, and in March 1625 the Border Commissioners were called to a meeting to consider a letter from Charles I containing instructions for the overhaul of the system. The ports of Kirkcudbright, Portpatrick, Ayr and Irvine were still proving to be easy exits to Ireland for "fugitives and malefactouris from the hand and stroake of justice".[4] On his accession to the throne in March 1625, Charles had inherited a war with Spain and saw Ireland as a potential danger to England. The attempts at repression of Roman Catholicism in Ireland had produced a nation which would probably welcome rather than obstruct any invading Spanish forces. The same policies against religious freedom had also produced an atmosphere of insurrection.

Again, in 1627, Charles wrote from London to the Privy Council in Edinburgh demanding that effect be given to the arrangements of the Warrant of 1616. The Scottish end of the route was proving particularly troublesome. New legislation was drawn up which restricted the ports that could be used for travelling to and from Ireland to Whithorn, Portpatrick, Kirkcudbright, Ballantrae, Ayr, Irvine, Largs, Glasgow and Dumbarton. Once more, the on-the-spot supervision of this operation was placed in the hands of Hugh Montgomerie. His fee for this office was to be half the beasts forfeited as a result of violation of the regulations.[5]

At the same time, the Privy Council made provision for the upkeep of the harbour at Portpatrick since it was "the most usuall and frequentit port within this kingdome" for communication between Scotland and Ireland. The job of keeping the harbour in good repair was entrusted to Montgomerie and in return for this undertaking he was entitled to charge a customs levy on all goods to Ireland leaving the coast between Whithorn and Ballantrae.[6] The following year, Montgomerie gave up this right at Whithorn, Kirkcudbright and Ballantrae.[7]

What was to be kept "in good repair" at Portpatrick is unknown: possibly a stone breakwater had been thrown up between the shore and St Catherine's Isle at the south side of the natural harbour. Certainly no major building had been carried out at Portpatrick. A harbour had, however, been built by Montgomerie at Donaghadee. This took the form of a crescent and was constructed of large stones. It was some 390 feet long and 20 feet wide.[8] The harbour was built to last since it was still in regular use in 1775.

A contemporary account conveys to us the level of traffic crossing between Portpatrick and Ireland at this time. On arriving at Portpatrick on the evening of 4 July 1636, Sir William Brereton relates that only one boat was found to convey parties to Ireland, whereas on the previous evening, he was told, fifteen boats had been available. Sir William was none too impressed with the facilities offered at Portpatrick and described it as "a most filthy, craggy passage, and very dangerous for horses to go in and out". On the return trip from Ireland the horses were landed by the simple expedient of throwing them overboard and letting them swim ashore.[9]

MAIL ROUTE ESTABLISHED

In 1641, rebellion broke out in Ireland and, at the request of the English Parliament, Scotland sent 10,000 troops to Ulster. The first party of 2,500 men left from the Ayrshire coast, a "place between the town of Ayr and the roads of Fairlie" on 17 February 1642 and landed at Carrickfergus where the garrison had been handed over to the Scots for their use.[10] A result of the Ulster uprising was a flow of refugees to Scotland and the presbyteries of Ayr and Irvine alone had to absorb more than 4,000. A more rapid means of communication was required between Edinburgh and Ireland now that the army was occupied in Ulster, and the Committee appointed to investigate the matter had their recommendation approved. The Privy Council on 27 September 1642 ruled that postal stages should be established between Edinburgh and Portpatrick and between Carlisle and Portpatrick. The former journey was to have the following stages: Blackburn, Hamilton, Newmilns, Ayr, Girvan, Ballantrae and Portpatrick; for the latter: Carlisle, Annan, Dumfries, Urr, Gatehouse of Fleet, the "Pethous", Glenluce, and Portpatrick.[11] John McCaig was appointed postmaster at Portpatrick and, like the other postmasters appointed to the route, he received £50 sterling per annum. McCaig was instructed to obtain a "post bark".[12] This, the first, attempt at a regular mail service would not appear to have lasted many years.

In the Privy Council records of the summer of 1642 we find another indication of the traffic passing through Portpatrick in the supplication lodged by a John McClellane. McClellane had built and kept in good repair and equipped with a good cellar a large inn at Portpatrick in which "three score hors and foot an once" could be accommodated. This had been burned down and the supplicant had borrowed money to rebuild since there had been every indication that traffic and trade would continue to be good. The "troubles" in Ireland following the uprising had so reduced his trade that he could not meet his commitments and he appealed to the Privy Council for help. The Council commended the unfortunate McClellane to the Christian charity and judgment of all noblemen, barons, gentlemen, magistrates of burghs, synods, presbyteries and sessions of kirks on the north side of the Forth. The recommendation was to last for one year.[13]

By an act of Parliament of 25 August 1662, arrangements were made to re-establish a postal service between Scotland and Ireland with eight stages on the route from Edinburgh to Portpatrick, viz. Linlithgow, Kilsyth, Glasgow, Kilmarnock, Ayr, Drumbeg (Turnberry), Ballantrae and Portpatrick. The Privy Council made Robert Mein, Keeper of the Letter Office at Edinburgh, responsible for the establishment of the postal route. His commission was two Scottish shillings for each Edinburgh to Glasgow letter, and six shillings for each letter going to Ireland.[14] Further "because he will be at great expensses in establishing these postes and building of a boatt to goe betwixt Portpatrik and Dannachadie, they doe therfore for his encouragment ordaine the soume of tuo hundreth pounds sterling to be payit unto him, the one half at Martimes nixt and the other at Whitsonday, 1663, provydit he cause make the said boatt for that service sufficient and that the publick packett be frie of any charges".[15]

The act contained provisions allowing Mein a monopoly of the mail from Edinburgh for a year but within a month Mein had to petition the Privy Council on account of repeated violations of his monopoly. A committee investigated and a proclamation duly appeared warning the public that it was at their peril that they infringed this statutory monopoly and at the same time Mein was vested with authority to arrest any offenders he encountered.[16]

The arrangement with Mein seems to have gone the same way as all the earlier attempts, for at their meeting in January 1668 the Privy Council considered a letter received the previous May from Charles II demanding action for "setleing ane correspondence betwixt this kingdome and Irelande".[17] A committee was set up, but we hear nothing more until the meeting of 26 November 1677, when plans were announced to replace the foot post on the

Edinburgh–Portpatrick route with a horse post. The postmaster at Portpatrick was instructed to keep a boat for a twice-weekly crossing. The Council wrote to Viscount Granard in Ireland advising him of their arrangements and asking him to see what could be done at Donaghadee. The Postmaster-General was advanced £150 sterling to enable him to hire or have built a suitable boat for the crossing.[18]

The Restoration Settlement of 1660 did not have the support of all Scots and there was a constant movement of Covenanters fleeing from Scotland and then returning once things quietened down. In the summer of 1679 an uprising in Galloway met its end at Bothwell Bridge, near Glasgow, and after this suppression many fled to Ireland. Hundreds were captured and returned to Scotland, landing at Portpatrick, Greenock and Port Glasgow (then called New Port).

The unrest in Ireland and Scotland continued and on 15 September 1684 instructions were sent from the Privy Council to the masters of ships using Portpatrick that they must lodge with the Collector of Customs at Portpatrick a list of names of all passengers crossing between there and Ireland.[19] The following month, Archibald Gray, "a sciper in Donachadie", was summoned to appear before the Commissioners of Council at Wigtown charged with carrying a renegade Covenanter from Portpatrick to Ireland and back.[20]

The accession of James, Duke of York, to the throne in 1685 provoked further discontent, and his deposition three years later precipitated revolution in Ireland, the outcome of which was decided at the battle of the Boyne on 1 July 1689.[21] This has been described as the "decisive battle of modern Ireland".[22] Certainly it meant that for centuries the Protestant minority were to rule Ireland.

Following the outbreak of revolution in 1688, an embargo on all shipping to Ireland would appear to have been imposed, for on 19 June 1689, the Privy Council heard a petition from the widow of a Robert Hamilton. Hamilton had fled from Ireland and died in Scotland. He had expressed the wish to be buried in Irish soil and his widow had arranged for the conveyance of the body to Portpatrick, but on account of the embargo no one could be found to carry the body over to Ireland. The Council agreed to lift the embargo for this macabre cargo.[23]

With the troubles of the 1680s the postal arrangement of 1677 must have been abandoned, for in August 1689 the Collector of Customs at Portpatrick, William Fullerton, was instructed to make arrangements to secure a boat to convey mail for the King and his subjects to Ireland.[24] Once again a mail service was established between Edinburgh and Ireland using horse post and boat via Portpatrick. This service was mainly for the purpose of keeping contact with the Duke of Schomberg who, with his troops, was in Ireland to keep control. Among the papers in the Manor House at Donaghadee is an account of the expenses of sending on the mail from Donaghadee.[25]

The mail arrangements would appear to have quickly fallen into disuse again, for in 1691 we find the Privy Council writing to the Lord Chancellor and Chief Justice of Ireland making the following arrangement: "We shall wryte to your Lordships every fourtnight and oftner upon any important occasione during this campaigne and shall transmitt our letters by the post to Portpatrik and cause the collector of the customes ther dispatch them by boat to Donachtidee as soon as can be".[26]

By the end of the seventeenth century the military, to be ready for any eventuality, had three sloops of their own based at Portpatrick and these could be hired by anyone wishing to cross. If there was space when the sloops were crossing on official business the public could be accommodated.

In 1695, in a further act "anent the Post Office", the Privy Council once again made arrangements for a postal service between Portpatrick and Donaghadee. This service was to be weekly.[27]

Following the Post Office Act of 1711, the post offices of Scotland and England were united under one Postmaster-General and a Deputy-Postmaster-General was appointed for Scotland. The second encumbent of this position was James Anderson who, in 1716, as one of his first tasks, visited Portpatrick. The Act of 1711 prescribed a daily service between Portpatrick and Donaghadee but the communication was proving difficult to maintain. As a result of his visit, an agreement was entered into between Anderson and the owner of the land on which the natural harbour at Portpatrick was situated, Mr. John Blair of Dunskey. For his part, Blair undertook to maintain the harbour, though, as with Montgomerie in 1627, it is unclear as to what structure, if any, was to be tended. It is also unclear as to what privileges fell to John Blair in return for the agreement.[28]

All remained quiet until about 1759 when no one could be found willing to take over the responsibility of supplying the boats for the mail contract at Portpatrick and the Post Office had to step in and operate its own craft. But the establishment of a regular mail packet owned by the Post Office did not remove the difficulties. Not only was there no adequate quay at Portpatrick but the crews of the packets knew they would be paid whether they sailed or not and, as the Reverend John McKenzie of Portpatrick wrote in 1791, "often chose to rest themselves".[29]

PREACHERS AND WRITERS

John Wesley embarked on his ministry of itinerant preaching in 1741 and, with the world as his parish, he soon visited Ireland. In 1765, Wesley made his first visit to Portpatrick when, on Tuesday, 30 April, he arrived at the port from Glasgow. His party received many offers of transport for the crossing, but the wind being "full in our teeth", it was the following day before they set out. "It seemed strange to cross the sea in an open boat, especially when the waves ran high," Wesley records in his diary. "I was a little sick, till I fell asleep. In five hours and a half we reached Donaghadee."[30] On this occasion the return was made from Dublin to Whitehaven.[31]

Two years later, John Wesley was forced to use the Portpatrick route when he could find no ship at Bristol or Liverpool. On Sunday, 29 March 1767, after the boat had awaited the mail for several hours, he and his colleagues were carried over to Donaghadee in three hours. On Wednesday, 29 August, John Wesley travelled to Donaghadee for the return journey, but found all the packet boats were on the Scottish side. He negotiated with the captain of a "small vessel" and made the crossing to Portpatrick[32] in five hours.[33]

An affair of the heart took James Boswell to Ireland in 1769, and on 1 May his cousin and he engaged the boat *James* and joined it late in the day. Boswell knew sickness was inevitable and hoped by sailing late to be able to sleep, since the boat had a "good cabin". He was indeed sick, and Boswell remarks, "It was pleasant to see the Irish coast". The breeze was moderate and the crossing achieved in five hours. By the time Boswell reached Dublin in pursuit of his "Grecian nymph", his passion had evaporated and he returned north, enjoying some riotous hospitality on the way. He would appear to have left Belfast Lough around 7 June for Glasgow.[34]

JOHN SMEATON AND DANIEL DELACHEROIS

Between 1766 and 1768 the military road was re-made between Dumfries and Portpatrick and, in 1769, Parliament released more money for improvements and plans drawn up by the civil engineer, John Smeaton. Smeaton had visited Portpatrick in October 1768 and found the harbour "entirely in a state of nature, a small platform for the more commodious landing and shipping of passengers, &c excepted". Smeaton's original plan of 1770 was to build a three-armed breakwater/pier. A breakwater of 120 feet in length was to be erected from a rock outcrop on the shore across a gully and on to St. Catherine's Isle. On the isle, the breakwater divided into two arms, one running for 280 feet in a WSW direction along the top of St. Catherine's Isle and designed to provide additional shelter for the harbour, while the other arm ran for 180 feet in an ESE direction along the isle and into the sea.[35]

Work was well advanced when, in January 1774, Smeaton wrote to his engineer at Portpatrick enclosing revised plans for the harbour. The breakwater running WSW along the spine of St. Catherine's Isle was abandoned and the ESE pier widened and strengthened. When work was completed in that year there had been created an inner harbour between the new pier head and the rocks on which the old platform was situated. The entrance to the new harbour was of the order of 100 feet. Some rocks were blasted and it was made possible for ships drawing 8 feet of water to berth alongside the new stone pier, except for an hour or so each side of low water. It was expected, however, that ships would still use the old platform as the principal place of loading and unloading, and the rocks on which the platform had been built were blasted to produce a fairly straight, vertical surface and wooden fenders fitted to the face. Steps were included in the new pier and small boats had access to these at all states of the tide. Smeaton reckoned the new harbour provided accommodation for up to 15 ships of 40 tons or less.[36]

The ingenuity of even John Smeaton, builder of the Eddystone Lighthouse, was not equal to the strength of the sea at Portpatrick, and twice, in 1786 and 1792, the north pier had to be strengthened by adding a bulwark on the seaward side. In 1802, the engineer John Rennie was called in by the army to repair the harbour.

In 1775, Daniel Delacherois, on whose land the harbour at Donaghadee was situated, petitioned the Irish Parliament for a grant of £1,500 towards the cost of repairing Montgomerie's harbour of 1626. It was not disputed that repairs were urgently required, and a grant of £1,000 was made. On starting the work, Delacherois discovered that almost complete rebuilding was necessary and this he commenced. In 1777, Delacherois petitioned for a further grant and received an additional £1,705. At the date of his second appeal the rebuilding had been carried out to the extent of 219 feet with another 221 feet to be done. The rebuilt harbour was completed in 1785 and followed the outline of the earlier structure. The area of the harbour was now in excess of 1,000 square yards.[37] The rebuilt harbour at Donaghadee possessed a lighthouse and, four years later, in 1789, Portpatrick was similarly equipped when a wooden lighthouse was erected at the angle of the two piers.

THE DONAGHADEE PACKET COMPANY

Little information survives of the vessels engaged in the carriage of mails in the period before the closing decade of the eighteenth century. An isolated cutting from *The Belfast News-Letter* of 2 May 1783 includes a report of Donaghadee Port Intelligence for a few days previous, and it appears that the daily service was covered by two vessels, *Kilwarlin* and *Sisters*, sailing "with the packet and passengers".

In July 1791, the Post Office entered into a contract with a Donaghadee company headed by the Marquis of Downshire, to provide a daily service between Donaghadee and Portpatrick, using half-deck cutters. The Donaghadee Packet Company supplied the route with four Thames-built ships of 40 feet length along the keel, *Hillsborough*, *Palmer*, *Downshire* and *Westmoreland*, each with a crew of six. The Packet Company received £700 per annum for the carriage of the mail, plus the passenger revenue. In 1821, the mail fee was increased to £925, and a year later rose to £1,000 per annum.[38] Agents were based at Donaghadee, a Mr. Lemon, and at Portpatrick, a Mr. Hanney. The two agents and the ships' masters were obliged each to place £50 in the Packet Company, and they received dividends, but they had no say in the company's policy.[39]

In addition to the complaints over the crews' propensity to "rest themselves", a very real objection under the pre-1791 arrangement had been that mail and passengers often took second place to livestock. England was finding it increasingly difficult to meet its own beef requirements and proved a good market for the farmers of Ireland. After a prohibition of nearly a hundred years, free importation of cattle and horses was again allowed in 1765, and it slowly built up and brought into being a small fleet of boats. For no apparent reason, 1784 saw a sudden increase, when over 18,000 cattle and 1,200 horses passed through Portpatrick. This was to prove an exceptional year, but for some time the annual movement was to exceed 10,000 head of cattle and horses. In 1790, the year before the Donaghadee Packet Company put its four sailing packets on the crossing, over seventeen thousand beasts were carried across to Scotland.[40] This traffic in livestock resulted in prosperity for Portpatrick and an attempt was made to establish a small shipbuilding business. The enterprise did not last long, but a number of sloops did come from the Portpatrick yard.[41]

But the four sailing packets introduced in 1791 were exclusively for mail and passengers and were described as "elegant vessels fitted with every accommodation". We have a record of the various charges raised in 1808 by the company: a cabin passenger single journey was 10s 6d (52½p) and a "hold" passenger 2s (10p). By comparison, a cabin passenger using the Newry–Liverpool packet was charged £1 11s 6d (£1·57½). In addition, there were harbour dues at Donaghadee, for example, 6d (2½p) per cabin passenger.[42]

In the same year as the Postmaster-General made this more satisfactory arrangement for the Scottish–Irish mails, there was a hint of what was to come when Parliament agreed to expenditure of £10,000 for the repair of the reinforcing bulwark of the north pier at Portpatrick.

UNREST IN IRELAND

International and home affairs increased the need for good communication between Britain and Ireland. Following the outbreak of war with France, in 1794, the prospect of an invasion of Ireland became very real. This was especially so in the light of the domestic scene in Ireland, where demands for reform were becoming louder. Some, however, did not wish to rest at reform but aimed more at the ending of the monarchy in Ireland and the establishment of a republic on the same principles as applied in France. Thus, an invading army from France could be assured of support from certain sections of the Irish population. The pointlessness of working for reform by constitutional means had been demonstrated for many by the recall in March 1795 of Fitzwilliam as Viceroy of Ireland after only two months in office. Fitzwilliam had recognised the reasonableness of much of the demands being made and had set about instituting some degree of reform. But he went too far for Westminster and was replaced by a safer man.

The situation steadily deteriorated, with minor insurrections in the north. The arrest of a French agent in Dublin, in February 1796, increased the realisation of the threat from France and, in fact, a French invasion force of between six and seven thousand men arrived off Bantry Bay in the following December. Less than half the force that had set out from Brest arrived in Bantry Bay, since the remainder had been separated by fog and never saw the Irish coast. By chance, there was no landing, due to a combination of bad weather and squabbling leaders, but it was a close shave for the Westminster Government.

On 23 May 1798, insurrection broke out, led by the United Irishmen, a movement aimed at radical reform and which drew its support from both Catholic and Protestant quarters. This achieved a short-lived success, but the arrest of the leader a few days before the outbreak produced a lack of impetus in the uprising. The United Irishmen had proceeded, depending on the arrival of aid from France, but Napoleon had to choose between Ireland and Egypt. He favoured the latter, and made only a token gesture of sending 1,000 men in August, but by then it was all over apart from isolated pockets. In mid-September another force left Brest but was intercepted off the coast of Donegal by units of the British Navy. County Down was greatly affected by this trouble, and from 26 June till 20 November 1798 the mail station was transferred from Donaghadee to Carrickfergus on the north shore of Belfast Lough.[43]

Part of Westminster's solution to the Irish unrest was the suppression of the Dublin Parliament by the Act of Union of 1801. This made rapid and reliable connection between Ireland and Britain even more urgent.

PORTLOGAN AND BANGOR

Because of the apparently insurmountable difficulties in making a safe harbour at Portpatrick, a move was made in 1802 to transfer the packet station to Portlogan Bay,[44] some ten miles south of Portpatrick. This bay was used on occasion as a haven by the sailing ships (and the steam packets when they arrived on the route) in the event of strong, northerly winds preventing entry into Portpatrick Harbour. The Irish base for the service was to be Bangor, a few miles north-west of Donaghadee.

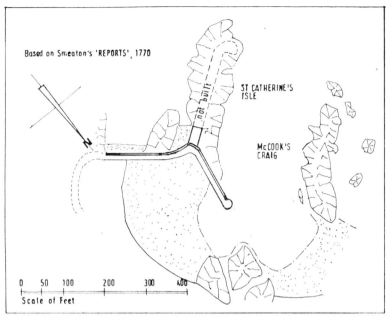

Portpatrick.   Above: John Smeaton's harbour.
Below: John Rennie's harbour with James Abernethy's North Basin indicated.

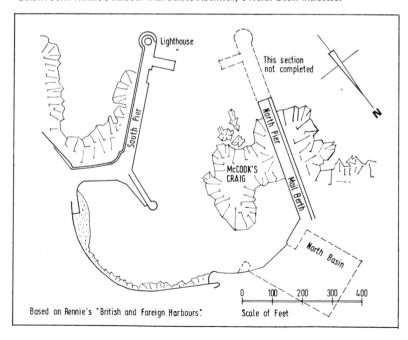

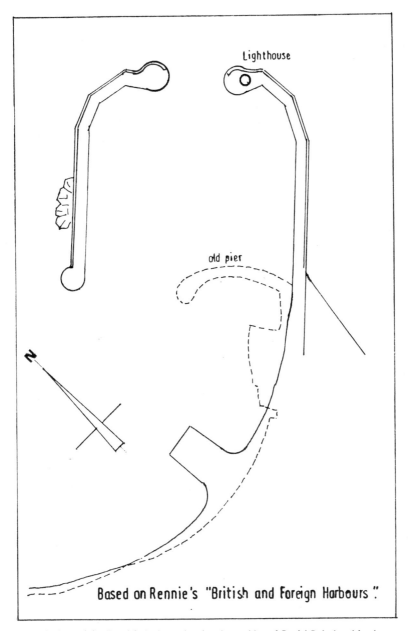

Lighthouse

old pier

N

Based on Rennie's "British and Foreign Harbours".

Donaghadee. John Rennie's harbour showing the position of Daniel Delacherois's pier.

It is interesting to note that as early as 1685, the limitations of Portpatrick were proving a problem when the Privy Council heard a petition from Robert McDowall, laird of Portlogan, seeking assistance with the building of a harbour, since it was considered impossible to extend the harbour at Portpatrick. This had restricted the harbour to small boats and had resulted in "much loss of life and cargo". The Council approved of the plan for a harbour at Portlogan and authorised a voluntary subscription within the dioceses of Galloway and Glasgow.[45] A small pier was subsequently built at the north end of the bay, but a hundred years later was reported as having been in ruins for some time.[46]

In 1715, the Geographer for Scotland, John Adair, was to express himself certain that Portlogan was the only place on the south-west tip of Scotland that had the potential of a safe anchorage.[47]

The Government, in 1807, requested the engineer Thomas Telford to investigate the requests for the abandonment of the traditional route between Portpatrick and Donaghadee in favour of Portlogan and Bangor. In March 1808, together with Captain John McKerlie of the Royal Navy, he issued his report which recommended strongly the building of piers at Portlogan and Bangor.[48] Considerations of wind, tide and expense all pointed to the benefit of the new route despite its greater length. The landowner at Portlogan, Andrew McDowall, had indicated his willingness to subscribe £3,000 towards the estimated cost of £8,400. In addition, he promised to establish an inn for travellers and to build a suitable road from Portlogan. Telford's plans for Portlogan involved a curved pier on the south side of the bay and a loose stone breakwater to the north, just beside the remains of the earlier pier. A slightly smaller version was built and completed in 1818 and the harbour enjoyed a modest livestock trade for some years.[49] The harbour soon silted up and access was available only around high tide.[50]

Bangor had a small tidal harbour built in 1757 for the protection of fishing boats. A sizeable livestock trade had developed from Bangor to Portpatrick and Workington. The ships involved in the Workington traffic were, in the main, colliers returning to England from Belfast. In the peak year, 1801, 192 ships sailed from Bangor with cattle for Portpatrick and 134 for Workington.[51] If a proper harbour was built at Bangor, Telford argued, it would cost, at £20,000, half the cost of making Donaghadee usable. Telford saw a great increase in the livestock traffic out of a new harbour at Bangor, but further, the Commander of Forces in Scotland had written to Telford indicating that Bangor would be an ideal port for the purposes of troop movements between Scotland and Ireland. For many years Portpatrick had been used, and the village possessed a barracks, but Portpatrick was soon to be abandoned in favour of Ardrossan, in Ayrshire, where a new harbour was being built to Telford's design. The Commander also favoured a pier at Portlogan, as this could serve as a secondary port and also for troops from the north of England. Bangor could serve both Portlogan and Ardrossan for troop shipments. He vehemently denounced Portpatrick. In 1806 it had taken nearly six weeks to move a troop of the 7th Dragoon Guards to Donaghadee.

In his report, Telford gave a first-hand account of some of the difficulties encountered at Portpatrick. In 1802, Telford had been at Portpatrick, and once his work there had been completed he had awaited passage to Ireland. It was the turn of *Palmer* to sail for Donaghadee that day and the vessel spent two hours in warping out of the harbour. The wind was from the west, but only moderate. The practice would appear to have been that when the wind was from South to WNW two small boats rowed out from the harbour, one carrying an anchor and the other 250 fathoms of rope. An end of the rope was secured to the anchor, which was then dropped, and the other end carried back into the sailing packet, which then began waltzing to clear the harbour.

Telford came out strongly against the Cairnryan–Larne Lough route for the mails on the grounds of adverse currents and the danger of the Maidens Rocks off the entrance to Larne Lough. He agreed Cairnryan might prove of use for troops since the anchorage was good.

In his conclusion, Telford suggested that the building of harbours at Portlogan and Bangor offered many advantages, not the least of which was the possibility of an improvement of the mail service. Paradoxically, however, he recommended the retention of the Portpatrick–Donaghadee route and suggested the mail should use the routes on alternate days or whichever route the weather dictated. Telford suggested that packets of length ten feet greater than those currently being used be built and a company corresponding to the Donaghadee Packet Company be established at Bangor. The two routes would introduce an element of competition which, he maintained, would remove much of the alleged inefficiency of the mail service.

A Select Committee, in 1809, considered the report from Thomas Telford and also heard other evidence concerning the question of the best ports for communication between Scotland and Ireland. The case for the use of Portavoe, $1\frac{1}{2}$ miles north of Donaghadee, was heard, but the bulk of the committee's considerations centred on Telford's plans. The Secretary and Treasurer of the Donaghadee Packet Company, Edward Hull, was vehement in his detailed rejection of Telford's findings. He produced figures which indicated the packet company had carried out its duties with exemplary regularity. In 1807, he maintained, the packet failed to leave Portpatrick with the mails on only nineteen days. The official returns from the Post Office in Ireland are also included in the published report and, rather surprisingly, we find, in 1807, only seventy-five days on which a mail packet is recorded as arriving at Donaghadee. There were gaps of as much as six days between arrivals. But even Hull had to admit that Portpatrick had its limitations and he suggested that Ardwell, between Portpatrick and Portlogan, could prove a suitable emergency port in the event of weather closing Portpatrick.

Edward Hull and his company must have carried weight in high places, since the committee in their report gave only qualified approval to Telford's plans. The committee recommended the immediate improvement of Portpatrick and Donaghadee harbours and also the building of harbours at Portlogan or Ardwell and Bangor. But "it appears to your committee that a diversity of opinion prevails respecting the making of new harbours". While acknowledging that the matter had been under consideration for seven years, the committee weakly recommended that further survey work should be carried out before any major expenditure was embarked upon.[52]

Some years passed until, in 1814, as a result of a further House of Commons Inquiry, John Rennie was asked to report on the best ports for mail communication between Scotland and Ireland. John Rennie had just taken his second son, also John, into the business, and the son, then nineteen years of age, relates how he was sent north in the spring of 1814 with one of his father's assistants, Francis Giles, to learn the business of surveying. They examined different places where it might be practical to build artificial harbours on those shores with little natural protection for ships. On the Scottish side they looked at Portlogan, Ardwell and Portpatrick, and on the other side of the channel investigations were made at Donaghadee, Ballyhone and Bangor.[53]

Having completed the surveys of the various possible harbours and charted the currents of the channel, John Rennie, Sr. recommended to the Government that the results of his work be placed before the Trinity Board, the lighthouse authority for England and Wales, who would make the final decision on the matter. In 1818, the board decided on Portpatrick and in the following year their vote went to Donaghadee as the Irish base. In 1819, the Rennies submitted plans to the Post Office for the building of harbours at Portpatrick and Donaghadee.[54]

JOHN RENNIE AT PORTPATRICK AND DONAGHADEE

John Rennie, Sr. died in 1821 and son John fell heir to the civil engineering business. Thus it was the son who transferred the plans from paper into stone and mortar.

Work commenced on the execution of the Rennies' plans at Portpatrick in 1820 and at Donaghadee in 1821. But, perhaps with the benefit of hindsight, we can see the tragedy of this expenditure. Both ports were obsolescent before they were fully operational. Both were designed with small sailing packets in mind. But the steamboat had arrived, and while this revolutionary means of transport was to prove a source of expansion for many ports, for Portpatrick especially the steamboat was to prove to be its undoing. As early as June 1815, Portpatrick received its first call from a steamboat when *Elizabeth*, bound from Port Glasgow for the Mersey, was forced to shelter in the harbour. She was stormbound for three weeks and eventually continued on her journey, only to suffer paddle damage that necessitated a stay in Ramsey Bay, Isle of Man. *Elizabeth* reached the Mersey on Wednesday, 28 June 1815, and for some time thereafter plied between Liverpool and Runcorn.[55]

At Donaghadee, the old harbour works were to be removed and two piers built at right angles to the shore. These piers were built out over reefs of rocks and considerable blasting was carried out to provide berths alongside the new piers. The south pier was built partly over the site of the old harbour wall and, unlike the north pier, was connected with the shore. The south pier extended for 900 feet in four cants or angles. The north pier, likewise, consisted of four cants and its total length was 820 feet. An entrance 150 feet wide was provided between the pierheads and the depth of water at spring low tides was 15 feet. By 1823 the south pier and lighthouse were completed and the whole project by 1834. The plans for the south pier included an entrance archway which incorporated a house for the lighthouse keeper, but this archway/house was not built.[56]

In 1820, Harbour Commissions for Donaghadee and Portpatrick were appointed and consisted of local gentry and landowners, and they were made responsible for the supervision of the construction work at the harbours.

The plans for Portpatrick called for the building of breakwaters/piers extending outwards from the existing harbour. Two piers were to be built over the rocks forming the natural boundary of the harbour. Each pier was to have a jetty 80 feet long and 30 feet wide at right angles to itself from a point approximately 120 feet within the extremity of the breakwater. The south pier was to be 500 feet in length and built in a south-west direction from the angle of Smeaton's pier. The south pier was completed in 1833, and the lighthouse built at the seaward end of the pier was functioning by the end of 1836. The northern pier was to be 300 feet longer than the southern pier. The two jetties would have reduced the south-west facing entrance to a width of 150 feet, but as it happened the north pier was never completed. In later years, Sir (as he was then) John Rennie criticised the Government for the piecemeal way in which money was made available for the construction, and often damage caused by the vulnerability of the incomplete works was left unrepaired for so long that further destruction and extra expense arose. In January 1839 the head of the south pier was breached in a severe north-westerly gale and the lighthouse undermined. Money allocated for the north pier had to be utilised in making the south structure sound, since an additional grant for the extensive repairs was refused. The light was not used after this and the work on the north pier never resumed.[57]

The work at Portpatrick was especially demanding, involving the difficult engineering feat of building breakwaters in water which at low tide was 21 feet deep. Much of the work required the use of diving bells. The editor of the local newspaper in Dumfries, John McDiarmid, was fascinated by the scale of the undertaking. "To obtain even a faint idea of the bustle and animation that prevailed at Portpatrick a few years ago", he wrote in 1830, "the reader must picture to himself from seven to eight hundred labourers, digging, building, quarrying". An added difficulty for the engineers was the isolated location of Portpatrick, since everything had to be brought in either over sea or land. For McDiarmid, "a visit to Portpatrick serves to elevate our conception of human ingenuity".[58]

But the local population viewed the progress with mixed feelings. A contemporary newspaper report from Portpatrick reads: "Though we are all delighted with the improvements that are going on, we regret the loss of a number of antiquities which time has rendered sacred in our eyes—the rock called the Old or St. Patrick's Kirk with the impression of the saint's foot three inches deep on it having yielded to the merciless attacks of boring irons and barrels of gunpowder. And his pole upon St. Catherine's from which he unloosed his barge when he set sail for that land—not of milk and honey but of potatoes and buttermilk—must soon give way to the same sacrilegious powers."[59]

CHAPTER TWO

Mail Steam Packets at Portpatrick

AT the beginning of the nineteenth century there were three mail routes crossing the Irish Sea. These were Dublin–Holyhead, Dunmore (for Waterford)–Milford Haven and Donaghadee–Portpatrick. Following the Act of Union of 1801 and the events leading up to it, improvements in the mail services were urgently required, and in the first instance Westminster looked to possible improvements in the road between London and Holyhead and at the harbour at Holyhead. (In 1818, Howth was to be substituted for Dublin as the Irish terminal for the route via Holyhead.)

Hitherto these routes connecting Ireland and Britain had been maintained by private operators under contract to the Post Office, but now the Post Office preferred to place its own ships on the mail routes. This change in policy was caused partly by the view of the Post Office that steam packets would give a more efficient service than had been possible with sailing ships, and partly because the private operators had neither the finance nor experience to promote this development. In 1820 the Post Office sought tenders for suitable steam packets from shipyards on the Clyde and the Thames. Wm. Evans of Rotherhithe quoted the best terms, and from this Thames yard the Post Office ordered its first two Irish mail steam packets. The ships' side lever engines were constructed by Messrs. Boulton & Watt of Soho, and the paddle steamers, *Lightning* and *Meteor*, took up service at Holyhead on 31 May 1821.[60]

The Post Office placed their own steam packets on the Waterford–Milford station in 1824. For some time the service continued without terminals at either end of the route with all the attendant problems that this brought with it: boating of passengers, mail, coaling from hulks, and so forth. In 1836, as a result of an enquiry conducted by Captain George Evans (no relation of the Rotherhithe ship-builder), a pier was built at Hobb's Point (known officially as Pembroke), and his suggestion that Waterford Quay be used in preference to Dunmore was adopted.[61]

LINKING SCOTLAND AND IRELAND BY STEAMBOAT

As with Milford Haven and Holyhead, the road access to Portpatrick was a considerable problem in the speeding up of the mails to and from Ireland. A Select Committee was appointed in 1823 to consider the road between Glasgow and Portpatrick, and their report included plans by Telford for a new road between Girvan and Stranraer to replace the barbarous track then in existence.[62] A bill was introduced into Parliament in 1824 whereby tolls from certain bridges around Glasgow were to be applied towards improvements on the road connection between Glasgow and Portpatrick. The justification for this lay in the contention that much of the traffic using these bridges was heading for Ayrshire and Wigtownshire; also the capital cost of the bridges had been all but recovered from the dues. This proposal brought immediate protests from many prominent merchants in Glasgow, who saw no good reason for the expenditure since for them the route to Ireland was now direct from the Broomielaw in the heart of the city.

From 1818, Glasgow had had a direct sea link with Belfast. In that year *Rob Roy* commenced a regular schedule of sailings between the two ports. Subsequently, many other ships appeared on the service, each surpassing its predecessors in speed, comfort and reliability. In 1825, the year the Post Office placed steam packets on the Portpatrick station, the steamships sailing between Glasgow and Belfast were *Swift*, *Ailsa Craig*, *George Canning* and *Aimwell*. In July 1825, the public were entertained, through the correspondence columns of *The Glasgow Herald*, to a rather unbecoming battle between the owners of *Swift* and *George Canning* concerning the merits of their respective ships and the defects of the other. *George Canning* seems to have carried the day in the battle of words, but in the summer of 1826 her sailings were between Glasgow and Inveraray and this might indicate the true outcome of the dispute.

The competition between the owners was fierce and fares were reduced to ridiculous levels. In June 1824, *Swift* offered fares to Belfast at cabin 2s (10p), steerage 10d (4p) and deck 5d (2p), and one can understand the satisfaction of the Glasgow merchants with this route rather than see their city's tolls spent on rebuilding a road to Portpatrick for the mail crossing, which at that time was still maintained by sailing ships. One unexpected result of the low fares was the mass arrival at Greenock and Glasgow of Irish beggars. The magistrates at Greenock advised the owners of the ships that in future these beggars would be returned to ships and carried back to Belfast at owners' expense. This produced the following statement from *Swift*'s owners on 11 June 1824: "In consequence of the difficulty of conforming to the provisions of the Act of Parliament regulating the number of passengers at the present very low rates of passage money between Glasgow, Greenock and Belfast, we have a new fare scale: cabin 7s 6d (37½p), steerage 5s (25p) and deck 3s (15p)." The economic regulator was introduced.

Another reason for Glasgow's lack of interest in the road to Portpatrick stemmed from that city having a regular sea link with Galloway via Stranraer and Portpatrick. In 1822, *Highland Chieftain* introduced the passenger and cargo service between Stranraer and Glasgow, calling at intermediate ports. In 1819, *Robert Bruce* had opened a steam service between Greenock and Liverpool, with the shallow-draught steamer *Post Boy* connecting to and from Glasgow. *Robert Bruce* called off Portpatrick and Ramsey, Isle of Man. In 1825, when the steam packets took up at Portpatrick, *James Watt* and *Henry Bell*, with *Post Boy* connecting with Glasgow, and *Majestic* and *Superb*, with *Sovereign* connecting with Glasgow, were all calling off Portpatrick and the Isle of Man while sailing between Liverpool and Greenock. In 1822, *Britannia* began a weekly service between Londonderry and Greenock, and in the following year a steamer link was established between Dublin and Greenock with *Emerald Isle* and *St. George*. Thus we can see that Glasgow had very adequate connections with Ireland by direct sea route and, into the bargain, had a service to Stranraer and Portpatrick for those travelling to Galloway.

The disinterest of the Glasgow merchants in the road link to Portpatrick and the mail route to Ireland is also understandable in the light of the Post Office Act of 1815. By this enactment the Postmaster-General gave implicit recognition to the services being provided by private shipowners when he consented to mail being sent by "ship letter" bags. Under this arrangement, the owners

C

of the ships were paid in proportion to the number of letters carried. But the use made of the direct route between Glasgow and Belfast would not appear to be as great as might be expected. For example, in the ten months to 5 February 1824, 1,630 letters went via the Broomielaw and 422 via Greenock to Belfast. This compares with over 8,000 going annually via Portpatrick.[63] But the level of postage charges was so high that we must assume that there was a considerable traffic in illegal letter carrying by the ships sailing from the Clyde to Ireland. Certainly the Act of 1815 was an attempt to stop ships carrying letters on which postage had not been paid to the Post Office, and it was declared a misdemeanour so to carry letters and customs officers were empowered to search ships for irregular letters.

Under the terms of the Act the ship's master paid a 3s (15p) deposit on receipt from the Post Office of the ship's bag and this was repaid when he handed the bag to the agent at his destination. The master received 2d (1p) per letter carried.

The bill proposing the utilisation of the Glasgow bridge tolls was thrown out in the House of Lords and the improvements on the road to Portpatrick had to be financed locally.

"ARROW" AND "DASHER" SAIL NORTH

The remit of the Select Committee on the Glasgow and Portpatrick Roads had included the consideration of the advantages and practicalities of placing steam packets on the Portpatrick–Donaghadee mail crossing. Their report, in 1823, came out in favour of the establishment of steamships on the crossing, but the fuller report in June 1824 shows the Committee unable to display the same confidence and the opinion is given that no great benefit could come from the expenditure involved in supplying the route with steamships until the road connection to Portpatrick was greatly improved. As we noted above, the bill designed to secure the necessary funds for the road works had not reached the statute book.

Another, and lesser, factor which led to the Committee's hesitation was the condition of Portpatrick Harbour. Work on the Rennie's plans for Portpatrick had commenced in 1820 but by the date of the Select Committee's inquiry little additional protection had been provided for the mail ships. There is no suggestion from the Committee of a need to reconsider the design of the harbour in view of the increasing size of cross-channel steamships. This is more understandable when one reflects on the division in opinion many years later by which time the points at issue had become clearer. For example, in 1842, Sir John Rennie was still claiming that no alterations were required to the original plans, as the needs of sailing ships and steamships were not markedly different. For him the ideal size of a steam mail packet was 110 feet in length. By that time the ships being built for the Clyde–Belfast services were 40–50 feet longer.[64]

The Post Office, in discussions with the Select Committee in April 1824, expressed themselves willing to try Cairnryan as a temporary station until the harbour facilities at Portpatrick were nearer to completion. In the autumn of 1823, the Post Office had purchased the Holyhead packet *Ivanhoe* and arrangements were put in hand for this vessel to travel north from her new station at Milford to try out the route between Cairnryan and Donaghadee. Whether

Ivanhoe came to Loch Ryan remains unconfirmed. If she did, she would not appear to have carried any mail between Scotland and Ireland. It is most likely the same fate befell these arrangements as the plans made the previous autumn to have *Ivanhoe* move north for the route. The Post Office's intention in the autumn of 1823 to try out the Portpatrick–Donaghadee route with their newly-acquired *Ivanhoe* had to be put aside following strong objections from the Donaghadee Packet Company.

The responsibility for the mail packets fell on the shoulders of George Freeling, Assistant Secretary at the Post Office, and in the spring of 1824 he visited Liverpool to inspect two steamships on the FOR SALE list, *Albion* and *Cambria*, with a view to their possible employment at Portpatrick. But they were found to be in poor shape and not adequate for the route.

One of the mail packet masters from Dover, Captain Hamilton, in giving evidence to the Select Committee on the Roads, recommended *Dasher* and *Arrow* of the Dover–Calais route for the Portpatrick station. They were small enough for the harbours and also were about to be replaced by new tonnage at Dover. *Arrow* had been earmarked for the Ostend station but could be freed until new ships were built for the Portpatrick crossing.

Despite the misgivings of the Select Committee, on the last day of 1824 the Treasury authorised the Postmaster-General to establish his own steam packets on the Portpatrick–Donaghadee service. *Dasher* and *Arrow* were to be transferred permanently to the route and the Post Office was to contract for the building of two packets for the Ostend route.[65]

The Donaghadee Packet Company, who at that time were still maintaining the mail service, had expressed their desire to continue to serve the route and investigated the practicality of chartering or purchasing a steamship for the route while maintaining two of their sailing packets as auxiliaries. In February 1823, David Napier offered the Glasgow Belfast ship *Rapid* to the company at a daily rate of £3 or an outright purchase at £4,000. But the company's treasurer, Edward Hull, had to declare to the Post Office that his company simply could not take on the considerable increase in costs involved with the steamship, and further their financial resources had been stretched by the recent loss of one of their sailing vessels. For many years, he maintained, the route had barely broken even, and with a steamship it could not help but run at a loss, at least in the early years of its operation.[66]

But, as elsewhere on the Irish Sea routes, the Post Office was to place their own ships on the route, and in 1826 the Donaghadee Packet Company received a half-year's fee of £500 as compensation for the loss of the mail contract. The one Irish Sea route which was left in the hands of private contractors was the Liverpool–Isle of Man service.

On 30 April 1825 the two ships from Dover—*Dasher* and *Arrow*—arrived at Portpatrick and took over the mail service from 4 May 1825. One is struck by the smallness of these sister ships. Measuring exactly 100 feet in length, they drew 6 feet of water and had a breadth of 17 ft. 3 in. Each ship was fitted with two side lever engines of 20 h.p. each which ran at 34 revolutions per minute. The paddle wheels are of interest, each being 10 feet in diameter and having twenty non-feathering floats. For comparison, consider the last Clyde paddler *Waverley* of 240 feet length with wheels of less than 14 feet diameter and each with eight feathering floats. The contracts for *Dasher* and *Arrow* had been placed with Wm. Evans of Rotherhithe in June 1821. *Dasher* was launched on 13 September and entered service on 17 October 1821 at Dover, where she was joined by *Arrow* on 25 January 1822. They were the pioneer steamships on the Dover–Calais mail route.

Captain Luke Smithett was transferred from Dover to Portpatrick and brought *Arrow* to the Scottish base, while *Dasher* came under the command of Captain E. R. Pascoe of Milford. As neither of the captains was familiar with the route, the masters of the sailing mail packets, *Hillsborough* and *Palmer*, transferred as "sailing masters" to *Arrow* and *Dasher*. Each of the ships had, in addition, an engineer, a mate, a fireman and three or four seamen. There was also a steward, but with such a short journey and the sailing being in daylight there was not much work for him, though we are told that breakfast was provided. The master of the ship collected the passage money and any money for freight brought to the ship.

Shore establishments were set up at Portpatrick and Donaghadee. Captain James Little was appointed agent at Portpatrick and he had local responsibility for the packets. There was also a carpenter who attended to minor repairs to the ships. At Donaghadee, a Mr. Lemon, who had been agent since 1791 for the Donaghadee Packet Company, was appointed harbourmaster. At each port there were employed about half-a-dozen boatmen, who not only assisted the packets in and out of the harbours but also attended to the coaling of the ships. These shore establishments changed slightly over the years. For example, a storekeeper was later appointed at Portpatrick.

Until the north and south piers at Portpatrick were completed, temporary provision had to be made for the steamboats and John Rennie arranged for excavations within the upper end of the new north pier. Here an area 200 feet by 110 feet was cleared and had 8 feet of water at low tide. A temporary breakwater was built connecting McCook's Craig and the north pier. This berth at the north pier was ready for the steamboats when they arrived. It was soon found that the northerly arm of Smeaton's harbour structure deflected the seas into the new steamboat berth, but nothing was done until after the mail service had ceased, when a storm badly damaged the old pier and it was dismantled and the waves allowed to break on the shore.

LOSS OF "DASHER"

Sunday, 19 December 1830 was a stormy day and as *Dasher* approached Donaghadee it was apparent that an attempt to enter the harbour would be dangerous, and so the mail packet lay off while a boat came out. The transfer of mail was accomplished, but it proved impossible to carry out an exchange of passengers, and those bound for Ireland were forced to remain on board *Dasher* for the return trip. When, between Donaghadee and Portpatrick, a boiler explosion put the engines out of use, the sails had to be set. On approaching Portpatrick a combination of the seas running and a sudden change of wind during a squall rendered *Dasher* temporarily unmanageable and she ran on the rocks two hundred yards south of the harbour entrance and became a complete wreck. One lady lost her life but the other passengers and crew managed to scramble ashore. Part of the wreckage and the mail bag were eventually picked up on the Isle of Man.

In January 1831 a Court of Inquiry ruled that the loss was in no way attributable to negligence on the part of the ship's commander, Captain William

Henry, or to the ship's sailing master, Captain McConnell (formerly of the sailing packet *Palmer*). In December 1837, a second *Dasher* was launched for the Post Office service, but her time was to be spent on the Weymouth–Channel Islands route.[67]

A replacement for the lost *Dasher* was quickly sent from Dover in the shape of *Fury*. *Fury* had been built in 1824 for the Dover station and at 94 feet was 6 feet shorter than the vessel she replaced. Her horse power was the same, with two side lever engines, each of 20 h.p.

Arrow was transferred back to Dover in 1833. In an attempt to meet the increasing competition there from private vessels, *Arrow* was lengthened by seven and a half feet and was fitted with new wheels, new boilers and more powerful engines. Captain Luke Smithett, who had commanded her at Portpatrick until 1831, took over *Arrow* at Dover. She was subsequently renamed *Ariel* and by 1848 was listed as an "old packet laid up at Woolwich".[68] The place of *Arrow* at the Scottish base was taken by *Spitfire*, sister of *Fury*, which was transferred from Dover.

It was clear from the Report of the Select Committee on Postal Communication, in 1832, that the ships were underpowered. *Spitfire* received new boilers in 1834 and her side lever engines given a thorough overhaul and larger cylinders fitted. *Fury* had also been taken in hand by the Post Office dockyard at Holyhead, and in 1832 had received new boilers and paddle wheels, and in the following year new cylinders were fitted. Both ships now had engines that gave each ship a total of 50 h.p. *Spitfire* and *Fury* were small ships (even smaller than *Arrow* and *Dasher*—a tonnage of 110 against 130) when compared with the Post Office packets on other stations in the Irish Sea. In addition, they were still underpowered. The 100 tons and 50 h.p. of the Portpatrick vessels compares with the Milford packets, where the tonnage ranged between 189 and 237 and the horse power was 80. At Holyhead the tonnage range was 230 to 237 and the horse power 100, and at Liverpool 300 to 327 with horse power at 140.[69]

One feature which distinguished the four ships selected for the Scottish–Irish mail service was that all were built with wooden sheathing instead of copper. All originally had sailed out of Dover, where the ships often took the ground, and it was considered that copper sheathing would be pulled or twisted away from the wooden hulls, thus adversely affecting the speed of the ships. This factor probably carried weight in the choice of these four ships for the northern station since the packets often had to be run on to the beach (for servicing and unloading) at Portpatrick, while a sandbar off the entrance to the harbour made grounding a frequent risk. To avoid this, the packets would leave earlier than scheduled and lie at moorings "in the roads", and a rowing boat would carry the mail out.

THE REPORTS OF 1830 AND 1832

Even though the mail steam packet service between Portpatrick and Donaghadee operated from 1825 to 1849, very little has been recorded about it. Perhaps, significantly, our main sources are the frequent inquiries into the Irish Sea postal services. Two important reports were the Twenty-Second Report of the Commissioners of Revenue Inquiry[70] and the Report from the Select Committee on Post Communication with Ireland.[71] The former was laid before Parliament in 1830 and the latter in 1832.

The Select Committee heard evidence concerning the abilities of the various packets on the Portpatrick station. Captain Smithett recounted that on one occasion *Dasher* while crossing to Donaghadee had been carried down as far south as Portaferry before she was able to make any progress north. He also reported that in 1830 the average passage time between Portpatrick and Donaghadee was 3 hours 18 minutes, while that for the return trip was 2 hours 56 minutes. The longest passage from Scotland to Ireland in 1830 had been 9 hours 10 minutes, and from Ireland to Scotland 7 hours 43 minutes. The shortest journeys recorded were 2 hours 28 minutes and 2 hours 26 minutes, respectively.[72]

These figures are fairly representative of the other years. Exceptionally, in 1826, *Dasher* is credited with a crossing of 2 hours 10 minutes, while the mail that left Donaghadee at 12.25 on 16 January 1828 did not reach the Scottish shore until the following morning at 10.40. The ship, name not recorded, landed the mail at Port Mullen at the north end of the Rhinns of Galloway.[73] On other occasions the packets were forced to use Loch Ryan when weather prevented entry to Portpatrick Harbour.

Even so, the reliability of these little ships was quite remarkable. In October 1825, Captain Smithett had to travel to Glasgow in an attempt to secure a chartered vessel for the route, while *Dasher* was at Holyhead for repairs. He must have been unsuccessful, for between November 1825 and the following February on a total of thirty days the mail was carried by sailing packets, principally *Friends* and *Prince Regent*, between Donaghadee and Portpatrick when *Arrow* was not available. At the beginning of March 1826, *Dasher* returned from Holyhead to Portpatrick.[74]

By 1829 there were only nine days on which one of the steam packets failed to leave Portpatrick, and on one of these, a day in February, the packet did not sail because the mail from Glasgow was delayed by snow. On the other days the packet could not put out because of the stress of weather. This reliability contrasted forcibly with the performance of the earlier sailing packets when, for example, in the year to 28 February 1823 there had been 97 days when the packets could not make the crossing. Likewise, the time occupied by the sailing ships on the crossing could range from $2\frac{1}{4}$ hours to a whole day.[75]

Captain Smithett reckoned that ships of the size of *Arrow*, but with engines of 30 h.p. each, could reduce the average passage by twenty minutes and the longer passages by considerably more. But the unfinished nature of Portpatrick Harbour made the Post Office hesitate before requesting the Treasury to authorise expenditure on ships. Once both the north and south piers at Portpatrick were completed there would be berths with 15 feet to 16 feet of water at low tide, but both piers had to be complete before the berths would be usable. Then, and only then, could the Post Office consider larger and more powerful craft for the route. At the time of the report the mail packets often had to take the ground on arrival at Portpatrick while they waited for the tide to rise and allow access to the mail berth on the north side of the harbour. £20,000 had been expended on building the north basin for the steam packets, but it quickly filled up with rubble and sand. Of the original estimate of £122,000 expenditure required for Portpatrick, by 5 January 1832, £120,200 had been spent and Sir John Rennie reckoned a further £15,000 and three and a half years would see the job finished.[76]

A happier story can be told of Donaghadee where, by 1832, the reconstruction work was well on the way to completion and there now existed a berth with 14 feet of water at low tide. The original estimate for the work had been £145,000, and by 5 January 1832 the outlay amounted to £135,000 with a further net expenditure expected of £10,000. Work additional to the original plans had been carried out. This consisted mainly of removing the old pier, widening the south pier by 10 feet and placing four landing stairs in the north and south piers.[77] In February 1838 the Harbour Commissioners considered their work was finished and they intimated their retiral. The Irish Board of Works was appointed in their place to attend to the maintenance of the harbour.[78]

Within the Report of the Select Committee we have the financial results for 1830 and 1831, and it is probably of sufficient interest to reproduce these in full:

	1830			1831		
1 Packet Agent	£300	0	0	£300	0	0
2 Captains	500	0	0	500	0	0
Cost and Wages of 12 Seamen	794	19	9	811	7	3
Cost and Wages of 4 Engineers	218	8	0	218	8	0
Coals	636	18	6	603	1	0
Repairs to vessels and stores supplied	446	6	3½	476	0	8½
Repairs to engines	95	17	6	29	17	3
Rent	5	9	0	8	16	6
Incidentals	83	13	10½	246	3	7½
	3,081	12	11	3,193	14	4
Receipts from Passengers, &c.	2,126	5	0	2,113	16	8
Excess Expenditure	£955	7	11	£1,079	17	8

We are forced to regard these figures as approximate since the total expenditure figure, here taken from Appendix 2 of the Report, differs from the corresponding figure given in Appendix 23. The Excess Expenditure/(Income) figures for the other mail routes to Ireland are:

	via *Holyhead*	*Liverpool*	*Milford*
1830	£12,042	(£2,359)	£9,534
1831	13,806	9,126	10,171

The losses at Portpatrick were, therefore, fairly modest when compared with other packet stations.[79]

But the peculiarity of the Post Office accounting is that no attempt was made to credit, actually or notionally, any route with the revenue generated by the mails carried. One writer has estimated the revenue from mails which could be credited to the Portpatrick route as at least £10,000. This figure produces a substantial surplus for the route.[80]

Of the Irish mail routes, Portpatrick had the greatest number of passengers. In the 1830s the passengers averaged over 10,000 a year, but a peculiarity of the traffic, which adversely affected the financial results, was that most of the passengers travelled deck rather than cabin. For example, in 1831 against 12,628 deck passengers at 2s (10p) each, there were only 1,020 cabin passengers at 8s (40p) each. No doubt the fact that the passage was a daylight crossing worked against revenue, but further, a large proportion of those travelling were harvesters and other labourers. This is borne out by the figures for, say, 1828, where 27 per cent of the year's traffic crossed in the months of August and September, and these 3,300 passengers, plus 29 carriages and 49 horses, produced only £567 revenue. In addition, there was a small, but probably not insignificant, traffic in students. Until the establishment, in 1849, of the Queen's University in Ireland, with colleges at Belfast, Cork and Galway, many students were forced to travel to one of the Scottish universities, where fees were lower, scholarships available to Noncomformists and the oppressive Anglican atmosphere of the University of Dublin (Trinity College) was absent. It is interesting to see that these small craft during the twenties and thirties managed to carry on average 60–70 four-wheeled carriages each year. Even in those distant days the road vehicle required to be catered for.[81]

The scale of charges which applied in 1832 is of interest:

Cabin passengers and female servants	8s (40p)
Children under 10	5s (25p)
Deck passengers	2s (10p)
4-wheeled carriages	£2
2-wheeled carriages	15s (75p)
Horses	8s (40p)

The after cabin could be hired for a party of not more than six for £3.[82]

These rates compare unfavourably with the charges operating in the summer of 1832 on the direct Glasgow–Belfast route. A price war was in progress with G. & J. Burns offering a cabin fare to Belfast of 2s 6d (12½p) and a steerage of 6d (2½p). The opposition maintained a semblance of economic sanity by charging double these amounts and appealed to the public for their support "to prevent any unjustifiable attempt at monopoly".[83] The 1832 Select Committee recommended a reduction in the fares on the Portpatrick packets, e.g. cabin passengers down to 4s (20p). They also proposed that a charge of 6d (2½p) should be introduced for dogs![84] The various recommendations do not seem to have been adopted, but a two-tier fare structure was introduced for deck passengers—5s (25p) and 2s (10p)—"according to the appearance of the individual". The ships' masters were given no guidelines as to the execution of this bureaucracy.[85] It was March 1837 before a significant reduction was made in the fares applying on the crossing between Portpatrick and Donaghadee.[86]

The Select Committee of 1832 gave consideration to the mail coach connections for the mail packets. The bulk of the mail using the Portpatrick route came from the Glasgow and Edinburgh areas. The mail coach left Glasgow at 1645 and arrived in Ayr at 2100. From Ayr, a gig conveyed the mail to Portpatrick, where it was expected to arrive at 0506. The mail coach left Edinburgh General Post Office at 2130 and reached Dumfries at 0630. From Carlisle a coach left at 0620 and arrived at Dumfries at 1003. At 1015, the mail from Edinburgh and Carlisle left Dumfries and after a half-hour break at Newton Stewart for refreshment at the Grapes Inn was due at Portpatrick at 2147. The packets were scheduled to leave Portpatrick at 0550, and this normally gave ample time for the mail from Edinburgh, Carlisle, and also for the small amount of mail from London that travelled on the 0620 coach from Carlisle, but the packets were often delayed by the late arrival of the gig from Ayr conveying the Glasgow mail. At Donaghadee the mail coach left for Belfast as soon as the mail had been transferred from the steamer, the coach taking about two and a half hours for the eighteen mile journey. Over the years the departure time for the packets from Portpatrick became steadily earlier and by 1848 the mail sailed at 0440 in summer and 0500 in winter.

On the return journey, the mail left Belfast by coach at 0845 and the packet was scheduled to leave Donaghadee at noon. The mail for Glasgow left Portpatrick at 1600 and reached the city at 0530. A 1900 departure was made from Portpatrick for Dumfries, arriving at 0626. The coach for Edinburgh left Dumfries at 0730 and arrived at the General Post Office at 1540. The mail for Carlisle and England left Dumfries at 1400, arriving at Carlisle at 1743. The precise timing to the minute seems incredible, though from the disparity of the timings appearing within the report one is led to treat all times as approximate.

In their report, the Select Committee were critical of the arrangements for the Ayr–Portpatrick leg of the journey between Glasgow and Portpatrick and saw potential for time-saving on that section.[87]

LOCH RYAN–LARNE LOUGH

Part of the remit of the 1832 Select Committee was the consideration of a petition from the merchants of Belfast seeking the transference of the mail route to the longer crossing between Belfast Lough and Cairnryan. But various reasons were put forward by the Select Committee for the refusal of this request. Shoals at the entrance to Belfast Lough prevented vessels from approaching within three or four miles of the town at certain states of the tide. The passage from Cairnryan to either Belfast Lough or Larne Lough would be right into the prevailing south-west wind. But the overwhelming factor was the expenditure already incurred at both Donaghadee and Portpatrick, where £255,000 had been spent in an attempt to improve the harbours. The main factor, in the view of the Select Committee, which caused the delay in the mails was the Glasgow mail, and the Committee urged the Post Office to examine this weak link and to make better arrangements than a gig between Ayr and Portpatrick. The road between Ayr and Portpatrick had been greatly improved, apart from a four mile stretch between Ballantrae and Cairnryan. The money had run out and the maximum credit available on the strength of future tolls had already been secured. The local commissioners were encouraged to make every endeavour to complete the road.[88] It was October 1836 before the gig was replaced by a mail coach.[89] A compromise plan to develop Carrickfergus as a port for Belfast was also rejected and plans prepared by John Rennie, in 1832, for the port were put aside.[90] The advocates of Larne as a packet port for the Ulster capital were also disappointed. It was admitted that the haven possessed only a tidal quay, but the approach to the lough had been made much safer by the recent building of lighthouses on the Maidens.

The complaints over delays and requests for change continued unabated, and, in 1835, a Post Office Inquiry was set up to look into the matter again and advise on the route between Cairnryan and Larne. On 24 January 1836, one of the commissioners of the Post Office Inquiry, Captain George Evans, R.N., visited Stranraer and Portpatrick. He happened to pick a day which was claimed to be the stormiest for more than twenty years. The mail boat could not put out from Portpatrick, but in his opinion a suitable steam vessel could have crossed to Ireland from Loch Ryan. His recommendation to the Inquiry was that on the Scottish side the packet station should be situated in Loch Ryan. This had two advantages. The loch provided excellent shelter and the cost of building an adequate quay would cost less than a quarter of the sum still required to complete the harbour at Portpatrick. Following the inspection of Portpatrick and Loch Ryan by Captain Evans, *The Glasgow Herald* reported confidently that "We have the greatest authority to state that the memorial from the merchants of Glasgow will be immediately attended to and that the packet station will be removed from Portpatrick to Loch Ryan".[91]

When the report of the Inquiry was published in 1836, a strong recommendation was made for the adoption of the Loch Ryan–Larne Lough route. The case for Larne had been considerably strengthened following the building of a pier, in 1835, which was free of any tidal restrictions. This pier, described as being of "rather a cheap and temporary nature" consisting of rough pieces of timber driven down into the mud "in a simple, plain manner", had been built at the request of the owners of the ship *Glen Albyn*, which in 1835 had began trading regularly between Glasgow, Brodick, Lamlash, Campbeltown, Larne and Oban. *Coleraine*, of the Portrush Steam Navigation Company also made calls regularly at the pier while she plied between Portrush and Liverpool. The owner of the pier at Larne had indicated that the pier was available to the mail packets free of charge.[92] No doubt stemming from optimism over the transfer of the Irish packet station from Donaghadee to the north side of Belfast Lough, two proposals were published for railways from Belfast. One was to have Carrickfergus as its terminus with regular communication to Scotland and England, transforming the village into "the Kingstown of Belfast". The second project saw Larne as potentially "an admirable packet station".[93]

But the recommendation of the Inquiry and the offer of the Larne Pier owner were put on the shelf to join all the other reports and money continued to be spent at Portpatrick and the complaints filed away. Captain Evans's advice may have been accepted regarding the Waterford service, but his counsels on Portpatrick went unheeded.

Six years later, yet another Select Committee reporting in 1842 came out strongly in favour of the Cairnryan–Larne route for the mail service, but after the money spent at Portpatrick a change of policy would have amounted to an admission of defeat on the part of the engineers. Sir John Rennie was still adamant that there was no reason why Portpatrick could not be rendered a safe port for the mail packets. Captain Evans also gave evidence and stated bluntly that attempts to build the piers out from the rock face was "a useless expense, just the same as throwing the money into the sea". When the report was considered the engineers carried the day against the navigators.[94]

In 1845, the patience of Captain George Evans must have been sorely tried when he was asked once again to report on Portpatrick and Donaghadee Harbours. On 17 December 1845, he crossed from Donaghadee on the mail packet *Pike* and five days later sailed on *Albion* from Stranraer to Belfast. "Portpatrick can never be made safe", he wrote. Larne he described as an "excellent port. A lighthouse has been erected on the eastern side of the entrance and there is a quay 200 feet long with jetties projecting on piles, having 16 feet water at low spring". In Loch Ryan a tower had been built at Cairn Point and a lantern was to be placed in it during the summer of 1846. He considered Finnart Bay and Stranraer as possible packet stations but still preferred Cairnryan.[95]

Criticism of the Post Office was nothing new. The Report of a Special Commission appointed in 1787 and the Seventh Report of the Select Committee on Finance issued in July 1797 complained of abuses and inefficiencies highlighted in earlier reports which had been left undisturbed, even following a reconstruction of the Post Office management in 1793.

The Reports of Special Commissioners appointed in 1787 and the Seventh Report in 1797 both exposed a system groaning under the weight of inefficiency, corruption and sinecures. Ever since the Post Office Act of 1711, the postal service had been looked upon as a source of revenue. Francis Freeling, Secretary to the Post Office from 1797 to 1836, wrote just before his death, "To make the Post Office as productive as possible was long ago impressed upon me by successive ministers as a duty which I was under a solemn obligation to discharge. And not long ago, is it not within the last six months that the present Chancellor of the Exchequer has charged me not to let the revenue go down?"[96] This attitude, plus an aristocracy whose birthright it was to hold well paid, nominal appointments bled the Post Office dry. Postal rates had been pushed upwards in an attempt to meet the financial needs of the day and this resulted in an increasing amount of evasion. Thus the revenue for 1835 was less than that of 1815—despite an increase of a third in the size of the country's population.[97] The malaise applying to the Post Office in general also applied to the Packet Service in particular. Many still could not see the Post Office at St. Martin's-le-Grand as the ideal body to be running steamships.

The floodgates to change were swung full open following the Reform Act of 1832. Apart from its sweeping changes in franchise, it reflected the admission of the Government that reform in all areas was demanded—parliamentary, ecclesiastical and in public services such as the Post Office.

Greenock sent as its first representative to Parliament one Robert Wallace. Wallace was involved in trade at home and overseas and became a strong critic of the unwillingness of the Post Office to improve its services. In the autumn of 1833 his campaign started and by perseverance he saw in 1835 a commission appointed "to inquire into the management of the Post Office Department". Their Sixth Report, issued in 1836, to which we already made brief reference, covered the packet boat operations and confirmed Wallace's contention that all was not well.

The Commission criticised the Post Office severely for the way in which the dockyard at Holyhead was run. The dockyard had been established by the Post Office for the maintenance of its Irish Sea and Channel Islands steam packets. These journeys were not without their hazards, and we have a record that in 1827 both the Portpatrick packets, *Dasher* and *Arrow*, had to shelter at Douglas, Isle of Man, while returning north from Holyhead.[98]

A sailing cutter, *Iris*, was based at Holyhead as reserve ship but did little actual work. Originally on the Milford station, her last spell in service was from October 1826 until July 1827 on the Weymouth–Channel Islands mail route. She was displaced on the arrival of the first steam packet on the route.[99] From the beginning of 1831 until the date of the Commission's inquiry she had not moved from Holyhead. *Iris* did visit Portpatrick on at least three occasions: twice in July 1829 with the agent from Holyhead and the following month with the Assistant Secretary of the Post Office, George Freeling, who had responsibilities for the packets and again with the Holyhead agent. It was revealed that the administration of the dockyard was so bad as to invite corruption. But this criticism was also applied to the packet stations themselves and the Post Office was severely censured for the "evil consequences which have resulted at the different stations from the absence of proper superintendence".[100]

The Sixth Report of the Commissioners on the subject of the Post Office packets reinforced the adverse reports of previous years. All had advocated a change of route. But this was not accepted. A new recommendation emanating from the April 1836 Report was, however, adopted. The Commissioners "considered it expedient . . . that this Branch of the Establishment should be transferred to the Board of Admiralty".[101] Since 1823, the longer-haul mail boats operating from Falmouth had been under the jurisdiction of the Admiralty, and from 16 January 1837 the mail ships on the Irish Sea, Channel Islands and English Channel routes were transferred to the same body. The seat of management moved from St. Martin's-le-Grand to Somerset House, where Sir Edward Parry had been appointed Comptroller of Steam Machinery and Packet Services. We are told the "and Packet Services" was handed to Sir Edward as an afterthought and he found this area of his responsibilities a continual trial.[102]

The responsibility for the operating of the ships now rested with the Admiralty, but the Post Office still stipulated the hours of sailing. Whether the Admiralty gave a more efficient and economic service is a moot point. Throughout the inquiries the approach to the financial and economic aspects of the packet operations appears to us today as inadequate. As we noted earlier, in striking a deficit or surplus no credit is included for the mail carried on the routes and the only sources of revenue included are passenger fares and the income from the small amounts of cargo carried. Some years later, when the mail was once again being carried across the Irish Sea under contract, the Post Office found itself paying out sums of money to the carriers (except between Greenock and Belfast) which if included, at least notionally, in the considerations leading to the reports of the 1830s would have produced a significantly healthier financial situation than that actually laid before Parliament. Lord Auckland, First Lord of the Admiralty, maintained that Portpatrick covered its costs if credited with the postage earned.[103] Shortly after the Admiralty took over responsibility for the management of the services, the mail packets were renamed. At Portpatrick *Fury* and *Spitfire* became *Asp* and *Pike*, respectively.[104]

The Sixth Report on the Management of the Post Office Department of 1836 had favoured returning to the practice of offering the carriage of mail out to contract rather than continuing with established packets, whether Post Office or Admiralty operated. At the same time the Commissioners had recognised that it would be neither safe nor expedient to throw all six stations open to competition at once. The recommendation that the Liverpool–Dublin route be opened to public contract was accepted while the Admiralty, as we have noted, took over the responsibility for the other routes.

An invitation to tender was put out for the Liverpool route, but only one offer received. This was from the City of Dublin Steam Packet Company who asked for £34,000. Negotiations were eventually completed and the company carried the mail from 20 June 1839. For the agreed £9,000 the company provided a daily evening packet scheduled at times to suit the company within a three hour range, while the Admiralty continued to give a daily morning sailing. The bulk of the passengers travelled on the City of Dublin's ships and this corrects the superficial view that at £9,000 the Admiralty and the Post Office had driven a good bargain. "The conclusion is inescapable that under the new arrangement the contribution of the taxpayer was greater while the packet service had deteriorated in respect of regularity of sailings."[105]

But the principle had been accepted that contract was better than establishment. As time passed the future of Portpatrick became increasingly in question. It looked as if the work on building the harbour was never going to be finished. Strong recommendations for the transfer of the mail to another route had been made in 1830, 1836 and 1842, as already noted, and these ignored. A further protest came from the merchants of Glasgow in 1844 listing the inconvenience caused by the mail being routed via Portpatrick. This again went unheeded, but a new factor had entered the debate.

DEFEAT AT PORTPATRICK CONCEDED

The period of the 1840s was the era of railway expansion. For example, *The Galloway Advertiser and Wigtownshire Free Press* of Thursday, 6 November 1845 gave over practically its entire front page to railway prospectuses. These sought subscriptions for the British and Irish Union Railway, the Glasgow and Belfast Union Railway, the Scottish Southern Railway, the Ayrshire and Galloway Railway, the Glasgow, Dumfries and Carlisle Railway, the Lochryan Harbour and British and Irish Railway Terminus, the Limerick and Belfast Direct Union Railway. The first two indicated that the port would be in Loch Ryan for their ships sailing to Belfast. The previous month there had appeared the prospectus for the Lochryan Harbour and Stranraer General Railway Terminus. This revealed most ambitious plans for the £50,000 capital sought. It was proposed to erect a quay to the east of the small tidal quay at Stranraer. This was to be the site selected fifteen years later for the new pier at Stranraer and it is perhaps no coincidence that the Stair family had a large stake in the 1845 proposals and the later railway and shipping developments at Stranraer. In addition to the new quay at Stranraer the 1845 plans envisaged a jetty at Cairnryan. The prospectus goes on to tell us that a company was already in course of formation to place powerful steam packets between Stranraer, Cairnryan and Inveraray and via the Crinan Canal to the Western Isles. Inverness was to be a destination for ships sailing from Stranraer via the Crinan and Caledonian Canals. The quay at Stranraer was to be of such dimensions that from it trade was to be developed with Canada and the United States of America. This ambitious prospectus may seem a digression but it serves to indicate not only the enthusiasm that came in the wake of the railway but also once again that Loch Ryan and not Portpatrick was seen as the ideal base for shipping to Ireland.[106]

In May 1844, Captain Edward Hawes was appointed supervisor for the Admiralty at Portpatrick, and in 1847, Lord Auckland, First Lord of the Admiralty, requested a confidential report from Hawes as to the situation. Captain Hawes could only report that despite the great expenditure the harbour had not been rendered safe. He had been struck on his arrival by the conflicting opinions of engineering and naval experts. The engineers were influenced by the short distance of the route, while the navigators were more conscious of the narrow, exposed entrance with heavy, broken seas at Portpatrick.[107]

The Portpatrick Harbour Commissioners, no doubt despairing of their work of superintendence ever being ended, petitioned successfully in 1847 to transfer their responsibilities over to the Admiralty. In September, the Commissioners handed over to Captain Hawes, who accepted the duty (without any increase in salary, he pointed out to the First Lord) in the hope that he might be able to effect some improvements in the harbour. He quickly set about making some fairly inexpensive alterations, including some dredging at the north berth which eased the situation for the mail packets. He relates dramatically the difficulty in stormy weather of the mail boat leaving the north berth tucked inside McCook's Craig to turn through 180° and head out to sea between the unfinished breakwaters. Drenched by sea spray, Captain Hawes would stand on the north pier and when a lull in the seas came word was passed to the packet to leave its berth. By means of a check rope the small craft was swung round McCook's Craig and the bow pointed into the seas. The engineer then had to get up sufficient speed to take the packet clear of the two piers.

Lord Auckland had asked Captain Hawes for specifications for two new mail packets, and these he duly received, but everything was working against the retention of Portpatrick as a mail packet station. In 1848, mails from England to Ireland were all routed via Holyhead, as this port now had a rail link with London. The other services to Ireland, via Milford Haven and Liverpool, were abandoned in August and September 1848 respectively.

Lord Auckland gave evidence to the Select Committee on Navy, Army and Ordnance Estimates in May 1848 and agreed that he was in favour of the mail service being carried out under contract with private shipowners, but "as a general principle, I should say that it may be more cheaply done by contractors, though I think in most cases it may be most efficiently and certainly done by the government". It was expected that the opening of the railway link to Holyhead would affect the Portpatrick route, but in March 1848, before the same Committee, H. G. Ward, the Secretary to the Admiralty, stated that there was no intention of abandoning Portpatrick.[108]

But on the first day of 1849, Lord Auckland died, and with a change in First Lord came a change of heart. Captain Hawes's specifications for two new packets for Portpatrick were never to reach the drawing board.

Towards the close of 1848, Mr. George Burns, the Glasgow shipowner, had an interview with Lord Clanricarde, the Postmaster-General, and in the new year, Colonel Maberley, the Secretary to the Post Office, was instructed to write to George Burns asking him to confirm his offer to convey the mail between Greenock and Belfast free of charge. It is recorded that Maberley's reaction to Burns's offer was to dismiss him as a fool.[109] But Burns was no fool. The Ardrossan Steam Navigation Company increased their service in 1848 with *Fire Fly* and *Glow Worm* to five times a week between Ardrossan and Belfast. Lord Eglinton of the Steam Navigation Company indiscreetly divulged that Lord Clanricarde had indicated that it was his intention to transfer the Scottish-Irish mail contract to Lord Eglinton's Company. For Burns, the inevitable loss to be incurred in the free conveyance of the mails was better than allowing the rival company win for itself this official stamp of approval.

Messrs. G. & J. Burns, as early as 1836, had offered to convey the mail from Glasgow via Greenock and were willing to forego the statutory 2*d* per letter if they had no competition from the mail packets for the passenger trade.

On that occasion the outcome of the inquiry had been to recommend that the Liverpool route only be handed over to public contract with the other stations being transferred to Admiralty management.[110]

George Burns successfully resisted pressure from the Post Office that the service should continue to be offered on seven days a week. Burns was a staunch evangelical and would not countenance his ships leaving port on a Sunday— though he did allow them to arrive on Sunday morning! A special train was introduced between Glasgow and Greenock in connection with the mail boat. The contract arrangements allowed the Postmaster-General the right to stipulate the times of the ships' sailing. Burns purchased the paddle steamer *Camilla* and her first departure from Greenock for Belfast was on the evening of Monday, 16 July 1849. In the conducting of the daily (except Sunday) service *Camilla* was partnered by two other paddlers already in the Burns fleet, *Lyra* and *Thetis*. Burns's *Aurora* also featured for a few weeks but proved too slow. Following the opening of the second section of the Victoria Channel in 1848 and extensive dredging in the harbour in 1849, Belfast could be approached at any state of the tide by ships of up to 10 feet draught. This made a fixed time schedule possible for the Greenock–Belfast sailings.[111]

There was held to be an immediate annual saving to the Treasury of between two and three thousand pounds, and contrary to Lord Auckland's fears the service was greatly improved. Formerly the Irish mail had been despatched from Glasgow at 1630 for Portpatrick and, if there was no delay, it reached Belfast about 0915 the following day. Going via Greenock, the mail left Glasgow at 1800 and reached Belfast before 0500, producing a saving of nearly six hours. In the reverse direction the time saved was more than seven hours. An additional benefit from the new service was that the mail was now in the two cities in time for distribution in the first delivery in the morning, and also gave more suitable evening despatch times.[112] Figures prepared in 1856 calculated the average time in the first six and a half years of the service of the Greenock–Belfast voyages as 9 hours 14 minutes 45 seconds and the return journey as 8 hours 46 minutes 5 seconds. Perhaps the precision shows how important seconds were![113]

With no mails from the south and none from the north, the mail stations at Portpatrick and Donaghadee were allowed to close at the end of September 1849, and the steam packets sailed for Portsmouth. *Pike* moved to Devonport and was laid up for many years. In 1862 she became a tender to H.M.S. *Royal Adelaide*. Four years later she was laid up again and in June 1868 was broken up. *Asp* was employed as a survey ship in the Irish Sea for several years, being based at Holyhead and then at Milford. In March 1865 she became a tender to H.M.S. *Saturn* at Devonport and after four years there was transferred to Chatham and used as a harbour craft during the extension of the dockyard. *Asp* was broken up in the early 1880s.[114]

An attempt was made in October 1849 to provide a service—probably by sailing boat—on an alternate-day basis between Portpatrick and Donaghadee for passengers and cargo, but this would not appear to have lasted long. The weekly steamboat service between Stranraer and Belfast was to prove adequate for local needs.

Captain Hawes stayed on as superintendent of the harbour works but the actual construction work at the harbour ceased in 1849. The position of Harbour Master had been suppressed in 1832 as an economy measure, but the post was recreated in 1849 and Captain Hawes appointed. On Monday, 3 December 1849 there was a sale at Portpatrick of the redundant naval stores, but Captain Hawes was allowed to retain one of the large row/sail boats as an emergency boat. This boat, manned by a volunteer crew, was quickly on the spot in the early hours of 18 June 1850 when the Burns's steamer *Orion* went on the rocks outside Portpatrick Harbour while bound from Liverpool for the Clyde.

At the Board of Trade Inquiry into the loss of *Orion* it was maintained that the light on the inner tower at Portpatrick misled the officers into thinking they were farther off the shore than events subsequently proved to be the case. The Admiralty urged the re-introduction of the light in the lighthouse at the extremity of the south pier. This light had been out of use since the pier was damaged in January 1839.[115]

The Northern Commissioners who were responsible for the lighthouses reacted to this request by closing down the inner light, thus leaving the harbour without any lighthouse in use. The inner lighthouse was handed over to Captain Hawes for his superintendence. In 1856, following another casualty, the Admiralty themselves established a light in the inner tower. The lighthouse at the seaward end of the south pier was kept in good condition, and in 1871 it was dismantled and shipped to Colombo, Ceylon. Work on this had commenced in the summer of 1869 and the local press surmised wearily that the dismantling of the beautiful and strongly-built lighthouse would probably cost more than its building. A lighthouse on the site of the old inner lighthouse was built in 1883.

At the *Orion* inquiry Captain Hawes had recommended strongly that one or two lifeboats be based at Portpatrick. This was eventually done in 1877. Portpatrick and Donaghadee are still lifeboat stations to this day.

All was quiet at Portpatrick. A few fishing boats plied from the harbour and one or two coasting ships called each month, most of these in connection with the Dunskey estates which surrounded the harbour. The large livestock shipments through Portpatrick were also a thing of the past. In 1812, 20,000 cattle and horses had crossed by sailing packets via Portpatrick, but once the direct steamboat services were introduced from Belfast to Liverpool and Glasgow the traffic dropped off gradually, and in 1837, for example, just over a thousand head of livestock moved through the port.[116] In February 1828, Portpatrick lost its status as a customs port and became a creek of Stranraer. In June 1855 another order of the Commissioners of Customs terminated any customs interest in the port. We now move north from Portpatrick and consider the links between Stranraer and Ireland.

LONDON
415.
P. PATRICK
1.
STRANRAER
7.
DUMFRIES
83.

CHAPTER THREE

Between Belfast and Stranraer

IN the pioneering days of the steamboat it was the exception rather than the
rule for timetables to be published giving dates and timings of sailings for
weeks or months ahead. Some companies and owners inserted their vessels'
sailings in the press but most relied on their customers picking up the information by word of mouth at the quay or by consulting the bill-boards. Tidal
restrictions applied at most harbours, heavy weather delayed the low-powered
steamers. Ships changed owners and routes with bewildering frequency. With
this situation, which contrasts with our contemporary scene of regularity and
stability, plus the lack of primary sources, it is dangerous to be dogmatic about
the date of something happening for the first time. Bearing this in mind, we
must now consider when the first service occurred from Stranraer to Ireland
and vice versa.

"HIGHLAND CHIEFTAIN" TO DONAGHADEE

It is in the context of the Glasgow–Stranraer passenger/cargo trade that
we find the earliest services between Stranraer and Irish ports. In April 1822
Highland Chieftain opened the first regular service between Glasgow and
Stranraer, calling at Greenock, Largs, Ardrossan, Saltcoats, Ayr and Girvan.
Built in 1817 as *Duke of Wellington* for work on the Clyde, she took over the
Glasgow–Fort William route following the loss of the pioneer steamboat,
Comet, in December 1820, having received her second name. A second *Comet*
took over in July 1821 and *Highland Chieftain* spent the summer months on a
weekly service between Liverpool, Douglas, Whitehaven and Dumfries. She
was a small craft for this exposed stretch of water but proved herself a "very
staunch and excellent seaboat", according to the FOR SALE notice that appeared
in *The Glasgow Herald* of 14 January 1822.

The service *Highland Chieftain* gave in her first year between Stranraer
and Glasgow was weekly—out from the Broomielaw on Tuesday and returning
from Stranraer on Thursday. Her arrival on Friday, 19 April 1822 at Glasgow
within fourteen hours of leaving Stranraer was worthy of mention in the press.
Each year the service was withdrawn in November and reintroduced in early
spring.

The establishment of a Glasgow–Stranraer steamboat service was no doubt
helped by the building in 1820 of the stone (west) Burgh quay at Stranraer.
The quay, which cost £3,800, was inaccessible some hours each side of low
water.

Highland Chieftain continued to serve Stranraer from Glasgow in 1823,
and in 1824 we encounter the first advertised service from Stranraer to Ireland.
The Glasgow Herald of 14 May 1824 carried an advertisement to the effect that
Highland Chieftain would sail from Glasgow on Thursday, 20 May, with
passengers and goods for Stranraer and on the following day would proceed
to Donaghadee. The return trip from Donaghadee was on Friday and she left

Stranraer on the Monday for Glasgow. This was to be the schedule "until further notice". How long this roster was carried out is open to conjecture. D. B. McNeill mentioned "a few months" [117] but the next advertisement for *Highland Chieftain*, that of 14 June 1824, shows a twice-weekly Glasgow–Stranraer timetable with no mention of Donaghadee.

The next appearance of *Highland Chieftain* in the columns of *The Glasgow Herald* was in the FOR SALE column when on 24 September 1824 she was offered at an upset price of £700, later reduced to £500.

Highland Chieftain returned to the western isles in 1825, being employed between Glasgow and Oban. At Oban she connected with *Maid of Islay* for Islay. *Maid of Islay* deserves a line in the Stranraer story since in the winter of 1826–27 she gave a weekly sailing for passengers and cargo between Glasgow, Largs, Girvan and Stranraer in addition to her Glasgow–Islay duties.

"DUMBARTON CASTLE" TO NEWRY

In 1823 another wooden paddler commenced a summer service between Glasgow and Stranraer. This was *Dumbarton Castle* of 1815. Captain James Williamson relates the occasion when James Watt on his last visit to Greenock made a voyage in 1816 to Rothesay on board *Dumbarton Castle* and in conversation with the ship's engineer discovered the means of reversing a steam engine.[118]

Dumbarton Castle appeared on the Stranraer station in late July 1823 and she at first offered two sailings a week between Glasgow and Stranraer. Thus between *Dumbarton Castle* and *Highland Chieftain* there were four sailings each week between Glasgow and Stranraer in 1823. In September, however, one of *Dumbarton Castle*'s Stranraer trips was dropped and the steamer headed for Campbeltown after leaving Ayr. In her programme for 1824, *Dumbarton Castle* gave a weekly sailing to Stranraer while Arrochar now featured in her schedule from Glasgow.

An incident concerning *Dumbarton Castle* tells us something of the times. In November 1827 Ezekiel McHaffie, master of *Dumbarton Castle*, was brought before the High Court of Admiralty and charged with violation of the regulations for steamboats on the river as no proper watch was kept. The charge arose out of an accident on 18 September 1827 when *Dumbarton Castle*, "running before the wind, with all sails set and the steam on" ran down a fishing boat at anchor off Gourock Quay. The fishing boat sank and one man drowned while another was injured by the paddles of *Dumbarton Castle*. The disaster was held to be "all in consequence of the culpable, negligent and reckless conduct of the said Ezekiel McHaffie" and the Judge Admiral had him committed to Stranraer Jail for six months. The Judge commented on the "general negligence in the management of the steamboats" and hoped the trial and its outcome would serve as an example and warning to others.[119] *Dumbarton Castle* was none the worse of the collision and in June 1828 we find her resuming her weekly trip to Stranraer.

In 1829 *Dumbarton Castle*'s schedule followed the usual pattern of one sailing from Glasgow to Stranraer each week and then in October an isolated trip is advertised from Stranraer to Portrush, leaving Stranraer on Friday, 16 October. The ship then returned to Stranraer and Glasgow. Later in the month there was a further development which justifies the inclusion of

Dumbarton Castle in this chapter. *Dumbarton Castle* was advertised to sail from Stranraer on Thursday, 29 October 1829 to Newry, arriving back in Glasgow via Stranraer on the following Tuesday. This service was to operate "until further notice". But early in the morning of Friday, 13 November, *Dumbarton Castle*, bound from Glasgow for Stranraer and Newry, ran into dense fog near Bowling and grounded on the dyke that marks the dredged channel. *Dumbarton Castle* was badly damaged and this finished her days of sailing to Stranraer and Newry, but she appears to have been salved for further work elsewhere since Duckworth & Langmuir record the dismantling of *Dumbarton Castle* at Leith in 1841, though in a recent article Ian McCrorie reports the loss of *Dumbarton Castle* off the Irish coast in 1838.[120]

The adoption of the Newry route by the owners of *Dumbarton Castle* was probably prompted by the hiatus in the network of services caused by the wreck of *Britannia*. This vessel had been employed by Messrs. Alex. A. Laird & Sons for some years between Glasgow, Campbeltown and Londonderry, but in 1829 had switched to a new service between Glasgow and Newry. On Sunday, 11 October 1829, after leaving Newry, she was caught in a gale and tried to put into Donaghadee, but grounded inside the harbour and became a complete wreck.

Following the disappearance of *Dumbarton Castle* from the Glasgow–Stranraer station, two steamers, *Hercules* and *Argyle*, stepped in. But these steamers, like various other Glasgow–Stranraer steamers of the 1830s, *Ayr*, *Nimrod* and *Northern Yacht*, were never to extend their route from Stranraer to Ireland.

THE STRANRAER STEAM SHIPPING COMPANY

During the 1830s a steamer based at Belfast, *Superb*, offered occasional excursions which for those days were ambitious. As well as local destinations such as Glenarm, Portrush, Donaghadee and Carrickfergus, this little ship ventured on pleasure trips to Menai Bridge, Ramsey, Whitehaven, Fort William —and Stranraer. On Saturday, 11 August 1832, *Superb* gave what appears to be the first steamboat crossing between Belfast and Stranraer. She sailed from the Corporation Dock at noon and returned to Belfast on the following evening. The trip must have proved a success for it was repeated later in the month, on Monday, 20 August, when the fares were increased by about 30 per cent. The return crossing was to be the same day or the next, "agreeable to the wishes of the passengers".

It was 1835 before a regular service was introduced between Stranraer and Belfast. On 27 June, *Lochryan* arrived at Belfast on her first call of what was to be a weekly service during the summer months. Two days later, Captain Gillespie took *Lochryan* from Belfast to Stranraer and Glasgow.

Lochryan, a wooden paddler, had been built at Dumbarton in 1830 and took up the all-year-round Stranraer–Glasgow sailing for passengers and cargo, entering service for the Stranraer Steam Shipping Company in September 1830. The new steamer was the largest ship to date employed on this route and this may be the reason for the abandonment of regular calls at Portpatrick by the ships plying between the Clyde and the Mersey. *Lochryan* is described as being of quarter-deck design with two masts and a female figurehead. In 1839, *Lochryan* was lengthened from 106 feet to 125 feet.

Lochryan was joined in August 1836 by the larger single-decked paddle steamer *Maid of Galloway* and both served Glasgow and Belfast from Stranraer. With two ships operating, the Stranraer Steam Shipping Company was able to expand its area of trading, and in the summer of 1837 a Belfast–Whitehaven service was introduced in addition to the weekly Belfast–Stranraer–Glasgow run. In the following year, *Maid of Galloway* gave some sailings from Belfast to Port Carlisle in addition to the Whitehaven and Stranraer sailings. Furthermore, the ships now sailed with liberty to call at the Isle of Man between Belfast and Whitehaven. The sailings between Belfast and Whitehaven continued into 1842.

In the autumn of 1836 there came about a transport development in Galloway which opened up various possibilities for travellers. A branch mail coach began running in October 1836 between Newton Stewart and Stranraer. The coach left Newton Stewart daily around 1630 as soon as the London mail arrived and travelled via Wigtown, Garliestown, Whithorn, Port William and Glen of Luce, reaching Stranraer the same evening. On the return journey the branch mail coach left Stranraer at 0600 and reached Newton Stewart early in the afternoon. It was now possible for travellers between Liverpool and Glasgow to avoid a tossing off the Mull of Galloway by embarking at Liverpool on the paddle steamer *Countess of Galloway*. This ship had been built in the previous year for the Galloway Steam Navigation Company. *Countess of Galloway* crossed to Wigtown or Garliestown where the new coach could be joined for Stranraer where either *Lochryan* or *Maid of Galloway* carried the traveller on to Glasgow. Alternatively, the mail coach for Glasgow could be boarded at Stranraer and the journey via Kilmarnock and Ayr completed in this way. This coach had also been introduced in October 1836 and replaced the previous arrangement for the mail which involved a one-man gig.

Another possibility was available for those travelling between Belfast and Liverpool. The sea mileage could be reduced to a minimum by using the mail packets, *Fury* or *Spitfire*, between Donaghadee and Portpatrick, having travelled from Belfast by the eight-passenger mail coach. From Portpatrick the traveller was conveyed to Stranraer where the new mail coach was joined for Wigtown or Garliestown. Here *Countess of Galloway* would be waiting to carry the traveller on to Liverpool.

The first edition of *The Galloway Advertiser and Wigtownshire Free Press* appeared on 5 January 1843 and included an advertisement for the Stranraer Steam Shipping Company's packets *Maid of Galloway* and *Lochryan*. At this time and for the next eighteen years the usual service was weekly from Glasgow to Stranraer and every two weeks from Stranraer to Belfast. The Stranraer–Belfast leg of the ships' roster involved two days: outward to Belfast one day and returning to Stranraer the following day. Apart from occasional excursions, a round trip within one day had to await the arrival of more powerful ships.

In late July 1843, *Lochryan* disappears from the advertisements, leaving *Maid of Galloway* alone. *Lochryan* was sold to coal traders of Newcastle-upon-Tyne in October 1843 and in May 1846 was registered in the name of individuals trading as the Netherlands Steam Navigation Company between London, Rotterdam and Hamburg. *Lochryan* sailed from Maaslandsluys on the River Maas on the evening of 7 October 1846 with between 80 and 100 head of cattle. She left in a storm and the weather so deteriorated that *Lochryan* sought shelter for two days in Helvoetsluys. Her master, Captain Larkins, thinking the gale had blown itself out, left the harbour on the 9th, but the weather quickly worsened and *Lochryan* was lost. No trace of the ship or crew was ever found, but *Rainbow*, of the General Steam Navigation Company, sailing from Rotterdam to London, sailed through a number of drowned cattle.

At the end of April 1844 a new paddle steamer, *Albion*, appeared from the yard of Tod & McGregor for the Shipping Company. *Albion* arrived at Stranraer on the evening of Monday, 28 April, having completed her journey from the Broomielaw in 7 hours 45 minutes. On the Tuesday she gave a special excursion from Stranraer and Girvan to Campbeltown. In July, *Albion* gave an excursion to Dublin from Stranraer, leaving on the evening of Saturday, 20 July, and remaining at Dublin until the Monday evening. *Maid of Galloway* remained in the fleet during 1844 and she relieved *Albion* in December, but in March and April 1845 she was advertised to sail between Wigtown, Kirkcudbright, Fleetwood, Liverpool and Garliestown. She was trading under the flag of a new company, the Galloway, Liverpool and Lancashire Steam Navigation Co., until their own ship, *Cheviot*, was completed.

In early 1845, *Maid of Galloway* was sold to a Preston shipowner but, according to Duckworth & Langmuir, saw further service in Scottish waters around 1846 when she was employed trading out of Ardrossan to Stornoway, calling at Campbeltown, Port Ellen, Oban, Tobermory and Portree.[121] On 31 March 1850, while sailing in ballast from Liverpool to Goole, *Maid of Galloway* was immobilised by a boiler explosion and the gale drove her on to the beach at Balbriggan, north of Dublin. She was a total loss.

THE GLASGOW & STRANRAER STEAM PACKET COMPANY

A new ship appeared at Stranraer in August 1845 when *Scotia* commenced operating from Ayr. The Glasgow, Paisley, Kilmarnock & Ayr Railway was completed between Ayr and Glasgow on 12 August 1840. At that time Ayr Station was situated at the harbour and Ayr became a packet port for many routes, and on Tuesday, 6 April 1841, the wooden paddle steamer *James Oswald* opened a service for passengers and cargo between Ayr and Stranraer, operating in connection with the new railway from Glasgow to Ayr. The sailings from Stranraer were on Monday, Wednesday and Friday, returning the following day, and called at Girvan and Ballantrae. The equally small iron paddler *Queen of Scots* took the summer service from Stranraer in 1842 and 1843. In 1844, it was the iron paddle steamer *Lady Brisbane*, transferred from the Glasgow–Largs and Millport station, that operated a daily service from Stranraer connecting into the 1100 train from Ayr to Glasgow, and she left Ayr again on the arrival of the 1330 train from the city. During the winter of 1844–45 the service continued but on an alternate-day basis. In March 1845, *Lady Kelburn*, also of the Glasgow, Largs & Millport Union Steamboat Co., allowed *Lady Brisbane* off for overhaul. In mid-July 1845, *Lady Brisbane* sustained paddle damage and she had to be taken off the station for repairs in the Clyde. By the beginning of August she was back and, as if to show her renewed strength, gave two lengthy excursions from Stranraer. These were to Rothesay on 9 August 1845 and to Campbeltown on 16 August. The sailings were routed via Ayr and required a 0430 departure from Stranraer.

Without warning, *Lady Brisbane* ceases to feature in the advertisements and *Scotia*'s immediate appearance on a very similar schedule between Ayr and Stranraer and connecting with trains at Ayr would indicate that she was an arranged successor to *Lady Brisbane*. *Scotia* took over on 30 August 1845 and, like *Albion*, was an iron paddler from the Tod & McGregor yard. By December 1845, both *Albion* and the slightly smaller *Scotia* had the same agent at Stranraer, and in March 1846 both appear for the first time in the same advertisement under the heading "Glasgow & Stranraer Steam Packet Company". The two ships tended to concentrate on their original routes, with *Albion* sailing Glasgow–Stranraer–Belfast and *Scotia* Ayr–Stranraer. Prior to 1862, *Scotia* did make occasional trips to the Irish coast, but these were usually excursions. From January 1847, Campbeltown was included in *Scotia*'s time-table and twice each week she sailed from Ayr to Campbeltown, again in connection with trains at Ayr Harbour.

A third ship, *Briton*, was added to the Glasgow & Stranraer Steam Packet Company fleet in 1847. With this addition, another destination was included in the rosters, and in January 1849 *Albion* made a sailing from Stranraer to Liverpool. *Maid of Galloway* had made trips to Liverpool, but it now became a feature of each winter and spring that sailings were given to Liverpool usually from Stranraer, though occasionally from other ports such as Drummore and even Islay. The main cargo on these trips was livestock, but sometimes they were advertised as excursion week-ends. *Briton* also took the Liverpool sailings on occasion. In July 1849, *Briton* gave her first long-distance excursion when she sailed from Ayr to Douglas, Isle of Man, calling at Portpatrick, Drummore and Port William. The fleet movements began to include an increasing number of excursions and special sailings.

Like her stablemates, *Briton* came from the Tod & McGregor yard. The Art Gallery and Museum, Glasgow, have in storage a 1:48 half model of *Briton*. The model is devoid of detail but serves to show the hull lines of this iron paddle steamer.

Albion again broke new ground for the Steam Packet Company when in August 1849 she sailed for Corpach. From there, *Albion* brought back livestock to winter in Galloway. In subsequent years these livestock sailings took all the units of the Stranraer fleet, with the exception of *Scotia*, to such distant places as Stornoway, Islay, Glenelg, Fort William, Ardrishaig, and elsewhere.

In the summer of 1845 and 1846 the service between Stranraer and Belfast was stepped up to a weekly frequency, while from the summer of 1847 the service was weekly practically the whole year until 1853, after which it was only in summer that a weekly service was offered, and for the rest of the year a fortnightly schedule was operated. This increase in the number of sailings between Ireland and Scotland is no doubt related to the Great Famine in Ireland which followed on the failure of the potato crop. The worst year was 1847, but every year from 1845 to 1849 was affected. In August 1847 over three million people in Ireland were being fed at the public expense. Since the beginning of the century there had been a regular emigrant movement from Ireland but the numbers had been comparatively small: between 1841 and 1844 they averaged about 50,000 a year. After the second potato failure in 1846, emigration was in the mind of everyone. Previously, the emigrant sailings to the new world from Scotland and Ireland had been in the spring and summer months, but from the autumn of 1846 the traffic continued throughout the year. The Gold Rush on the west coast of America in 1849 further accelerated the emigration from the poverty of Ireland. The peak year was 1851, when a quarter of a million left Ireland for the United States of America and Canada.

Some of this traffic would pass through Stranraer on its way to Greenock or Glasgow to join the ships sailing west.[122]

In November 1853, *Briton* suffered paddle damage while crossing to Belfast and had to be taken to Glasgow for repairs. Mr. Alex Langlands, the Company's agent at Stranraer since 1851, chartered the Campbeltown & Glasgow Steam Packet Company's *Celt* to cover *Briton*'s sailings for a few days. In May 1854, while returning to Stranraer from Liverpool, *Briton*'s mainshaft broke and the ship had to be towed back to Liverpool. On this occasion, *Glow Worm*, of the Ardrossan Steam Navigation Company, was brought in to fill the gap. This involved *Glow Worm* sailing from Stranraer with livestock for Islay.

Glow Worm was almost at the end of her career on the Ardrossan–Belfast service. This route has always proved to be a source of competition for the steamers sailing from Stranraer to Ireland. The railway reached Ardrossan in 1840 and brought Glasgow within an hour's journey, and this gave Ardrossan great potential as a packet port for the lower Firth of Clyde, Ireland and the Isle of Man. A short-lived service operated between Ardrossan and Liverpool in 1840 by *Fire King*. The Ardrossan–Liverpool sea journey was advertised as part of a Glasgow to London service using the Ardrossan railway and also the train between Liverpool and London. The journey between Glasgow and London was covered in twenty-four hours. A service between Ardrossan and Belfast was introduced in 1841 by the Glasgow and Stranraer steamer *Ayrshire Lassie*, but this did not last long and the ship was transferred to Liverpool. In 1844 the Ardrossan Steam Navigation Company was formed and the chartered steamer *Isabella Napier* was put on the station between Ardrossan and Belfast until the arrival of the company's first steamer, *Glow Worm*, in September 1844. A consort, *Fire Fly*, entered service the following year. It is to *Fire Fly* that the distinction goes for the first day excursion from Glasgow (via Ardrossan) to Belfast. This was on 13 July 1850, Glasgow Fair Saturday. Both ships were withdrawn in October 1855 and the service by the Ardrossan Steam Navigation Company discontinued. *Glow Worm* was eventually lost in 1859, and *Fire Fly* broken up in 1867. After a gap of a few weeks, the overnight Ardrossan–Belfast service was reopened in December 1855 when the paddle steamer *Cambria* was placed on the route by, paradoxically, the Belfast Screw Steamship Company.

Briton was approaching Ballantrae on the last day of January 1855 when she struck a rock and quickly sank, becoming a complete wreck. The passengers, there were about thirty, managed to transfer themselves and their luggage into the boats that had come out from Ballantrae to meet *Briton*. The rock was not charted but was well-known locally. Many years before, *Maid of Galloway* had struck the same rock but without fatal consequences. *Duke of Cornwall*, of the Campbeltown & Glasgow Steam Packet Co., was chartered in temporarily, and from the end of March 1855, *Albion* and *Scotia* alone covered the traffic. Another paddle steamer was ordered from the Tod & McGregor yard at Partick, and in March 1856, *Caledonia* made her first call at Stranraer from Glasgow. The Art Gallery and Museum, Glasgow, have a 1: 48 half-model of *Caledonia* in store.

Albion remained the principal Stranraer–Belfast steamer, although *Caledonia* did appear on the route occasionally. *Caledonia* also undertook an occasional trip to Liverpool from Stranraer just as *Briton* had done before her.

The new ship was used to assist in the livestock movements to Stranraer in the autumn of each year. Although neither *Scotia* nor *Caledonia* featured regularly in the main Belfast timetable, excursion trips did cause them to visit the Irish coast. On 22 July 1858, *Scotia* gave an excursion from Ayr to Belfast and on 5 August *Caledonia* left Stranraer at 0600 on an excursion to Donaghadee. The same news report reads, "*Caledonia* is now a swift boat, having lately had additional power bestowed on her machinery".[123] On 14 July 1859, *Caledonia* reversed the route, bringing an excursion party over from Donaghadee to Stranraer.

Working down the exposed Ayrshire coast, it is not surprising that accidents occasionally happened. The loss of *Briton* off Ballantrae has already been noted. In November of the same year, 1855, *Albion* grounded near the Cumbraes and her passengers and cargo had to be taken off by a tug. *Albion* was refloated and taken to Greenock. In February 1860, it was the turn of *Scotia* when she was caught in a gale between Stranraer and Ayr and tried to make into the lee of Arran. The wind was too strong for her and *Scotia* headed for Girvan. The harbour was safely entered but she took the bottom inside the harbour entrance and some hull plates were broken. The passengers were safely landed and *Caledonia* took over.

The Glasgow & Stranraer Steam Packet Company decided to order a new ship for their trade and *Albion* made her last sailing from Stranraer on Monday, 23 April 1860, before being handed over to her new owners. *Scotia* was still off for repairs after her accident at Girvan, and for a time the services were maintained by *Caledonia* alone. On 18 October 1860, a new *Albion* was launched from the Tod & McGregor yard and her first arrival at Stranraer Quay was on 15 November. The ship was credited with a speed of fourteen knots and her accommodation was considered outstanding for a passenger/cargo boat.

The new *Albion* was given a schedule on 22 July 1861, which not only showed her capabilities but also opened up the old "Short Sea Route" for the day. *Albion* had been chartered by the Belfast & County Down Railway for an excursion from Donaghadee in connection with their newly-opened railway branch. The Glasgow & Stranraer Steam Packet Company took the opportunity of making some extra cash by advertising her outward run from Stranraer as an excursion to Donaghadee with a train connection to Belfast. *Albion* left Stranraer at 0600 and called at Portpatrick at 0800 before crossing to Donaghadee for her B & C D R excursion which brought her back to Stranraer via Portpatrick. Thus, by the time *Albion* reached Stranraer around 2300 she had made two round trips between Stranraer and Donaghadee and made four calls at Portpatrick.

But there had been a significant change in the Stranraer scene. The railway reached Stranraer on Monday, 11 March 1861, and this had great repercussions for the whole area and the Glasgow & Stranraer Steam Packet Company.

CHAPTER FOUR

A Railway for Portpatrick

THE long-established mail route between Portpatrick and Donaghadee may have been abandoned in 1849, but there was no lack of individuals determined to realise the potential of the short crossing. In the mid-1850s various plans were formulated. On 14 September 1853 the steamer *Telegraph* crossed from Belfast to Cairnryan with a party "interested in establishing a route between Belfast and Cairnryan", but in June 1854 it was reported that a company was being formed in Northern Ireland to re-open the Donaghadee–Portpatrick route and prospectuses had been circulated on both sides of the channel. Nothing came of either, but a more promising event was a meeting on 30 April 1856 when there was convened the annual meeting of the Commissioners of Supply for the County of Wigtown (part of the local government system then in operation). At this meeting the advantages deriving from Wigtownshire being linked by railway with the outside world were outlined and it was agreed to investigate further. To the east, a railway was being promoted to run from Castle Douglas to Dumfries, and it was to this line, the Castle Douglas & Dumfries Railway, that the Wigtownshire planners saw their rails joining.

THE TREASURY MINUTE

The western objective of the line was Portpatrick and the re-establishment of the mail service to Ireland. In 1855, the First Lord of the Admiralty had indicated he favoured the re-opening of the route once there was a railway connection on each side. Early in 1856, the Belfast & County Down Railway had received powers to extend their line from Comber to Downpatrick with branches to Ballynahinch, Bangor and Donaghadee. In 1853, the B & C D R had asked Captain Hawes for his views on the capabilities of Portpatrick Harbour. Captain Hawes, as Government Superintendent of the Harbour, had made a reply sufficiently optimistic for the railway to be hopeful of the eventual re-establishment of the route from Donaghadee. In supporting the B & C D R Bill, the Admiralty had submitted a report in which the hope was expressed that "the enterprise might lead to a revival of the packet communication between Portpatrick and Donaghadee". The time was ripe for a move on the Scottish side.

But everybody was not happy at the prospect of the resurrection of the old route, and on Monday, 11 August 1856, the Belfast Harbour Commissioners and a "large number of influential merchants and inhabitants of Belfast" crossed over to Cairnryan on the steamer *Semaphore*. The reason for their trip was to ascertain the progress made with the plans of the railway to Portpatrick and to discuss the best point for establishing a steamship route to Belfast. The voyage from Belfast by *Semaphore* to Cairnryan was completed in 3 hours 35 minutes and the travellers were met by Mr. George Guthrie, the convener of the railway committee, and Mr. Alex Ingram, the interim secretary. The steamboat agent, Mr. Alex. Langlands, was also present. The majority of the party from Ulster favoured Cairnryan as the terminal for the Belfast service, but Mr. Guthrie had to report that Portpatrick must be reached by the railway, but that this did not preclude a direct service from Belfast which would connect into the railway on the shores of Loch Ryan. On being assured that the railway would touch Loch Ryan, the party "expressed satisfaction" and *Semaphore* returned to Belfast.

Events were moving quickly. In May 1856, a deputation from the B & C D R and from Galloway had attended the Treasury to deliver a memorial on the subject of promoting the short-sea passage between Portpatrick and Donaghadee. This memorial, along with an appeal from the inhabitants of Ballantrae that the mail route should operate between Ballantrae and Belfast, were passed to the Admiralty for examination and comment. On 22 July 1856, Captains Vetch and Washington submitted their report in which they argued for the re-establishment of the Portpatrick–Donaghadee service, since (i) it was the shortest, being 19 [sic] miles against 32 between Larne and Cairnryan and 44 between Belfast and Ballantrae, (ii) only a small outlay would be required to bring Portpatrick and Donaghadee up to the standard required for ships of 150 feet length, and (iii) the B & C D R were about to construct a branch line to Donaghadee and there was a proposal to link Portpatrick with Dumfries by rail. The estimated expenditure at Donaghadee was £10,000 and at Portpatrick £15,000.

On the basis of this report the Treasury issued a Minute of 15 August 1856. Should private enterprise be prepared to put steamships on the route and link Donaghadee with Belfast and Portpatrick with Glasgow and with Dumfries, then the Admiralty undertook "to inquire as to the best and cheapest way in which these ports may be made suitable for the purpose", and the Government guaranteed the use of the route for mail. The leader in *The Galloway Advertiser and Wigtownshire Free Press* of 28 August 1856 declared, "All questions, all differences, all rivalries are now at an end". But this was wishful thinking. Both the editor and Mr. Guthrie made repeated pleas for agreement, as any disputing over rival routes could have resulted in no undertaking by the Government to prepare the harbours for the service.

The railway to Portpatrick, initially styled "The British and Irish Junction Railway", received the Royal Assent for its Act on 10 August 1857 under the more modest title of the Portpatrick Railway. The length of the main line from Castle Douglas to Portpatrick was 60 miles 60 chains with two branches. One branch was to the (west) quay at Stranraer and the other from Portpatrick down to the north pier of Portpatrick Harbour. Contained in the Act was an authorisation for involvement of certain railway companies in the capital of the P R, and at the date of the Act the B & C D R, Glasgow & South Western Railway and Lancaster & Carlisle Railway (its line was leased to the London & North Western Railway) had guaranteed to subscribe £15,000, £60,000 and £40,000, respectively. In response to a Government request for a guarantee of the line to Portpatrick being built, the promoters agreed to the inclusion in the Act of a clause prohibiting any payment of dividend before the line to Portpatrick was opened.

In May 1858, the first contracts for the building of the line were placed and work started very quickly. For a full description of the planning, execution and operating of the P R the reader is directed to David L. Smith's book, *The Little Railways of South-West Scotland.*[124]

WEST QUAY AND EAST PIER

Included in the plans of the P R was the building of a short branch to the quay at Stranraer. In the spring of 1855 the Town Council had started work on the improvement of this quay to provide facilities for ships at all states of tide. The work for 1855 was to include the construction of a wharf extending the existing stone quay, and an embankment formed behind a wharf wall to be erected some 80 feet from the existing shore line. (This infilled area was to form part of the site of the proposed railway station and yard.) Also, the existing quay was to be widened by some 15 feet and dredging was to give 4 feet of water at low tide. It was contemplated that in the following year the wooden pier would be extended by about 200 feet and a strong breakwater was to be placed at the extremity of the lengthened pier. The inside of the breakwater was to be so constructed that ships could berth at it with 8 feet of water at low tide. By the beginning of August 1855, a good part of the sea wall forming the wharf was up to high water mark and dredging of the harbour had commenced.

The following year, dredging began in earnest in October when *Caledonia* towed the "dredging machine" from Ayr. Work was not allowed to continue without interruption and the estimated date of completion was repeatedly revised. In July 1857 the coffer dam gave way and work was suspended temporarily. Work was also interrupted by objections to the plans. The building of the breakwater met serious opposition, as it was maintained that it would effectively close the harbour by silting, since no dredged approach was included in the plans. An appeal was made to the Admiralty and they appointed Captain Hawes from Portpatrick to investigate and report. Captain Hawes confirmed the complaints and also viewed the breakwater as a serious obstruction for shipping using the harbour. Not much attention seems to have been paid to the Admiralty censure, since later plans appeared which still featured the breakwater.[125]

But progress with the building was made and at half-tide on Saturday, 29 May 1858, *Caledonia* was able to land her passengers from Ayr on the new wooden pier. But this would appear to have been part only of the projected extension to the pier, since in August 1859 a plea is made in the local press for the work on the wooden pier to be finished. The occasion which prompted the press mention was Thursday, 28 July, the Cattle Show Day at Stranraer, when in the evening nearly a thousand passengers had to be boated out to the steamers waiting to take them home. We have to wait until 31 May 1861 to read that, "the timber wharf is now carried out to its full extent, and only requires a portion of planking to be laid and a protecting hand-rail to make the job complete". Thereafter, boating was to be but a memory.

A schooner arrived at the quay in August 1859 with rails for the new railway, and it was followed by another with other equipment for the permanent way. To expedite the unloading, a railway was laid along the stone quay and across the new embankment bordering the infilled area. And it transpired that this was the only railway that the quay was to see, as at a P R Board meeting on 8 September 1859, it was agreed that for railway traffic it would be more convenient to deviate from the plan in the company's Act and erect a pier in the deep water to the north of the old quay. In December, negotiations started between the P R and the Harbour Commissioners at Stranraer to agree an annual payment which would be acceptable to the Town Council in exchange for building a new pier.

By an agreement dated 5 and 6 March 1861, the P R undertook to pay £1,100 annually to the Stranraer Town Council in lieu of petty customs and harbour dues on goods passing through Stranraer. In return the Town Council were to outlay the "whole capital sum and interest which the said annual payment . . . will produce in erecting and maintaining harbour works for the accommodation of the railway traffic".[126] Three weeks later the Town Council entered into a contract with Thomas Nelson & Co., of Carlisle, to erect a timber pier with accommodation for two steamers. Stone-work extended for nearly 1,700 feet out into the bay, where a wooden gangway and pier were built 860 feet long. The single railway line, which comprised the branch from the main line, was doubled when it reached the stone neck and at the seaward end of the stone was erected a single platform. The lines ran on to the wooden pier and a small goods shed was erected on the pier, but engines were not permitted on to the wood, not so much because of their weight as their ability to start a fire. A small office was provided on the pier for the harbour staff.

Work went ahead quickly, and by mid-August 1861 the local newspaper could report that the "railway portion of the eastern works is carried down about half-way and the contractors are now making preparation for commencing the timber gangway and low water pier".

SECOND THOUGHTS AT PORTPATRICK

The same could not be said of Portpatrick. Following the Treasury Minute of 15 August 1856, it had appeared as if all the problems were over and the improvement of Portpatrick and Donaghadee Harbours for the accommodation of swift mail steamers with rail connections would be speedily put in hand.

At first, however, nothing happened, but on receiving in 1857 an assurance that work at Portpatrick would soon start, the P R agreed to guarantee that the railway would reach the harbour by 1862. The building of the railway commenced in 1858. In the following month a rather disturbing letter was received by the P R. This included a second Treasury Minute. This letter had been precipitated by a deputation to London to press for a start on the harbour works. The Treasury Minute of 26 July 1858 read:

> However willing to carry our fairly the arrangement proposed in the Minute of 15 August 1856, my Lords are not prepared at present to embark in an expense for the improvement of a harbour estimated in 1856 at £15,000, in 1857 at £30,000, and in 1858 at about £40,000.
>
> The experience of such works has shewn that unless great caution is used before engaging in them, it becomes almost impossible subsequently to check or limit the expenditure.
>
> Having regard to the nature of the communication and service and to the report of July 1856, my Lords hesitate to suppose that so large an expenditure as that now proposed can be necessary for the improvements contemplated when the Minute of the late Board was made, and they therefore request that the Lords of the Admiralty

will take immediate steps to ascertain by what means at the smallest expense the harbour at Portpatrick can be rendered sufficiently safe and commodious for the purpose intended.

It was a case of once bitten, twice shy. In the early part of the century the expenditure had outstripped estimates and the project at Portpatrick even then had to be left in an incomplete state. In their investigation into the "best and cheapest manner in which the ports may be made available for the purpose" the Admiralty had obtained a detailed estimate from the Office of Public Works at Dublin for the work required at Donaghadee. The figure was £9,900 and was incurred in dredging the harbour. Captain Vetch had visited Portpatrick on 1 September 1856 to begin a detailed survey, but it was June of the following year before his estimate of cost arrived at the Admiralty. This had now increased from the £15,000 of 1856 to £30,000 and covered the repair and completion of the north pier, the building of a large basin in the harbour and the dredging of a channel to this basin. In Captain Vetch's detailed report of twelve months later the cost had increased by a further £10,000.

At this the Treasury requested the Admiralty to reconsider the project and advise if it was possible to make Portpatrick Harbour safe at a cost which was not much in excess of the £15,000 of the original 1856 report. Captain Vetch agreed that the north breakwater was not indispensible, and if this part of his plan was discarded, the remaining work on the basin and dredging should not cost more than £20,000.

Mr. James Abernethy, C.E., was engaged by the Admiralty to report on the Portpatrick project, and in February 1859 submitted an estimate for £19,491. 2s. 5d. for the building of the new basin and dredging a channel. Mr. Abernethy asked for twelve months to complete the job. He agreed with Captain Vetch that a completed north pier was desirable, if not absolutely necessary, and reckoned £17,000 would be involved.[127]

On 15 July 1859, £20,000 was voted for the work at Portpatrick, but the project was beset with problems. Four years and £40,000 later the contract with James Abernethy was terminated and the work handed over to Captain Hawes.

The new basin was to be cut out of the land to the north of the north berth, formerly used by the mail steam packets. The dock, rectangular in shape, was to extend northwards for over 200 feet, and its area was just in excess of an acre. The height of the coping from the bottom was to be 32 feet. James Abernethy effected an economy by rescuing portions of the masonry displaced from the disintegrating north pier and using the blocks in the building of the quay walls in the new basin. The depth of water in the basin was to be never less than 10 feet and the vessels intended for the mail service would have access at all states of the tide.

There were still doubts about the wisdom of spending money at Portpatrick. In April 1857 an appeal had gone to the Treasury from gentlemen of County Antrim who pointed out the "insuperable natural disadvantages of Donaghadee and Portpatrick" and the "enormous sums already spent upon them, having failed completely to accomplish the desired purpose". In this and other correspondence the Treasury's attention was drawn to the various reports which had recommended the abandonment of the traditional route in favour of Larne–Cairnryan. The memorial and other correspondence was referred to the Admiralty and ignored.[128]

Colonel James McDowall, of Portlogan, wrote to the Admiralty and the Treasury in October 1858 requesting that instead of more money being wasted at Portpatrick, Telford's plans of 1808 for the development of Portlogan should be reconsidered. The railway, he argued, could be easily replanned and diverted from Portpatrick to the village of Portlogan, and this would prove in the long run to be a cheaper project. The Treasury sought the opinion of Captain Vetch, who agreed that Portlogan, if it had been adopted in the first place, would have been a better port than Portpatrick. But he estimated £100,000 would be required to equip Portlogan as a mail packet port, whereas the Treasury was prepared to spend only £20,000. On the grounds of cost and speed of completion, it had to be Portpatrick.

In 1859 the Admiralty received a petition from the Ayr & Maybole Junction Railway Committee. Their complaint was that not enough consideration had been given to the possibilities of other ports along the Wigtownshire and Ayrshire coast. The sole purpose of the Ayr & Maybole Junction Railway and the Maybole & Girvan Railway was to link Glasgow and its environs with Ireland. The latter company was well on with its extension from Maybole towards Girvan, which was the intended port for Ireland. The G & S W R lay behind this railway project. The A & M J R further complained that in the agreement between the Treasury and the P R there had been stipulated that Portpatrick should be linked with Glasgow. This link, the A & M J R hoped, would join the M & G R line at Girvan. After correspondence among the Treasury, the Admiralty and the P R, the Treasury had to admit that in the various negotiations and agreements the link with Glasgow had been allowed to fall by the wayside. As far as the P R was concerned the link with Glasgow would be provided via Dumfries. If the line was to be extended south of Girvan the P R would be pleased to have it join their line, but they did not feel under an obligation to build the line.

Work on the railway to Portpatrick and the branch down to the harbour continued. In *The Galloway Advertiser and Wigtownshire Free Press* of 8 March 1860 is reported the arrival of two schooners at Portpatrick with "engines, wagons, barrows, &c., for railway works". The work at Portpatrick was to start within a few days. But nothing happened to give any encouragement concerning the improvement of the harbour. This lack of inactivity did not go unnoticed across the water, and in September 1860 the Burns's steamer *Giraffe* was chartered by the B & N C R to convey "a large and influential deputation" from the railway company. The ship left Belfast at 0800 and reached Donaghadee within the hour. Thence *Giraffe* sailed to Portpatrick, crossing in 1¼ hours. After a brief look at Portpatrick, the ship proceeded to Cairnryan, taking just over an hour. There the deputation met representatives from the P R and insisted that Stranraer be the base for the cross-channel service. At the Irish end, in May, Parliamentary approval had been given at Westminster for plans to link Belfast by rail with Larne via Carrickfergus. Larne, the B & N C R deputation suggested, was the ideal base for a mail service from Stranraer.

26 July 1860 was the day of the Agricultural Exhibition at Stranraer, and the small steam tug *Wonder* was chartered from Donaghadee to Portpatrick, arriving at noon after a two-hour crossing. Behind this charter was a Mr. John Jamieson, a staunch supporter of the Donaghadee route, and whom we shall encounter again.

The P R had been asked by the Admiralty to act as its agents in obtaining the land required for the basin at Portpatrick. The Admiralty refused to allow the work to start until the land had been conveyed to them. There was some haggling with the Dunskey Estate, which owned the land, and it was November 1860 before the conveyance was actually completed. On 17 November 1860, the P R's contractors for this section, Thomas Nelson & Co., wrote to the railway company complaining that work on the branch at Portpatrick had ceased since the plans for the new basin had still to be agreed. On 17 January 1861, and again two months later, the P R secretary, Alex Ingram, wrote to the Admiralty asking when work was going to start. In March, the Admiralty replied that the improvements "will be commenced as early as practicable", while by May the response was, "I am directed to acquaint you that the subject is under consideration".

A further opportunity for delay was discovered by the Admiralty in June when the secretary wrote to the P R complaining that the plans submitted by the railway showed railway lines effectively cutting in two the Admiralty yard at Portpatrick. This virtually derelict piece of ground suddenly acquired value and full compensation was being demanded for its loss. A valuer had been instructed to visit the harbour and report on the land. On 19 June the suggestion of the P R was accepted that £1,000 be taken as a deposit on the value of the land pending the valuer's report. There then ensued for some years a correspondence accompanied with plans in pink, blue and red, endeavouring to find a suitable substitute piece of land for the Admiralty.

The next matter taken up by the Admiralty was a booking office being built on the new quay wall. On 30 September 1861, the Admiralty wrote protesting against this building since it would take up 10 feet of the 50 feet clear space surrounding the quay and thus cause congestion since "no doubt the traffic will become very great". The P R Board replied that to move the office 10 feet involved a complete realigning of the permanent way with resulting inconvenience and cost. But the firm reply came back that there had to be a clear 50 feet quayage right round the basin. This correspondence continued for some time and then inconclusively fizzled out.[129]

The time of the Admiralty at Portpatrick was running out. By the Harbours Transfer Act of 1862 the responsibility for the harbour was vested in the Board of Trade from 1 January 1863. Thus the real culprits were let off the hook and the whole matter fell for reconsideration by the Board of Trade. The P R enquired of the Board of Trade what the position was, and were rather surprised to be asked in return what provision the P R had made for the opening of the route. In a lengthy reply, the Chairman of the P R outlined the history of the project, but the Board of Trade were unconvinced, and by 1866 expressed their opinion in very clear terms when they requested of the Treasury that "The Board of Trade trust that they may no longer be the instruments of wasting public money by carrying out an undertaking which was originally vicious, and which can never be, in their opinion, of any public service."[130] But we jump ahead.

By April 1861 it would appear that work had finally started at Portpatrick Harbour, and at that time two years was expected to be sufficient to see the job done. In 1861, a Bill was passed empowering the Admiralty to close the harbour during the work. By February 1862 the excavation of the new basin was almost complete, but nothing had been done about widening the entrance to the harbour and dredging a channel to the basin. On Saturday, 25 July 1863, the day announced for the opening of the new basin, a large crowd had travelled to Portpatrick to observe the spectacle, only to discover that for once the work had been completed ahead of schedule and the water admitted to the basin the day before. In the middle of August the dredger from Ayr was towed to Portpatrick and began deepening the harbour and remained until December.

The branch line from Newtonards to Donaghadee had been opened on 3 June 1861, and this now linked Belfast and Donaghadee by rail, the line being single track from Newtonards, though the bridges were constructed to accommodate double tracks should this subsequently prove necessary. The line, in fact, remained single track during its life of eighty-nine years. The B & C D R were understandably concerned about the lack of progress at Portpatrick, and in March 1861 the company arranged for *Giraffe* to try out the crossing for them. In April 1861 it was reported that the railway had purchased a "fast and beautiful steamer" to ply between Portpatrick and Donaghadee. It is unlikely that the ship was *Giraffe*, since her length of 270 feet would preclude her use of Portpatrick Harbour. "A number of commodious omnibuses" were to be placed on the eight miles of road since the line was still incomplete between Stranraer and Portpatrick. But the P R managed to persuade the B & C D R to hold its hand until the harbour works at Portpatrick were completed.

A couple of weeks before the railway to Donaghadee was opened to the public, a special party of the B & C D R officials travelled over the line and joined the steamer *Wonder* at Donaghadee to cross over to Portpatrick to see if the advice of the P R board was justified. This trip was on 23 May 1861, and they would receive little encouragement from what they saw at Portpatrick.

A public excursion was organised by the B & C D R for Thursday, 27 June 1861, again using *Wonder* between Donaghadee and Portpatrick. On Monday, 22 July 1861, *Albion* called at Portpatrick on her way with an excursion from Donaghadee to Stranraer. The following year *Briton* did the same on 24 July.

Two excursions were given from Donaghadee to Portpatrick in the late summer of 1862. The first of these was on 28 August and was to celebrate the opening of the railway from Stranraer to Portpatrick. Most of the six hundred excursionists climbed up the hill to the main station at Portpatrick and joined trains for Stranraer. The crossing was made by *Heroine*, a new and fast paddle steamer employed on excursions from Belfast along the County Down coast. Like so many of her contemporaries, her speed made her attractive as a blockade runner, and in 1863 she crossed the Atlantic.

The second excursion in 1862 was provided by *Wonder* on 30 September.

But events had overtaken Portpatrick. The railway had now reached Portpatrick but there was no possibility of mails passing through until the harbour was nearer to completion. In the previous year the railway from Castle Douglas had reached Stranraer and the P R Board diverted their energy to securing a link between Stranraer and Ireland.

Donaghadee Harbour *c.* 1880

Portpatrick Harbour *c.* 1880

(The Galloway Advertiser and Wigtownshire Free

5 *(above)* Advertisement of August 1870
6 *(left)* Advertisement of July 1868
7 *(below)* *Dolphin* at Portpatrick in 1868

(WIGTOWNSHIRE COUNTY LIBRARY, STRAN

J. M. Brownlee, Photographer, Portpatrick

8   *Dolphin* as *Islay*

9   (*below*) John Rennie, Jr.

bove) ~~George Smeaton~~ John Smeaton

elow) An excursion steamer at
ortpatrick, possibly *Terrible*

(*The Galloway Advertiser and Wigtownshire Free Press*)

12   Advertisement of July 1871

(*The Belfast News-Le...*)

13   Advertisement of March 1867

(WOTHERSPOON COLLECTION, MITCHELL LIBRARY, GLASGO...)

14   *Alice* in L & S W R colours

Princess Louise off Stranraer

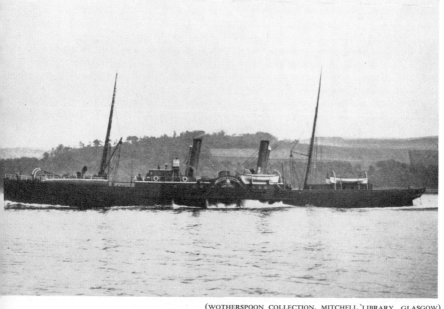

Princess Louise as *Islay*, off Inverkip

"PRINCESS LOUISE."

PLEASURE EXCURSION
TO
LARNE AND BELFAST.

THERE will be a SPECIAL EXCURSION to LARNE and BELFAST by the Splendid New Steamer, "PRINCESS LOUISE," on SATURDAY the 29th June curt., leaving Stranraer at 8 A.M. ; returning by train leaving Belfast at 4 P.M., Irish time, and Steamer from Larne at 5 P.M.

	1st Class & Cabin.	3rd Class & Steerage.
Stranraer to Larne and Back, ...	4s.	2s.
Stranraer to Belfast and Back, ...	6s.	3s.

SHORTEST SEA PASSAGE
BETWEEN
GREAT BRITAIN AND IRELAND,
Via LARNE AND STRANRAER.

DAILY SAILINGS to Commence on 1st JULY, 1872. Sea Passage under TWO HOURS. Loch Sailing about 40 Minutes. Trains go alongside Steamer at Larne and Stranraer.

The above Service will be Opened by a New Paddle Steamer, "PRINCESS LOUISE," built expressly for this Service. It is expected she will be the Fastest Steamer in the Channel.

London and Belfast,......................about 16½ Hours.	
Birmingham and Belfast,................. ,, 15 ,,	
Manchester or Liverpool and Belfast, ,, 12 ,,	
Carlisle and Belfast,......................... ,, 7½ ,,	

For information as to Passenger Fares and Goods, and Cattle Rates, apply to WILLIAM CAWKWELL, London and North-Western Railway (Euston), London ; JAS. SMITHELLS, Caledonian Railway, Glasgow ; EDWARD J. COTTON, Northern Counties Railway, Belfast ; or the several Station-Masters of the London and North-Western, Caledonian, or Northern Counties Railways.

(The Galloway Advertiser and Wigtownshire Free Press)

STEAM COMMUNICATION
BETWIXT
BELFAST AND STRANRAER

THE EXCELLENT AND SUBSTANTIAL STEAM-PACKET

LOCH RYAN,
JAMES GILLESPIE, Commander,

CONTINUES to Sail regularly once a week, with GOODS and PASSENGERS, between STRANRAER and GLASGOW; leaving STRANRAER & GREENOCK and GLASGOW every TUESDAY and returning from GLASGOW to STRANRAER every FRIDAY; calling off BALLANTRAE & GIRVAN, wind and weather permitting. The *LOCH RYAN* will also Sail every SATURDAY from STRANRAER to BELFAST, and return from BELFAST to STRANRAER, every MONDAY.

Fares and Freights very Moderate.

FROM STRANRAER FOR BELFAST.	FROM BELFAST FOR STRANRAER.
Saturday, July 18, 8 m.	Monday, July 20, 9 m.

Cabin Fare, 6s.—Steerage, 2s.

JAMES BRUCE, Oswald-street, Glasgow ; A. R. CAMPBELL, Queen-street, Stranraer ; ALEX. BRENAN, 55, York-street ; or, R. HENDERSON, 29, Donegall-Quay, Belfast.
324) STRANRAER, 14th July, 1835.

(The Belfast News-Letter)

17 (*left*) Advertisement of June 1872

18 (*above*) Advertisement of July 1835

19 (*below*) *Princess Beatrice* off Larne

(NATIONAL LIBRARY OF IRELAND)

(NATIONAL MARITIME MUSEUM, negative A4238)

20

Princess Louise and *Princess Beatrice* at Stranraer
The photograph shows the pier and station as extensively rebuilt in 1878

(ABERDEEN UNIVERSITY negative C1108)

21

Princess Victoria (1890) and *Princess Beatrice* at the railway pier
and *Argyll* at the West Quay, Stranraer

(The Galloway Advertiser and Wigtownshire Free Press)

London & North-Western Railway.

Shrewsbury
Crewe
Stafford
Tamworth
Wolverhampton
Walsall
Dudley
Birmingham
Coventry
Leamington
Rugby
Stamford
Peterborough
Northampton
Bedford
Oxford
Dunstable
LONDON — Euston Station ... arrive

Middlesborough
Stockton
Darlington
Barnard Castle
West Hartlepool
Shields—North or South
Sunderland
Newcastle-on-Tyne
Carlisle
Annan
Dumfries
Castle-Douglas
Newton Stewart
Stranraer ... arrive
Larne ... arrive
BELFAST ... arrive

Trains go alongside Steamer at Larne and Stranraer.

LARNE TO STRANRAER.............. CABIN, 6s.; STEERAGE, 3s.

Steamer leaves Larne Every Evening at 4.45 Irish time.

CHANGE OF CARRIAGES.—All change at Carlisle; those for Stations marked † change at Rugby; those marked * change at Stafford. Passengers to Stockton, Darlington, and North-Eastern Railways, break journey at Carlisle in each direction.

Passengers are Booked Through

To Dumfries, Carlisle, Newcastle-on-Tyne, Sunderland, Shields—North or South, West Hartlepool, London, Birmingham, Manchester, and Liverpool

From Londonderry, Portrush, Coleraine, Ballymoney, Ballymena, Cookstown, Magherafelt, Randalstown, and Antrim

By Train leaving Londonderry Daily at 12 noon.

HORSES are also Booked Through from Belfast or Larne to Stranraer, Dumfries, Annan, Carlisle, Newcastle, Darlington, and Stockton.

For other information, either as to Through Cattle Rates, or Through Goods Rates, or other matters, apply to Mr CUTTON, Belfast and Northern Counties Railway, Belfast; or to Mr GRAFTON, Portpatrick Railway, Stranraer.

Portpatrick Railway Manager's Office, Stranraer, September, 1862.   BY ORDER.

(SCOTTISH RECORD OFFICE, reference BR/GSW/4/4)

London, Euston...le
Bristol (n. S. Tunnel)
Birmingham
Stafford
Liverpool
Manchester, L.N.W.
Preston
Newcastle on Tyne
Carlisle, Cale.
Carlisle, G. & S.W.
Aberdeen
Dundee (West)
Perth
Stirling
Greenock
Gourock
Paisley
Glasgow, Central
Edinburgh, Prin. St
Moffat
Beattock
Lockerbie
Dumfries ...... leave

Castle-Douglas
Crossmichael
Parton
New Galloway
Cromore
Creetown
Palnure
Newton-Stewart dep.
Wigtown
Whauphill
Garlieston
Whithorn
Newton-Stewart for Stranraer ...... dep.
Kirkcowan
Glenluce
Dunragit
Castle-Kennedy
Stranraer Harb'r...ar
Stranraer Station..ar
Stranraer...... leave
Colfin
Portpatrick...arrive
Larne...... arrive
Belfast...... arrive

22 (above) Handbill for *Briton's* October 1862 service

23 (right) Advertisement of July 1892

24   *Princess Victoria* (1890)

25   *Princess May*

26

(*left*) Chief Engineer C. T. Henderson

27

(*right*) Captain Andrew Hamilton

LARNE AND STRANRAER STEAMBOAT COMPANY, LIMITED.

ROYAL WEDDING.

GENERAL HOLIDAY,
THURSDAY, JULY 6th.

ON above date the Steamer "PRINCESS VICTORIA" will leave the RAILWAY PIER, Stranraer, at 1.30 p.m., for a Trip along the

AYRSHIRE COAST
AND ROUND
AILSA CRAIG,

arriving back at Stranraer about 4.30 p.m.

FARE, - - - - ONE SHILLING.

EDWARD J. COTTON, General Manager.

Belfast, June, 1893.

(The Galloway Advertiser and Wigtownshire Free Press)

* (*above*) Advertisement of June 1893

* (*right*) Advertisement of July 1891

* (*below*) Advertisement of July 1908

(The Galloway Advertiser and Wigtownshire Free Press)

LARNE AND STRANRAER STEAMERS.

Salubrious Sailing on the Sapphire Sea.

ON SATURDAY, 11th July, at 2 p.m., the Princess Victoria will make a Cruise from Stranraer Harbour

ROUND SANDA.
FARE—TWO SHILLINGS. Getting back about 6 p.m.

In connection with this Cruise, the 1.30 p.m. Train from Portpatrick will run on to Stranraer Harbour Station with passengers for the Steamer.

THE USUAL TRIP ROUND AILSA CRAIG

on the CATTLE SHOW DAY will be given on FRIDAY, 17th, leaving the Pier at 2 p.m. Fare, 1/-.

WILLIAM M'CONCHIE, Traffic Manager.

21 Waring Street, Belfast.

LARNE & STRANRAER STEAMERS.

MAGNIFICENT NEW TRIP TO CAMPBELTOWN,
"THE GARDEN OF KINTYRE,"
On TUESDAY, 21st JULY.

LEAVING Stranraer Harbour at 9.20 a.m., getting back at 6.30 p.m., allowing about 4 hours ashore Campbeltown.

KEEN CUT RETURN FARE, 3/.

Giving access to Saloons of Ship. Train connections and Cheap Fares from all Stations, Whithorn to Portpatrick inclusive.

WILLIAM M'CONCHIE, Traffic Manager.

21 Waring Street, Belfast.

EXCURSIONS.

CHEAP SUMMER TRIPS
TO

PORTPATRICK,
VIA DONAGHADEE,
COMMENCING ON SUNDAY, 12TH JULY.

A STEAMER WILL SAIL FROM DONAGHADEE on Sundays on arrival of 10-0 a.m. Excursion Train from Belfast, and on Week-days on arrival of 9-25 a.m. Excursion Train from Belfast, as under (weather and other unforeseen circumstances permitting) :—

On Week-days at   ..   10-30 a.m. Irish Time.
On Sundays at   ..   11-15 a.m. Irish Time.

RETURNING FROM PORTPATRICK

On Week-days at   ..   6- 0 p.m. English Time.
On Sundays at   ..   4-30 p.m. English Time.

AT THE FOLLOWING FARES—

	Cabin.	Steerage.
Single	2s. 6d.	1s 6d
Return	4s 0d	2s 6d

CHEAP RETURN TICKETS

Are issued to Donaghadee by Trains and at Fares as under, thereby enabling Passengers to proceed to Scotland and return on same day.

From	Trains. On Sundays. a.m.	On Week-days. a.m.	Railway Return Tickets. 1st Cl.	2nd Cl.	3rd Cl.
Belfast	at 10- 0	9-25	2/6	1/9	1/3
Knock	" 10-10	9-35	2/6	1/9	1/3
Dundonald	" 10-17	9-40	2/6	1/9	1/3
Comber	" 10-25	9-50	1/9	1/3	9d
Newtownards	" 10-38	10- 2	1/6	1/-	7d

Tickets available for return on date of issue only.

A Train will leave Donaghadee for Belfast and intermediate Stations after the time the Steamer is expected to arrive from Portpatrick, as under :—

On Sundays, Donaghadee dep. 7-30 p.m. Ord. Tr.
On Saturdays,   "   " 9- 0 "   "
On other days,   "   " 8.45 " Spel. Tr.

(The Newtonards Chronicle)

Princess Victoria (1890) arriving at the rebuilt Stranraer Pier and Station

Larne Harbour Station after rebuilding

Princess Maud (1904) on trials off Skelmorlie

35

36   *Princess Victoria* (1912)

37   *Galtee More*

CHAPTER FIVE

Briton, Fannie, Alice, Dolphin and other attempts

ON 11 March 1861, the Portpatrick Railway was opened from Castle Douglas to Stranraer (Town) and arrangements had been made with the Glasgow & Stranraer Steam Packet Company for an augmented service to Belfast from Stranraer. *Albion* now left Stranraer at 1300 on Saturdays and *Scotia*, not hitherto a frequent visitor to Ireland, left on Wednesdays at the same hour. *Albion* returned from Belfast on Mondays and *Scotia* on Thursdays, both at 0830 I.T. (Until March 1916, Irish Time was 25 minutes behind Greenwich Mean Time.) These sailings operated in connection with the Portpatrick Railway, and a 2100 departure from London (Euston) by the London & North Western Railway meant a 1700 arrival in Belfast the following day, while the 0830 sailing from Belfast made a 0530 London arrival possible. In June, *Albion*'s days of sailing were altered to a Friday departure from Stranraer and Saturday from Belfast. The Steam Packet Company still maintained its sea link with Glasgow and also its Ayr–Campbeltown service. But the two days a week service to Ireland was not really what the P R wanted.

SAILING WEST

A daily service between Stranraer and Belfast was required for the traffic the Railway expected and needed. In November the Board met Mr. Langlands, of the Steam Packet Company, but in spite of this, the service for the winter dropped to once weekly. From 16 May 1862 the service was stepped up to an alternate day frequency, with *Albion* leaving Stranraer on Monday, Wednesday and Friday at noon, returning from Belfast at 1300 the following day.

The railway branch to the harbour was nearing completion in the summer of 1862, when a minor crisis was produced by a letter from the Packet Company intimating that the Belfast service was to be discontinued from the end of August. After discussion the withdrawal was postponed until the end of September.

Without an adequate shipping connection to Ireland the Railway could not hope to attract the traffic required and a committee was set up by the Railway Board to scour the land for a suitable vessel. In December 1861 the P R had been offered a spare ship by the L & N W R. The ship—it would seem to have been the 1836 paddler *Ocean*—was no longer employed on the Holyhead and Dublin service, but the P R's Act did not include powers to own ships and the offer was declined.

The steamer for the route came to the Committee rather than the Committee having to go looking for it. The Steam Packet Company had ordered a new paddle steamer for its services and, launched on 2 June 1862 from the Tod & McGregor yard, *Briton* arrived at Stranraer from Glasgow on 26 June. *Briton* displaced *Caledonia* from the Stranraer fleet. During 1863, *Caledonia* found summer employment on the Glasgow–Largs and Millport and excursion station, and in late December 1863 left for the Confederate States of a divided

America, where she was to be used as a blockade runner. A sketch, probably executed for the U.S. Consul, shows her leaving Cork and is dated 31 December 1863.[131] *Caledonia* managed four trips before being captured on 30 May 1864 by *USS Keystone State* and *Massachusetts* and her cargo of bacon and medical supplies jettisoned.

When, in April 1861, President Lincoln declared a blockade on the ports of the states of Florida, Alabama, Mississippi, Louisiana and Texas, which had seceded from the Union, the Confederate Government set about devising methods of maintaining communications with the outside world. In August 1861, the Confederate Government's financial agents in England, Fraser, Trenholm & Co., of Liverpool, initiated plans to break the blockade, and by showing its ineffectiveness it was hoped to encourage others to trade with the Southern ports. The screw ship, *Bermuda*, was chartered. Of 1,000 tons gross, she had just been completed at Stockton-on-Tees, but she was slow, being capable of only 8 knots. Her first voyage was successfully completed when Savannah, Georgia, was reached on 18 September. Her second trip was not so lucky, as on 27 April 1862 she was captured and taken to Philadelphia. She was renamed *General Meade* and some years later traded between New York and New Orleans.[132]

But the blockade had been demonstrated as vulnerable and the trade became a popular and lucrative one. The Clyde steamers were especially well suited to the traffic on account of their combination of speed and shallow draught. The ships in this trade could carry no armaments to defend themselves from capture, since to have done so would have resulted in their being treated as pirates. Speed and the ability to run over the shoals was their only defence against the Yankee ships.

The runners sailed for the Confederate ports from Nassau in the Bahamas, St. George's in Bermuda, and also from Cuba and Matamoras, Mexico. Cargoes brought over from Britain would be transferred at these ports into the blockade runners for the last lap. On the return journey the little ships would bring out cotton for Britain. Some ships made the voyage straight from Britain into the Southern ports. Blockade running came to an end in the spring of 1865 with the fall of Wilmington and Charleston to the Union forces. The magnitude of the trade is indicated by 1,149 blockade runners being captured during the four years. Of these, 210 were steamers. In addition, 355 vessels were lost at sea, of which 85 were steamers. Later in this chapter we shall meet two that got away.[133]

Reverting to the relative calm of Loch Ryan, the new *Briton* was an iron steamer of raised quarter-deck design, ten feet longer than *Albion* and greater in the beam. The journey from Greenock to Stranraer was completed in six hours. After a spell on the Glasgow–Stranraer trade, *Briton* took over the Stranraer–Belfast run on 8 August 1862. This was to be the ship selected by the Committee for their Irish sailings from Stranraer, but the destination was to be Larne and not Belfast.

In 1860 an Act had been passed creating the Carrickfergus & Larne Railway, which was empowered to build fourteen and a half miles of railway from the Belfast & Northern Counties Railway at Carrickfergus to Larne. The B & N C R had subscribed 10 per cent of the £125,000 capital of the C & L R and the former company was to manage and work the line. In the summer of 1862 this line was nearing completion and would provide a fast connection between Belfast and Larne. The Manager of the B & N C R, Edward J. Cotton, early in 1862, had contacted the P R and opened up discussion about using Larne as the Irish port for any steamers sailing in connection with the P R. This was agreed and *Briton* selected as the ship for the route, but neither the P R nor the B & N C R at that time had powers to own ships and *Briton* became the property of a consortium headed by Colonel James McDowall, of the P R. Her operating was covered by a guarantee completed in August 1862 by the L & N W R, Caledonian Railway, P R, B & N C R, and the Castle Douglas & Dumfries Railway. The Glasgow & South Western Railway declined to enter into this guarantee, though they did provide rail connections and through bookings.

STRANRAER & LARNE STEAMBOAT COMPANY

1 October 1862 was the date fixed for the new daily Stranraer–Larne service by *Briton*, and the trade name of "Stranraer & Larne Steamboat Company" was adopted. At Larne the station and pier were almost ready for traffic, but at Stranraer the work was some months from completion as the big day drew near. After inspecting the Stranraer–Portpatrick line on Friday, 1 August, the Board of Trade Inspector, Captain Tyler, spent the evening examining the progress of the harbour branch at Stranraer and had expressed himself satisfied with the work so far carried out. But by 1 October, however, the Board of Trade stamp of approval had not been obtained for the branch. Not troubled by such legal details, the P R put up a temporary platform at the seaward end of the stone neck of the pier. Great emphasis had been placed on the fact that at both ends the trains would be positioned alongside the steamer. As soon as the passengers had transferred from the connecting train, *Briton* set out for Larne to inaugurate the new pier.

At Larne, the pier, described by *The Belfast News-Letter* as of a "somewhat temporary character and hardly equal to the requirements of the place and the expected trade" was crowded with those eagerly awaiting the steamer. The newspaper's correspondent contrasted the rather subdued atmosphere at Stranraer with the exuberance and flag waving of the crowds at Larne. For him this typified the differing temperaments of the two nations. The railway line from Carrickfergus had been opened for traffic in the forenoon and the first passenger train left Belfast (York Road) at 0930. The crossing was made by *Briton* in nasty weather and she lost fifty-five minutes on the journey, but the connection was still made at Carrickfergus Junction (later renamed Greenisland) with the train for Londonderry. For the return journey, an express left Belfast at 1600 and stopping only at Carrickfergus Junction, for passengers off the noon train from Londonderry, and at Carrickfergus Town, the train reached Larne Curran, as the harbour terminal was called, at 1645, and after a few minutes *Briton* was off for Scotland.

Thereafter, *Briton* provided a daily (except Sunday) service between Stranraer and Larne, leaving the Scottish port around 1030 on arrival of the 0830 P R train from Castle Douglas with connection from Dumfries off the 2115 L & N W R train from Euston. Passengers crossing by *Briton* were scheduled to reach Belfast at 1330 I.T. Passengers from the Irish side left Larne at 1645 I.T. once the 1600 I.T. train from Belfast had arrived. The arrival time in London was 0940. Despite the threat of complete withdrawal, the Glasgow &

Stranraer Steam Packet Company maintained a monthly service between Stranraer and Belfast, employing *Albion*.

The half-yearly meeting of the shareholders of the P R had been held on 30 September 1862, and a contingent of B & C D R shareholders crossed from Donaghadee to Portpatrick by the tug *Wonder* and then proceeded to Stranraer for the meeting. They had crossed in stormy weather and the vulnerability of Portpatrick to wind and sea was brought home when the tugmaster declined to leave port on the return journey. This forced some of the shareholders to cross with *Briton* on her first sailing on the despised Stranraer–Larne route while others waited at Portpatrick until *Wonder* managed to leave on 1 October.

Briton battled on during the winter months and managed to give a service with few interruptions. But some of the P R directors were impatient for increased traffic. The line had been completed to Portpatrick Harbour and the Company could now exercise its power to pay dividends—if there was any profit available for distribution. But apparently it came as a surprise to some that the ship was, initially at least, to run at a loss, and by March of the following year one of the directors moved that the steamer service be discontinued because of its losses. The majority of the Board were more inclined to give the service a longer period to show what potential it had. At the end of September 1863 the figures for the half year to date had shown a marked increase and it was decided to continue the service for the time being.

During the summer of 1863, *Briton* had maintained the service reliably and had even given an excursion from Larne. Early in July, after arrival at Larne, Captain George Campbell took the excursionists along the Antrim coast as far as Red Bay. *Albion* also provided occasional excursions from Stranraer to Belfast and vice versa.

On 23 November 1863, the B & N C R Board decided they had ventured as far as they were prepared to go and resolved that the service had to cease. The L & N W R were of the same mind. The P R Board at their meeting on 1 December 1863 agreed that the service by *Briton* should be discontinued as from 31 December. Some years later, it was reported that the service by *Briton* had cost the P R in the region of £2,000. But the chairman of the P R was of the opinion, "If we had gone on with it, it had the germs of a future success".[134]

Briton was sold in January 1864 to the Bristol General Steam Navigation Company, who placed her on their Bristol–Waterford run. Three years later she moved to the Wexford service. *Briton* was to remain on this station until she and the interest in the route was sold to the Waterford Steamship Company in 1890. On 8 March 1892 she stranded on the North Bar at Wexford and in view of her age was sold for breaking up.

THE HIATUS

At the general meeting of the P R on 30 January 1864, the blame for the withdrawal of *Briton* was laid at the door of the Irish, who wanted a bigger and faster ship, but who were, at the same time, unable to finance the running of the ship. At the meeting the shareholders were told of a Bill to be introduced to Parliament which would allow the P R to invest directly in ships to provide connections between Portpatrick and Stranraer and ports on the north coast of Ireland and Donaghadee and Belfast. Where the capital for this plan was to be obtained was not indicated, but having tried once, and failed, the P R had no alternative but to try again, and there was still hope that some tangible support might come from Westminster for a service from either Portpatrick or Stranraer.

The Stranraer–Larne service by *Briton* had come as a bit of a shock to the B & C D R. In November 1861, their chairman had been heard "at length" by the P R Board on the need for the establishment of the service between Portpatrick and Donaghadee. After all, this was why the B & C D R had taken up £15,000 of P R stock. But on that occasion, Larne had won the day. In the late summer of 1864, the B & C D R Board asked for a resolution to be passed by the P R Board that they had no intention of aiding the re-establishment of the Larne steamboat service. The P R Board instructed the secretary to reply that there was no such *present* intention.

Following the demise of *Briton*, *Albion*'s Stranraer–Belfast service was stepped up to twice a month, and in May 1864 the frequency became weekly: out and back on Thursday. These sailings connected with trains of the P R. Traffic on the Glasgow–Ayr–Stranraer steamers fell off following the completion of the railway, and in May 1863, *Scotia* had been sold, leaving *Albion* alone in the fleet of the Glasgow & Stranraer Steam Packet Company. Like her consort, *Caledonia*, *Scotia* was to sail west, having been selected as a blockade runner. *Scotia* left the Clyde in August 1863 and managed five successful trips before being captured by *USS Connecticut* off Cape Fear, North Carolina, on 1 March 1864.

Albion was due to have some time away from the Clyde herself, but not for the exciting life of blockade running. A new ship had been ordered for the Steam Packet Company and in April 1865, *Albion* was chartered by the Somerset & Dorset Railway Company for a new Poole–Cherbourg service. This employment lasted less than two years, and in February 1867 the vessel was purchased for a service between Hayle, Swansea, Ilfracombe and Bristol. Again, this was to prove of short duration and early in 1869, *Albion* was sold back to M. Langlands & Sons (who in 1864 had taken over the Glasgow & Stranraer Steam Packet Company).

A new screw *Albion* was being built when the paddler *Albion* left for Poole in April 1865, but it was to be some months before she was ready for the station. A vessel was chartered to fill the gap. This was *Staffa*, a screw steamer, built in 1863 for the Western Isles trade of David Hutcheson & Co. *Staffa*, as well as giving the weekly Stranraer–Belfast service, gave occasional excursions from Belfast to Stranraer in the summer of 1865. During the previous summer the steamers *Laurel* and *Electric* had each given an excursion to Stranraer from Belfast in September. On 8 August 1865, the new *Albion* arrived at Stranraer and took over the sailings, including the weekly Belfast trip, from *Staffa*.

CALEDONIAN TAKEOVER

In December 1863, the P R Board began the dangerous game of playing off one giant against another. The P R had had its tussles with the G & S W R and decided to accept the CR offer to take up £40,000 of P R stock and take over the rolling stock and plant and responsibility for the working and maintenance of the P R for a period of twenty-one years.

The agreement with the C R was effective only if the P R could obtain running rights over the stretch that separated the two companies lines. This was the Castle Douglas & Dumfries Railway, which was very much tied to the G & S W R apron strings. An Act of Parliament was necessary to obtain this running right, and on 29 July 1864, the Portpatrick Railway Act (No. 1) received the Royal Assent. This Act also legalised retrospectively the deviation of the Stranraer Harbour branch from the west pier to the new east pier. The Act increased further the borrowing powers of the P R. On the same day, the Act outlined at the general meeting in January the Portpatrick Railway (Steamboats) Act, received the Royal Assent. The P R now had authority to operate steamers between (a) Portpatrick and Donaghadee, and (b) Stranraer and Belfast or Larne. Thus the way was now open for ships owned directly by the P R to operate between Scotland and Ireland. The original intention was for the former route to be utilised for mail and passengers and the latter for cattle and cargo.

In February 1864, the G & S W R wrote indignantly to the C R protesting that the aid being given to the P R was inconsistent with the Articles of Agreement executed by the two companies. But the C R was not to have its foothold in the south-west corner threatened and blandly denied any inconsistency.

No time was wasted by the C R in its attempts to raise traffic for its new investment. In March 1865, the P R shareholders were told that it was expected Portpatrick Harbour would be completed by the summer and their company, in conjunction with the C R, were to provide a Portpatrick–Donaghadee service. But the harbour was not ready and nothing happened at Portpatrick that summer. In August, at a meeting in Glasgow with the C R, the P R were asked to consider a service between Stranraer and Belfast. The P R Board replied that they could not contemplate taking on the full financial load of such a service and also asked that if a service was put into operation one of the two ships to be purchased should be adapted for the Portpatrick–Donaghadee route, thus allowing both the Stranraer and Portpatrick stations to be maintained. After the meeting the P R Board went further and wrote to the C R "to let it be known by the Caledonian Railway that they cannot consider Stranraer–Belfast without Portpatrick–Donaghadee".

The vessels selected by the C R (without, it was subsequently claimed, any consultation with the P R) were two blockade runners just returned from Nassau to Liverpool. The asking price for the two paddlers was £27,000 and it was estimated that £2,500 would make them suitable for the Stranraer station.

Built in 1859 by Caird & Co., Greenock, as *Sirius* and *Orion*, these ships had operated on the mail route between Lubeck and Cronstadt for the St. Petersburg & Lubeck Steam Navigation Company. These two-funnelled, iron paddlers, now bearing the names *Alice* and *Fannie*, had arrived on 1 June 1863 at Nassau for blockade running, and Frank Burtt gives a brief history of their days operating into the Carolina ports. He records that *Alice* was so successful that her master was paid $5,000 a trip. The success of *Alice* is borne out by the detailed research of Marcus Price, who credits *Alice* with sixteen successful runs in 1863. *Fannie* was not far behind with fourteen. By the end of 1864, both had returned to the Clyde and were given extensive overhauls at Dumbarton, and in the early months set out for Nassau. But the blockade had been intensified and the two ships lay at Nassau. *Alice* and *Fannie* were eventually obliged to unload their cargo at Nassau and sail for Birkenhead, arriving during the summer.[135]

In July 1865, the C R Manager, Mr. C. Johnston, and Mr. Benjamin Conner, the C R Locomotive Superintendent, together with Mr. Rowan, of Aitken & Co., Engineers, went to inspect the ships at Birkenhead, and after considering their report the C R Board agreed at their meeting on 8 August 1865 to purchase *Alice* and *Fannie*. Until a suitable financial arrangement could be arrived at with the P R the ships were to remain C R property, but this posed a legal problem, since the powers of the C R did not include shipowning. To get round this difficulty the two steamers were registered in the names of Thomas Salkeld, a C R director who also served on the P R Board, and a C R solicitor.

The intention was that the P R should pay to the C R the cost of the ships plus the outlay involved in preparing them for the route—a total agreed at £30,000—with the C R guaranteeing the P R against any loss incurred when the ships were sold at the termination of the working agreement covering the ships. The agreement was initially for five years, but in September 1865 it was extended to seven years. For its part the P R agreed to pay a straight £800 annually to the C R.[136]

The appointment of Mr. John McKee as agent for the C R at Belfast was confirmed in November 1865, and it was agreed to spend £218 on erecting an office on the quayside at Belfast. In April 1867, Messrs. McGregor Bros. replaced Mr. McKee as C R agent. The advertisements in the press for *Fannie* and *Alice* always appeared under a C R heading with the title "Short Sea Passage".

The P R Board in November 1865 considered a request from the Belfast, Holywood & Bangor Railway that Bangor should be the Irish terminus, since the railway link between Belfast and Bangor had been opened in May of that year. The P R declined to entertain this request. But they in turn found that the C R was simply ignoring their stipulation that the Stranraer–Belfast route could not be considered unless the Portpatrick–Donaghadee crossing was also supplied. When *Fannie* arrived at Stranraer it was obvious that while she might be ideally suited for the crossing to Ireland her dimensions ruled out any possibility of employment at Portpatrick. The suggestion that her sister *Alice* was for the Portpatrick station must be dismissed as an attempt to keep the B & C D R from becoming too restless.

"FANNIE" AND "ALICE" ON THE CROSSING

On the first day of December 1865, *Fannie*, under the command of Captain Samuel Barker, arrived at Stranraer Railway Pier at 1300. She then crossed to Belfast. It is probable that Larne was not selected as the Irish port because of the absence of any C & L R or B & N C R capital in the enterprise. *Fannie* accomplished the journey to Belfast in 3¾ hours. She lay overnight at Belfast, and the basic schedule (excepting Sunday) was out in the morning from Belfast and returning in the evening from Stranraer. The 1000 departure from Belfast gave arrivals at Glasgow at 2130, Edinburgh 2110 and London 0550. There was no connecting London train advertised for the 1945 sailing from Stranraer, but connecting trains left Glasgow and Edinburgh at 1300. An agreement was drawn up between the L & N W R and the C R in June 1867 whereby the former would bear a third of the loss incurred by the latter in working the line from 1 October 1864.[137]

Whether we can detect feverish attempts by the C R to increase trade is an open question, but certainly the variation in schedules were numerous. The 1000 departure from Ireland proved to be unpopular and a 1400 departure was tried from February 1866. The retiming must have produced satisfactory results, since it was left undisturbed until March 1867, when another change was made, the vessel being billed to leave Belfast at 0930. From 1 August 1866, the steamer left Stranraer at 2300, arriving at Belfast at 0230. In March 1867, the departure from the Scottish side was moved to 1700.

When *Fannie* re-opened the daily service between Belfast and Stranraer on 4 December 1865, her sister *Alice* was being refitted for the station, and she arrived at Stranraer on 6 February 1866 under the command of Captain Primrose. The sisters were identical externally except, a contemporary report tells us, that *Alice* had a carving on her stern which featured a man with hounds. When *Alice* arrived, *Fannie* had a few days off service and then the pair began to sail on roughly alternate days. On occasion both would be in service, either conveying a special party from Stranraer to Belfast, or vice versa, or assisting one another when traffic was heavy.

In the summer of 1866 the P R received a request to charter *Alice* for a trip to the Highlands for sheep. This was agreed to, but nearer the time had to be cancelled because of repairs required to the ship. In August, considerable boiler repairs were necessary before her Board of Trade certificate could be renewed. The repairs were carried out and tenders sought for the reboilering of *Alice*. In November, the tender from A. & J. Inglis for £2,308 was accepted, but the work does not appear to have been carried out. In September 1866, *Alice* managed a trip to Inveraray for cattle.

All was not well. The expenses were far ahead of income and the C R Board, in June 1867, agreed to advertise both ships for sale. The following advertisement appeared in *The Glasgow Herald* of Thursday, 27 June:

For Sale

The *Fanny* [sic] or *Alice*, Clyde built iron paddle steamers, now trading between Stranraer and Belfast. Gross tonnage 639.52; register tonnage 402.90. Nominal horse power 260.

These steamers have been fitted for passengers, goods and cattle traffic, and are in excellent condition.

The steamers are of the same size and power; and if a purchaser desires to have the two, the owners would receive an offer for both.

Full particulars may be had on application to Mr. Conner, Locomotive Department, Caledonian Railway, St. Rollox, Glasgow.

But no one was interested. In December, the decision was taken to retain *Alice* until a replacement was available for the route. The C R wondered, however, if the P R would like to purchase or hire the substitute vessel. The loss in working the ships for the six months to the end of 1867 is recorded as £4,689. 8s. 1½d. Small wonder the C R wanted to end this operation, and the P R were slow in taking up the invitation.

But the trouble really began in January 1868. On Tuesday, 14 January, *Alice* was damaged when berthing at Stranraer in a strong east wind. Her wheels were obstructed by the damage but she managed to make off at 2300 for Belfast. At the same time, a high tide caused the paddle box of *Fannie*, berthed at the Railway Pier, to rest on the edge of the pier, and as the tide fell, damage was caused to the paddle box. Later in the same week, *Alice* was caught in a great storm on her crossing from Belfast and her floats damaged. Captain Barker managed to make Loch Ryan and *Alice* anchored for two hours off Cairnryan while temporary repairs were carried out. When she arrived at Stranraer, the locomotive foreman of the P R, Mr. Blackwood, had his men on board to repair the damage. It was 2000 on the Saturday before *Alice* was able to cross to Belfast.

But *Alice* could not continue in service for long, and it now became known that *Fannie*'s passenger certificate had been allowed to expire. It was announced that the service between Stranraer and Belfast would be discontinued for the time being, the last day of the service being Thursday, 30 January 1868. Both ships continued to lie at the Railway Pier and it was expected that the interruption to the service would be brief. *Albion*, once again, fitted in the occasional crossing to Belfast, the first being on Friday, 5 February.

At a meeting of shareholders of the P R on 24 March 1868, the directors reported, "Owing to a disaster which happened to one of the steamers during the tempestuous gales of last winter, after the certificate of the second steamer had expired, it was deemed necessary by the C R to suspend the sailings between Stranraer and Belfast at the end of January last". The directors also noted that the working company (C R) were under an obligation to maintain the passage since the agreement entered into had been for a period of seven years. The repairs to the steamers, the shareholders were told, were "now far advanced". One shareholder, Mr. John Jamieson, of Donaghadee, criticised the C R for its high-handed manner in the whole business with *Fannie* and *Alice* and counselled the P R to go it alone and use the Portpatrick–Donaghadee route.

Despite the promises, neither *Fannie* nor *Alice* were to touch the Irish coast again. *Fannie* left Stranraer for Bowling Harbour on the Clyde on 23 June 1868. In early June it was reported that Mr. Blackwood's staff had almost completed the extensive repairs necessary to put *Alice* back in service. On Friday, 26 June, Captain Barker took *Alice* on a trial run to Corsewall Point but then headed north to join *Fannie* at Bowling.

Fannie and *Alice* were offered for public sale on 23 September 1868, the upset prices being £7,000 and £8,500, respectively, but there were no takers. In April 1869, *Alice* was sold to the London & South Western Railway for £7,000 and *Fannie* joined the same fleet for £5,550 in June of the same year. In 1870 they entered service on the Southampton–St. Malo route. At that time, there had been a great increase in traffic to France, caused by the Franco-Prussian war. Their luck with the L & S W R proved better than it had been with the C R, for they remained in the L & S W fleet for many years and in 1874 were reboilered. *Fannie* was broken up in 1890 and her sister in 1898. The research of K. A. Williams shows that for her last ten years *Alice* lay as a re-fitting hulk at Northam for the L & S W R. Duckworth & Langmuir record that *Fannie* also saw service under charter to the North of Scotland & Orkney & Shetland Steam Navigation Company.[138]

Because of the agreement between the C R and the P R, the difference between the initial cost of the ships, nearly £30,000, and the sale proceeds of £12,550 had to come out of the C R pocket. The C R were never, in fact, paid a penny of the £30,000 by the P R. The last straw for the C R must have been the presentation by a Glasgow shipyard of an invoice for £950 for work on *Fannie*. Undaunted, the C R was to turn to the Clyde in an effort to establish a marine foothold, and in the summer of 1870 chartered the steamers *Dunoon Castle* and *Vesta* with no greater success than marked their Stranraer enterprise. But the P R Board had its own headaches at this time.

COMPENSATION

The P R Board had meantime been continuing correspondence with the Treasury following the suspension of work at Portpatrick Harbour. On 2 August 1866, a deputation from the B & C D R and the P R and other interested parties had met Lord Derby, First Lord of the Treasury. Lord Derby had encouraged the railway companies with their plans for a Portpatrick–Donaghadee service and had asked for details to be sent to the Treasury. Before the month was out, the proposed schedule was in his hands. This service was to connect off the 2040 limited express from Euston with an arrival in Belfast at 1020. The return service would leave Belfast (Queen's Quay) at about 1800 and arrive in London at 0940 the next day. The mail service, Castle Douglas–Belfast, was offered at £14,690 per annum, or £12,595 if the service was restricted to six days a week.

In September 1867, a reminder was sent off to London, and in November a reply was received at Stranraer from the Treasury which dismissed the offer as not even forming a starting point for negotiation. The Treasury had now come to the conclusion that there was no hope of establishing a service between Portpatrick and Donaghadee. The Postmaster-General had shown no interest in the route, and a pessimistic report had been received from Captain Hawes. The P R Board were advised that legislation could be introduced into Parliament whereby the harbour at Portpatrick would be transferred to the railway company and in addition £25,000 offered to them unconditionally in satisfaction of all claims.

Earlier in the year, July 1867, the Treasury had come to an agreement with the B & C D R as to the compensation to be paid to them. The B & C D R had a debenture debt of £166,666, most of which had been incurred in building the Donaghadee branch. These debentures fell due for repayment in 1867–69 and the Treasury agreed to advance a loan of the same amount for the purpose of liquidating the debt. The rate of interest on the Government loan was $3\frac{1}{2}$ per cent as against the debenture rate of 5 per cent. So that when, in December 1867, the P R approached the B & C D R with a proposition to re-open the Portpatrick–Donaghadee route their chairman had to reply that his company must decline at present in joining to put ships on the crossing. Following their satisfactory arrangement with the Treasury, the B & C D R interest in the route waned.

Lord Stair, the P R chairman, had already written off to the Treasury declining to entertain their offer. Perhaps, he surmised, the Government was now finding it both troublesome and expensive, but the P R had taken the Treasury Agreement of 1856 as binding and it was iniquitous that a Government Department should try to wriggle out of its obligations. He described the compensation of £25,000 as paltry. The interest from it would barely cover the expense of maintaining the harbour which was now being palmed off on the railway. Lord Stair argued for a transfer of the mail route to Stranraer, reminding Lord Derby that in March 1867 this possibility had been received encouragingly by the First Lord.

In February 1868, the Treasury replied and noted with surprise that their offer to transfer Portpatrick Harbour to the railway was being refused. The harbour had always been described by the railway directors as an asset of great potential, but no one could be forced to accept property if they did not want it. They recommended the P R Board to accept the £25,000, as a straight payment was safer than an uncertain mail contract which would fall periodically for review.

In his reply, in March, Lord Stair maintained that the original agreement had envisaged not a temporary mail contract but one of some permanence and that compensation should be based on this loss. He still preferred a mail subsidy for the mail route via Stranraer. The P R chairman reckoned the compensation to the B & C D R amounted to £2,500 per annum—being the difference between 3½ per cent and 5 per cent on the debenture stock of £166,666—and if this was based on a mileage of the line from Newtonards to Donaghadee of 22 miles, a comparable figure for the 62 miles from Castle Douglas to Portpatrick was £7,000. This figure, he suggested, should be considered as a mail subsidy for the route via Stranraer.

The Postmaster-General was consulted and he was of the view that even £5,000 would be out of all proportion to the benefit accruing from the use of the route via Stranraer, whether straight to Belfast or via Larne. This subsidy to the P R was refused.[139]

At a meeting at London on 23 June 1868, the P R Board considered a Treasury Minute of 8 June offering to obtain for the company a grant of £20,000 together with a loan to the extent of the debenture debt (£153,000) of the company in satisfaction of the company's claims in consequence of the abandonment of the Portpatrick–Donaghadee route as a mail service. The Board authorised Lord Stair to accept.

At the next meeting of the P R Board, on 29 July 1868, a fly appeared in the ointment, for the C R had written asking how the P R Board intended to allow the C R to participate in the compensation. The curt reply was to the effect that the C R would participate in the same way as any other shareholder. Naturally, this did not satisfy the C R, who had burnt their fingers over the *Fannie/Alice* exercise and who now found themselves operating a railway line in which they had a substantial capital involvement but which led virtually nowhere. They replied that the Portpatrick–Donaghadee passage was "the very basis and foundation of the Caledonian Company undertaking to work the line at the low rates specified in the Agreement" (of 1864). It was pointed out to the C R Board that this simply was not so, as the C R had agreed to the rates, which were no lower than those offered by the G & S W R to the P R. The C R Board took legal advice, but the opinion of counsel was that the claim to participate in the compensation in any preferential way would not stand up in court and the matter had to be dropped.

THE DONAGHADEE & PORTPATRICK SHORT SEA STEAM PACKET COMPANY LIMITED

In the spring of 1867, agitation had started on the Irish side for a service between Donaghadee and Portpatrick. In May 1866, John Jamieson had organised an excursion by *Terrible*. This was a wooden paddle tug built at North Shields in 1866 and based at Glasgow. She earned extra revenue by taking occasional public sailings and charters on Belfast Lough or the Clyde. After *Terrible* berthed in the inner basin at Portpatrick, a train took the excursionists to Castle Kennedy. As we have already seen, Jamieson spoke out against the Caledonian intrusion with *Fannie* and *Alice* and set about organising a service for the summer of 1868. "We'll have no *Fannies* or *Alices*", he declared. To demonstrate the shortness of the route, he had reached the general meeting at Stranraer in March 1868 by crossing with four others from Donaghadee to Portpatrick in a rowing boat and completed the crossing in 3½ hours.

At the meeting in July 1868, the P R Board considered a prospectus received from The Donaghadee & Portpatrick Short Sea Steam Packet Company Limited.[140] The objects of the Company are what one would expect, viz., to establish a steam packet service between the ports named in its title. The Company's capital was to be £10,000 in 2,000 shares of £5 each. A deputation was received, and this included Mr. John Jamieson, who had strongly advocated the Portpatrick route at the P R general meeting the previous March. The P R Board agreed to recommend to their shareholders that a loan be advanced to the Short Sea Steam Packet Company. The loan was to be £5,000 or half the cost of the steamer to be purchased, whichever was the lower, and was to be interest-free for five years. The loan would be secured by a mortgage on the ship. The P R was to nominate two directors for the D & P S S S P Co. Board and Mr. Alexander Ingram, the P R's secretary, and Lord Garlies were selected.

Representatives of the C R had met the D & P S S S P Co. promoters in June 1868, and seeing here a slight chance of salvaging something from their investment in the P R, the C R agreed to co-operate with through bookings and rates. From 11 September 1868, the Permanent Way and Traffic Committee of the C R arranged for carriages to travel down from Portpatrick Station to the Harbour, and the seven weeks following appear to be the only time during which the harbour branch at Portpatrick was used.

Advertisements in the latter half of September and in October carried the note that "the train now comes alongside the steamer at Portpatrick". The C R suggested to the P R that they might like to have a suitable shed built for passengers to shelter in. On the Irish side, the B & C D R advertised train connections to and from Belfast with through fares.

The ship purchased in 1868 by the D & P S S S P Co. for their service was *Dolphin*, a paddle steamer built in 1849 by Tod & McGregor and formerly engaged, as *Islay*, on trade to the Western Isles of Scotland.[141] In February 1868, David Hutcheson & Co. had purchased the vessel and renamed her *Dolphin*, but her duty with the company was brief. For the last two weeks of April, *Dolphin* sailed on the Glasgow–Islay route, replacing her successor, *Islay*, while during the middle two weeks of June *Dolphin*, again presumably under charter, replaced *Albion* on the Stranraer–Glasgow route. On Saturday afternoon, 11 July 1868, *Dolphin* made her first arrival at Portpatrick, having crossed from Donaghadee in less than two hours. She was greeted by a gun salute and once berthed, "gentlemen met in her cabin and drank to the success of the venture".

A double daily service (excepting Sundays) commenced on Monday,

13 July, leaving the Irish side at 0900 and 1515 and Portpatrick at 1225 and 1840. The cabin single fare was 3s. (15p) and the steerage 1s. 6d. (7½p). An excursion fare of 5s. (25p) applied between Belfast and Portpatrick. Train connections were laid on at both ends of the route. *Dolphin* had her busy days. On Friday, 17 July, the day of the Stranraer Cattle Show, two hundred passengers were carried over to Portpatrick, where they joined a train for Stranraer. In addition to her two round trips, on every Thursday in August, *Dolphin* sailed from Portpatrick at 0700. This connected with the 0850 train from Donaghadee to Belfast and provided an excursion from the Scottish side with four hours in Belfast, returning by the 1350 train and 1515 sailing from Donaghadee. This sailing was also provided on Saturday, 15 August 1868, when about two hundred excursionists left Stranraer by special train shortly after 0600 to join *Dolphin*.

At a meeting of the D & P S S S P Co. at their offices in Queen's Square, Belfast, in late September, it was reported that since the commencement of the service four thousand passengers had travelled by *Dolphin*. In September 1868, the frequency was reduced to one round trip daily, leaving Ireland at 1100, though by the end of the month and during October the time was 0900, and leaving Scotland at 1730. The loss sustained by the company during its short life was £2,500. *Dolphin* was sold to London owners and no service operated from Portpatrick in 1869, while at Stranraer there was only *Albion* crossing twice a month or so.

The D & P S S S P Co. had no ship sailing in 1869, but in October it was resolved to approach the P R and B & C D R with a view to re-opening the Donaghadee–Portpatrick route in the spring of 1870 under the joint management of the three companies. Nothing came of this. At the same time, the P R Board were asked to consider a plan emanating from Liverpool for the establishment of a steamboat service between Portpatrick and the North of Ireland. Early in 1870, the P R received a draft prospectus for the Portpatrick & North of Ireland Steam Packet Company Limited. But the matter was allowed to drop. The same fate befell another attempt to interest the P R in a service between Stranraer and Londonderry. Something approaching a service between Stranraer and Londonderry was offered in the autumn of 1868, when *Druid* fitted in a round trip on Thursdays between Belfast and Stranraer while employed principally on a Belfast–Londonderry service.

In March 1869, M. Langlands & Sons (who had taken over the Glasgow & Stranraer Steam Packet Company) purchased back their paddler *Albion* of 1860 and ran her alongside her screw namesake. The local press "hoped that the company will develop further the Stranraer–Belfast trade which the Caledonian Railway Company has abandoned". But the twice-monthly programme from Stranraer continued.

Stranraer received the occasional attention of the former Clyde steamer *Earl of Arran*, which in 1868 had been displaced from its Ardrossan–Arran station by new tonnage and forced to make a living elsewhere. In 1869, *Earl of Arran* was on Belfast Lough sailing principally between Belfast and Bangor. On Wednesday, 23 June, *Earl of Arran* gave an excursion from Ardrossan, Ayr and Stranraer to Belfast. The journey each way was spread over two days, with the intervening night being spent at Stranraer. On 27 July 1869, the same steamer brought an excursion party from Belfast to Stranraer. The Ayr Races on 16 September 1869 brought *Earl of Arran* back to Stranraer, whence she sailed at 0700 on a cruise to Ayr, calling off Cairnryan and Ballantrae. *Earl of Arran*'s Belfast–Bangor sailings commenced on Saturday, 15 May 1869. On the previous two days she had sailed on day excursions from Donaghadee to Portpatrick, leaving the Irish side at 0845 after the arrival of the 0730 train from Belfast. *Earl of Arran* sailed from Portpatrick at 1630. An excursion to Castle Kennedy was advertised by the 1010 train from Portpatrick. As often happened, the presence of a brass band on the steamer was promised. *Earl of Arran* spent only one summer based at Belfast and by 1871 she was sailing between Penzance and the Scilly Isles. She was lost by stranding in July 1872.

FURTHER ATTEMPTS AT DONAGHADEE

After an uneventful year, another attempt was made in mid-July 1870 to to re-open the route between Donaghadee and Portpatrick. The vessel was a wooden paddler, *Reliance*, built the previous year at North Shields. She was based at Donaghadee and left the Irish port daily, except Sunday, at 0900 and completed the crossing in 1½ hours. *Reliance* returned from Portpatrick at 1700. A Sunday service was arranged, leaving Donaghadee at 1100. Train connections by the B & C D R left Belfast at 0730, except Sunday, and 0955 on Sunday. The railway offered return tickets at single fare. On Monday to Saturday a train left Portpatrick at 1230 for Stranraer and Castle Douglas. *Reliance* gave one excursion from Portpatrick to Donaghadee. This was on Saturday, 13 August 1870, the Newtonards Fair Day, when she left Scotland after the arrival of a special train from Stranraer, leaving at 0730. The return trip started from Donaghadee at 1900 and was expected back in Stranraer at 2130. With *Dolphin* the P R and C R had co-operated to the full, but with *Reliance* there is no sign of similar co-operation. On the occasion of the special excursion the advertisement warns, "Usual fares will be charged on Portpatrick Railway".

Reliance was a small steamer—she appears to have been a passenger/tug vessel—but a press report maintained that she was "well adapted for passenger trade during the summer months". After about two months, on Saturday, 3 September 1870, the service ceased. Contrary to expectations, *Reliance* did not appear at Donaghadee in 1871. It was considered that the operators had antagonised many by sailing on Sunday. Nothing is known of *Reliance*'s career subsequent to her brief appearance on the Short Sea Route.

In April 1871, an advertisement appeared in the local Stranraer paper which promised the re-opening of the Donaghadee–Portpatrick route, but the service was not to operate on a regular basis until August 1871. *Shamrock*, a ship very similar to *Reliance* and built in 1870 at North Shields, made occasional appearances on the station in 1871. On Saturday, 13 May, *Shamrock* left Portpatrick at 0700 and returned from Donaghadee for a second sailing four hours later with a return to Portpatrick in the evening. *Shamrock*'s next crossing was on 22 June, when she again made two round trips. This was repeated on the following day. *Shamrock* also took time off from her normal sailings between Belfast and Holywood on the shores of Belfast Lough on the Queen's Birthday Holiday, Wednesday, 24 May, when an opportunity was given for a day excursion from Portpatrick to Peel, Isle of Man, while on Wednesday, 5 July, *Shamrock* brought two hundred trippers from Belfast to Stranraer. On the following Saturday, *Shamrock* appeared at Stranraer to assist *Albion* on an excursion from Stranraer to Ayr. *Shamrock* remained on Belfast Lough until 1894.

Yet another paddler appeared at Donaghadee in August 1871. This was the wooden paddle steamer *Aber*, built at Sunderland in 1867. Grahame Farr relates that during 1868 this ship ran excursions from Swansea to Ilfracombe, Appledore, Clovelly, and also Gower Coast cruises.[142] Captain Walls, who had commanded *Reliance*, was master of *Aber* while she was at Donaghadee. *Aber* commenced on the route on 18 August 1871 and gave a daily crossing from Donaghadee. But her time was to be brief, for on Tuesday, 29 August 1871, while between Portpatrick and Donaghadee, she was run down and almost cut in two by the liner *Prussian*. *Aber* sank in five minutes but there was no loss of life, her seventeen passengers and crew of eight being all picked up. Thus ended dramatically yet another attempt to maintain the Donaghadee–Portpatrick station.

This activity at Portpatrick should not lead us to believe that nothing was happening at Stranraer. After long negotiations, the P R let it be known, through *The Galloway Advertiser and Wigtownshire Free Press* of 14 September 1871, that measures had been taken "to have a suitable paddle steamer on Larne–Stranraer next spring". After the attempts of 1862–63 and 1866–68 was it to be a case of third time lucky?

CHAPTER SIX

The Larne & Stranraer
Steamboat Company Limited

BY March 1869, correspondence was flowing once again between the P R and the B & N C R seeking the re-establishment of the Stranraer–Larne route. The B & N C R manager, Mr. Edward J. Cotton, was also engaged on the same topic with the L & N W R.

At a P R Board meeting in March 1870, it was decided to put a proposition to the shareholders at the general meeting to be held at the end of the month. At that meeting it was successfully moved that the P R use part of the £20,000 compensation received from the Government in financing half the capital required for a steamboat company to operate the Stranraer–Larne route. This amount was not to exceed £7,500 and the B & N C R were to raise the other half. The Irish promoters, headed by Mr. James Chaine, chartered the steamer *Semaphore* to take them on 23 August 1870, from Larne to Stranraer. At the subsequent meeting with the P R, it was decided that the sum required from the P R was now reckoned at £10,000, and the B & N C R was not going to invest its own capital but would arrange for £10,000 to be raised among private individuals.

FINDING A SHIP

The service was going ahead and to operate it several ships were considered as possibilities. One of these was *Scud*, a paddle ship built in 1862 for the London Chatham & Dover Railway, but it was decided that she was unsuitable. The same opinion was held concerning *Herald*, of the Barrow Steam Navigation Company. This paddle steamer had been built at Greenock in 1866 and for a few months had traded for J. Little & Co. between Greenock and Campbeltown before being placed, the following year, on the Barrow Company's Isle of Man service from Morecambe. In 1870, the B S N Co. had taken delivery of *Antrim* and *Herald* was considered spare. But she was to remain with the B S N Co. until 1891, when, for a season, she returned to the Clyde and sailed, rather erratically and slowly, between Fairlie and Campbeltown.

In March 1871, the decision was taken to advertise for a ship, and for the first time the name of the steamboat company was used. In *The Glasgow Herald* of 23 March 1871 we find the advertisement:

To charter, with option of purchase, a first-class steamer not above 250 tons register, and draft of water loaded not to exceed 9 feet, capable of performing the passage between Larne and Stranraer, in all weathers, in three hours, with good accommodation for 1st and 2nd class passengers, and complete cargo and cattle arrangements.

Offers, stating terms of charter, description of steamer, horse-power, consumption of fuel, when built, details of cabin accommodation and

64

how soon she could be ready for sea, to be addressed to the undersigned, on or before 28 March inst.

Charles Stewart, Secretary *pro tem*,
Larne & Stranraer Steamboat Co.,
Belfast.

21 March 1871.

From the minutes of the P R it appears that several ships were offered
but again none was found suitable. Tenders for building were sought and considered in September. There were four tenders submitted for a paddle steamer:

Tod & McGregor	£19,000
A. & J. Inglis	£18,800
Thos. Wingate & Co.	£18,500 or
	£18,000
	(depending on engines fitted)

The Board resolved to accept the lowest offer of £18,000, but two weeks
later "deemed it necessary to accept the offer from Tod & McGregor" at the
lowered price of £18,500. The first entry in the cash book of the L & S S Co.
is of 7 November 1871, "By Tod & McGregor remitted them on account of
first instalment, *Princess Louise* £2,000".

THE LARNE & STRANRAER STEAMBOAT COMPANY LIMITED

It was not until 23 December 1871 that The Larne & Stranraer Steamboat
Company Limited was registered under the (Irish) Companies Act of 1862.
The nominal capital of the company was £20,000 in £10 shares and the P R
subscribed for half the capital. The balance was to come from gentlemen in
Ireland, but in fact only £9,250 was taken up. This resulted in the L & S S Co.
being, in today's terms, a subsidiary of the P R. The share capital was called
up in four instalments: £1 in October 1870, £2. 10*s*. a year later, £5 in March
1872, and £1. 10*s*. in August 1872, making £10 in all. Among the leading shareholders was Mr. James Chaine, who took up £1,000 capital. James Chaine had
acquired Larne Harbour in 1866 and was largely responsible for the development of the harbour. As well as being a strong supporter of the Larne–Stranraer
crossing, he worked on the establishment of links between Larne and the
United States of America. When he died, at the early age of 44, a monument,
in the form of a lighthouse, was erected at Larne, and this can still be seen on
the west shore of the harbour.

Mr. Charles Stewart, secretary of the B & N C R, was also appointed
secretary of the L & S S Co., and the steamboat affairs were managed from
the B & N C R offices at Belfast with Mr. Edward Cotton serving as manager
of the L & S S Co. while still retaining his position as manager of the B & N C R.
The enterprise was especially fortunate in having the services of Edward Cotton,
as his reputation was high in railway circles in Ireland, Scotland and England.
In 1858, he had been appointed to his post with the B & N C R at the age of
28.[143] Mr. Stewart and Mr. Cotton both had small financial stakes in the
L & S S Co. Mr. William Grafton, manager of the P R, was appointed Stranraer agent for the company in 1873. The manager at Belfast and the agent at
Stranraer each received a salary of £100 per annum, while the secretary received

F

£50. Small payments were also made to two clerks and the cashier at the York Road office, Belfast, for steamboat work they carried out.

The P R Board was of the opinion that a separate marine superintendent was not required and the master of the ship was expected to carry out these duties. Likewise, no engineer superintendent was appointed, though during the building and introduction of the new ship, a Mr. R. M. Beath was retained as consultant engineer. In June 1873, the P R Board requested their secretary to make inquiries about the cost of a visiting marine engineer. He also was to find out how much the Caledonian locomotive foreman at Stranraer, Mr. Blackwood, knew about marine work. Mr. Blackwood had carried out repairs on *Fannie* and *Alice*, but in September 1873, the P R Board appointed Mr. Alex McGibbon, marine superintendent of the Glasgow & Londonderry Steam Packet Company, as visiting marine superintendent. This position he held until his death in 1876. Thereafter, Messrs. G. & J. Weir, Engineers, of Glasgow, took over the responsibilities.

THE "PRINCESS" LINE

Most of the steamers that had headed out of Loch Ryan for Ireland had first seen the light of day on the ways of the Partick yard of Tod & McGregor, and it was to this yard that the order went for the first ship of the L & S S Co. The name *Princess Louise* was approved in January 1872. Princess Louise was the daughter of Queen Victoria, and in 1871 her marriage to the Marquis of Lorne, eldest son of the eighth Duke of Argyll, had been an occasion of great rejoicing.

Princess Louise was built to the highest standards for passenger comfort. The accommodation for cabin passengers was situated aft, with a saloon, a smoke-room and a state-room. The decor was in true, heavy Victorian style. The panelling of the walls and ceiling of the saloon were painted in imitation satin wood and the cornicing consisted of gilt cable with pendant medallions of the Royal lady whose name the vessel bore. The gable panes of the deck lights for the saloon were adorned with stained glass representations of the Marquis and Marchioness of Lorne. The bows, stern and paddle boxes were decorated with shields bearing the arms of Argyll, heraldic insignia and en-larged medallions *alto relievo* portraits of the Marquis and Marchioness, the latter surmounted by a royal coronet. Steerage accommodation, with wooden benches, was provided forward, and it was claimed to equal the cabin accom-modation of many ships then plying. Space for cattle was also forward.

The "Louise" was fitted with a steeple engine and, as far as can be ascertained, her two funnels were painted red with black tops. She proved to be a heavy coal eater and also required a steady supply of brass bushes for the paddle wheels, and the P R workshops were regularly casting new ones. The bridge of *Princess Louise* spanned the paddle boxes and had a canvas dodger as its only form of protection. When entering or leaving harbour or in heavy weather two helmsmen had to be on duty. The L & S S Co. adopted as their flag a scarlet pennant, having angled in the middle a white square on which was set the Red Hand of Ulster. *Princess Louise* was initially registered at Belfast, but in September 1872 her port of registry became Stranraer, and this practice was followed for all subsequent "Princess" ships until the arrival of *Ailsa Princess* in 1971.

Delivery of *Princess Louise* had been expected early in 1872, but her construction was delayed by labour disputes in the yard and it was 7 May before
the ship was even launched. After testing compasses in the Gareloch on 25 June,
she completed trials with her engines driving her at 14 knots while, we are
told, her machinery "was not yet in top working order". The ship had been
rushed away from Glasgow with craftsmen still on board putting final touches
to her ornate decoration and she had to make a special call at Wemyss Bay
Pier to land them before she headed for Stranraer.

The company was lucky with personnel. The manager of the engineering
shop of Tod & McGregor had at one time served as engineer on *Albion* and so
knew first hand the beating the engine and paddle wheels would take on the
crossing. The services of an experienced master were also obtained for *Princess
Louise*. Captain George Campbell, who had commanded *Briton* during her time
at Stranraer, joined *Princess Louise* at Glasgow. In the summer of 1864, Captain
Campbell had been master of the North British Railway Company's *Waverley*
sailing between Silloth and Dublin, and in the following year had moved to
the next *Waverley* for that vessel's equally short career on the same route.

At ten o'clock in the evening of Tuesday, 25 June 1872, the first of the
"Princess Line" arrived at the Railway Pier, Stranraer. The following day,
Princess Louise crossed to Larne and on the Thursday and Friday gave excursions from Larne to Stranraer with trains conveying passengers from
Belfast to join the steamer. For the benefit of the excursionists, the chairman
of the P R, Lord Stair, opened the grounds of his home, Castle Kennedy. On
Saturday the "Louise" gave an excursion from Stranraer to Larne, where 500 of
the 800 passengers disembarked and made for Belfast. *Princess Louise* then
gave a cruise to view the channel fleet lying in Belfast Lough.

THE SCHEDULE

Princess Louise settled down to her basic service on Monday, 1 July 1872,
leaving Stranraer at 1000 and returning from Larne around 1700. At Larne,
trains connected with Belfast and Londonderry, while at Stranraer there was a
railway connection with Castle Douglas and beyond. The departure from
Belfast (York Road) at 1600 provided a 0940 arrival in London (Euston) the
following day. The 2100 L & N W R train from Euston connected into the
morning sailing from Stranraer. Travellers to and from Glasgow and Edinburgh had an overnight stay in Dumfries, Castle Douglas or Stranraer. Traffic
was encouraging: on several evenings in August the "Louise" landed two hundred
passengers at Stranraer, but the mainstay of the service was to be cargo and
livestock. In her first three months, 4,561 passengers were carried and 202
horses and 6,349 cattle transported. On each of the first two days an extra
sailing had to be provided to clear the cattle from Ireland and special luggage
trains had to run to cope with the traffic. At the end of September 1872, at the
half-yearly general meeting of the P R, the chairman was able to say that
considering the route was still virtually unknown traffic had exceeded expectations. After years of frustration the route via Stranraer was showing its
potential. At the meeting the death of Colonel McDowall was intimated. The
Colonel had always been a staunch advocate of the Stranraer route and had had
a considerable financial stake in *Briton* while that ship had run in conjunction
with the P R and B & N C R / C & L R during 1862–63.

RELIEF SHIP "GARLAND"

At the meeting in September 1872, a discordant note was sounded when the question of the speed of *Princess Louise* was raised. In October 1872, Mr. Tod, of Tod & McGregor, visited Stranraer and inspected the "Louise" and agreed to carry out alterations. In early December, *Princess Louise* was taken, rather surprisingly, to Belfast for the work to be carried out. Tod & McGregor's yard was short of manpower after the strike and could not handle the work. During the three weeks 6 to 27 December, the service was maintained by the paddle steamer *Garland*, of the Glasgow & Londonderry Steam Packet Company. Built by Caird & Co., of Greenock, in 1863 to the order of G. & J. Burns, she had been sold while still on the stocks for blockade running. As *City of Petersburg*, she completed a successful spell on the other side of the Atlantic. In 1863 she made three successful runs through the blockade; in 1864 eleven runs were chalked up; and in 1865 a single trip was made before the blockade was over.[144] On her return, *City of Petersburg* was purchased by the Liverpool & Dublin Steam Packet Company and renamed *Bridgewater*. In 1868 she was sold to the Glasgow & Londonderry Steam Packet Company, which gave her the name *Garland*. Captain Campbell brought *Garland* from Glasgow and then took *Princess Louise* off to Belfast, reversing the operation when the work on the "Louise" was completed. These positioning runs caused Captain Campbell to be absent from the Stranraer–Larne route for a few days, and during these periods the Stranraer Harbour Master, Captain Haswell, was responsible for the navigation of the service. Captain Haswell knew the area well, having served for many years with the Glasgow & Stranraer Steam Packet Company. The following year, in December, while *Princess Louise* was being overhauled at Glasgow, *Garland* was once again obtained as relief ship.

In December 1873, at the end of *Garland*'s second spell on the Larne service, word got round of a free trip to Glasgow, and on Saturday, 20 December, just as *Garland* was about to leave Stranraer, over three hundred piled on board. Captain Campbell put about two hundred of them ashore but allowed the balance to sail up to Glasgow on *Garland*, returning on the Sunday with *Princess Louise*. The passage from Greenock to Stranraer occupied seven hours and it was noted that the ship was travelling at barely twelve knots on the measured mile.

On the Tuesday before her departure from Stranraer, Captain Campbell had involved *Garland* in an attempt to rescue the crew of a 300-ton brigantine, *John Slater*, of Barrow. When the gale was at its height, a lifeboat was launched from *Garland* for the purpose of securing a hawser to the disabled craft, but the attempt was unsuccessful. The brigantine was lost but the crew of three were safely landed at Stranraer by *Garland*. The efforts did not pass unobserved.

General Manager's Office,
Belfast.
16 January 1874.

Captain Campbell
Dear Sir,
I have the pleasure to inform you that the Liverpool Shipwrecked Mariners Association have agreed to present you with a silver medal and vote of thanks for the heroic conduct displayed in rescuing the

crew of "J. Slater", of Barrow, and a bronze medal to each of the
crew who manned the boat. Names of the latter will be engraved on
the medals. Please let me have a list of their full names.

Yours truly,

E. J. Cotton.

"Princess Louise",
Larne Harbour.

On the afternoon of Tuesday, 16 March, the presentation was made in
the new Court House at Stranraer. It was quite an occasion, with the Provost,
magistrates and members of the town council attending, as well as the public.
It turned out to be a double presentation, since, as well as the silver and bronze
medals, the Board of Trade had awarded a telescope to Captain Campbell and
£2 to each of the lifeboat's crew.

ANOTHER ATTEMPT AT DONAGHADEE

The "Louise" was not left in peace for long. With a large, new ship
running regularly on the Stranraer–Larne route, one would not have expected
the appearance of a rival service, but in June 1873 an attempt was made to
revive the traditional route via Portpatrick and Donaghadee.

Andrews & Company, of Belfast, were behind this. In December 1865,
they had approached the P R with a view to operating the Donaghadee–Portpatrick route, but the P R had the Caledonian masters breathing down their
necks and had to decline. All their energy had to be put into making a go of
Fannie, which had just been placed on the Stranraer–Belfast station. Andrews
paddle steamer *Avalon* was placed on the Donaghadee–Portpatrick crossing
from 5 June 1873, leaving the Irish side at 0900 and Portpatrick at 1730 daily.
The ship crossed in 1½ hours, a full hour less than *Princess Louise*. Railway
connections were expected but did not materialise. *Avalon* proved slow and
small for the route and gave up after Saturday, 12 July. Eighteen years passed
before a service operated again between Donaghadee and Portpatrick. By an
Act of Parliament, responsibility for the maintenance of Portpatrick Harbour
passed from the Board of Trade to the local authority in 1873.

The potential of the short sea crossing between Portpatrick and Donaghadee had proved impossible of realisation. The shortness of the route can be
recognised in the achievement of Mr. Tom Blower who, in July 1947, swam
from Donaghadee to Portpatrick in 15 hours 26 minutes, while in August
1957, Mr. J. Norman Barclay, of Helensburgh, completed the crossing on
skis in 1 hour 20 minutes, but the harbour at Portpatrick proved too difficult
for ships bigger than coastal fishing boats. These fishing boats continue to
carry small parties on trips as far as Donaghadee and the Isle of Man.

Occasionally, Portpatrick and Donaghadee were still to enjoy brief spells
of employment as mail stations, while the main route via Stranraer was closed
for some reason or other. The seas have continued to reduce the Portpatrick
piers to rubble until now there is virtually nothing left of either. In 1953, action
had to be taken to protect the west side of the harbour, when erosion by the
sea threatened the basin wall and surrounds. During the Second World War,
air–sea rescue boats were stationed at Portpatrick, but because of the entrance
they had to be of the smallest type.

To tie up a loose end, it should be recorded that on 1 September 1874, the P R Board agreed to lift the rails of the Portpatrick Harbour branch and use them for sidings at Newton Stewart Station. In May 1889, a piece of waste land at Portpatrick was rented from the railway to make a bowling green. The nominal annual rent was 50p. This "waste land" was the site of the harbour terminus. Thus, today we find tennis courts and a bowling green where should have stood the *raison d'être* of the P R.

Donaghadee was not to die so quickly. It still received calls by excursion steamers from Belfast up until the First World War. In 1889, it was considered as the Irish destination of a service from Peel, Isle of Man, but on that occasion the eventual choice was Bangor. Donaghadee did, however, receive occasional excursions from the Isle of Man. *Fenella*, of the Isle of Man Steam Packet Company Limited, was probably so employed when she struck a rock off Donaghadee on 25 August 1900. After thirty-five minutes, *Fenella* refloated and proceeded to Peel under her own power. Cargo ships called from time to time but they are now very few in number. For example, after *Finvoy*'s call in October 1955, eleven years elapsed before another cargo ship visited the County Down port—*Dutchmate* on 7 June 1966.[145] Until the evacuation of the Copeland Islands in the late 1950s there was a ferry service of sorts between Donaghadee and the Islands. Tourist launches still operate in summer to the Islands.

With the service by *Avalon* abandoned in July 1873, *Princess Louise* was left in peace at Stranraer, as *Albion* had ceased in the previous month crossing from Stranraer to Belfast. In January 1873, the frequency of these crossings by *Albion* had been reduced to once in each month and her last crossing from Stranraer to Belfast was scheduled for 20 June 1873. *Albion* continued to give occasional excursions to Belfast from Stranraer.

However, regular crossings to Belfast were never again to feature in the timetable of Langlands's steamers. The screw *Albion* was sold in 1873 to the London & Edinburgh Shipping Company and traded between London and Berwick. The paddler *Albion* was laid up in November 1877 and eventually left the Clyde in January 1880, when she was towed to Liverpool. *Tuskar*, a screw ship, made her first call at Stranraer for Langlands on Thursday, 22 November 1877. In addition to the weekly service between Stranraer and Glasgow, *Tuskar*'s duties for a time included a rump of the Solway Firth schedule of the paddler *Countess of Galloway*, which had become a member of the Langlands's fleet. The opening, in March 1875, of the Wigtownshire Railway, which ran from Whithorn and Garliestown to Newton Stewart, where it joined the P R, had eroded the trade of *Countess of Galloway*, with the result that the Galloway Steam Navigation Company agreed, in the autumn of 1875, to sell the ship and wind up the company. Thus, *Tuskar* offered a weekly service from Stranraer to Liverpool, calling at Garliestown and Kirkcudbright alternately. But *Countess of Galloway* was not quite finished. After a surprisingly extensive overhaul, she joined *Tuskar* and between them they continued to serve Stranraer, the Solway ports and Liverpool as well as provide occasional connections between Ayr, Campbeltown and Liverpool. *Countess of Galloway*'s last spell in service—September and October 1879—was spent on the Glasgow–Stranraer–Liverpool passenger and cargo service. She was broken up in January 1880. The service between Glasgow and Stranraer by *Tuskar* terminated with her departure from Glasgow on 23 December 1879, though an intermittent service between Stranraer and Liverpool continued for some years.

Various attempts were made to revive the passenger and cargo service between Glasgow and Stranraer, but most lasted for only a short time. For example, John McCallum & Co. ran their passenger and cargo steamer *Lady Ambrosine* for the month of November 1883, before she was replaced by the cargo-only *Telephone*. For the same month, F. M. McLarty, of Greenock, ran the paddle steamer *Terrible* between Glasgow and Stranraer. This would appear to be the same *Terrible* as John Jamieson chartered for his excursion from Donaghadee to Portpatrick in May 1866 and which we shall again encounter on the route. But once the rail link between Stranraer and Girvan was completed, in 1877, the potential for passengers was nil, and for cargo not much better.

MECHANICAL TROUBLE

Princess Louise was still causing headaches, however, and in April 1874, the paddle steamer *Albion* had to be chartered for three days to cover the Stranraer–Larne service. Again, on 21 September, *Albion* had to cross in place of the "Louise". By the autumn of 1874, it had been agreed that the only solution to the "Louise's" ailment was reboilering, but the L & S S Co. had no money and its financial position was so dire that in the summer of 1874 guarantees for an increasing overdraft had to be obtained from the P R and the Irish directors. The reboilering of the two-year-old ship was shelved and she had to limp on as well as she could.

But *Princess Louise* had to be off service for nearly two months in the winter of 1874–75, as extensive repairs were required. From the beginning of December 1874, until the end of January, and again for the second week of February, *Garland* maintained the service. *Princess Louise* was repaired at the Belfast yard of Victor & David Coates, who duly submitted their invoice for £1,277. Harland & Wolff also spent time on the "Louise", and this cost the steamboat company £234. After returning to service for a few days, *Princess Louise* had to be taken in hand by Barclay Curle & Co. at Glasgow for repairs to her paddle shaft. An invoice for £130 soon reached Mr. Cotton. The financial state of the L & S S Co. was such that they had to pay off the Coates's account in instalments and did not complete payment until the following October. This extensive programme of repairs did not, however, include reboilering.

On 7 December 1874, the chartered vessel *Garland* could not sail because of wheel trouble, and we read in the cash book that each of the six passengers nconvenienced received a shilling. When *Princess Louise* failed again in February, *Garland* was brought back to cover the sailing, and pending her arrival, *Albion* was again chartered and crossed to Larne on 8 February 1875.

A SECOND VESSEL

In the autumn of 1874, wheels were set in motion to obtain another vessel for the route. Whether this vessel was to replace or assist *Princess Louise* is not clearly stated, but certainly the "Louise" was now viewed as a liability and not adequate for the standard of service required. In November 1874, Captain Campbell set off for Glasgow and inspected *Islay*. The L & S S Co. Board were considering the possible long term charter with option to purchase. *Islay* was a two-funnelled paddle steamer owned by Messrs. C. Morrison, T. G. Buchanan and John Ramsay and employed by them sailing between Glasgow, Portrush and Islay. This possibility did not materialise and the ship was left to be bought in 1876 by David Hutcheson & Co. Looking ahead, it is interesting that *Princess Louise*, when her Stranraer days were over, was to be sold into the fleet of David MacBrayne, the successor of David Hutcheson & Co., as a replacement of *Islay*. In January 1875, an advertisement was inserted in *The Shipping Gazette* for a steamer to purchase for the Stranraer station.

In November 1874, plans for a new ship had been considered, and when in February 1875, after two months at Belfast, the "Louise" lasted only a week before more work was required, the matter was resolved and it was agreed that a new ship had to be built for the run.

The new ship could not be in service before the beginning of 1876, and in the meantime arrangements had to be made to have *Princess Louise* taken in hand once again for repairs. The Irish directors had delivered an ultimatum that unless repairs were immediately taken in hand, they would publicly repudiate any responsibility for the consequences of keeping the "Louise" in service. In October 1875, the screw steamer *Midland*, of the Ardrossan Shipping Company, was chartered for two weeks, and *Princess Louise* went to Belfast for condenser and boiler repairs.

Harland & Wolff, of Belfast, received the order for the new ship, the cost being £24,000. The hull was to be based on that of *Princess Louise*, but the machinery was to be two diagonal direct-acting surface condensing engines. The P R Board advanced the balance of the compensation it had received, viz. £10,000, to the L & S S Co.

Lady Templeton, wife of the chairman of the C & L R, named the ship *Princess Beatrice* at the launching from the Queen's Island yard on Thursday, 4 November 1875. The future of the route was looking brighter. A more direct rail connection between Stranraer and Glasgow was soon to become a reality. The original plan to extend the line from Girvan along the coast to Stranraer had been abandoned in favour of a line from Girvan joining the Portpatrick line at East Challoch. This was expected to be finished by March 1876. At the reception following the launch of the "Beatrice", plans were announced for a double daily service to Larne plus a Sunday crossing. As a last ditch stand, the Belfast & County Down Railway's representative asked if the Sunday service could be to Donaghadee. But harsh reality made short work of this planning.

After much endeavour, the Stranraer route was being used for mail. One of the original intentions of the P R was thus realised when, from the beginning of February 1875, mail crossed between the north of England, Scotland and the north of Ireland via Stranraer and Larne. When *Princess Louise* returned from her two month stay at Belfast the words "Royal Mail" featured conspicuously on her paddle boxes. The principal Scotland–Ireland mail service was left undisturbed with G. &. J. Burns via Greenock and Belfast. In December 1883, the Burns Company offered to establish a mail service direct between Stranraer and Belfast, as this, they reckoned, was the most efficient route for mail between England and the north of Ireland. Their offer was not taken up, but in 1884 a quantity of London parcels mail began to move through Stranraer. It was 1891 before letter mail was to travel by this route to any degree.

The trial trip of *Princess Beatrice* was on Thursday, 3 February 1876, when she sailed from Belfast, Spencer Dock, to Larne. On the following day, the first Irish-built mail steamer took over from *Princess Louise*, which was laid up for the time being. Captain Campbell and his crew moved over to the new ship. On the evening of Wednesday, 16 February, Captain and Mrs. Campbell entertained fifty guests to supper on board the new steamer at Stranraer as part of the welcome programme.

Princess Beatrice got off to a shaky start. She was off the run from mid-March till the middle of June. The second half of July she was out of service and again for three weeks in September. During these gaps, *Princess Louise* was on the run. During February and March, the "Louise" had again visited Belfast and brought back from V. & D. Coates a bill for £1,100, which Harland Wolff followed up with an account for £520.

At least, with two ships at Stranraer the service could be maintained with a degree of regularity, and from 1 April 1876 an accelerated service was operated. The train now reached Belfast fifteen minutes earlier, at 1300, and left at 1610 instead of 1600. In July, the acceleration was extended to London and an arrival at Euston was now possible at 0900, forty minutes earlier than previously.

Apart from filling the gaps while the "Beatrice" was off, the spare vessel, the "Louise" was used for the occasional special trip. For example, on the day of the Stranraer Cattle Show, 21 July 1876, *Princess Louise* gave a day excursion from Larne to Stranraer. This special sailing for the Cattle Show was given every year until 1889 by *Princess Louise*, with the exception of 1883, when *Princess Beatrice* was absent at Glasgow for reboilering and the "Louise" was employed on the main service.

The reboilering of *Princess Louise* was eventually taken in hand, and on 8 April 1878 she set off for the Glasgow yard of Barclay Curle & Co. The new boilers cost £4,500. The "Louise" returned to Stranraer in the middle of June and took over the service for four weeks. With two reliable ships now available, plans had been made to have both ships sailing in the summer months. In April 1878, the L & S S Co. Board had decided to run both ships on the route during July, August and September. But all that was managed was the provision of excursion sailings from Larne to Stranraer on the last three Saturdays in July, viz. 13, 20 and 27. These sailings had train connections at Larne from Belfast and at Stranraer. The trippers had time to visit Castle Kennedy.

THE GIRVAN RAILWAY

After many delays the line from Girvan to Challoch Junction was opened on Friday, 5 October 1877 and there was introduced a service of four trains daily from Glasgow (St. Enoch) to Stranraer. It was now possible to leave St. Enoch's at 0615 and arrive in Belfast at 1300. The return journey could also now be completed in a day with a 1610 departure from Belfast making a 2345 arrival at Glasgow. These trains used the Harbour Station at Stranraer while the others arrived and left from the Town Station. The boat train from Glasgow was given 3 hours 25 minutes for the journey, but by 1879 the train was expected to complete the journey in three hours.

Very soon after Ayr was linked by railway to Glasgow in 1840, plans were mooted to extend the line southwards with an eye to trade with Ireland. The plans of the Glasgow & Belfast Union Railway incorporated in an Act of

1846 to build a line from Ayr to Cairnryan were abandoned and in the 1850s the intention was to operate a sea route between Belfast and Girvan with a rail link from that port to Ayr and so to Glasgow. The line to Girvan was opened on 24 May 1860, but no attempt was made to establish a steamer service. On 5 July 1865, the Girvan & Portpatrick Junction Railway received the Royal Assent, but for various reasons it was 1870 before work actually started on the line from Girvan. In 1872, powers were obtained for the G & P J R to run over the line of the P R from East Challoch where the Girvan line joined the Portpatrick line. The financial arrangements arrived at required the G & P J R to pay interest on half the cost of the "Stranraer Section", viz., the line between East Challoch and Stranraer Harbour and Stranraer Town Stations. The cost to the Girvan railway was $4\frac{1}{2}$ per cent on £42,000 per annum. The Stranraer Section was to be managed by a committee, the Portpatrick and Girvan Joint Committee, which had three representatives from each of the railway companies.

But there were to be many headaches before a train ran from Girvan to Stranraer. In their dealings with the G & P J R neither the P R nor the C R can be considered epitomes of the good host. Both saw increasingly the threat that this new line could be to their traffic. The C R holding sway at Stranraer saw itself outflanked when, through Caledonian obduracy, the G & P J R had to sign a working agreement with the G & S W R, thus providing access for this rival right into Stranraer.

For the saga of the planning, building and operating of this line of thirty-one miles the reader is directed to *The Little Railways of South-West Scotland*.[146]

ACTIVITY ELSEWHERE

1878 was the first year to feel the full benefit from the Girvan route and the results of the L & S S Co. showed increased revenue of £2,400. The operating loss for the year was almost a third of the previous year's, at £1,160 compared with £3,360. With a few setbacks, the results for each year were to show improvement. Much of the traffic passing through Stranraer on its way to Ireland was at the expense of the other routes, that is, those via Ardrossan, Greenock and Glasgow. This new competition to these established routes was not allowed to pass unchallenged.

Since the departure of *Fire Fly* and *Glow Worm* from Ardrossan, various ships had maintained the connection between Belfast and Ardrossan for varying lengths of time. Two new screw ships were placed on the route in 1866 and 1867 for the Ardrossan Shipping Company and these ships—*Countess of Eglinton* and *Earl of Belfast*—with a thrice-weekly service, soon gained for the route a reputation for reliability. Both ships were sold for further service, the former in 1869 to the Newry Steam Packet Company for whom, renamed *Newry*, she traded until 1911 from the port whose name she bore, the latter in 1870 to the North British Silloth Steam Packet Company for their Silloth–Isle of Man–Dublin service.

Two larger ships took over the route for the Ardrossan Shipping Company: *South Western* in 1870, and *North British* in the following year. In 1874, another ship was built for the Ardrossan trade, *Midland*, and this allowed *South Western* to be transferred to a new Ardrossan–Silloth–Isle of Man–Dublin schedule.

The arrival of *Caledonian* in 1874 for the Ardrossan–Belfast station allowed *North British* to be transferred also to the Dublin service from Ardrossan or Silloth. *South Western* was sold to foreign owners in 1882 and *North British* was wrecked off the Isle of Man in 1879. A daily overnight service to Belfast was instituted upon the arrival of *Caledonian* and this continued until 1936. All the Ardrossan Shipping Company ships were iron vessels driven by single screws, and the spell by *Midland* on the Stranraer–Larne route in October 1875 was to be the only occasion a ship of this type maintained the service for more than an odd day.

Thus, upon the opening of the railway route via Girvan to Stranraer, there was a daily overnight service between Ardrossan and Belfast for passengers and cargo with the ships *Midland* and *Caledonian*. In addition, there was direct contact with the south of Ireland by *South Western* and *North British*. In anticipation of the increased competition, two new ships for the Belfast station were ordered for the Ardrossan Shipping Company. Continuing the practice of naming their ships after railway companies with access to Carlisle, the company took delivery of *North Eastern* and her maiden voyage from Ardrossan was on the first day of November 1877, four weeks after the line via Girvan to Stranraer had been opened. *North Western* joined her sister before the end of the year and this allowed *Midland* and *Caledonian* to be transferred to the south of Ireland service. The tonnage of the 1877 pair was almost double that of the ships of ten years before, *Countess of Eglinton* and *Earl of Belfast*, and this indicates the improvements that the decade had seen. The challenge of the Stranraer route had been accepted.

When G. & J. Burns took over the mail contract between Greenock and Belfast in 1849 the paddle steamer *Camilla* was acquired for a nightly Glasgow–Greenock–Belfast route. *Camilla* remained on the route for two years and had as consorts *Lyra* and *Thetis*, also iron paddle steamers. By 1877 the ships employed on the Glasgow–Greenock–Belfast mail service were the paddle steamers *Buffalo*, *Llama*, *Camel* and *Racoon*, built in the four years 1865–1868. *Racoon* was the largest, fastest and last paddler to be built for the Burns's overnight services. But, as at Ardrossan, the grass was not to grow under the feet of G. & J. Burns, and in 1878 two screw steamers, *Walrus* and *Mastiff*, were delivered for the Glasgow–Belfast overnight service. Further, a direct Glasgow–Larne schedule was introduced for passengers and cargo with the small iron screw steamer *Rook* in 1878 and 1879. This latter development was aimed largely at the suppression of a Larne-owned ship, *Larne*, which in January 1877 had started a thrice-weekly service between Larne and Glasgow. *Rook* effectively squeezed out *Larne* and the service quickly became cargo-only and continued until the First World War.

Again, as we found on the Ardrossan station, a rapid succession of new ships bears witness to the increasing facilities on the route. After only three years, *Walrus* and *Mastiff* were replaced in 1881 by three ships of greater size, *Alligator*, *Dromedary* and *Gorilla*, and in the same year three cargo-only ships were acquired for the Belfast route. The work of the L & S S Co. was cut out for them when the standard of the alternative routes is considered.

From geographical considerations there was a third route between Scotland and Ireland which might be thought to have provided competition for Stranraer. That is the route from Ayr to Larne and Belfast. Dating from 1875, the Ayr Steam Shipping Company operated a number of ships offering cargo and passenger accommodation. Rail connections were made at Ayr from Glasgow, but the ships were always primarily cargo carriers with some accommodation for passengers, and the route never proved popular with travellers.

The opening of the Glasgow–Stranraer via Girvan route certainly had a great potential for the steamboat company, but the competition was fierce. Similarly, new ships were continually appearing on the routes between Belfast and England. The Belfast Steamship Company Limited had modernised its Liverpool–Belfast fleet of cargo and passenger ships. The same can be said of the railway backed North Lancashire Steam Navigation Company and Barrow Steam Navigation Company, trading to Belfast from Fleetwood and Barrow, respectively.

MEANWHILE ON THE GIRVAN LINE

But all was not well with the G & P J R. The receipts were not as great as the expenses, and on 7 February 1882 the Girvan route to Stranraer was closed following an interdict obtained by the P R. The line was to remain closed until August 1883.

In July 1879, less than two years after the opening of the G & P J R, the company's creditors had petitioned the Court of Session and a Judicial Factor had been appointed to manage the Girvan railway and safeguard the interests of the creditors. The matter dragged on until, in 1882, a Bill was proposed to allow the G & P J R to raise a loan, partly to pay off the outstanding debt to the P R for the agreed interest on the Stranraer Section and partly to provide the finance necessary for the G & P J R to purchase its own plant and rolling stock. This last provision would enable the company to free itself of the crippling terms of the G & S W R, who had been operating the line for the G & P J R.

After some haggling over the amounts outstanding in respect of the Stranraer Section to the P R by the G & P J R, the matter was referred to arbitration and on 11 June 1880 the decree was issued by Sir Thomas Bouch. This decree laid down the amount on which the interest was to be calculated and should have put an end to the delaying tactics of the G & P J R.[147] But almost a year later, with no action from the G & P J R, the P R petitioned the Court of Session, and on 1 February 1882 a Notice of Interdict was served on the G & P J R denying them the use of the Stranraer Section after 7 February.

With bewildering resilience the G & P J R quickly made alternative arrangements to maintain the link with Stranraer. The G & S W R operated the rail service as far south as New Luce and between there and Stranraer passengers and goods were conveyed by road.

But a horse and cart was no permanent solution to the problems of the G & P J R. In 1882, the company obtained powers for further borrowing and also managed to negotiate a more attractive agreement with the G & S W R for the working of the line. On 1 August 1883, the interdict was withdrawn and the service through to Stranraer commenced once again. At last, the railway seemed to have a fair wind behind it and in 1884 actually paid its first dividend —1 per cent. But the history of the Girvan line is one of lurching from crisis to crisis. Both the G & P J R and the P R had become pawns in a game played by the railway giants. The G & S W R intimated late in 1885 that the agreement for working the Girvan line was to be terminated, and after more trouble the line between Girvan and Challoch Junction once more lost its service from mid-April 1886. Mr. Meikle's coach service between Stranraer and Girvan was reactivated with a coach from Stranraer at 0900 to connect with the 1500 train out of Girvan, while a coach met the 0700 from Glasgow and was due in Stranraer about 1500. The choice before the G & P J R was either to go it alone or put up the shutters and sell out to the G & S W R at an extremely low figure. The former course was adopted and the company obtained its own rolling stock and plant and after a gap of two months a service between Stranraer and Girvan was once again operating.

In October 1886 the G & P J R was advertised for sale and a hope of greater stability for the line was created by its being purchased by the Ayrshire & Wigtownshire Railway, a London-based concern formed for the sole purpose of acquiring the bruised hero of so many battles. On 1 June 1887, the full service of trains between Glasgow and Stranraer was re-introduced. Five years later, an Act was passed empowering the G & S W R to acquire the A & W R. On the deal being concluded the G & S W R set about immediately putting the line between Girvan and Challoch Junction into good shape and an acceleration of the timetable between Glasgow and Stranraer soon resulted. By this date the G & S W R had a double incentive for encouraging traffic over the Girvan line since not only had a considerable capital been expended in the refurbishing of the line but also, since 1885, the G & S W R had a direct financial stake in the line between Challoch Junction and Stranraer and in the L & S S Co. itself.

LARNE AND STRANRAER PIERS

A new steamer berth at Larne for *Princess Louise* had been completed in June 1873 to the order of James Chaine, the proprietor of the harbour. Delay in building new station accommodation at Larne was caused by the intention of the Ballymena & Larne Railway to open a line between the towns forming its title. This railway was built with a gauge of 3 feet, in contrast to the 5 feet 3 inches of the B & N C R and C & L R. The B & L R was opened for traffic in August 1878 and ran boat trains in summer to the harbour at Larne.[148] Work was then put in hand for a new station to serve both the B & N C R and B & L R trains. This building was to be "of as cheap a character as possible consistent with efficiency".[149] But even this was only after much disagreement. So great was the rift, that in 1877 the B & N C R had embarked on investigations into making a packet port out of Magheramorne on the shores of Larne Lough, about four miles south of Larne.

Not long after the L & S S Co. began its service from the east pier at Stranraer the condition of the pier became a cause for concern. At the ordinary half-yearly meeting of the P R shareholders in March 1875 the state of the pier was discussed but no course of action agreed upon. The P R Board, in July 1875, instructed their Secretary to write to Stranraer Town Council listing the repairs required at the east pier and stating that if the Town Council did not carry out the work the railway company would do so and deduct the cost from their annual payment. The Town Council asked for a renegotiation of the agreement since a larger payment was required each year. The Board declined, and nothing was done.

Threats of legal action in 1876 likewise brought no response from the

Town Council, and in November a Bill was drafted for the compulsory acquisition of the east pier. At that date it was estimated that repairs costing about £6,000 would be required to put the pier into order.

By the Portpatrick Railway Act 1877, the P R acquired the east pier from Stranraer Town Council. The railway, as part of the deal, took over the capital debt incurred by the Council in the building of the pier. This Act also granted the G & P J R the right to use the east pier and the line leading to the pier while the management of the pier was entrusted to the Portpatrick and Girvan Joint Committee. Work on the repairs was put in hand right away and completed at a cost of £7,000 the following year. It is by no means certain but it could well have been at this time that the platform was transferred from the stone neck to the wooden gangway. A covering over this platform on the wooden gangway was part of the work, but the main line locomotives were still not allowed to travel beyond the stone neck. David Smith relates the arrangements made to overcome this difficulty. The two boat trains, of the G & S W R and the C R, coupled together would be brought down to the harbour and pulled on to the wooden pier by a small tank engine. The P R Board had agreed in March 1873 that this engine alone would be allowed to travel on the wooden section. The G & S W R section of the train would be on the shore end and so stationed that the G & S W R engine could couple on without leaving the stone section. Once it had left, the C R section of the train remaining was pushed up to allow the C R engine to receive its carriages, again without leaving the stone neck. This clumsy system would appear to have been in force until the extensive rebuilding of the pier in the 1890s.[150] The west pier at Stranraer remained the responsibility of the Royal Burgh until 1975.

From its inception the L & S S Co. had supplied the staff for both Larne and Stranraer piers. The men wore jerseys emblazoned "Larne & Stranraer Steamers".

TAKEOVER OF THE PORTPATRICK RAILWAY

Compared with the present day, nineteenth-century boilers had short lives, and in 1882 the L & S S Co. accepted a tender of £6,700 for the reboiling and refurbishing of *Princess Beatrice*. The work was entrusted to David Rowan & Co., of Glasgow, at whose suggestion the engines were to be altered to a compound arrangement with a resulting 25 per cent saving in fuel and an increase in speed. During the first week of March 1883, *Princess Louise* went to Glasgow for a quick overhaul at the hands of Barclay, Curle & Co. and then returned to Stranraer to allow *Princess Beatrice* to come to Glasgow. This was to prove to be *Princess Louise*'s last prolonged period in service at Stranraer and she maintained the station from the middle of March until the middle of September. *Princess Louise* would appear to have conducted the service satisfactorily.

A remodelling of the accommodation of *Princess Beatrice* was carried out by Rowan's and the cabin-class fittings were relocated in the steerage area forward. An improved refreshment room was also installed for the steerage passengers. This was situated on the port side, while a ladies' cabin was placed on the starboard side. Part of the cabin saloon was partitioned off to form a dining saloon. A novel feature of the partitioning was that the panels forming the partition were 6 inches from the floor and 18 inches from the deck head to give ventilation. The seating in the main saloon was altered: that around the hull shell was wider and placed out from the plating, so that a wide ledge for light luggage was now available. Three double rows of seating, fore-and-aft, back-to-back, were provided.

While the L & S S Co. continued upgrading its ships, the parent company, the P R, was finding itself in the uncomfortable role of spoils for the railway giants. Apart from the C R, G & S W R and L & N W R, a new party was in the field—the Midland Railway. From 1 May 1876, the M R had provided an alternative route to London for travellers using the Stranraer ships. Until this time the route to London from Stranraer was by the C R-worked trains to Dumfries and then on to Carlisle by the G & S W, where passengers changed to the L & N W R train for Euston; but now they could join the M R train at Dumfries for St. Pancras. Just as the C R and L & N W R could co-operate together, so could the G & S W R and the M R. The original working agreement between the C R and P R was due to expire on 30 September 1885, and the M R and G & S W R joined forces to get what they could in the ensuing scrap. The P R had little say in what followed: it was a silent victim before the vociferous appetites of the four. After deliberations in London at which all five companies were represented, a compromise solution was reached, the victim to be divided into four equal shares. Before the necessary Act received the Royal Assent in August 1885, the other railway in the south-west corner of Scotland, the Wigtownshire Railway, was included in the carve up.

The vesting date in the Act was 1 August 1885, and from that date a new entity came into being to own and manage the two railways, the Portpatrick and Wigtownshire Joint Committee with headquarters in Citadel Station, Carlisle. Under the terms of the Act, the Portpatrick and Wigtownshire Railways (Sale and Transfer) Act, a new stock was created—Portpatrick and Wigtownshire Guaranteed Stock. This stock bore interest at $3\frac{1}{2}$ per cent and was jointly guaranteed by the four railway companies making up the P & W J C. The holders of P R stock were entitled to a one-to-one exchange, while the W R stockholders received one share of the new guaranteed stock for each two W R shares held. Each of the constituent companies appointed two directors to the P & W J C.

THE MANAGING COMMITTEE

Following the takeover of the P R by the four large railway companies and the establishment of the P & W J C, thought was given by the newly constituted L & S S Co. Board to the most efficient means of managing the ships. At a meeting of the Board on 15 April 1887 in Belfast, it was resolved to set up a Managing Committee, which would consist of eight directors, one half nominated by the Irish shareholders and the balance by the P & W J C. This committee was to meet at least once every three months and on alternate sides of the Irish Sea. The first meeting was in Belfast on Thursday, 21 April 1887.

At this meeting, the committee looked at an anomaly which had existed since the inception of the service in 1872. The catering on board the "Princess" ships had been conducted by Captain George Campbell, the company's senior master, on his own account, and the L & S S Co. had no direct financial benefit from this. After discussion with Captain Campbell, he agreed to make an annual payment of £50 to the company for this privilege. The company paid the two stewards and the stewardess and supplied the silver, cutlery, crockery, etc. This arrangement took effect from 1 May 1887 and continued with amended fees until 30 September 1897, four months before Captain Campbell's retiral from the service.

In August 1887, the Managing Committee reviewed the salaries of the officials of the L & S S Co. and voted substantial increases. The Secretary, Charles Stewart, had his salary increased from £50 to £125. In return, Mr. Stewart had to "find the company an office" and also take over the work of two clerks then receiving £20 and £10 each per annum. Mr. Edward Cotton, the Manager, had his salary increased from £100 to £150. Both gentlemen continued to hold parallel appointments with the B & N C R.

SHIPS TO HOLYHEAD

One of the assets taken over by the P & W J C was the P R's 1,000 £10 shares in the L & S S Co.; and in August 1885 the committee had appointed seven new directors to the steamboat board. One of the results of the change in control of the company was that the ships were for some years to be over-hauled at Holyhead under the supervision of the L & N W R. Messrs. G. & J. Weir, of Glasgow, had acted as marine superintendents of the L & S S Co. since 1876 and their services were now no longer required.

Before their involvement ceased, G. & J. Weir had submitted specifications for proposed alterations to *Princess Louise*, covering new boilers and com-pounding of the machinery and sundry other changes. In December 1885, the L & S S Co. Board considered the letter from Weir's but decided against their recommendations and left unopened the six tenders obtained for the work. It was resolved to have the "Louise" sent to the L & N W R yard and have Admiral Dent examine the ship and carry out the repairs he considered absolutely necessary for the ship to be passed by the Government surveyor.

At the sixteenth meeting of shareholders, held at the York Road offices of the L & S S Co. on 19 August 1886, the Secretary read a report in which he stated "the boats are in a very good working order, both steamers were sent to Holyhead in the spring for overhaul and renewal of certificates. The boats, when there, had the advantage of a thorough examination, and it is satisfactory to know that when examined found to be in a very creditable condition".

No doubt, the Chairman, the Earl of Galloway, had few qualms about having a hired official read this report, rather than deliver himself what turned out to be a document having little connection with the reality of the situation.

The "Louise" was far from being in "good working order" or "in a very creditable condition". On 8 October 1886, the matter could not be deferred any longer when the Board met to consider a report from Captain Campbell. In this he stated, "tubes in the boiler of 'Louise' have got far decayed and are now neither safe nor reliable". The engineer was also adamant that something had to be done immediately. The Board accepted Captain Campbell's suggestion that work on retubing the boilers should be started right away, and by doing one boiler at a time, the "Louise" would still be available should an emergency occur. The retubing may have increased the safety of the ship but no appreciable improvement in speed was noticed.

While surveys and annual overhauls were now conducted at Holyhead, emergency repairs were carried out wherever a berth was available. Thus, on

9 December 1886, *Princess Beatrice*, while lying at Stranraer, was damaged by *Telephone*, a cargo steamer plying between Glasgow and Stranraer, and later that month went to the yard of the Ailsa Shipbuilding Company at Troon. On other occasions the ships visited Ayr, Dumbarton, Belfast and various Glasgow shipyards.

THE GLASGOW EXHIBITION OF 1888

There was to be an exhibition at Glasgow during the summer months of 1888 and a considerable increase in traffic to the city was expected. The Chairman of the G & S W R suggested that there was possible employment here for *Princess Louise* by putting her on a service from Larne to Stranraer during the three months of the exhibition. The L & S S Co. Board agreed readily to this suggestion and Mr. Cotton was left to arrange the details of timings and train connections. As well as a train connection with Glasgow, the Managing Committee later requested that he also investigate the possibility of a connection between Stranraer and the North of England and London. Captain Campbell was instructed to get the ship up to a satisfactory standard for the anticipated traffic.

By the middle of May, Captain Campbell had engaged most of the crew required for *Princess Louise* and the ship was now clean and freshly painted. Mr. Cotton had made arrangements for a train leaving Stranraer at noon for Carlisle with a connection there for the south. Two alternatives for the Belfast–Glasgow journey were laid before the Managing Committee: either leave Belfast at 0645 and arrive at Glasgow 1415, or leave at 0720 and arrive 1530. The earlier departure won the committee's approval.

But difficulties now appeared at the Scottish end. G. & J. Burns soon got wind of this planned service and saw it as a threat to their direct service between Belfast and Glasgow. Mr. John Burns, eldest son of George Burns, together with his son George, attended the G & S W R Board meeting on 15 May and outlined the detrimental effect the extra Larne service would have on the Burns's steamers from Belfast. The Burns family carried some weight with the G & S W R, for the steamboat Managing Committee were called to a meeting on 18 May to hear Charles Stewart, their Secretary, read the following telegram which had been received from the Passenger Superintendent of the G & S W R, "To Cotton, B & N C R, Belfast. Mr. Burns has seen my directors this morning and fully discussed proposed service via Larne and Stranraer and they are diposed to accept Mr. Burns's offer to exchange tickets instead of making arrangements for second service. Mathieson". G. & J. Burns had agreed to accept tickets issued by the Stranraer steamer as valid for return by their steamers to Belfast if the return trip was made within the week. In the letter that followed the telegram the G & S W R did not go so far as to say, however, that they would not run trains in connection with the morning sailing from Larne.

Mr. Cotton quickly sounded out the other railway companies interested in the steamboat operation, and opinion was that the service should go ahead as planned and start on 1 June. The 0720 departure from Belfast was now selected, as it would suit existing trains between Stranraer and Glasgow. Mr. T. Wheatley, of the G & P J R, undertook to accelerate the passage of the trains between Stranraer and Girvan as much as possible.

G

On the 20th, Mr. Cotton crossed over from Belfast and met top G & S W R officials—Mr. Thomson, the Chairman, Mr. Morton, the General Manager, and Mr. Mathieson, the Passenger Superintendent. They now made their objections to the second service quite explicit and stated that if the service ran, no provision would be made for special trains and ordinary fares would apply.

The following day, Mr. Cotton reported back on his meeting and the Managing Committee decided that, without the full co-operation of the G & S W R, the scheme could not be carried out efficiently, and it was agreed, with regret, to abandon the plans for the second service. The committee was at a loss to understand this last minute change of mind on the part of the G & S W R, especially as the suggestion had come, in the first instance, from the G & S W R Chairman. Perhaps John Burns being a major shareholder in the G & S W R is relevant.

A NEW COMPANY FOR A NEW SHIP

Princess Beatrice was on her outward run from Stranraer on the morning of Saturday, 26 January 1889, when she suffered a fracture to the main frame of the port engine. She managed to limp back from her position six miles off Corsewall Point to the railway pier. Alex. A. Laird & Company's screw ship *Elm* was hurriedly chartered for the evening sailing from Larne, and from the Monday morning *Princess Louise* took over the sailings and remained so employed until Saturday, 9 March. During this spell on the route her time-keeping was very poor and the Board were forced to give serious consideration to a replacement.

1889 was to see an intensification in competition from the fleet of G. & J. Burns. In the spring of that year the fast paddler *Cobra* had been launched for the Burns's fleet and this ship had been designed for a daily daylight round trip between Ardrossan and Belfast. Difficulties arose with the G & S W R over train connections at Ardrossan, and this caused *Cobra* to use the newly-built C R pier at Gourock. The crossing was completed in five hours and one hour was given ashore for day trippers from Scotland. But *Cobra*'s career on the Irish Sea was to be brief, since in 1890 she was sold to the Liverpool & Llandudno Steamship Company Limited. On 18 April 1890, a larger and faster paddler, *Adder*, was launched from the Fairfield yard for the daylight sailing, though her Scottish base was moved to G & S W R Princes Pier at Greenock. In 1892, *Adder* was transferred to Ardrossan, where she berthed at the C R Montgomerie Pier, and this reduced further the journey time between Glasgow and Belfast. A train left Glasgow (Central) at 0905 and *Adder* was due at Belfast Princes Quay at 1335, and nearly $2\frac{1}{2}$ hours was given ashore with an arrival back in Glasgow at 2130. Very soon the excursionists' time at Belfast was restricted to two hours with the Glasgow departure and arrival times virtually unchanged.

In the light of arrival of *Cobra*, it was generally agreed that a new ship was required for the Stranraer route, but the question was how was it to be financed. An opinion shared by the railway companies and certain of the Irish shareholders was that it would be better all round if the individual shareholders could be bought out by the companies, who could then inject the necessary capital into the steamboat company for the new ship. The question was what was a fair price.

The B & N C R and C & L R, not directly interested in the capital of the L & S S Co., were prepared to have the loans they had made to the company converted into capital, but they were not able to increase their financial involvement either by direct investment or by buying out the independent shareholders.

One of the Irish shareholders, Mr. William Valentine, had written to the steamboat Board outlining a scheme for repayment. A new company should be formed, he suggested, by the four companies comprising the P & W J R plus the B & N C R, which would purchase for £25,000 the two steamers and the goodwill of the trade. From this fell to be deducted net liabilities of the L & S S Co. of £10,611, leaving £14,389 available for distribution. This was equivalent to £7.40 per £10 share on the issued £19,250 capital. Part of the net liabilities was £23,815 of loans outstanding to railway companies, and this, once repaid, would be returned as capital for the new company. But the Managing Committee could not see its way to recommend the adoption of this scheme, nor would they entertain Valentine's suggestion that the Belfast Steamship Company Limited be allowed to take over the private shareholding.

Substantial loans had been made to the L & S S Co., but when surplus cash had arisen in the steamboat company's cashbox, no attempt was made to reduce these loans. Instead, the money was placed on loan with the B & N C R, and by April 1887 the loan to the B & N C R had risen to £14,000. As if to hasten a decision by the steamboat Board, the Chairman of the B & N C R indicated that his company would probably be repaying part of the loan at an early date. The Chairman suggested that, as the L & S S Co. did not require the money for working capital, part of the loans made to the L & S S Co. by the B & N C R, C & L R and P & W J C, totalling £23,815, should be repaid on the understanding that the money could then be returned to the L & S S Co. for the purpose of building a new steamer.

There was more delay, but in principle the suggestion from the B & N C Chairman was adopted, as well as the request from Mr. Valentine that the private shareholders be bought out. In March 1889, the Irish directors were asked to ascertain at what figure the fifty-five outside shareholders would be prepared to sell their stock. The majority of the shares would be available, it transpired, at £6.25 per £10 share. The stock had yielded no dividend and a capital loss of £3.75 per share was acceptable in the circumstances.

At a Board meeting of the L & S S Co. on 29 March 1889, the motion was adopted to wind up the steamboat company and establish a new and larger company. The new company would take over all the liabilities of the old company and pay off the loans to the railway companies and purchase the Irish shareholders out at £6.25 per £10 share. The new company would also take over the assets of the old company, including the two ships. At the meeting, the chairmen of the B & N C R and C & L R indicated that their respective boards were prepared to take up to £6,000 capital in the new company. This amount corresponded almost exactly to the net sums owing by the L & S S Co. to the two Irish companies. The representatives of the L & N W R, M R, G & S W R and C R stated their companies were prepared to take up shares for any further capital required for the purchase of a new steamer. So the nettle had been grasped. At the same meeting a sub-committee of directors was set up to obtain designs and prices for a new steamer for the Stranraer–Larne route.

In the middle of April 1889, a circular was sent to all shareholders advising them of the forthcoming purchase of their shares. But the signature at the foot of the letter was W. R. Gill, Acting Secretary. Charles Stewart, the first and only Secretary of the L & S S Co., had died on 8 April. By the end of September 1889 all the shareholders had been paid off and the shares purchased were registered in the names of two members of the P & W J C until such times as the old company was finally wound up. The books of the P & W J C were amended to reflect the reduction of the share value from £10 to £6.25.

Until the new company was formed, the management was left in the hands of the Managing Committee, although the number of representatives from the Irish side was reduced to two from the B & N C R, reflecting the imminent takeover by the B & N C R of the C & L R. This committee, to all intents and purposes, was trading as a partnership, with the five partners acting as trustees for the interests of their respective railway companies. The committee was given capital of £100,000, just under £20,000 coming from each of the P & W J R companies and £21,000 from the B & N C R.

Correspondence concerning the new company continued with and between solicitors for a few years and then quietly died and the new company never saw the light of day. The interregnum arrangement was regularised by an agreement completed in May 1893 between the B & N C R, C R, G & S W R, L & N W R and M R, whereby was established the Larne & Stranraer Steamship Joint Committee. This committee had six members, one from each of the P & W J C companies and two from the B & N C R. The agreement was deemed to have commenced on 1 January 1890.

CHAPTER SEVEN

The Larne & Stranraer
Steamship Joint Committee

THE sub-committee set up on 29 March 1889, to arrange for the building of a new steamer for the Larne route, met on the last day of May 1889 and opened the tenders received. The tenders for a paddle steamer ranged from £43,000 to £68,000, while those for twin-screw ships were from £45,000 to £54,000. As with every Stranraer "Princess" for the next seventy years the order went to Messrs. William Denny & Bros., of Dumbarton. For £46,500 the firm offered to build a steel paddle steamer of 280 feet length with a speed of 18 knots consuming $2\frac{3}{4}$ tons of coal per hour. Delivery was to be seven months from the signing of the contract.

PADDLE OR SCREW

There had been much discussion as to whether the ship should be paddle or twin-screw. The limiting factor on all Stranraer ships is that of draught. A shallow-draught steamer with a high-standing triple expansion engine was likely to prove tender and a bad sea boat, while a paddle steamer would be more susceptible to storm damage and delay by heavy weather. Nevertheless, the new ship for the route was to be a paddler.

On entering the water from the Dumbarton yard on 23 January 1890, the ship was named *Princess Victoria*. She was ready for trials on 22 April (four days after the launch of her Ardrossan rival *Adder*) and maintained a speed of $19\frac{3}{4}$ knots over a distance equal to that between Stranraer and Larne. On 24 April, guests arrived at Craigendoran to join the Clyde Shipping Company's tug, *Flying Scotsman*, which was acting as tender to *Princess Victoria*. The new Stranraer paddler then set off on a special trip around the Firth and, after a call at Wemyss Bay Pier, handed her party back to the tender for landing at Craigendoran Pier by five o'clock. Captain Campbell anchored his ship in the Gareloch for the night and in the morning sailed for Larne. Reflecting the departure of the old steamboat company, the new ship's two funnels were painted buff instead of the red and black of the first two "Princesses". *Princess Beatrice* was at Holyhead for overhaul when the "Victoria" arrived to take up the run, and on 1 May 1890 the "Victoria" took over from the pioneer *Princess Louise*. *Princess Louise* had sailed for the last time on the Stranraer station. The first day in service was marred for *Princess Victoria* by her running into a schooner, causing considerable damage to the victim but little to herself.

In all respects *Princess Victoria* introduced new standards to the Stranraer route. She was fitted with electric light and, contrary to the usual practice in paddle steamers, saloon accommodation was provided amidships and in the forward region of the ship. On the upper deck, between the funnels, four private cabins, each with accommodation for two, were provided as an innovation. In the same area there was a large cabin for ladies, while forward of the funnels there was a beautifully upholstered general cabin. Ample accommodation was provided, we are told, below the forecastle for deck passengers. Special provision was made for the carrying of livestock and seven hundred cattle could be accommodated, as well as a number of horses. The elaborate scale of the accommodation was possible because of the greater size of the "Victoria" when compared with her two older consorts. She was 70 feet longer than the "Louise", and using gross tonnage as a rough and ready indication of enclosed accommodation, the "Victoria's" 1,096 contrasts with the 497 for the "Louise" and 556 for the "Beatrice". Alongside concern for the comfort of the passengers we see a developing concern for their safety, and *Princess Victoria* was built with seven water-tight bulkheads all carried up to main deck level. Four ordinary marine type return-tube boilers supplied steam to the compound surface condensing machinery. Forced draught was employed in the stokehold.

With the old company no longer in use and the new company not likely to be in existence for some time, the question arose as to who owned the ship for registration purposes. It was agreed that *Princess Victoria* should be registered in the name of the Secretary of the L & S S J C, Mr. John Thomson, as individual and managing owner.

SALE OF "PRINCESS LOUISE"

The L & S S J C Manager, Mr. Edward Cotton, had been instructed in February 1890 to receive any offers for the sale of *Princess Louise*, and in June 1890 the offer of £2,250 was accepted from a Mr. Lowther, of Belfast. She had taken over from the "Beatrice" on 17 April and remained in service until the end of the month. By authority of the Board of Trade dated 17 January 1891, her name was changed to *Islay*, since she was now a member of the MacBrayne fleet. *Islay* was to be employed on the Glasgow–Islay route in succession to a ship of the same name wrecked in December 1890 at Red Bay, County Antrim. The new *Islay* made her first departure from Glasgow on 16 February 1891 and continued on this route, where speed was of secondary importance, until about 0200 on Tuesday, 15 July 1902, when she ran aground in dense fog on Sheep Island, near Port Ellen. Passengers were safely landed but the ship was a total loss. Three months later a gale caused the wreckage to break up and the after end disappeared into deep water.

This opportunity is taken to correct a mistake concerning *Princess Louise* which has crept into Grahame Farr's excellent book, *West Country Passenger Steamers*. He writes that *Princess Louise* was used for a time on the Penzance–Scilly Isles service while on charter to the West Cornwall Steamship Company. But this proves to be a case of mistaken identity. Through the help of the honorary secretary of the Isles of Scilly Museum Association, a photograph has been obtained of *Princess Louise* leaving St. Mary's, but it is not the Stranraer ship of that name. It is the *Princess Louise* owned by Mr. Alexander Paterson, of Oban, from 1898 until her sale to David MacBrayne Ltd. in 1934. This small screw steamer was the regular relief ship on the Scillies route during several winters before the First World War. No doubt those crossing would have preferred the larger *Princess Louise* from Stranraer. Also, the cargo carrying facilities of the Oban steamer were extremely limited and on one occasion the traders of the Scilly Isles petitioned the Great Western Railway to take over the service, probably from Plymouth. The Great Western declined.[151]

THE "DAYLIGHT SERVICE"

Princess Victoria brought increased speed and reliability to the service, and an additional round trip between Larne and Stranraer was introduced during the summer of 1890. The large financial outlay involved in building the new steamer made the L & S S J C determined to squeeze the maximum work out of her. The earliest date by which train connections could be arranged was 14 July, and from that date until the end of September 1890, *Princess Victoria* doubled back in the morning from Larne to Stranraer, where a train left at 1240 for Glasgow. A train leaving Glasgow at 0950 connected into *Princess Victoria* for her return trip to Larne, where a train met her with an arrival time at York Road, Belfast, of 1600.

Although, after the troubles of the G & P J R were solved, the full Glasgow–Stranraer train service had been re-introduced, it had proved impossible to provide a morning connection from Glasgow for the mail steamer, since the morning departure was now around 0700. But with the additional service by *Princess Victoria* it was now possible to make the journey in either direction between Glasgow and Belfast within the same day. It was still a longer journey timewise than the Burns's Daylight Service by the new, fast *Adder* via Princes Pier and Princes Quay, but the Stranraer route had the attraction of the short open sea crossing. In 1890, 10,200 passengers used the daylight service offered by *Princess Victoria*, and during the same period the new ship saw an increase of 200 passengers using the mail service, thus removing fears that the new daylight schedule would prove detrimental to the mail sailing.

For comparison, the services offered in the summer of 1890 by *Princess Victoria* and *Adder* between Glasgow and Belfast are shown:

	Princess Victoria Via Stranraer and Larne				*Adder* Via Greenock	
Glasgow (St. Enoch)	lv 0950	1615	ar 1600	2345	lv 0800	ar 2133
Belfast (York Road)	ar 1600	1000*	lv 0900	1645		
Belfast (Princes Quay)					ar 1330	lv 1500

* Following day.

A couple of years later, in July 1892, *Princess Victoria* was returning from overhaul at Belfast and by chance followed *Adder* down Belfast Lough, and once open waters were reached a trial of strength ensued, with both ships going flat out as far as Ailsa Craig, when the Stranraer ship left off and headed for Loch Ryan. The contest was inconclusive, but it was with great vehemence that the "Victoria's" owners refuted the inference in the press that their ship had been the loser.

Despite the chronic shortage of cash that attended the Girvan line, the Ayrshire & Wigtownshire managed to have six new coaches built, and these were placed on the express morning train from Glasgow to Stranraer, stopping only at Girvan, Maybole and Ayr, for the "Daylight Service", as it was called. These coaches also worked the 1240 return service from Stranraer.[152.]

The daylight service started on Monday, 14 July 1890, and the following day saw the continuance of an innovation of two years previous—excursions by the Stranraer steamers. 15 July was the day of the Stranraer Cattle Show

Day, in 1890, and an excursion was offered along the Ayrshire Coast. In 1888 and 1889, *Princess Louise* had given the excursions after bringing day trippers over in the morning from Larne for the Show. In 1890, *Princess Beatrice* was roused and sailed in the afternoon on the excursion. The 1890 excursion did not meet with universal approval and complaints were made through the press that the object of the Show Day was to bring people to Stranraer, not take them away. Whether for this reason or not, the excursion was not repeated in 1891 and it was left to the small screw steamer *Argyll*, of the Argyll Steamship Company, to provide some excursion sailings. On Saturday, 18 July, she sailed round Ailsa Craig; on Monday, 20, to Corsewall Point; and on the Show Day itself, Tuesday, 21 July, short cruises on Loch Ryan were offered.

Argyll had given occasional short excursions from Stranraer before. She had been built in 1886 and operated a service between Glasgow, Greenock, Fairlie, the west coast of Arran and Campbeltown. During many of her years in service on the Clyde she made a weekly return trip from Campbeltown to Glasgow via Stranraer, thus providing a weekly service of sorts for cargo and passengers between Stranraer and Glasgow. *Argyll* was lost on Sunday, 17 September 1893, when she struck rocks near Cairnryan during fog. A replacement, *Pirate*, was quickly obtained and took up *Argyll*'s sailings from the following Tuesday, but *Pirate* did not advertise any facilities for passengers, though she carried a few when required.

It had always been part of the function of the small passenger/cargo ships trading between Stranraer and Glasgow to give occasional excursions from Stranraer. We have already noted the excursions offered from Stranraer by ships of the Glasgow & Stranraer Steam Packet Company. A small screw steamer, *Ayrshire Lass*, operated for the Girvan Steam Packet Company in opposition to the G & S S P ships on a, usually, weekly schedule between Glasgow and Stranraer, calling at intermediate ports. She so traded from 1849 until the opening of the railway link in 1861 between Glasgow and Stranraer via Dumfries. *Ayrshire Lass* was succeeded on this station by the cargo-only *Norseman*. *Ayrshire Lass* gave excursions from Stranraer to Culzean Bay and to Ailsa Craig during her time on the station.[153]

A few years were to pass before excursion sailing became a regular feature of the programme of the "Princess" ships, but the daylight service was to remain. In 1891, it commenced on 11 July and again *Princess Victoria* supplied the two round trips, while *Princess Beatrice* remained at Stranraer Railway Pier as stand-by steamer.

A TWO-SHIP SCHEDULE

For any service requiring two ships, both must be of the same standard and have similar capabilities. If one of the pair is inferior, the utilisation of the lesser ship must be kept to a minimum and negates the benefit of retaining a spare ship. *Princess Beatrice* was not deemed a fit consort for *Princess Victoria*, and in August 1891, the decision was taken by the L & S S J C to invite tenders for a sister for *Princess Victoria*.

An important factor leading to this decision was the news from the Post Office that after many years of discussion a mail contract was to be offered to the Stranraer–Larne route. The aspirations of the 1860s were to be realised.

Out of the contract price, the steamship section was to receive £8,000 per year. The mail contract was effective from 1 September 1891. The route proved able to handle the mail efficiently, and in September 1895 a satisfactory report was made to Parliament on the punctuality of the service. In the sample four months to 31 July 1895 the mail arrived in Belfast almost always on time.[154]

A condition of the mail contract was the requirement at all times of a stand-by ship for the route. Thus a decision in April 1892 to dispose of *Princess Beatrice* was rescinded and this vessel retained for another twelve years to cover the periods when one of the larger paddlers was absent for overhaul.

Despite their poor experience with the "Victoria", the L & S S J C went back to Denny's for their next ship. The shipbuilders' offer to build a repeat of *Princess Victoria* for £48,000 was accepted. For an extra £2,000 the builders were prepared to fit triple expansion machinery in preference to the obsolescent two-crank compound engines. But after discussion it was decided to adhere to the traditional compound machinery. Also at these discussions the representatives from Dumbarton agreed to reduce the price for the ship to £47,000 and undertook to deliver the ship in the following March. In January 1892, it was agreed to bestow the name *Princess May* on the new steamer.

During the course of construction of the "May", modifications were made to the plans in the light of continuing experience with the "Victoria". In the "Victoria" the wheels were a source of continual trouble and paddle wheels of stronger build were incorporated into the "May". These wheels were never to give any trouble. In addition, a small shelter deck around the two funnels was added to the "May". The "Victoria" received this small improvement in 1893. The cost of fitting sleeping berths to both *Princess Victoria* and *Princess May* was investigated but the estimate of £2,000 killed the idea. In 1898, a more modest proposal for sleeping berths, costing £600, was adopted for the sisters.

Although promised for March, it was 4 May 1892 before *Princess May* was on trials on the Clyde, when over a distance of 28 miles an average of 20·02 knots was maintained with engines running at 47½ r.p.m. The following day the ship set off for Stranraer and on her way to the head of the loch passed another fine ship from the Dumbarton yard—the paddler *Duchess of Hamilton* of The Caledonian Steam Packet Company Limited—returning to Wemyss Bay with an excursion party. When the "Victoria" arrived back from Larne she welcomed her new sister by setting off rockets and firing guns.

On Monday, 9 May 1892, *Princess May* took over from *Princess Victoria* on the mail service and allowed *Princess Beatrice* to sail to Ayr for overhaul and survey. On the return of the "Beatrice" the "Victoria" crossed to Belfast on a similar errand. On the afternoon of the first day of the "May" a presentation was made to Captain Campbell at Larne by over two hundred regular travellers on the route. The presentation of silver plate took place in the Olderfleet Hotel, just beside the mail berth. Included was a silver salver with a representation of *Princess May* at the top and the flag of the old steamboat company which had been adopted by the L & S S J C.

The pattern of the summer service was changed in 1892 with both new ships being in service. Each ship gave one round trip, with *Princess Victoria* being based at Larne and *Princess May* at Stranraer for the mail service. This basic pattern of summer employment remained until 1962, when *Caledonian Princess* reverted to the practice of undertaking the double schedule single-handed.

With a train departure from Belfast at 0905, the daylight service steamer, in 1892, left the Irish side at much the same time as in 1890 and 1891, but with two ships in service a later return trip from Stranraer was possible. Instead of a departure from Glasgow (St. Enoch) at 0950 as applied in 1890, a train for the evening sailing left at 1640, since the steamer did not leave Stranraer until 1955. The ships would pass each other in Loch Ryan, since the mail steamer left Larne at 1815 (GMT). This recasting of the outward schedule from Glasgow removed a clash in timing with the Burns's Daylight Service by *Adder*. In 1892, *Adder* transferred to Ardrossan and her train left Glasgow (Central) at 0905 for the Caledonian terminal at Ardrossan, Montgomerie Pier. The evening return timings of *Adder* probably proved more attractive to passengers for Glasgow than the mail steamer to Stranraer, since by leaving Belfast at 1600 an arrival at Glasgow was possible by 2130. The 1700 train from Belfast (York Road) for the mail steamer at Larne meant a 2355 arrival in Glasgow. In the spring of 1896 the B & N C R and G & S W R representatives on the L & S S J C argued for the operation of the double service all year round, but their opinion did not carry the day.

The outline of the services between Belfast and Britain offered by the Stranraer steamers and by the Burns's fleet remained almost unchanged until the 1930s (allowing for interruption by war) and the timetables for 1892 are reproduced. For completeness the relevant London times are shown for the Stranraer–Larne schedules.

					a			a
London (St. Pancras—M R)	......	......	......	lv. 0945	1740	ar. 0415	0750
London (Euston—L & N W R)	......	......	,, 1000	2000	,, 2250	0720
Glasgow (St. Enoch—G & S W R), via Girvan	......	,, 1640	2130	,, 1535	2355
Glasgow (Central—C R), via Dumfries	......	......	,, 1401	1750	,, 1800	0918
Stranraer Harbour	......	......	......	......	......	,, 1955	0634	,, 1220	2015
Larne Harbour	......	......	......	......	ar. 2130	0810	lv. 0955	1750
Belfast (York Road—B & N C R)	......	......	,, 2225	0910	,, 0905	1700

	b	c				
Glasgow (Broomielaw) lv.	1830	ar. 0600				
Glasgow (St. Enoch) ,,	2105	,, 0506	d	f	a	a
Glasgow (Central)		lv. 2200	ar. 0551	ar. 1651	lv. 0905	ar. 2130
Greenock (Princes Pier),,	2152	,, e				
Ardrossan (Montgomerie Pier)				,, 1515	,, 1000	,, 2030
Ardrossan (Winton Pier)		,, 2310	,, e			
Belfast (Princes Quay)				lv. 0900	ar. 1335	lv. 1600
Belfast (Donegall Quay) ar. 0430	lv. 2000	ar. 0500	lv. 2130			

a—Operated in summer only; b—leave Broomielaw 1600 on Saturdays; c—leave Belfast 2130 on Saturdays; d—except Saturdays; e—time of call not published; f—on Mondays only. Local time is shown.

Traffic between Britain and Ireland was increasing but the Stranraer route had to cope with increased competition from new ships on other routes. In addition to the fast, popular, passenger-only paddler *Adder*, Burns placed two new screw ships on its Belfast routes. In 1891, the cargo ship *Grouse* was allocated to the Glasgow–Belfast station and was joined two years later by the fine passenger-cargo steamer *Hound*. The overnight service between Ardrossan and Belfast, which had passed from the Ardrossan Shipping Company to G. & J. Burns in 1882, was operated until the close of 1893 by *Seal*, formerly *North Eastern*, and *Grampus*, formerly *North Western*. On the opening of the

Manchester Ship Canal, these ships were transferred to a service between Glasgow and Manchester. Their duties were taken over by the newer and faster screw ships, *Mastiff* and *Hare*.

Even the Ayr Steam Shipping Company, normally a cargo-orientated company, had begun to advertise their alternate-night services to Larne and Belfast as "Another Route to Ireland" with train connections from Glasgow (St. Enoch).

In the summer of 1893, therefore, a traveller from Glasgow to Belfast had several options open to him: by the 0905 train from Glasgow (Central) to Ardrossan for the daylight crossing by *Adder*, or *Hound* from the Broomielaw at 1830 or via Princes Pier by the 2105 train from Glasgow (St. Enoch); again, the 2200 train from St. Enoch connected into *Mona*'s overnight sailing from Ayr; and the 2300 from Central to Ardrossan connected into *Seal* or *Grampus*. In addition, there was the 1640 from St. Enoch to Stranraer for the daylight service by *Princess Victoria*. A similar variety of services was available for those from London and the north of England via Barrow, Fleetwood, Liverpool, as well as via Stranraer. The early 1890s had seen a considerable investment in new tonnage on the English routes also. The L & S S J C were finding they had to run very fast just to stand still.

A "PRINCESS'S" PROBLEMS

Princess Victoria was not allowed to settle down to a quiet life at Stranraer. She was dogged by weather, mechanical difficulties and sheer misfortune. We have already noted her altercation with a schooner on her first day in service. This brought a bill for £122. In August of her first season we hear that Messrs. Dennys had to be called in when one of her paddle wheels failed. Also, through negligence on the part of a seaman, the bow rudder was damaged and the "Victoria" had to be beached to allow repairs to be carried out. Captain Campbell reported encountering severe weather on 7 November 1890, and stated that *Princess Victoria* behaved well, but on 22 January 1891, heavy seas carried away part of her top deck and damaged the bridge and engine telegraphs.

While on the morning mail run on 4 June 1891, *Princess Victoria* was disabled when ten miles from Larne through her port wheel striking some floating wreckage. The hull and paddle box also sustained some damage. Her plight was seen from the Irish shore and two ships, *Annie* of Liverpool and *Mona* of Ayr, came out and towed the steamer into Larne. A letter to *The Belfast News-Letter* praised the coolness of John McCracken, who was sailing as master of the "Victoria". After he had ascertained the extent of the damage, he stood back and unhurriedly lit his pipe. This action, the correspondent reflected, restored calm to the ship's passengers. As soon as arrangements could be made, *Princess Victoria* was moved to Dumbarton to spend a month or so in the repair yard. As luck would have it, the stand-by vessel *Princess Beatrice* was at Ayr for annual overhaul and so was not immediately available. Until she took up the service on the 8th, the route had to be covered by chartered tonnage, the return sailing from Larne on the evening of 4 June being taken by *Mona*, of the Ayr Shipping Company, while the service on 5 and 6 June was covered by *Armagh*, of the Barrow Steam Navigation Company.

Princess Victoria left Larne with some three hundred passengers on the morning run on Saturday, 3 September 1892, and once outside the harbour felt the full force of a gale. All went well until the ship was nearly within the shelter of Loch Ryan, when Chief Engineer Henderson was forced to stop the engines following a great crashing in the port paddle box. He discovered that one of the outer arms had broken and this left a paddle float hanging loose. Normally it would have been a simple job to disconnect completely the float, but in the gale this was impossible. Captain McCracken dropped anchor and the ship swung to in Port Mullen Bay, near Corsewall Point. Distress signals were sent up. The lighthouse at Corsewall Point failed to see these, but they were seen in Ballantrae and the lifeboat launched. Also a telegram was sent to the railway office at Stranraer. The lifeboat was half-way to the "Victoria" when the crew saw a ship approaching the disabled paddler and they headed into the shelter of Loch Ryan. The ship approaching the "Victoria" was the tug *Gamecock* and the master of the tug offered to tow *Princess Victoria* to Stranraer for £300. Captain McCracken would not go above £250. *Gamecock* lay off to see if resistance would break down, but before long smoke of another ship was seen heading for Port Mullen. Captain Campbell, on board the "Victoria's" younger sister at Larne, has received word of the accident and brought *Princess May* over. Captain Campbell dropped anchor and allowed the "May" to swing round to within sixty feet of her sister. A boat was launched and a rope passed from the "May" to the "Victoria". *Gamecock* lingered for a short time to see if there might be any pickings, but soon headed off in a cloud of smoke!

Because of the gale, *Princess Victoria* could not be manoeuvred alongside the pier at Stranraer and so she was anchored off the pier and the passengers transferred to *Princess May* and landed at the railway pier at 2130. The "May" then left Stranraer again at 2300 for Larne to take back the handful of day excursionists on the "Victoria". On arrival at Larne, Captain Campbell discovered a large number of cattle and horses and a few passengers awaiting the evening mail sailing to Stranraer. Once these were on board, he set off for Stranraer, arriving at 0700 on the Sunday morning. At Stranraer special trains were laid on for passengers bound for Glasgow and Carlisle. Later on the Sunday, *Princess May* brought her disabled sister alongside the railway pier and the Stranraer railway engineer's staff set about repairing the wheel.

Both steamers had slipped their anchors in Port Mullen Bay, and on Monday the "May" returned from Larne and recovered these. *Princess Victoria* took up service again on the evening of Friday, 16 September. In the meantime, the reserve steamer *Princess Beatrice* had been in service—it would appear on the mail schedule.

In 1899, it was fog that almost put *Princess Victoria* ashore. Returning from Larne on the evening of 31 July, the "Victoria" ran into dense fog in Loch Ryan. Captain Cumming suddenly realised how close to the shore he was when a couple of men waded out from the shore at Cairnryan and shouted up to the ship. Boats were lowered and acted as feelers to guide the ship along the main channel. On the following night the story was repeated at Larne with *Princess May*. Captain McNeill could discern neither Island Magee nor the light in the Chaine Memorial and decided to lie off until the fog lifted. Around 0400, a farmer on Island Magee had his sleep disturbed by the steamer's fog horn, and crossing to the beach saw the "May" almost on the rocks. His shouting was heard on *Princess May* and a grounding avoided. She eventually reached Larne at 0600.

In November 1901, weather again brought trouble to *Princess Victoria*. On Tuesday, 12 November, a south-east gale damaged both *Princess Victoria* and *Princess Beatrice* as they lay on the east side of the pier at Stranraer. The concrete wall of the pier caused over £1,000 damage to the "Victoria". Both she and the "Beatrice" were sent to Harland & Wolff's yard at Belfast and returned to Stranraer at the beginning of December. The mail boat, *Princess May*, could not leave Larne until the following morning.[155]

In January 1892, Captain Campbell had to draw the attention of the L & S S J C to the following points: the coupling bolts on the crank shaft were repeatedly coming loose, one of the floats had cracked, one of the driving arms was showing signs of failure, heavy seas had caused the paddle floats to twist at the centre, with resultant loosened and broken bolts. Heavy seas had also stove in the decking of the fore sponsons. In December 1892, while at Dumbarton, *Princess Victoria*'s steel paddle wheels were replaced by wheels of wrought iron and the sponson decks strengthened. These items and sundry other repairs produced a bill for £3,000 for a ship not yet three years old. By November 1893, cracks in three paddle arms were reported.

When the "Victoria" was about to leave Dumbarton after her 1897 overhaul, a serious defect was found in the crank shaft of the ship and repairs had to be put in hand immediately. The decision had to be taken in November 1897 to replace the ship's two piston shafts, since both were cracked at the neck.

Certainly *Princess Victoria* was an ambitious ship when built, but she proved an expensive ship to keep in service. It would appear that the "Victoria's" builders and owners learned much from their experience with this steamer, for her sister, two years junior, was to prove a most successful ship.

EXCURSION EXPANSION

The early 1890s witnessed a considerable increase in excursion trade around the coast of Britain, and this resulted in the building of some fine ships. At Stranraer both new ships were in service during the summer months, but their schedules left them idle for a large part of the day. Thursday, 6 July 1893, was a public holiday, celebrating the wedding of the Duke of York and Princess May, and two special excursions were offered at Stranraer. *Princess Victoria*, having sailed over from Larne on the daylight service, carried about a thousand passengers along the Ayrshire Coast and round Ailsa Craig, while the Barrow Steam Navigation Company's *Manx Queen* sailed to the Isle of Man with two hundred passengers from the railway pier at Stranraer. *Princess May* had been well-loaded on the morning mail run to Larne with excursionists bound for Belfast and Portrush. *Argyll* does not appear to have given an excursion sailing but satisfied herself by letting off some rockets in the evening while she lay at the West Pier.

The Annual Agricultural Show was to become a regular day for excursions from Stranraer by the railway steamers, and in 1893, on Thursday, 18 July, *Princess Victoria* repeated her Ayrshire Coast and Ailsa Craig trip. Likewise on Tuesday, 17 July 1894.

The excursion programme was expanded in 1895 to the extent that every Saturday in July and August, afternoon excursions were provided from Larne along the Antrim Coast and from Stranraer round Ailsa Craig.

1895 also saw a new feature which was to become an annual event. Mr. George Watson, the agent at Stranraer for *Argyll* and *Pirate*, chartered a steamer for a public trip to the Firth of Clyde. On 1 August 1895, it was the G & S W R *Glen Rosa* that paddled her way from the West Pier to Rothesay, but this duty soon fell on the same company's *Juno*. An exception was 1910, when, on Thursday, 4 August, the Laird Line *Olive* gave an excursion to Campbeltown and Tarbert. But the weather was bad and the ship poorly prepared for the excursionists, and in 1911 it was back to *Juno* for Dunoon and Arrochar.

From the summer of 1887 on, the P & W J C combined with The Isle of Man Steam Packet Company Limited to provide an excursion at least once a a year from Galloway to the Isle of Man. Trains conveyed the excursionists from Stranraer and other stations to Garliestown, where they joined the steamer for the three-hour crossing to Douglas. In 1909, in addition to two trips to Douglas, an excursion was offered from Stranraer via Garliestown to Fleetwood with a train connection for Blackpool. There are isolated instances of the excursions from Garliestown to Douglas being taken by vessels not of the Isle of Man fleet. For example, in August 1887 and 1888, and May 1892, the trips were given by the Laird Line *Elm*, which at that time was normally employed on the Liverpool–Garliestown route.

The energetic Mr. Watson drew up a most ambitious excursion for Friday, 18 August 1899, when he offered a day excursion from Campbeltown via Stranraer and Garliestown to the Isle of Man. He chartered the paddle steamer, *Carrick Castle*, and she left the Kintyre port at 0500 for Stranraer. A special train at 0800 conveyed her passengers from the railway pier to Garliestown, where they embarked for Douglas. On the return crossing from Stranraer, *Carrick Castle* was held up by fog and did not reach Campbeltown until 0200 on the Saturday. Having chartered the steamer, Mr. Watson used her to the full by offering an afternoon excursion from Stranraer to Lamlash on the island of Arran. A year later, Friday, 10 August 1900, the sale of *Carrick Castle* to the Russian Government was announced and this opened another chapter in the varied career of this steamer.

In 1896, The Isle of Man Steam Packet Company Limited joined with the P & W J C to provide another excursion possibility for the folk of Stranraer. Passengers boarded the Isle of Man steamer at Stranraer and sailed round the Mull of Galloway to Garliestown. This attractive circular trip was completed by train from Garliestown back to Stranraer. This outing from Stranraer was part of a tour from the Isle of Man. The passengers from Douglas left their steamer at Stranraer and crossed to Garliestown by train, where they rejoined the steamer for the return crossing to Douglas. On Monday, 6 July 1896, the paddler *Prince of Wales* left the railway pier at 1430 for Garliestown. On Thursday, 6 August, *Tynwald* gave the same excursion, but her departure from Stranraer at 1600 reminds us that Garliestown was tidally restricted. This excursion was repeated occasionally in the following years. On Saturday, 19 July 1899, *Princess May* left the railway pier on an excursion to Ailsa Craig at the same time as *Queen Victoria*, bound for Garliestown. The "May" followed the Isle of Man steamer down Loch Ryan and soon overtook her, but

Queen Victoria was "not amused" and easily put the Stranraer ship in her place before turning south for Garliestown.

On her closing excursion two years previously *Princess May* had cause for more than a blush. At 1430 on 25 September 1897, she set out for Ailsa Craig with less than two hundred on board. All went well until the ship was off Ailsa Craig, when two paddle arms broke, immobilising the ship. Captain McCracken decided to make the return journey on one paddle wheel and seven hours were spent disconnecting the damaged wheel from the crankshaft. Two local engineers on board for the cruise found themselves at work alongside the engine-room crew. The weather was fair, and although several passing ships offered help, none was accepted. While everything was calm on the "May", the steamboat office at Stranraer was besieged by people awaiting passengers returning from the excursion and telegrams were sent to Ayr, Cairnryan, Corsewall, Campbeltown, Lamlash and several other ports. A reply came from Ayr that the ship could be seen stopped off Ailsa Craig.

On her return on the evening mail run from Larne to Stranraer, *Princess Victoria* was sent off to Larne around 2100 with passengers and mail that the "May" should have taken. About 2330 the "Victoria" left Larne to make contact with her sister and, if required, tow her back to the mainland. In the darkness the "Victoria" missed the "May", which by now had drifted in towards the Ayrshire coast. Around midnight Cairnryan had passed to Stranraer a message from a shepherd, "Ship at anchor under Bennane Head and a lot of hammering". The shepherd, sensing something was amiss, had walked some eight miles to deliver the message. He was later to receive a gift of £5 from the steamboat company. Eventually the "May" managed to get under way and arrived back at Stranraer about lunchtime on the following day— eighteen hours late. *Princess May* was taken to Dumbarton for repairs and the "Victoria" maintained the double service single-handed for the remaining four days of the summer timetable.

Why *Princess Beatrice* did not appear is not known. Probably traffic at the end of the season was so light that it did not justify awakening the steamer from its slumbers. But certainly *Princess Beatrice* did see duty on the Daylight Service in the following June for three days following a collision between *Princess May* and the coasting steamer *Bay Fisher*.

Princess May was normally a very reliable vessel and incidents like that off Ailsa Craig were exceptional. She did, however, have one or two accidents during her time. Some were trivial, such as the time in June 1892 when she dented the Ayr steamer *Mona* at Larne, or on 26 June 1902, when the "May" and *Logic* of the Belfast Steamship Company had a disagreement in Larne Harbour and each was slightly damaged. A more dramatic occurrence was on 27 November 1905, when *Princess May*'s outward mail run to Larne stopped short as a result of her high-pressure connecting rod breaking. *Princess Victoria* was sent out and towed the disabled ship back to Stranraer and took over the mail service. The most costly mishap to the "May" occurred while the ship was laid up in December 1894. During a storm on the 22nd, the ship was torn from her moorings at Stranraer and driven ashore on the sandy beach. The force of the storm pushed her so far up the beach that it took three weeks and the use of tugs to free her. The cost incurred for refloating and repairs amounted to £2,700. In the normal way this would have been recoverable from insurance underwriters, but one had fled the country and the Steamship Profit & Loss

Account had to accept a debit of £1,100 for the balance of the expense not recovered.

The increase in excursion traffic in the twenty-five years preceding the first world war was experienced to a lesser extent in the Belfast Lough area than in regions such as the Clyde, Thames or Mersey. But one of the manifestations of what increase there was is relevant to our account.

In *The Newtonards Chronicle* of 27 June 1891, an advertisement appeared intimating that from Monday, 29 June, there would be a daily excursion service from Donaghadee to Portpatrick. For the first two weeks the steamer left Donaghadee at 0900 and returned from Portpatrick at 1815 in time for the evening train to Belfast. From Sunday, 12 July, however, a revised schedule was operated leaving Donaghadee at 1115 on Sundays and 1030 on other days in the week. The Sunday train connection left Belfast (Queen's Quay) at 1000, while Monday to Saturday it was thirty-five minutes earlier. The return crossing from Portpatrick left at 1630 on Sundays and 1800 during the rest of the week, with trains at Donaghadee for Belfast. The cabin return fare for the crossing was 4s. and the steerage 2s. 6d.

The vessel employed on the service was the Clyde tug *Terrible* operating under charter. We met *Terrible* earlier, when in May 1866 she gave an isolated excursion on the route and in November 1883 when a short-lived service was operated between Glasgow, Greenock and Stranraer. On 18 July, *The Newtonards Chronicle* noted that "If the merits of this trip were better known we could, with confidence, predict a good season for the promoter, Mr. McGladdery". The last mention in the press of the service was a routine advertisement on 1 August 1891. No attempt was made in 1892 or subsequent years to re-open the route for excursionists.

Terrible was a member of the once-popular category of coastal craft—the passenger carrying tug. Once it became economically possible to build steamers purely for excursion traffic these dual-purpose vessels began to fade away, and their demise was further expedited by increasing regulations for passenger certificates. A few isolated examples did linger on in the Clyde, Mersey, Solent and East Coast.

A feature of the Stranraer–Larne route was that all sailings were in daylight for the most part of the year. But this benefit was nullified to an extent by the lengthy journeys over land between Stranraer and the centres of population. From 1898, provision was made for sleeping berths on both *Princess Victoria* and *Princess May*. Until this time a passenger leaving Glasgow by the evening train for Stranraer had to find overnight accommodation in Stranraer and make an early start for the mail steamer's departure before seven o'clock. Now first-class passengers could occupy one of the sleeping berths until the arrival of the steamer at Larne around 0800. Likewise, on the return journey, it might be more convenient for a traveller to remain on board the mail steamer at Stranraer and make an early start from Stranraer in the morning than travel up on the evening train connection which arrived in Glasgow around midnight.

In each of the two ships, a ladies' deck sitting room was converted into four cabins, each with two berths. A cabin was also constructed on each side of the engine-room skylight and each fitted with two berths. The space appropriated had hitherto formed part of the engine-room. Denny's completed the work for £600 and the charge made for a berth was 2s. 6d. In the first five months of the facility, to 31 March 1899, 502 berths were reserved.

This new feature of *Princess Victoria* and *Princess May* rendered *Princess Beatrice* even less suitable as a stand-by ship for the route. But nothing was done immediately except that the work on the "Beatrice" was minimal. In 1898, Harland & Wolff, at Belfast, managed to have her overhauled and surveyed for £120. In 1902, the Board of Trade surveyor expressed dissatisfaction with the state of *Princess Beatrice*'s boilers and the pressure had to be reduced to 90 lb. This gave the vessel a top speed of less than fourteen knots, and in April 1903 the L & S S J C resolved to sell *Princess Beatrice*. But she remained at Stranraer during 1903 and it was February 1904 before the ship was put in brokers' hands. Four months later she realised £1,600 for breaking up.

Reverting to the Steward's Department, a brief look at the catering arrangements is in order. From the inception of the service in 1872 until the end of September 1897, the management of the catering department was in the hands of Captain George Campbell, the master of the mail steamer. Until 1887, he managed the "Cabin" on his own account, hiring his staff and arranging for the supply of provisions, though the steamboat owners supplied the crockery and silverware. It was agreed by the Managing Committee that from 1 May 1887, Captain Campbell should pay a fee to the L & S S J C for this privilege. Initially this was at a rate of £50 per year, but by 1893 Captain Campbell was paying £250 per year for the two ships. Just before his retirement in 1898, the catering was taken out of Captain Campbell's hands and for a year, from 1 October 1897, the B & N C R, a member of the L & S S J C, managed the catering on the ships from their Laharna Hotel at Larne and paid a fee of £500. The committee paid the wages of the staff and also supplied the crockery, etc. When the year was completed, the L & S S J C took over the catering itself but retained the B & N C R as superintendents and passed over to them 5 per cent of the catering receipts as a fee. In the first decade of this century the net annual revenue accruing to the L & S S J C from the catering department was in the region of £500, though in 1908 it fell to £136.

In 1906, the position of Shore Superintendent at Stranraer was created, and one of the steamer masters, Captain John Cumming, was appointed. The catering arrangements became part of his responsibilities, and as Catering Superintendent he received an additional salary of £100 per year. Captain Cumming remained in this office until his retiral in 1922, when the Marine Superintendent of the G & S W R, William Fraser, exercised oversight for a few months from his office at Princes Pier, Greenock. A new arrangement of superintendence came about after the absorption of the Stranraer shipping into the London Midland & Scottish Railway in 1923.

The Marine Superintendent of the C R, Captain James Williamson, had been requested, in 1909, by the L & S S J C to investigate the catering arrangements on the Stranraer ships. Apart from small adjustments concerning crew catering, he expressed himself satisfied with the running of the Steward's Department. Captain Williamson had had a great influence in the building up

H

of the Clyde fleet of the C R's shipping subsidiary, The Caledonian Steam Packet Company Limited, and this company's enviable reputation for a high standard of catering has continued into the present decade.

Following the absorption by the B & N C R of the Ballymena & Larne Railway in 1889 and the C & L R in 1890, improvements were put in hand at Larne Harbour. Approval was given by the B & N C R Board in 1890 for a new station costing £3,000. The new terminal had an island platform serving two lines—one narrow and one broad gauge. On the covered concourse was an interesting clock with two minute hands. One gave Irish Time and the other Greenwich Mean Time, the latter being twenty-five minutes ahead of the former. The platform adjoined the steamer berth, the mail berth being extended by 70 feet to receive *Princess Victoria*.

Belfast (York Road) was also taken in hand for modernisation in the 1890s. This work involved the building of extra staff accommodation, refreshment rooms, an extension of the city's tramway system into the station, and an increase in the number of platforms from two to five. The programme was completed in November 1898, when the Station Hotel opened for business.

In March 1893, the P & W J C received Parliamentary approval to proceed with considerable alterations at Stranraer. Some initial difficulty with the local authority was overcome when it was "leaked" that the P & W J C were considering building a terminal at Cairnryan. It was said that as ships became larger the railway pier at Stranraer could prove an obstacle because of the shallow approaches. The sailing time from Cairnryan would be 15–20 minutes shorter, and either the G & S W R would build a branch off the Girvan–Stranraer line which would serve Ballantrae and come round the coast to Cairnryan, or the P & W J C would extend their line from Stranraer to Cairnryan (as was done in emergency during the Second World War). The "sabre-rattling" had the desired effect and all obstacles in the way of improvement were removed.

The pier was to be widened by 12 feet on each side and lengthened by 20 feet. The wooden pier and gangway were to be filled in and the whole pier faced with concrete. The station was to be practically rebuilt, the single platform being replaced by two, connected by an overhead bridge. The platforms were to be covered in and a wooden building was to be erected to the west of the lines which would house waiting-rooms, a booking office, a refreshment room and other office accommodation. Additional sidings also formed part of the scheme, which had an estimated cost of £20,000. The execution of the project was protracted. Although work started in late 1892 on certain preliminaries, it was 1898 before the job was completed and the bill for nearly £60,000 received. In September 1902, the P & W J C received Parliamentary approval to extend further the railway pier at Stranraer. A wooden extension 18 feet wide was built out from the west side and round the head of the pier in preparation for the route's first turbine steamer. The contractors completed the work by mid-July 1904 at a cost of £14,700.

Dredging had also to be carried out. In December 1895, the area round the pier was dredged following grounding by *Princess May* twice in November. Extensive dredging was required in 1903, and the estimate of £1,500 proved to be a sixth of the final cost. In the twelve years following their takeover of the east pier at Stranraer, the P & W J C spent over £83,000 on work connected with it.

THE MIDLAND RAILWAY MOVES IN

The years 1903 and 1904 saw the M R make considerable inroads into Irish railways and shipping. On 1 July 1903, its takeover of the B & N C R became effective. For the management of the railway there was established a Northern Counties Committee with the last chairman of the B & N C R, John Young, appointed as chairman. Both the B & N C R and M R had been represented on the L & S S J C, and in order that parity might be retained, the N C C continued to send representatives to the L & S S J C meetings, but these representatives no longer had voting rights.

The M R had a substantial stake in the Stranraer–Larne route and also in the Barrow Steam Navigation Company which operated to Belfast and the Isle of Man from Barrow, but up until this time it had not directly controlled any shipping routes. Now the decision was taken to extend the railway from Morecambe to a new harbour at Heysham, and on 1 September 1904 the M R opened a new route to Ireland (and the Isle of Man in summer) and placed on the station four fine passenger/cargo ships.

Possibly because of their interest in traffic travelling via Larne, the M R introduced a new train in 1903, the "Stranraer Express", which left St. Pancras at 2030. But either traffic was below expectations or it was preferred to maximise traffic via Heysham, and in 1910 the service was reduced to a sleeping car and a through carriage attached to the 2015 express to Glasgow.

FIRST TURBINE ON THE IRISH SEA

In June 1901, the L & S S J C requested their Marine Superintendent, Captain Binney, of the L & N W R shipyard at Holyhead, to give both *Princess Victoria* and *Princess May* a thorough survey and comment on their potential life. Captain Binney reported that he saw these ships as having only a further three years in top-line employment and indicated that major repairs, including the reboilering of both ships, would be necessary to prolong their lives. The committee went ahead with some minor repairs but the cost of reboilering, estimated at £7,000 combined with £3,000 for new cylinders for the "Victoria", was too much. The Marine Superintendent also made the observation that the reserve steamer *Princess Beatrice* was quite inadequate. In order to keep two ships in service at a high level of repair it was necessary to have a satisfactory reserve steamer. The ideal situation was to have three ships of equal ability. The L & N W R certainly followed out this policy on their Holyhead–Dun Laoghaire service where with a quartette of ships only two were in service, with a third off for refit and the fourth in reserve with banked fires. Captain Binney recommended to the L & S S J C that a ship be built for the route fitted with reciprocating machinery driving twin screws. He pointed out that such a ship would require at least 13 feet of water and would necessitate alterations at Stranraer and Larne Harbours. The committee agreed with the principle outlined and recognised the increasing unsuitability of *Princess Beatrice* as stand-by for the route. The decision to build was deferred, however, until the extent of the work at the piers could be quantified.

William Denny & Bros. Limited launched from their Dumbarton yard a ship in May 1901 that brought a revolution to the world of marine propulsion. This was *King Edward*, the first commercial ship to be driven by turbine machinery. The possibilities of the turbine-driven ship had been demonstrated with ships of the Royal Navy, but in 1900 the Turbine Steamer Syndicate was formed with the purpose of testing the machinery in a commercial ship. The ship proved an immediate success. Not only did she prove mechanically sound, but additional speed was achieved without any corresponding increase in coal consumption. *King Edward* was to visit Stranraer in 1928, 1929 and 1930, when she gave excursions from the Firth of Clyde towns to the Galloway port.

The introduction of *The Queen* in June 1903 on the Dover–Calais service for the South Eastern and Chatham Railway demonstrated the potential of the turbine steamer on the more exposed cross-channel routes. In the same year the S E & C R's rival, the London Brighton & South Coast Railway, placed their Denny turbine, *Brighton*, on the Newhaven–Dieppe crossing. One factor which made the turbine steamer attractive to the Stranraer route was the possibility of shallow draught ships. The turbine machinery lay in a horizontal rather than vertical plane and this avoided the need for a deep ship to compensate for the high centre of gravity.

Accordingly, in June 1903, following the decision of the L & S S J C to build a new ship for their route, when tenders were considered, it was a turbine steamer that was agreed upon. The order went to William Denny & Bros. Limited, the builders of *King Edward*. The original specifications were modified to include a single-ended boiler in addition to two double-ended boilers, and this was guaranteed to produce a minimum speed of 20 knots. Denny's offered to build the ship for £66,000 and she was to be ready within ten months of the contract being signed. The final cost was to exceed the estimate by £600.

On 20 February 1904, the daughter of Mr. Miles MacInnes, chairman of the L & S S J C, named Denny's fifth turbine steamer *Princess Maud*, after the sister of King Edward VII. On 27 April, official trials were completed with a mean speed of 20·7 knots being achieved. The following Tuesday, 3 May, *Princess Maud* sailed with two hundred and fifty guests from the Tail of the Bank between the Cumbraes, round Garroch Head and up to East Loch Tarbert in Loch Fyne.

Princess Maud had two covered decks and the promenade and boat decks. The boat deck extended to the side of the steamer and this provided shelter for the promenade deck below. Aft on the promenade deck was to be found the ladies' lounge for steerage passengers, while below that was a combined lounge and tea-room and below that again a general steerage lounge. As became the tradition for so many years, all the steerage accommodation was situated aft of the after hatch and connected with the rest of the ship by a hinged gangway. (In the previous Stranraer ships the steerage accommodation had been for'ard.) Most of the first-class accommodation on the promenade deck was devoted to four staterooms plus dormitory-style sleeping accommodation for twenty-five. There was also a ladies' cabin and the first-class bar. On the main deck there was situated a dining saloon with seating for sixty-four, while the balance of the space on this deck was occupied by staterooms and officers' accommodation. The crew's quarters were forward on this deck and on the deck below. A considerable area aft on the main deck was given over to cattle pens, while the deck below was almost exclusively devoted to cattle.

Inevitably, some problems were experienced. After her first season, cowls were fitted to her two funnels and vibration was to cause concern for several years after her introduction into service. Another, and perhaps related, problem was continuing defects appearing in the stern rudder. The situation improved after the replacement in April 1909 of two of the "Maud's" three propellers.

On 1 June 1904, the first turbine steamer on any of the Irish Sea services took over as mail steamer at Stranraer. *Princess Maud* soon showed that ten minutes could be knocked off the paddlers' schedule on the crossing. But other turbines very quickly appeared on the Irish Sea. In September of the same year the M R commenced their service from Heysham to the Isle of Man and Belfast, and of the four ships built for the route, two, *Londonderry* and *Manxman*, had engines incorporating the turbine principle. *Manxman*, designed for the Isle of Man trade, was capable of 23 knots.

With *Princess Maud* in service, *Princess May* became the Larne-based ship for the summer daylight service, which in 1904 extended from 1 June until 15 October, *Princess Victoria* became reserve steamer and *Princess Beatrice* was sold for breaking up.

Princess Maud had an interesting diversion on 6 July 1905, when she conveyed the newly-married Marquis and Marchioness of Bute from Dundalk Bay, County Louth, to Stranraer. The wedding took place in Castle Bellingham and the wedding party joined the steamer anchored two miles out in the bay.

Burns's daylight service between Ardrossan and Belfast was entrusted from 1906 to a new turbine steamer, *Viper*, capable of 22 knots. *Viper* replaced the paddler *Adder*, which had maintained the route every summer since 1890—except for most of 1901 when *Vulture* had filled the station. 1906 also saw the placing of *Woodcock* and *Partridge* on the overnight route from Ardrossan. These two ships were of the traditional triple-expansion, single-screw class but were a considerable improvement on the ships they displaced—*Magpie* and *Vulture*.

EPISODE WITH "PIRATE"

The winter of 1906–07 was a difficult time for *Princess Maud*. On the evening of 30 November, while sailing on the evening mail run from Larne in heavy weather, an "exceptional sea" hit the ship with such ferocity that the "Maud" heeled over, causing part of the after-deck to be flooded, and three of her passengers were injured. On 18 December, on the same run, the "Maud" struck a floating object which damaged her bow rudder. Proceeding very slowly, *Princess Maud* arrived at Stranraer $3\frac{1}{4}$ hours late. Repairs were managed at Stranraer.

But a more serious accident occurred on the morning of 6 August 1909. While proceeding down Loch Ryan on the morning run to Larne, patches of fog obscured the anchored cargo ship *Pirate* until the "Maud" was on top of her. The engines were reversed, but the mail steamer sliced into *Pirate*, which sank within ten minutes. *Pirate*, built in 1884, had been engaged since the autumn of 1893 on a Glasgow–Campbeltown–Stranraer cargo service, and on this occasion she had on board four passengers for Arran. A rope ladder was lowered from the "Maud" and the passengers managed to climb this to the safety of the mail steamer. One of the passengers was in poor health and subsequently died. Her widower sued the L & S S J C but it was decided by the Court of Session in 1912 that her death was no doubt hastened by the events of 6 August but could not be attributed to them. Some of *Pirate*'s crew left in their ship's boat and took with them the lady's cat, while other members of the crew managed to climb the ladder to the "Maud" before the two ships parted. *Princess Maud* returned to Stranraer and transferred her passengers and mail to the morning boat from Larne. *Princess May* then set out for Larne at 1330 while steam was being raised on *Princess Victoria*. The Shore Superintendent, Captain Cumming, took over command of *Princess Maud* and she left for Greenock to be drydocked and her twisted stem put right. The owners of *Pirate* sued the L & S S J C, but a settlement was made out of court costing the committee £2,600. Although some of the passengers defended the mail steamer's master, he was dismissed. Some blame was attached to *Pirate*, since the steamer had anchored in the fairway and the ship's bell had not been sounded regularly. At low tide the mast, funnel and accommodation aft of the bridge of *Pirate* were visible. Very quickly two Ross & Marshall puffers, *Starlight* and *Sealight*, were on the scene with pumps and salvage apparatus and a week after sinking she was raised and beached to the east of the railway pier to allow her hull to be patched up temporarily. On 19 August, she managed to proceed under her own steam to Glasgow for full repairs, and on 18 September, *Pirate* took up once again her twice-weekly service from Glasgow to Campbeltown and Stranraer.

CALEDONIAN STAND-BY

With a fine turbine steamer in service knocking ten or fifteen minutes off the crossing, the question once again arose about the adequacy of the other two ships. In October 1909, the L & S S J C were advised that it would cost between £12,000 and £14,000 to keep *Princess Victoria* in service. *Princess May* was also in poor shape when compared with *Princess Maud*, and ideally both ships would be disposed of and replaced by two turbine steamers. But this proposition could not be entertained and a compromise solution was reached.

Princess Victoria was sold to the Shipbreaking Company Limited of London, who paid £3,000 for the ship and removed her from Stranraer on 23 February 1910. A second turbine steamer was to be built for the route, and in January 1911 tenders were sought for a steamer similar to *Princess Maud*. Four months later the tender of William Denny & Bros. Limited for the delivery of a ship in April 1912 was accepted at a price of £71,000. But in the meantime there was the problem of satisfying the condition of the mail contract that required that there should always be a stand-by ship available.

The daylight service came in for scrutiny. Figures indicated that the service was justified but the question was whether both remaining ships should be committed to the timetable. The compromise was to reduce the length of the summer season, and the daylight service, instead of starting on 1 June, began on 13 June in 1910 and finished two weeks early on 17 September. On the Clyde the pooling of vessels of the C S P and the G & S W R had produced spare vessels, and in the spring of 1910 the L & S S J C reached an agreement with the C S P whereby their turbine steamer *Duchess of Argyll* would be available for the Stranraer route if required during the period 1 April to 15 October. This would cover the main overhaul and autumn docking of *Princess Maud* and also the overhaul of *Princess May*. Certain alterations were required to render the "Argyll" suitable for the route, mainly the plating up of the main deck at bow, and the cost of £425 was met by the L & S S J C. A retaining fee of £100 was paid and the daily rate for charter was agreed at £50. In 1910, *Duchess of Argyll* had no cause to visit Stranraer and spent the summer on the pooled C S P/G & S W R Ardrossan–Arran service. In 1911, however, her services were required at Stranraer.

On the morning of Friday, 9 June, *Princess Maud*, on completing the mail run, collided with the quay at Larne and "burrowed her nose" to a depth of fourteen feet. The quay was of wooden construction and to those on board the collision was barely perceptible, but when the "Maud" went astern it was seen that one of the cross beams had torn a large hole in the port bow of the ship. The "Maud" was taken off service and despatched to the Dumbarton yard for repairs. *Princess Maud* returned to the mail run with the evening service from Larne on Saturday, 17 June. The mail run in her absence was taken by *Princess May* while *Duchess of Argyll* was brought into service. On Saturday, 10 June, a special excursion was to operate from Larne to Stranraer and the "Argyll" was at Larne in time for this sailing. An excursion had been advertised for that afternoon from Stranraer and the "Argyll" took 165 passengers round Ailsa Craig. *Duchess of Argyll* then took the 1933 return Stranraer to Larne sailing. On Monday, 12 June, the daylight service from Larne commenced and *Duchess of Argyll* operated this service until replaced by *Princess May* on the evening of Saturday, 17 June. The Caledonian turbine steamer was issued with a certificate for 592 passengers while on the Larne-Stranraer route.

After this incident with *Princess Maud*, it became standard practice for all Stranraer steamers to navigate into Larne stern first.

It was a happy coincidence that the steamer selected for stand-by duties at Stranraer was *Duchess of Argyll*, since the lady after whom the ship was named was none other than Princess Louise, whose name was bestowed on the first of the "Princess" Line. The husband of Princess Louise had acceded to the Dukedom of Argyll in 1900.

In 1912, the Stranraer fleet returned to its full strength of three and no arrangements were required for an outside stand-by vessel. In 1922, *Duchess of Argyll* was again retained as Stranraer reserve steamer, and to satisfy new Board of Trade requirements the Caledonian turbine was fitted with wireless telegraphy.

A SECOND TURBINE

Lady Bine Renshaw, wife of the C R chairman, launched the second Stranraer turbine steamer from the Dumbarton yard on 22 February 1912 and named the ship *Princess Victoria*. She was in most respects a sister to the "Maud" and incorporated some modifications found necessary in the pioneer Stranraer turbine. Cowls were fitted to the funnels, and the extra belting fitted on the bows of the "Maud" in 1905 were part of the "Victoria's" design. One distinguishing feature was the positioning of the steampipes on the older ship forward of the funnels, while in the new ship they were at the sides. On 16 and 17 April, the new *Princess Victoria* achieved a speed of 20·98 knots, and over a run of three hours' duration averaged 20·4 knots. On 20 April 1912, she berthed at Stranraer and took over the mail run on 29 April.

Maiden voyages are usually festive occasions, but not this one. Two weeks previously the White Star liner *Titanic* sank while on her first voyage, and this cast a gloom over the maiden trip by *Princess Victoria*. One lady refused to board the ship on Monday morning when she learnt that this was to be a maiden voyage. A more lasting result of the *Titanic* disaster was the tightening up of lifeboat requirements. In 1913 both turbine steamers were fitted with an additional lifeboat, buoyant deck seats were added, and two cutters on each ship were converted into lifeboats. (During overhaul in the spring of 1907 two lifeboats had been removed from the after deck of *Princess Maud*.)

A year later reductions were made in the passenger complements for the Stranraer route. The new figure for *Princess Victoria* was 1,081 against 1,426, for *Princess Maud* 1,081 against 1,455, and for *Princess May* 664 against 964. Special "daylight sailing" certificates were obtained allowing 1,361 passengers on the turbine steamers and 839 on the paddler. The turbines had a crew of 39 and the paddle steamer three fewer.

The fate of the last Stranraer paddle steamer was sealed in October 1914, when Captain Holland, the L & N W R's Marine Superintendent, submitted a report on *Princess May* which indicated that expenditure of £28,000 was required. It was agreed that the ship should be disposed of and a third turbine steamer obtained for the route. But the country was at war and contrary to popular belief it was not over by Christmas. *Princess May* was sold and sailed under her own power from Stranraer on Thursday, 10 December 1914, and arrived at Swansea the following day. But the replacement was not to be built.

INCREASED TRAFFIC

The daylight service operated in July, August and September in 1912, but traffic requirements brought additional sailings into the regular programme. During these months an extra crossing was given from each end on Saturdays. This service became known as the auxiliary service. The ship providing the daylight service, usually *Princess Maud*, on arrival at Stranraer, returned from the railway pier at 1315 for Larne. This ship returned from Larne immediately, arriving at Stranraer at 1750 and then provided the 1933 return leg of the daylight service to Larne. This double round trip by the Larne-based ship was also operated on other peak days, such as Glasgow Fair Friday, 12 July.

Special arrangements were made for extra crossings on Saturdays in June. On these Saturdays the daylight and auxiliary service schedules were operated. The mail steamer on arrival at Larne in the morning provided the 1000 daylight service from Larne, then gave the auxiliary service sailing at 1315 back to Larne and completed her day with the return evening mail run to Stranraer. This left the return leg of the daylight service from Stranraer, which meant the use of a second ship on this run at 1933. As one of the turbine steamers was off in June for overhaul, we find *Princess May* being brought to life for this trip each Saturday in June, though on the last Saturday in the month the sailing was taken by the turbine steamer to be positioned at Larne for the full daylight service schedule. On the Saturdays when *Princess May* gave the 1933 sailing to Larne she returned immediately to Stranraer and this opportunity was taken of advertising the round trip from Stranraer as an evening cruise at a fare of 2s. with an arrival time at Stranraer of "around midnight".

This pattern of sailings was repeated in 1913 and 1914, except that in the latter year the auxiliary service left Stranraer at 1550, since this later time gave more suitable train connections. The 1230 train from Glasgow (St. Enoch) connected into the 1550 sailing. It is probable that *Princess May*'s last service run was the 1933 from Stranraer with its evening cruise on Saturday, 20 June, 1914.

The carriage of cars was becoming increasingly important. Provision for the stowage of cars had been incorporated in the design of the "Victoria", and in August 1912, 120 cars crossed the Irish Sea via Larne and Stranraer, representing a considerable increase on the previous year. Ten years previously, in 1902, only five cars were carried from Stranraer to Larne. Livestock movements were also on the increase, and in September 1913 a new landing place for livestock and a separate screened sidewalk along the pier, as well as six cattle sheds and other associated plant, were completed at Stranraer at a cost of £4,000.

The increase in traffic was also reflected in the excursion programme. Mr. William McConchie was appointed to the post of Traffic Manager of the L & S S J C on 1 April 1905. Early the following year the committee received a request from his Belfast office that the spare steamer should be utilised for occasional excursions from Larne and Stranraer to places in Ireland, Scotland and the Isle of Man. The board declined to entertain his suggestion at their meeting in April, but 1906 still proved a busy year for excursions and on at least one day it would appear that all three ships were in service. On Saturday, 14 July, there was a noon sailing from Larne to Rathlin Island, a 1330 from Stranraer to Larne, and a 1400 from Stranraer along the Ayrshire Coast and round Ailsa Craig. In 1906, the programme of excursions was expanded by various devices. Peak-day extra sailings to Larne were offered as excursions to both Larne and Belfast, and on four occasions when the mail steamer was scheduled to provide an afternoon cruise from Larne this was advertised as a through sailing from Stranraer.

New ground was broken in 1907, when two afternoon cruises were given from Stranraer to the Kintyre Coast and round the Island of Sanda. Again, Ailsa Craig and Rathlin Island via Larne featured. *Princess May* called at a new port for Stranraer ships on 21 July 1908, when the destination of her day trip was Campbeltown. She gave her three hundred passengers four hours ashore. In 1909, the Stranraer programme was even more extensive and included the first evening cruise by a Stranraer steamer. On Tuesday, 20 July, a trip was scheduled at 1930 for Ballantrae Bay—but it was cancelled because of the weather. It was to be 1912 before evening cruises became a regular feature of the programme and, as we previously noted, these were attempts to raise a little revenue for what would otherwise be light runs. Thus, on Saturday, 1 June, and the following three Saturdays in June 1912, *Princess May* gave an evening cruise from Stranraer to Larne, returning immediately. On Wednesday, 20 June 1912, the "May" gave an evening cruise along the Ayrshire Coast and round Ailsa Craig, with nearly four hundred on board. These evening cruises were repeated in June 1913 and 1914.

The excursion programme in 1912 appeared under the heading "Salubrious Sailings on the Sapphire Sea" and included yet another innovation. *Princess Maud* provided a "Grand New Panoramic Cruise" when she sailed from the railway pier at Stranraer at 1330 and cruised along the shores of Bangor Bay, Belfast Lough, Whitehead, Blackhead, Gobbins Cliffs, and arrived at Larne at 1545. There a connection waited for Belfast. Passengers could travel up to Belfast and return by the 1830 train for the evening mail crossing, or remain in Larne for the mail steamer, or return right away with *Princess Maud*.

The programme at Larne was not to expand so greatly as that at Stranraer. By 1906 Rathlin Island was featuring approximately thrice in each season. In 1907, the Island of Sanda was added to the cruise programme. In 1912, in addition to two cruises to Rathlin Island, a cruise left Larne at 1100 on Friday, 12 July, for Ailsa Craig, Ayrshire Coast and Loch Ryan. The steamer (unspecified) called at Stranraer—this was Glasgow Fair Friday—before returning to Larne. 1907 was a busy year for excursions from Larne—three round Rathlin, two round Sanda and one to Bangor Bay to view the warships. In addition, there was usually, each year, an excursion from Larne by one of the G. & J. Burns's fleet. In 1906, on the local holiday, Monday, 6 August, *Vulture* had taken trippers to Rothesay, and the following year *Hound* gave the trip to Rothesay. 1908 had no Burns excursion, but in 1909 *Magpie* sailed on 2 August and the destination was again Rothesay. 1910 and 1911 saw repeat performances by *Magpie*, but on 5 August 1912, *Magpie* sailed to Ardrossan, where a train carried the excursionists to Saltcoats. In 1913, it was back to Rothesay, but in 1914 *Magpie* sailed to Ayr.

This indicates the variety of cruises being offered from Stranraer and Larne by the L & S S J C steamers before the First World War. The reader is directed to Appendix F for detailed coverage.

CHAPTER EIGHT

The First World War and its Aftermath

O N 4 August 1914, war was declared, but coming events had cast their shadows before. A letter from the Admiralty had been received by the L & S S J C in June 1912 in which the views of the committee were sought as to the conditions attaching to the chartering as fleet messengers of *Princess Maud* and *Princess Victoria* by the Government in the event of war. The L & S S J C replied, explaining their obligation to the Post Office to have a stand-by vessel at Stranraer at all times. The committee were willing to offer the option to the Admiralty of chartering one of the turbine steamers if a suitable arrangement could be worked out with the Postmaster-General.

The railways in Great Britain came under Government control on the outbreak of war and the L & S S J C took its instructions from the Railway Executive Committee. But the impact of the war did not come home immediately and the daylight service from Larne was continued until 31 August. The auxiliary service operated on Saturdays had, however, been suspended from 1 August. From 1 September 1914, one trip each way was given daily (except Sundays, as always). During July and August both ships had given some additional sailings with military personnel.

TWO PRINCESSES GO TO WAR

In October a note was received at Stranraer that the Admiralty required the immediate release of *Princess Victoria*, and after giving *Princess Maud* a few days in dock the "Victoria" left Stranraer on 12 October 1914 for Dover, where she arrived at noon two days later. After a brief call for orders she sailed to Sheerness. For the next five years *Princess Victoria* was to be employed on the south coast. Initially she was based at Sheerness as a fleet messenger but did little sailing. On 7 December 1914, the South Eastern & Chatham Railway advised that they were having to withdraw their Dover–Dunkirk service because of pressure of traffic on other routes. The General Manager of the S E & C R suggested that the service could be continued if *Princess Victoria*, "which hitherto has done very little but lie at anchor at Sheerness", was made available to the railway. On 10 December, *Princess Victoria* sailed from Sheerness for Dover and at 0730 on Friday, 11 December, took up the service which had previously been performed by *Invicta* and *The Queen*. A cargo boat was based at Dover to supplement the "Victoria".[156]

In the early part of 1915 the German troops overran most of Belgium and the service by *Princess Victoria* between Dover and Dunkirk was abandoned and the steamer transferred to the Dover–Boulogne route, where she served as a leave ship. Part of 1916 was spent by *Princess Victoria* based at Southampton as auxiliary hospital ship. By 1918 the "Victoria" was back on the Dover–Boulogne route.

During September 1916, rumours reached Stranraer that the "Victoria" had been torpedoed, and this was given greater credence when it was discovered that the ship was no longer to be seen around Dover. But despite a near miss with a German torpedo, it was not the "Victoria" but the S E & C R's turbine steamer *The Queen* that had been sunk. *Princess Victoria* had been badly damaged during a severe gale and her absence from Dover was due to her being ordered to Southampton for repairs.

The appearance at Stranraer of crewmen on leave during October cleared up the matter.

Princess Victoria was released from Admiralty charter on the last day of 1919. During the war, *Princess Victoria* continued to sail under the red ensign with many Stranraer men on board, but the management of the ship was in the hands of the South Eastern & Chatham Railway.

Princess May was also to see war service, since her buyers, the Shipbreaking Co. Ltd., proved to be a "front" for the Admiralty. The "May" was converted and employed as an accommodation ship at Scapa Flow in the Orkneys. Official sources are silent on the "May's" Admiralty career, but it has been claimed that at one time during the latter part of the war she was in the Mediterranean. After the end of hostilities, *Princess May* (she retained her peace-time name) was laid up for some time in the Holy Loch and in January 1920 was sold by the Admiralty for scrapping.

With *Princess Maud* left alone to carry out the service between Stranraer and Larne, it was considered impossible to operate the daylight service and no extra sailings were given, even at holiday peaks. The Postmaster-General recognised that with both the "May" and "Victoria" away the L & S S J C could not implement the mail contract with regard to a stand-by vessel and left the committee to use its best endeavours to maintain the service without break. A gap in the service was brought about in 1916 following a dispute over wages, which spread from Fleetwood, Heysham and Liverpool. For three weeks, from Saturday, 8 April, *Princess Maud* lay at the railway pier. The service was resumed on Monday, 1 May.

The "Maud's" turn of speed was displayed one evening in 1917 when crossing to Stranraer with some senior military personnel on board. Her departure from Larne had been delayed by the late arrival of the military men, and once clear of the harbour the engines of *Princess Maud* were opened up to near full. She was accompanied by two ageing destroyers, who were hard put to keep up with her, and as they turned off Milluer Point, the leader signalled, "Au revoir, you escort us next time"!

Wireless telegraphy was fitted to *Princess Maud* in June 1917 and a Marconi operator borrowed until a youthful employee of the L & S S J C was trained. In April 1918, David Broadfoot was appointed wireless operator on *Princess Maud*. It was the morse from David Broadfoot that maintained the link between the car ferry, *Princess Victoria*, and a listening world on that fateful voyage on 31 January 1953. Wireless telegraphy had been installed on the "Maud's" sister in 1916.

Towards the end of the war, the submarine became a serious threat, and to give *Princess Maud* a degree of defence, she was equipped with a machine gun and smoke apparatus in July 1917. The Admiralty supplied a gun crew for the mail steamer. Instructions came from the Admiralty that all sailing in darkness was to be without lights and at full speed. So as to avoid this dangerous procedure, the timings of the steamer were amended between 1 November and 2 December 1918 to give a departure from Larne four hours earlier than normal with an arrival at Stranraer at 1715. On rare occasions the service would be suspended on Admiralty orders.

RELIEF SHIP "GALTEE MORE"

With *Princess May* and *Princess Victoria* away from Stranraer and the projected turbine replacement for the "May" shelved, an immediate problem was a substitute for *Princess Maud* during her overhaul. In April 1915, an offer was accepted from the L & N W R, a member of the L & S S J C, of the loan of their steamer *Galtee More*, "without any question of hire or charter being raised". This steamer had been built in 1898 by William Denny & Bros. Limited for the Holyhead–Greenore service of the L & N W R. *Galtee More* was a passenger/cargo twin-screw steamer with two sets of four-cylinder triple expansion engines, a type of propulsion not hitherto represented in the Stranraer fleet.

On the outbreak of war, the Holyhead–Greenore service had been downgraded to third-class passenger accommodation and cargo only when the two principal ships on the route, *Rathmore* (of 1908) and *Greenore* (of 1912) had been transferred to the Dublin route from Holyhead. *Rosstrevor* and *Connemara* (both of 1895) were left to maintain the link between Holyhead and Greenore, while *Galtee More* acted as stand-by for the Dublin and Greenore routes from Holyhead and the Larne route from Stranraer.

She also sailed in June 1915 for the Great Western Railway between Weymouth and the Channel Islands.

After the end of hostilities, *Galtee More* returned to her intended route but still found employment elsewhere in at least one summer when, together with *Rathmore*, she assisted on the London & South Western Railway's Southampton–Channel Islands service. In 1920, the passenger accommodation of *Galtee More* was removed and she served as a cargo-only ship on the Greenore station until she was broken up in 1926.

From its opening on 1 May 1873, the Holyhead–Greenore route had proved a rival for traffic to the Stranraer sailings, as both vied for passengers and cargo between London and Belfast. The L & N W R had a considerable stake in the P R and so indirectly in the L & S S C, but they guarded their own route to Ireland jealously. The Fleetwood–Belfast route was operated jointly by the L & N W R and the Lancashire & Yorkshire Railway, and when the L & N W R delegates met their P R colleagues prior to the opening of the "Princess" line route in 1872, they were keen to maintain rate differentials which favoured their routes via Holyhead and Fleetwood.

The passenger service to Greenore had been suspended for 1918 and 1919 and then resumed until the 1926 General Strike. It was not re-established after the strike, mainly because of the drastic reduction in passenger traffic which had followed the partition of Ireland. Passengers between Greenore and Belfast now required to pass through customs, since the port and the city it served were in different countries. The cargo sailings by railway steamers continued until the end of 1951, and served mainly for livestock movements.

Princess Maud was scheduled for docking each spring and autumn, and it became standard practice for *Galtee More* to sail north and replace the "Maud" for a couple of weeks or so as mail steamer. The first spell of duty at Stranraer for *Galtee More* was from 3 to 22 May 1915. *Galtee More* had just set out for Holyhead when the "Maud" developed a fault in the port turbine and had to return to Troon. *Galtee More* was recalled and continued on the mail route from 25 to 29 May, when *Princess Maud* was able to take over again. The pressure of war was experienced in the shipyards and the "Maud" was forced to visit a variety of repair yards for overhaul at Belfast, Troon and Govan. The last occasion on which *Galtee More* stood in as mail steamer at Stranraer was from 27 October to 8 November 1919. By the spring of 1920, *Princess Victoria* was again available and the Stranraer fleet was able to undertake their overhaul programme without having recourse to borrowing from other areas.

PEACE AND UNREST

The Admiralty released *Princess Victoria* on 31 December 1919 and the work of reconditioning was given to Messrs. Alexander Stephen & Sons Limited, of Linthouse, Govan. Stephen's rendered an account for £62,000, which was passed on to the Ministry of Shipping. *Princess Victoria* arrived back at Stranraer for duty on 22 April 1920, and took over from *Princess Maud*, which now went for overhaul also at Stephen's yard, and £5,000 was spent in bringing the "Maud" back up to standard after the rigours of war.

Naturally, travel to Ireland fell off during the period of the war, but trouble in Ireland had resulted in troop movements via Stranraer. On Easter Monday 1916, the Irish Republican Brotherhood took over the centre of Dublin and held it against Government troops for a week. From the steps of the General Post Office a proclamation was read declaring the establishment of a republic. The actual uprising was quickly suppressed, and the general feeling reflected in the press was that the insurrection did not have widespread support among the people. But the cause was supplied with martyrs and public opinion shocked when the Government executed fifteen of the leaders. Negotiations were started in 1916 and dragged on inconclusively for two years, the only result being that partition of the island was discussed for the first time as a possible solution.

In the spring of 1918, Westminster failed in an attempt to extend conscription to Ireland and, shaken by this defeat, the Government attempted to curb any further revolutionary movement by arresting the leaders: the Sinn Fein party was declared illegal and public meetings banned. At a general election following the restoration of peace in Europe, the Sinn Fein had a majority of the Irish members elected to Westminster, but these members, instead of heading for London, met in Dublin in January 1919 and declared themselves the Parliament of the Irish Republic and reaffirmed the declaration of Easter 1916. The republicans had time to dig themselves in and it was 1920 before a real clash came. Troops moved in, and after two years of bloodshed a political solution was reached in December 1921, when a treaty was signed establishing an "Irish Free State" and included provision for the separate status of Northern Ireland.

The compromise nature of the solution was unsatisfactory to some, and soon the Irish Free State was torn by civil war. In April 1923, fighting ceased and an uneasy truce began. The bitterness and mistrust remained, but the island was to have the longest period of peace there had been for nearly two hundred years.

A LOW EBB

This unrest had naturally an adverse effect on traffic over the Stranraer route and it was 1923 before any attempt was made to reintroduce the daylight service in the summer. In 1920, *Princess Maud* was disturbed from her idleness at the east pier to give an extra sailing to Larne on the Thursday and Friday before Glasgow Fair Week holidays. There were special return sailings on Saturday, 24 and Monday, 26 July. In 1921 a special sailing was provided to Ireland on the Friday only.

The severe drop in traffic between Scotland and Ireland was also experienced in the daylight service operated in summer by G. & J. Burns between Ardrossan and Belfast. This service had been suspended on the outbreak of war and the turbine steamer *Viper* was laid up for a time. *Viper* was later requisitioned by the Admiralty and saw service as a troop carrier on the English Channel. Upon release she was reconditioned in time for the 1919 season, which she opened with a special one-way sailing on Friday, 27 June, from Ardrossan to Belfast. The following day *Viper* gave an excursion sailing from Belfast to Rothesay, and on Monday, 1 July, the daylight service via Ardrossan commenced with *Viper* leaving at 1000.

The Glasgow holidays in July have always produced heavy traffic on the Irish routes, and despite the unsettled state of Ireland, 1919 was no exception in this respect. The crowds for the Ardrossan morning steamer were so great that the train was brought into Central Station before midnight on the Friday, 18 July, to allow the travellers to sleep in the carriages. Hundreds were unable to obtain a passage by *Viper* on the Saturday. On the Monday morning when Central Station opened, a large queue had formed and again many were disappointed and a queue started to gather for the evening boat train for the midnight sailing from Ardrossan to Belfast.

But this intensity of traffic was not typical of the 1919 summer, and when the Ardrossan daylight service finished on Saturday, 13 September, *Viper* was put up for sale. Her purchasers were The Isle of Man Steam Packet Company Limited who, after renaming her *Snaefell*, pressed her into service for the 1920 season. In 1920, the Ardrossan daylight service was operated but with the smaller ship *Graphic* transferred from the Belfast Steamship's Liverpool–Belfast berth, reflecting the inclusion within the Coast Lines Group of both G. & J. Burns and Belfast Steamship Company. Traffic was very light and the service abandoned after 20 July. No attempt was made to revive the daylight service from the Ardrossan until 1925, and even then the sailings were one way only each day.

From the outbreak of the war the overnight service between Ardrossan and Belfast had been entrusted to *Spaniel* and *Pointer*, passenger/cargo ships built in 1895. They replaced *Woodcock* and *Partridge* which were required for wartime duties elsewhere. During the early part of the war *Ermine*, built in 1912 for the Glasgow–Dublin run, appeared on the overnight service from Ardrossan and in 1915 was scheduled for a special daylight service to Belfast via Ardrossan for the Glasgow Fair Holiday, 16–24 July, but at the eleventh hour *Ermine* was requisitioned and sailed for the Mediterranean. In 1923, *Magpie* and *Vulture* returned to the overnight service, having been reboiled, converted to burn oil fuel and generally greatly improved. Following the attempt at uniformity consequent upon the merger in 1922 of the Burns and

Laird fleets, *Magpie* and *Vulture* were, in 1929, renamed *Lairdsgrove* and *Lairdsrock*. These two ships maintained the overnight service between Ardrossan and Belfast until it closed at the end of August 1936.

A result of the partition of Ireland was that from the spring of 1922 mail from England for Northern Ireland was conveyed via Stranraer and Larne instead of Holyhead and Dun Laoghaire. The Northern Ireland Government pressed for this change, since they alleged that the mail coming through the Free State was subject to delay and interference.

As well as the unrest in Ireland, industrial unrest at home had a detrimental effect on the Stranraer route. A railwaymen's strike closed the route from 29 September to 4 October 1919. A year later, a coal miners' strike caused the service to be suspended for five days, and in 1921, with the coal crisis continuing, the Ministry of Transport ordered the withdrawal of the service from 15 April to 11 July 1921. The overnight services of Burns from Glasgow and Ardrossan to Belfast were also cancelled and resumed on Wednesday, 6 and Monday, 11 July, respectively. The industrial problems which followed the war caused far more disruption to the sailings than the war itself had produced.

During the lengthy withdrawal of the Stranraer–Larne service in 1921 an attempt was made to revive the link between Donaghadee and Portpatrick. From 23 May three motor boats, each able to carry up to only twelve passengers, were placed on the crossing. The basic schedule entailed a 0900 daily departure from Donaghadee on arrival of the 0730 train from Belfast, returning from Portpatrick at 1500 with a train connection due in Belfast at 2035. The motor boats were managed from Belfast and required three hours for the crossing. The intention was stated of chartering a small steamer for the route, "should circumstances warrant the step". Presumably this *ad hoc* service between Donaghadee and Portpatrick ceased in July when the Stranraer–Larne route was re-opened.

LONDON MIDLAND & SCOTTISH RAILWAY

Part of the industrial agitation was a call for full nationalisation of the railways in Britain, but this was too big a pill to be swallowed and the compromise reached was the massive grouping of the various railway companies into four large companies still owned by private shareholders. By the Railways Act 1921, all the constituent companies of the Larne & Stranraer Steamship Joint Committee were tidily absorbed into the London Midland & Scottish Railway, effect being given to this in 1923.

The resignation of Captain Cumming, the Shore Superintendent, had been received with effect from 30 September 1922, but the vacancy was not filled until the situation after the grouping became clearer. In the meantime, the Marine Superintendent of G & S W R kept an eye on Stranraer affairs from his base at Princes Pier, Greenock.

The last meeting of the L & S S J C was held on 27 October 1922. The days of the red flag with white, angled square and Red Hand of Ulster were running out and soon a new houseflag—red with a white St. George's cross and in the centre a circle containing rose, thistle and harp, representing England, Scotland and Ireland—adopted by the L M & S R was to adorn the mainmast of *Princess Maud* and *Princess Victoria*.

8 *Princess Maud* (1904) in 1923–24 L M & S R colours

9 *Princess Victoria* (1912) in post-1924 colours at Larne

EXCURSIONS TO IRELAND
FROM STRANRAER HARBOUR.

CHEAP TRIPS EVERY WEEK-DAY from 1st JUNE to 30th SEPTEMBER.
☞ PLEASANT RECREATIVE FACILITIES FOR HOLIDAY RESIDENTS. ☜

The Service between Stranraer and Belfast is shown at page 131,

---

ONE-DAY RETURN FARES—SEA, RAIL, AND COACH. († ‡)
No Luggage Allowed.

TO	Cabin and First.	Steerage and Third.	TO	Cabin and First.	Cabin and Third.	Steerage and Third.
Larne Harbour	4/-	2/6	Antrim	6/6	5/6	4/-
Ballycarry			Parkmore	8/6	6/6	5/-
Whitehead	5/-	3/6	‡ Cushendall	13/-	10/-	8/6
Belfast			Portrush	10/-	6/6	5/-
† Garron Tower	7/-	5/6	Londonderry	12/-	7/6	6/-

† The Garron Tower Excursion includes a Magnificent Coast Drive of 36 miles from Larne to Garron Tower and back. The Antrim Coast Road displays many geological marvels.
‡ The Cushendall Excursion includes Rail Journey, Larne Harbour to Parkmore, Coach down the beautiful Glenariff to Cushendall (7 miles), and the Coast Road Coach thence to Larne (25 miles more). Starting by the 6 a.m. Steamer, the whole round can be accomplished in one day, with ample leisure for refreshments.

ONE-DAY COMBINED SEA, RAIL, AND CYCLE TOUR.
Including conveyance of Ordinary Bicycle at Owner's Risk.

	To Larne.	To Belfast.		To Larne.	To Belfast.
Cabin & First	6/-	6/6	Steerage & Third	4/6	5/-

N.B.—All Tickets at the foregoing Fares are valid for Return on day of issue only, but may be extended till following day, or from Saturday to Monday, by the extra payment at Station Booking Office, before returning, of half the Excursion Fare charged.

PLEASANT AFTERNOON EXCURSIONS TO IRELAND

May be made by the Special Steamer from Stranraer Harbour at 3.50 p.m. every Saturday from 30th May to 29th August inclusive; also on Friday, 17th July, and Wednesday, 22nd July, by Special Steamer at 1.20 p.m.

Fares as above.   See page 131 for Service.

EIGHT-DAY TOURS IN IRELAND.

At Stranraer Harbour Contract Tickets may be purchased at the following Fares, covering one journey to Larne or Belfast and back, and a Week's Travelling at will over certain of the Railways traversing the best part of "Ireland's Northern Playground."

For the Midland Railway (Northern Counties) System:—
Tour B.—Including Larne, Belfast, Parkmore, Portrush, Londonderry, &c.

Saloon and 1st Class.	Saloon and 2nd Class.	Saloon and 3rd Class.	Steerage and 3rd Class.
30/-	24/6	19/-	16/-

For the Great Northern Railway (Ireland) System —
Tour C.—Including Belfast, Warrenpoint, Greenore, Newcastle, Armagh, &c.

Saloon and 1st Class.	Saloon and 2nd Class.	Saloon and 3rd Class.	Steerage and 3rd Class.
29/9	25/-*	21/6*	17/-

*First Class between Larne Harbour and Belfast. Full particulars from the Agent at Stranraer Harbour.

POPULAR EXCURSIONS ROUND AILSA CRAIG, &c.
Weather and other circumstances permitting.

WEDNESDAY, 17th JUNE, at 6.30 p.m.—EVENING CRUISE. Extended Trip. Fare 2s.
TUESDAY, 21st JULY, at 2 p.m. Getting back about 5 p.m. for Trains. Fare 1s.
WEDNESDAY, 17th August, at 2.50 p.m. (To Port Logan Bay). Back about 6.30. Fare, 2s,

---

N.B.—See later Announcements for Grand Cruise on Thursday, 30th July.

---

40   A page from *Tours in Galloway*, 1912 edition

The Royal Mail Route and Shortest Sea Passage
Between GREAT BRITAIN and IRELAND is
Via Stranraer and Larne.

Open Sea Passage 70 Minutes : Port to Port under 2 Hours.
Through Express Connection with Principal Places in England and Scotland.

DAILY SERVICE (Sundays excepted) all the Year round; **TWO SERVICES** (Morning and Evening) each way; on Saturdays in June, and every Week-day from 1st July till **30th September.**

N.B.—Every Saturday from 30th May to 29th August inclusive, an Auxiliary Service leaves Carlisle at 12.50 p.m., and Dumfries at 1.40 p.m., arriving at Larne Harbour at 5.36 p.m. and Belfast at 7.15 p.m.

The "PRINCESS MAUD," a magnificently-equipped Turbine Steamer has by her splendid behaviour at Sea, made herself an intense favourite.

The "PRINCESS VICTORIA," new and superbly furnished, is a sister ship to the "Princess Maud," with all modern improvements added.

CONVEYANCE OF MOTOR CARS AND CYCLES.

Motor Cars will be conveyed between Stranraer and Larne by any Steamer, if alongside an hour before sailing time. For services see Page 131.

Rates and Charges.—The Owner's Risk Rates for the conveyance of Motor Cars and Motor Cycles between Stranraer and Larne, including all charges for Harbour Dues, Cranage, &c., are:—

MOTOR CARS AND CYCLE CARS.
Not exceeding 10 cwts. .. .. 25/- each.
Over 10 cwts. and not exceeding 25 cwts. .. .. 35/- each.
Over 25 cwts., 35/- plus 1/- for each cwt. or part thereof above 25 cwts.
Company's Ordinary Rates, 25 per cent. additional.

	Accompanied by Passengers.	Unaccompanied by Passengers.
Motor Bicycles each,	3/- O.R.	4/6, O.R. 5/9, C.R.
Motor Tricycles each,	6/- O.R.	7/6, O.R. 10/-, C.R.
Motor Cycles with Fore Carriages, Side Carriages or Trailers,	each 6/- O.R.	10/6, O.R. 14/9, C.R.

Supply of Petrol may be purchased on the Quay at Larne or Stranraer on arrival from the other side. Car and Cycle Tanks must be emptied before shipment.

LUNCHEON BASKETS.

Passengers travelling from Ireland by the Day Service can obtain on the Steamer **HOT** or **COLD LUNCHEON** in Baskets (2s 6d and 3s), which may be taken forward for use on the connecting trains to Carlisle and Glasgow. Requisition should be made to the Chief Steward on joining the ship at Larne Harbour.

SLEEPING ON BOARD SHIP.

Passengers intending to Sail from Stranraer to Larne by the Steamer at 6 A.M. may, about 10 P.M. the previous evening, obtain SLEEPING BERTHS on the Ship, thus avoiding the trouble and inconvenience of an early rise to catch the boat.

Passengers sailing by the Summer Evening Steamer from Stranraer to Larne, and not wishing or being able to continue their journey forward from Larne the same evening, may sleep on board till about 7.15 A M. the following morning.

The Charges for Accommodation are, in addition to the Saloon Fare:
One Berth in a Two-Berth Room 2/6
Exclusive use of a Two-Berth Room (when available) ... 5/-
Private State Cabin made up for Sleeping (Two Berths) 9/-

Sleeping Passengers and their Luggage are Conveyed by Train to the Ship's side. Berths may be reserved in advance on early application to the undersigned, or to any Stationmaster on the Route. **A Steward** and **Stewardess** are in attendance during the night, and **Food** is served at **Moderate Charges.**

Passengers holding Third Class Tickets desiring to travel First Class (Saloon) on the Steamers between Stranraer and Larne may do so on payment of the following additional Fares:—Single Journey, 3s 6d; Return Journey, 5s 6d.

For any further information desired, apply to

WILLIAM M'CONCHIE, *Secretary and Traffic Manager,* Stranraer.

A page from *Tours in Galloway*, 1912 edition

Larne Harbour and Station with *Princess Victoria* (1912) and *Princess Margaret*

42

CRUISE

Along Antrim Coast

AND ROUND

RATHLIN

By R.M.S. 'Princess Maud'

ON

MONDAY, 15TH JULY, 1929

(Weather and other circumstances permitting)

Leaving Larne Harbour at 12-15 p.m.
Arriving back about 4-30 p.m

RETURN FARE

3/6

JAMES PEPPER,
Manager and Secretary.

(The Larne Times)

(above) Advertisement of July 1929

(right) Advertisement of July 1935

(right) Advertisement of June 1934

L M S — N.C.C.

Attractive CRUISE

LARNE — BANGOR — STRANRAER

By Royal Mail Steamer,
" PRINCESS MARGARET "

SUNDAY, 14th JULY, 1935

(Weather and other circumstances permitting)

Return Fares from Larne Harbour
Saloon on Steamer:

TO STRANRAER **5/-** TO BANGOR **2/6**

Larne Harbour	.... dep.	11- 0 a.m.
Bangor	.... arr.	11-50 a.m.
"	.... dep.	12- 0 noon
Stranraer	.... arr.	2-30 p.m.
"	.... dep.	4-30 p.m.
Bangor	.... arr.	7- 0 p.m.
"	.... dep.	7- 5 p.m.
Larne Harbour	.... arr.	8- 0 p.m.

Luncheon and High Tea will be served on
board at a charge of 2/6 per meal.

Tickets are issued subject to the Conditions
shown in the Company's Time Table and Notices.

MALCOLM SPEIR,
Manager and Secretary.

(The Larne Times)

LONDON MIDLAND & SCOTTISH RLY.

ATTRACTIVE

CROSS CHANNEL TRIP

TO

BANGOR (Ireland)

Allowing about 2 hours on shore.

By Luxurious New Turbine Steamer

"PRINCESS MAUD"

On Sunday, 17th June

Leaving STRANRAER HARBOUR at 1.15
p.m. and arriving back about 8.15 p.m.

CHEAP RETURN FARE 5/-

Lunch and Tea served on board at a charge
of 2/6 per meal.

Trains in connection from Glasgow Central
10 a.m., Annan 10 a.m., Ardrossan (South
Beach) 9.58 a.m., Ayr 11.4 a.m., Carlisle
9.35 a.m., Castle Douglas 11.0 a.m., Dumfries
10.24 a.m., Fairlie 9.41 a.m., Girvan 11.45
a.m., Irvine 10.42 a.m., Kilmarnock 10.20 a.m.,
Largs 9.35 a.m., Maybole 11.21 a.m., Newton
Stewart 12 noon, Paisley (Gilmour Street)
10.12 a.m., Prestwick 10.40 a.m., Saltcoats
10.1 a.m., Stevenston 10.5 a.m., Troon 10.34
a.m., West Kilbride 9.50 a.m., Wigtown 11.38
a.m., Also from Creetown, Dalbeattie,
Dunragit, Gatehouse of Fleet, Glenluce,
Gretna Green, Kirkcowan, Kirkinner, Millisle,
New Galloway, Sorbie, Whauphill, Whithorn.

3rd and Cabin return fare from Glasgow or
Paisley 11/-. For fares from other stations
see handbills to be obtained free at stations.

(The Glasgow Herald)

Princess Margaret off Larne

(H. M. REA

(E. J. WYL

Princess Margaret in dry dock at Greenock, April 1962
prior to departure for Hong Kong

48   First-class lounge, *Princess Margaret*

49   First-class dining saloon, *Princess Margaret*

    Princess Margaret as *Macau*

51 (*right*) *Princess Maud* (1934) during Second World War

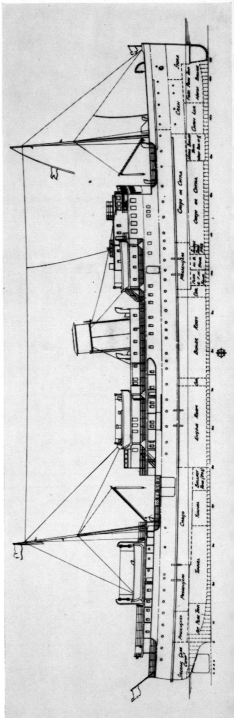

Rigging plan of *Princess Maud* (1934)

52

3   *Princess Maud* (1934) at Gourock

4   *Princess Maud* (1934) on Belfast Lough

Princess Maud (1934) leaving St. Peter's Port, Guernsey

(CYPRUS SEA CRUISES (LIMASSOL) LTD.)

56   *Princess Maud* (1934) as *Venus*

(H. M. REA

57   *Princess Maud* (1934) as *Nybø* at Copenhagen

58 (right) *Princess Victoria* (1939)

(C. LAWSON KERR)

Rigging plan of *Princess Victoria* (1939)

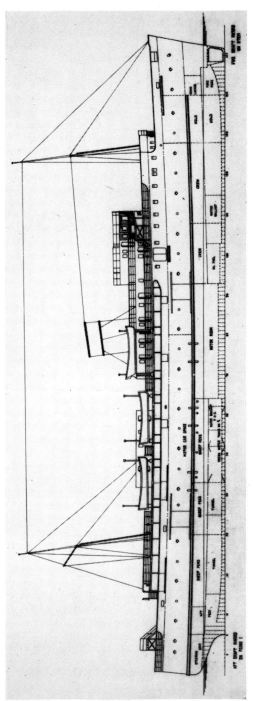

59

(*Shipbuilding and Shipping Record*)

Car deck of *Princess Victoria* (1939)

61   *Empress Queen* during Second World War

Hampton Ferry during Second World War

63   A view at Stranraer in June 1943

64   A view at Stranraer in June 1943

65   *Duchess of Hamilton* in dry dock, February 1946 after running aground near Corsewall Point

(MRS. M. FERGUSON)

6   Officers of *Princess Victoria* (1947) on press cruise, June 1947
(*left to right*) Third Officer William McInnes, Radio Officer David Broadfoot,
Captain James Ferguson, Chief Officer Shirley Duckels, Second Officer Leslie Unsworth.
All except Mr. Unsworth were lost with their ship on 31 January, 1953.

(H. M. REA)

Princess Victoria (1947) approaching Larne

68   *Princess Victoria* (1947) with milk tankers arriving at Stranraer

On Monday, 4 June 1923, when *Princess Victoria* resumed her duties on the mail run, the buff funnels which had given the Stranraer steamers a yacht-like appearance were seen to have been repainted in colours described as primrose, vermilion and black. The local newspaper pointedly remarked that "the new colour scheme for the steamers has evidently been chosen by the management in London. [The change] is adversely criticised on this side of the border, as the inharmonious combination offends the taste of all Scottish people who delight in a ship's good looks". With a change in owners had come a change in colour scheme. After two seasons, in common with most other components of the L M & S R fleet, the vermilion band was dropped, leaving buff funnels with black tops.

The L M & S R Board established a Scottish Local committee to handle affairs north of the border, and the Scottish marine business was handled by the Steam Vessels Sub-Committee meeting monthly (except August) in Glasgow. The word "Local" was omitted from the title of the senior Scottish committee from May 1937.

The District Manager's office was closed down at Stranraer in 1924, leaving a reduced marine department with a marine agent responsible to Mr. Charles Bremner at Gourock. Mr. William McConchie had retired as Secretary and Manager of the L & S S J C. Mr. J. Hope Smith, who had been appointed Station Master and Harbour Master in December 1901, was now given the additional position of Stranraer marine agent. Mr. Smith retired in 1932. In addition to the two Stranraer steamers, Mr. Charles Bremner had been made responsible, at Gourock in 1924, for the L M & S R Clyde and inland loch fleets which were produced by the amalgamation of the fleets of The Caledonian Steam Packet Company Limited and the Glasgow & South Western Railway. Prior to the grouping of 1923, Mr. Bremner had served as Manager and Secretary of the C S P since March 1919.

The L M & S R announced in June 1923 the re-establishment of the daylight service between Larne and Stranraer. From 9 July to 8 September, *Princess Maud* left Larne at 0955 and arrived at Stranraer at 1203, leaving in the evening at 1955, reaching Larne again at 2210. At the same time the over-night service to and from London was accelerated.

The pre-war practice of retaining a ship as stand-by for the route was revived, and in 1922 the C S P *Duchess of Argyll* once again acted as reserve while each of the "Princess" steamers was off service for overhaul. *Duchess of Argyll* had to be fitted with wireless telegraphy for the route, but she was not required and was allowed to remain undisturbed on the Firth of Clyde. In 1923 and 1924 the L M & S R Heysham steamer, *Duchess of Devonshire*, was earmarked if an emergency arose. Soon the practice was abandoned, since the pool of L M & S R ships, from which a substitute could be called, was sufficiently large for a ship always to be available.

As it turned out, a substitute was never required, while *Princess Victoria* was to leave Stranraer for a short time and act as reserve steamer for another route. At the end of November 1931, the Heysham–Belfast steamer, *Duke of Lancaster*, sank in Heysham Harbour as a result of a fire and was to lie on the harbour bed for two months before being salved. Her sister, *Duke of Argyll*, which had been acting as stand-by, was pressed into service and the rôle of stand-by vessel at Heysham fell to *Princess Victoria*. On the first day of December, a crew arrived at Stranraer from Heysham and on the morning of

I

the following day she sailed to Heysham. While south, she continued to serve
as stand-by for the Stranraer route, but was not required that winter for either
the Larne or Belfast services.

THE 1926 GENERAL STRIKE

Early in May 1926, railway and mine workers came out on strike and
crippled much of the country's transport. At Stranraer a reduced service was
introduced on Tuesday, 11 May 1926, when a round trip was offered on Tues-
days, Thursdays and Saturdays. The sailing times remained unaltered—leaving
Stranraer at 0630 and Larne at 1825. The mail steamers between Holyhead
and Dun Laoghaire were off service completely and all their mail travelled via
Stranraer and Larne.

Because of the dispute in 1926 the daylight service did not open that year
until Monday, 12 July, and was curtailed at the end of the season, *Princess
Maud* making the last round trip on Saturday, 18 September. In 1925, the
daylight service had lasted exceptionally into October, finishing on the 2nd.
In 1927, the daylight service was to start on 1 June, and the previous day,
Tuesday, 31 May, the positioning run of *Princess Maud* was advertised as an
excursion with train from Glasgow. The day trippers returned by the mail
steamer in the evening and this use of the otherwise light run was repeated in
several subsequent years.

Princess Maud gave the first post-war excursion from Stranraer on Saturday, 15 July 1922, when she sailed round Ailsa Craig. On the Stranraer
Merchants' Holiday, Wednesday, 23 August, the Isle of Man steamer *Tynwald*
took eight hundred passengers in a north-west gale to Douglas. A slim
excursion programme by the "Princess" ships was offered in 1923 and 1924
and slowly expanded.

The General Strike resulted in only one excursion being offered from Stranraer in 1926—on Monday, 2 August, when *Princess Maud* gave an afternoon
cruise round Ailsa Craig. A new excursion enterprise was available at Stranraer in 1926 when a small locally-owned steamer, *Galloway Lass*, offered trips
down Loch Ryan from the West Pier. But her sojourn at Stranraer was to be
brief. On Friday, 8 July 1927, *Galloway Lass* sailed for Belfast Lough, where
she was employed as a tug for coal barges.

In 1927, a new feature appeared in the Stranraer programme—Sunday
excursions. On Sunday, 19 June, *Princess Victoria* gave an excursion to Portlogan Bay. Connecting with this sailing was the first Sunday train south of
Girvan. These Sunday excursions, with train connections from Dumfries, Ayr
and Glasgow, became a regular and popular part of the programme.

Two excursions from Larne to Stranraer were arranged in 1922 for Friday,
14 July, and Monday, 7 August. The first was intended primarily to provide
an additional sailing from Stranraer for the Glasgow holidays, and despite
only 1½ hours ashore, it attracted six hundred trippers from Ireland. Six hours
ashore were offered on the August trip and the steamer arrived at Stranraer
with a full complement of excursionists.

Regular excursions were offered from Larne for the first time after the
war, in 1924, when *Princess Victoria* gave two excursions to Rathlin Island. In
1926, despite the General Strike, three excursions were given from Larne, and
one of these, on Monday, 2 August, was to Campbeltown. The first Sunday

excursion from Larne was by *Princess Victoria* on 25 July to Rathlin Island, while the following Sunday she gave a day excursion to Stranraer. Again, these excursions on Sundays became a feature of each year's programme, though those to Stranraer were often really extra ferry runs at peak week-ends.

The 1926 General Strike also affected the other routes between Scotland and Ireland. The Burns-Laird steamer, *Moorfowl*, had been taken in hand for modernisation and now burned oil fuel, and her passenger accommodation had also been extended and sleeping accommodation was now available for 91 passengers. *Moorfowl* operated a truncated daylight service from Ardrossan during the latter half of July and combined it with the overnight sailing. From Friday, 14 to 21 July, she sailed in the morning from Ardrossan and returned overnight from Belfast, though on the 21st she lay overnight at Belfast as from the following day until 2 August *Moorfowl* sailed in the morning from Belfast and returned overnight from Ardrossan. This arrangement was made for the benefit of the holidaymakers from Glasgow.

In 1927, *Moorfowl* operated a daylight service between Ardrossan and Belfast for the month of July, and it was now possible to sail out and back in the same day with about an hour ashore at Belfast. By 1929, when the ship was renamed *Lairdsmoor*, the season extended from the last week of June until mid-August.

THE CREST OF THE WAVE

The two main English routes to Belfast, via Heysham and Liverpool, received exceptionally fine new ships in 1928 and 1929. As part of their rationalisation, the L M & S R concentrated their Fleetwood and Heysham traffic at the latter port, and in 1928 the railway company took delivery of the Denny-built *Duke of Lancaster*, *Duke of Argyll* and *Duke of Rothesay*, all turbine steamers, for the overnight passenger/cargo service to Belfast. At their time of building their gross tonnage of 3,600 made them the largest ships on the Irish Sea routes. Late in the following year this distinction passed to *Ulster Monarch*, the first of three diesel-engined ships built by Harland & Wolff for the Belfast Steamship Company's Liverpool–Belfast line. In the case of both sets of new ships the accommodation for cabin passengers, at least, was outstanding.

The 1930s saw new tonnage appearing on all three routes from Scotland—Glasgow, Ardrossan and Stranraer—to Ireland. As around 1900, 1930 was the beginning of another crest of a wave of cross-channel traffic.

In the early and middle 1920s, Irish traffic was in the doldrums, but in the latter half of the decade traffic was building up on all the routes, especially at the holiday peaks. For example, at the Glasgow Fair Week-end in 1930 there were, from Ardrossan, two daylight sailings to Belfast on the Friday and three on the Saturday, as well as three overnight sailings. At Stranraer, on the Friday and Saturday of the week-end, the evening sailing to Larne required two trains from Glasgow. There was a special train from Glasgow at 2355 for the mail sailing at 0610 on the Friday and Saturday. On the Friday there were extra sailings from Stranraer at 1100 and 1330, and on the Saturday at 1330. The 1330 service operated on six peak Fridays in 1930.

To accommodate the month-end traffic and the Paisley holidaymakers, the two extra sailings were scheduled for Friday, 1 August, and Saturday,

2 August 1930. All went more or less according to plan on the Friday, but the overnight train from London for the Saturday mail sailing was delayed and the ship sailed nearly two hours late. With the tight timetable the ship was inevitably still 1½ hours late on the 1330 crossing from Stranraer. The 1330 sailing was also advertised as a day excursion from Glasgow to Belfast, but the only part of Belfast to be seen that day would be York Road Station, since the train from Larne arrived at Belfast at 1820 and the return connection left at 1825!

The late twenties saw the beginning of a change in the provenance of passengers on the Stranraer route and other areas, especially the Firth of Clyde resorts. The Clyde had been almost entirely the playground for Glasgow and its environs. But now holidaymakers from the North of England were being attracted to the Firth and the Glasgow folk were venturing farther afield, for example, to Ireland.

It appears as a paradox that at a time commonly called "The Depression" coastal shipping should enjoy a boom. Unemployment was high—three million at one time—and between 1920 and 1922 average wages fell by an astounding 28 per cent, but prices fell by the same percentage in the same period. The decrease in wages continued until the graph reached its minimum point in June 1933, by which time the percentage drop on 1922 earnings was 12 per cent. But the significant feature of the Depression was that retail prices dropped by 24 per cent on the 1922 level, i.e. double the drop in wages. This meant that those in employment during the 1920s and early 1930s were better off in real terms and were enjoying a new affluence which enabled more ambitious holiday plans to be considered. The deflation also caused reduced fuel prices, lower building and crew costs, thus allowing fares to remain unchanged.[157]

CHAPTER NINE

The Booming Thirties

A S part of the modernisation programme of the Irish routes of the Coast Lines Group, two ships of the British & Irish Steam Packet Company Limited were transferred to Burns & Laird's Glasgow–Belfast trade. Built in 1923 and 1924 at Ardrossan, the single-screw steamers *Lady Louth* and *Lady Limerick* were renamed respectively, *Lairdsburn* and *Lairdscastle*. Before their transfer to Scotland the ships had both undergone an extensive refit, including conversion to oil fuel. Each could carry approximately eight hundred passengers and provided sleeping accommodation for 128 in single and two-berth cabins. The move of the "Ladies" to Glasgow to replace *Woodcock* and *Partridge* on the Belfast service had been made possible by the arrival of *Ulster Monarch* for the Belfast Steamship Company and the resultant shuffle round of the ships. *Lairdscastle* took up service in late May 1930 and *Lairdsburn* followed in June.[158]

This was the first round in the struggle between Coast Lines and the L M & S R for the traffic between Ireland and Scotland. The L M & S R planned a two-pronged attack to recover the traffic lost to the Glasgow overnight service. A new ship was to be built for Stranraer, but also improved sleeping accommodation on board the ship and later train connections were seen as the means of attracting traffic away from not only the overnight route from Glasgow but also the overnight and daylight services operating via Ardrossan.

RE-ENTERING THE JOUSTING

On 5 May 1930, the month *Lairdscastle* took up her station at Glasgow, Wm. Denny & Bros. Limited received an order from the L M & S R for a passenger/cargo mail steamer for the Stranraer–Larne route. The cost was to be £180,000. At her launch on 21 January 1931 the vessel was named *Princess Margaret* after the first Royal princess to be born in Scotland for over four hundred years. A Miss Margaret Rose, daughter of the Chairman of the L M & S R Scottish Local Committee, actually named the ship.

Prior to 1931, passengers from Scotland for Ireland via Stranraer had travelled to Stranraer on the evening prior to their journey and found accommodation in the town. An early rise was required the next morning for the six o'clock departure. This was the usual procedure—unless the traveller happened to be lucky enough to secure one of the thirty-eight berths available for saloon passengers on *Princess Victoria*. It certainly compared unfavourably with joining a ship at Ardrossan or Glasgow and bedding down for the night to awaken in Belfast where there was ample time for breakfast before heading off into the city. Mail considerations dictated that the service from Stranraer remain an early morning departure, but the plans for the new ship incorporated greatly improved facilities for cabin and steerage passengers joining the ship for the following morning's sailing. In contrast to the previous ships, *Princess*

Margaret could provide sleeping accommodation for 161 passengers—107 in saloon cabins and 54 in steerage cabins. Of the saloon passengers, 53 could be accommodated in single cabins, while the remainder were in two-berth cabins. All cabins had hot and cold water. Deck machinery was electrically driven so as to minimise noise when cargo and mail was being loaded in the early morning.

The rest of the ship was built to the best standards of the day. On the boat deck forward there was an observation lounge which extended the full width of the ship, while on this deck aft was a smoke room. Beneath the observation lounge was another lounge into which opened the offices of the purser and the night stewards. Also on this, the promenade deck, was a small pantry to provide early morning refreshments, while further aft was a dining saloon with seating for 54. On *Princess Victoria* and *Princess Maud* this deck had been almost completely open to the elements, apart from the shelter provided by the spar deck above. As was the custom with the earlier ships, the steerage accommodation was concentrated at the stern of the ship and was joined to the first-class accommodation by a gangway over the starboard side of the after hatch. On the poop deck were the baggage and mail rooms, as well as a smoke room and separate ladies' lounge. A general saloon with pantry and bar was situated on the main deck, while on the lower deck there was a dormitory with two-tier bunk beds.

Below the main deck approximately 40,000 cubic feet of cargo could be stowed. Cattle stalls could be rigged to accommodate 236 beasts and, in addition, there were eight permanent horse stalls. As part of her equipment, the "Margaret" carried a portable platform for the speedy loading and unloading of cars. An electric crane was fitted aft, but this was removed in 1941.

Steam was generated by four water tube boilers and drove the ship's turbines, and so her twin propellers through single reduction gearing. Trials were completed on 17 March 1931, when a speed of 20·7 knots was achieved. *Princess Margaret* burned coal fuel, and in this policy the L M & S R appeared reactionary when compared to, say, Coast Lines, where diesel and oil fuel were being employed increasingly. But the lower capital cost of a coal burner, combined with the low cost of coal and labour, made the traditional fuel attractive to the railways, especially when so much of their revenue came from carrying the same coal.

However, in the early part of 1952, *Princess Margaret* was converted to operate on oil fuel. When built, *Princess Margaret*'s single funnel was fitted with a cowl top, but after two years this was removed. Whereas on her predecessors the lifeboats had been black on *Princess Margaret* and later ships the boats were painted white.

Princess Margaret took over the mail run on 1 April 1931, and on the previous day the L M & S R gave a lunch at Larne on board their new ship. After lunch, the "Margaret" carried the party over to Stranraer in boisterous weather but she was able to display her steady seagoing qualities.

To enable *Princess Victoria* to relieve the new mail steamer for overhaul, it was necessary to spend nearly £4,000 in increasing her cabin accommodation. The number of cabins was increased from 14 to 27 and this provided sleeping accommodation for 45 passengers as against 28. There had formerly been no provision made for sleeping in the steerage area of the ship, but now 44 open berths were added.

As if to emphasise that no expense had been spared, the gas lighting in Stranraer Harbour Station was replaced by electric!

THE PIONEER TURBINE RETIRES UNGRACEFULLY

The "Victoria" was now the Larne-based ship and the daylight service in 1931 opened on 1 June. On her arrival at Stranraer on the first day, she struck the pier and damaged her stem below the water line. The bow rudder was put out of action by the impact and a diver was immediately engaged to clear the obstruction to allow the vessel to remain in service until an opportunity arose for a visit to a dry dock. At first, it was arranged that the Heysham steamer *Duke of Abercorn* would take over from the "Victoria" on Tuesday, 16 June. But this plan was dropped and the "Maud", which had been laid up on the quiet side of the railway pier at Stranraer, was awakened.

On the evening of Tuesday, 9 June, *Princess Maud* took the return sailing to Larne, while *Princess Victoria* headed for dry-docking at Barrow-in-Furness. But this was to be the "Maud's" last sailing. Approaching Larne in a dense fog, the engines were at "Dead Slow" when she grounded at Barr's Point on Island Magee at the entrance to Larne Lough. *Princess Maud* was stuck fast and the 186 passengers and mail were landed on the "island" by ship's boat. They walked about a mile to the ferry that connects the peninsula with Larne. Most of the travellers were bound for Belfast and the boat train reached the city at about 0100 on the 10th, and the L M & S R laid on buses to convey their passengers to the various parts of Belfast. The "Maud" pulled herself off the shore at about 0500 on the 10th and by 0900 was safely berthed at Larne and was later taken to Barrow. No attempt was made to repair the "Maud", as her end was approaching, anyway, and she lay waiting for her passenger certificate to expire at the end of June. T. W. Ward Limited, of Sheffield, purchased *Princess Maud* for £2,150. The master of the "Maud" was severely censured and not allowed to take command for a twelve month period.

Princess Victoria was intercepted by wireless and headed back to Stranraer, and on the morning of the 10th she crossed to Larne to take up the 1000 sailing.

A FITTING CONSORT

As had happened before on the Stranraer route, the new ship highlighted the deficiencies of the older consort. In February 1933, after two years of operating the "Margaret" and "Victoria", the L M & S R Steam Vessels Sub-Committee discussed the matter and their first course of action was to investigate the possibility of working the route with one ship on one round trip each day. But the profit accruing from the daylight service, computed in 1932 as £5,000, swung the balance against this suggestion. The Sub-Committee then considered building a new ship only two years after the "Margaret". It was shown that by a small increase in dimensions—7 feet in length and 2 feet in beam—that an extra 53 berths could be provided as well as additional bathrooms and a ladies' lounge. The drop in building costs produced an estimate from Denny's of £160,000, £20,000 less than the cost of *Princess Margaret*.

No doubt still partly influenced by the cheaper capital cost, the L M & S R stuck to steam turbine propulsion with coal-fired boilers, but the design of the stokehold incorporated mechanical retort-type stokers which it was estimated would result in a saving in fuel of £1,200 each year. In 1932, such stokers had been fitted in the Heysham steamer *Duke of Lancaster* and the results encouraged the management to fit them to their new Stranraer–Larne steamer.

The contract for the new ship went to William Denny & Bros. Limited at Dumbarton, and on 19 December 1933, Lady Craigavon, wife of the Prime Minister of Northern Ireland, named the ship *Princess Maud*. At the Steam Vessels Sub-Committee's meeting in September 1933, the name had been agreed as *Princess Victoria*, but this decision was reversed the following month, "in case the public think the old ship is still on the run".

The new *Princess Maud* had sleeping accommodation for 223 passengers— 161 first class in single and two berth cabins and 62 third class in two and four berth cabins. A special feature of the first class two berth cabins was that the berths were on the same level, as against the old arrangement of upper and lower berths, and were all in a fore-aft position. The layout of the public rooms corresponded closely to that of the "Margaret". *Princess Maud* was the first British ship to be fitted throughout with a fire alarm and sprinkler system.

During fitting out, a cowl top was added to the "Maud's" funnel but this was removed before she went on trials on 15 February 1934, when a speed of 19·84 knots was reached. *Princess Maud* gave a special sailing on Tuesday, 27 February, for invited guests of the L M & S R and took over the mail service from the "Margaret" on 1 March 1934. Captain Andrew Hamilton transferred from the "Margaret" to the new flagship for the remaining weeks of his service on the route. When he retired in April, he was succeeded by Captain Munro; and Captain Hugh Montgomery was appointed to *Princess Margaret*.

Soon after leaving Stranraer on the morning of Tuesday, 20 March 1934, *Princess Maud* passed *Princess Victoria* under tow for Norway, where she was to be broken up. She had been sold for £3,000. Her last service run had been on Sunday, 17 September 1933, when she conveyed to Larne a party of football supporters who had been to an international match in Glasgow.

To minimise the idle time of these two smart steamers, *Princess Margaret* and *Princess Maud*, the possibility was investigated of employing *Princess Maud* on cruising work in the early and late summer. Her ample sleeping accommodation and speed made her ideal for this work. The operating powers of the L M & S R did not permit of such employment and a possible way round the restriction was to have the ship registered in the name of The Caledonian Steam Packet Company Limited, the Scottish shipping subsidiary of the L M & S R. The C S P were already involved with the Stranraer ships, since its management superintended the route on behalf of the L M & S R. But the plan for the new Stranraer ship was dropped and *Princess Maud* was registered as owned by the L M & S R. Cruising at this time formed part of Coast Lines' programme, with *Killarney* and *Ulster Prince* visiting various parts of the West Highlands and Islands. Some twenty-five years later cruising in the off-peak season was to become a recognised part of the schedule for the Heysham steamer *Duke of Lancaster*, and from 1958 to 1966 this ship gave up to six cruises each season in June and September.

BANGOR EXCURSIONS

Princess Victoria chalked up another first when on Sunday, 5 August 1928, she gave an afternoon excursion from Stranraer to Bangor. About a thousand visited this seaside resort of County Down. In 1929, the "Victoria" visited Bangor from Stranraer on three Sunday afternoons. The town's Mayor paid a courtesy visit on 17 August 1930 to *Princess Victoria* on her last call of the season at Bangor and expressed the hope that the sailings direct between Stranraer and Bangor would be increased in frequency once the new ship was introduced. The saving in time to holidaymakers was considerable, since the direct sailing avoided two train journeys and a change of railway stations in Belfast.

The Mayor's wish was granted, but perhaps not to the extent he had hoped. *Princess Margaret* sailed from Stranraer to Bangor every alternate Sunday in 1931 from 7 June until 16 August. Train connections on the Scottish side brought trippers from as far afield as Dumfries, Largs and Glasgow to join the steamer at 1315. About two hours were given at Bangor. In 1931, the Larne-based steamer also began to visit Bangor. On Sunday, 12 July, *Princess Victoria* gave an excursion from Larne and Bangor to Stranraer with about two hours in Stranraer. Excursion fares were also offered between Larne and Bangor. The ship sailed from Larne at 1100 and was due at Bangor fifty minutes later, leaving again at noon. *Princess Victoria* repeated this on Sunday, 9 August.

1931 was a busy year for Bangor Pier, since, after several blank years, a programme of excursions was offered by a Belfast Lough steamer. This was the paddle steamer *Cynthia*, brought round on charter from the Foyle to test out the market. The traffic must have fallen below requirements since, in 1932, *Cynthia* was transferred to Dublin.[159]

When *Princess Maud* took over the Stranraer-based roster she continued the fortnightly Sunday trips to Bangor, and *Princess Margaret* also continued the two annual trips from Larne to Bangor and Stranraer. Apart from 1931, these two trips were on Sundays when trips were scheduled from Stranraer, thus providing a busy day at Bangor Pier.

These trips from Stranraer to Bangor were very popular. In 1932, it was noted that the six Bangor cruises carried over five thousand passengers. David Smith writes of a train of sixteen coaches leaving Girvan for Stranraer and the steamer for Bangor on 5 August 1934. This, he believes, was the heaviest load to that date handled over the Girvan–Stranraer section.[160]

1935 was the last year in which excursions were offered by the "Princess" ships to or from Bangor. On Sunday, 18 August, *Princess Margaret* gave the final trip from Larne to Bangor and Stranraer, while four weeks later, on Sunday, 15 September, *Princess Maud* made the last call at Bangor while on an excursion from Stranraer. Pressure on the main route required that the Sunday trips be between Stranraer and Larne. In an attempt to retain some of the attraction of the Bangor trips, the first Sunday trip from Stranraer in 1936, on 14 June, was advertised to Larne via Bangor Bay and Belfast Lough, but subsequent trips were direct to the Irish port with longer ashore. 1935 had also seen the last attempt to base an excursion steamer at Bangor when, after a few weeks, the small paddle steamer *Whitsand Castle* gave up the struggle to eke out a living.

Bangor never quite made it as a cross-channel passenger port. In 1808, Telford's recommendation that it should be used as a mail packet station on a route from Portlogan went unheeded. In 1889, the Peel & North of Ireland Steamship Company established a link between the Isle of Man and Ireland with the co-operation of the Belfast & County Down Railway. This service was taken over by the Isle of Man Steam Packet Company Limited, but lasted only a few years.[161]

In 1911 and 1912 the Portpatrick and Wigtownshire Joint Committee were alerted by their manager to the intentions of G. & J. Burns to operate a direct service between Bangor and Scotland. But any apprehension experienced by the committee proved groundless.

A brief taste of cross-channel traffic was experienced again at Bangor on Saturday, 16 May 1970, when the turbine steamer *King George V*, of David MacBrayne Ltd., sailed from Ayr to Bangor and then gave a three-hour cruise towards Portpatrick, returning by Donaghadee and the Copelands Channel. This enterprising excursion was conducted under the joint charter of the Coastal Cruising Association and Mr. W. Paul Clegg. The original intention had been to retrace the old mail route between Portpatrick and Donaghadee, but it proved impossible to have the steamer call at either port.

In 1971 we read of an attempt to interest the Scottish company, Western Ferries Ltd., in opening a car and passenger ferry between Portpatrick and Bangor. Nothing came of this, and Western Ferries concentrated on their existing Scottish-Irish link between Campbeltown and Red Bay, County Antrim. In passing, it is interesting to note that the vessel employed on the Red Bay route, *Sound of Islay*, with an overall length of 142 feet, is of the size envisaged in the plans for the re-opening of the Portpatrick–Donaghadee service in the 1850s.[162]

Bangor continues to receive cargo ships and for the past few years has had a regular cargo link with Peel, Isle of Man.

As the 1930s progressed the excursion sailings from Stranraer and Larne became fewer. In 1936, all excursions from Stranraer were really extra ferry runs on peak Fridays, Saturdays and Sundays. In 1937, there was a trip to Ailsa Craig and this was repeated in the following two years. The only other excursion from Stranraer was the annual trip by the Campbeltown steamer *Dalriada*. Every year, from 1930, usually the second last Friday in July, *Dalriada* gave a day trip from Stranraer to Campbeltown.

Princess Margaret had an unusual charter sailing in 1932 when she conveyed a party from Larne to Dublin for the Eucharistic Congress there. She left Larne early on the morning of Sunday, 26 June, and returned to Larne on the following day, arriving about 0500.

In the midst of expansion we have to note one area of contraction. In June 1932, the narrow gauge railway between Larne Town and Larne Harbour was closed for passenger traffic, and eight months later the service between Larne Town and Ballymena ceased. But an improvement in train services resulted, as far as the steamer passengers were concerned. Not only was a much-needed second broad gauge platform built at Larne Harbour, but trains now ran through from Larne to Portrush via Greenisland, whereas before a change of train (and gauge) at Ballymena had been necessary. A goods service continued between Larne Harbour and Ballyclare on the narrow gauge until July 1950.

ROYALTY AND THE ROUTE

Members of the royal family crossing between the mainland and Ireland usually sailed on the royal yacht or a unit of the Royal Navy. But in November

1932, Edward, Prince of Wales, crossed on *Ulster Prince* from Liverpool to Belfast.[163] The return was made by *Princess Margaret* from Larne on the evening of Friday, 18 November.

Princess Maud was also to receive royalty, but her rôle was that of a gangplank! On the evening of Tuesday, 27 July 1937, King George VI and Queen Elizabeth arrived at Stranraer to join the royal yacht *Victoria and Albert* anchored in Loch Ryan. The Belfast Harbour Commissioners had sent over their new tug/tender *Duchess of Abercorn* to convey the royal party to the yacht. Possibly it was realised that a transfer direct from the pier to the "Duchess" would be difficult since there were no steps in the railway pier. But for whatever reason, the tender lay alongside *Princess Maud* at the pier and their Majesties passed through the "Maud" to join *Duchess of Abercorn*. Half an hour after midnight on Thursday, 30 July, the royal party arrived back in Loch Ryan on board *Victoria and Albert* and again *Duchess of Abercorn* was detailed to act as tender and *Princess Maud* served as a step to the shore and the train for London.

Other well-known people have sailed on the Stranraer route. In the early days of the steamboat company it was a publicity gimmick to list in the press the titled gentry who crossed by the short sea route. During the political unrest of 1912, Winston Churchill crossed and met an openly hostile reception when he stepped off the mail steamer on 8 February.

UNDER PRESSURE

Passengers carried on the Stranraer–Larne route in 1930, the last year with the two pre-war steamers, had totalled just over 130,000. By 1936 this figure had increased by 48 per cent. The operating profit on the route rose from £3,483 to £14,184 in the same period. Records were being broken each year. In 1931 an extra sailing every Friday in July and August had been introduced with the ships leaving Stranraer at 1330 and Larne at 1450. This was repeated in 1932, but in 1933 the additional sailings, at the same times, operated on Saturdays instead. In the following year the 1330 and (now) 1505 sailings were scheduled for Friday and Saturday. This was adopted in 1936 also, except that the Saturday sailing from Stranraer was at 1400.

In 1937, as well as the additional sailings on Friday and Saturday (Larne departure now reverted to 1450), the alternate Sunday sailings were included in the timetable as service runs, leaving Stranraer at 1330 and Larne at 1800. This pattern was repeated in 1938. Although passenger numbers in 1937 were up on 1936, the cost of carrying this increase produced heavier fuel and wages charges and the 1937 financial surplus was down to £8,800.

The times given above are at least what the timetables showed, but on the peak week-ends no serious attempt appears to have been made to adhere to published schedules. In the course of the Friday, Saturday and Sunday of the Glasgow Fair week-end in July 1936 nearly 11,000 passengers passed through Stranraer. The following year this figure was exceeded by 20 per cent and on the Saturday alone seven crossings were made by the two ships. From 1937 the Larne-based ship came over to Stranraer for the mail run on Glasgow Fair Saturday, thus allowing the Stranraer-based steamer to leave for Larne around 0400.

A letter from "Indignant" in *The Glasgow Herald* of 21 July 1937 indicates that all did not go according to plan that Glasgow Fair. The writer left Glasgow by the 1030 train on the Saturday. The train did not reach Stranraer until 1415—about an hour late. There was no steamer to be seen and "Indignant" did not leave Stranraer until 2000, by which time another train had arrived from Glasgow.

But "Indignant" tells only part of the story. As so often happened, the trouble started with the late arrival of the overnight train from London. Instead of reaching Stranraer at 0545, it steamed in at 0730. The length of the train caused the mail coaches at the end to be beyond the platform, and the shunting required, after the rest of the train was empty, resulted in the mail steamer sailing about 2½ hours late.

The saga continued at Larne with the train off the mail steamer being delayed by relief trains from other parts of the N C C system. On its return from York Road with passengers for the return sailing from Larne by the morning mail steamer, the train added to the comedy of errors by running into a lorry near Whitehead!

The 1030 train from Glasgow was comprised of twelve coaches and at Ayr a further three coaches were added. A pilot engine was detailed to assist the train from Ayr to Stranraer, but the train set off without the pilot and managed as far as Dalrymple Junction, where the train came to a halt. The pilot engine eventually caught up and pushed from behind. The pilot engine then uncoupled and, moving into a loop, allowed the train to back down until the pilot could be positioned at the front.

All went well until Pinwherry, where the train was brought to a halt to allow the 1230 from Stranraer Town to pass. Thirteen of the fifteen coaches were non-corridor stock and the stop provided a welcome opportunity for most of the passengers to visit the station toilet. Stranraer was reached 1½ hours late and the 1315 sailing was missed.

"Indignant" must have gone off in pursuit of food, as there was a steamer around 1800 from Stranraer.

In 1938 again new records were established. The overcrowding had become so blatant on the Irish routes that questions were asked in the House of Commons. The initial question cited the Glasgow–Londonderry sailings over the Glasgow Fair period, but soon the Glasgow and Ardrossan–Belfast and the Ardrossan–Isle of Man routes were also quoted as causing concern.[164] Certainly this was an exceptional year on all routes to Belfast. Seven sailings were required to carry all the passengers seeking passage between Ardrossan and Belfast on the Saturday of the Glasgow Fair. At Heysham, 1,000 people were stranded at midnight of the last Friday in July (August Bank Holiday week-end) and had to be accommodated overnight in a Morecambe ballroom.

The Stranraer route was under pressure. So also was the seat of superintendence for the route at Gourock. By 1937, as well as new tonnage built for the C S P in the previous few years, Mr. Charles Bremner had been given, in 1935, the responsibility for the five ships purchased by the L M & S R from the fleet of Williamson-Buchanan Steamers Limited. In May 1937, he requested that the maintenance and catering supervision of the Stranraer ships be transferred to the marine superintendent and catering officer at Heysham. The former work had been at Gourock since 1925, but the catering had only become Gourock's responsibility in 1931. Until then the hotel manager of the Northern Counties Committee of the L M & S R had supervised the stewards' department on the ships and had been credited with £300 each year for this service. The main reason behind the transfer of the catering to Gourock was to have all staff under the control of one office. The Steam Vessels Sub-Committee agreed, in June 1937, that some of the maintenance work could be transferred to the Heysham office but wanted the catering to stay with the C S P at Gourock in view of the great improvement there had been since Mr. Bremner's staff had taken over. In the financial aspect of the catering there had certainly been a marked improvement. The profit of £939 in 1930 was 15 per cent of gross receipts, in 1934 the profit of £1,370 was 17 per cent of the gross receipts, while in 1937 the profit of £2,443 represented 25·5 per cent. But the increased profit margin was not at the expense of the public palate, since the standard of food and service had also improved.

At Stranraer, records for passenger figures were being established, only to be broken the following year. But it should not be assumed that the L M & S R were having it all their own way in the trade between Scotland and Ireland.

THE NEW LAIRD

Lairdsmoor had gradually extended the summer daylight service between Ardrossan and Belfast from four weeks in 1927 to seven weeks in 1932. Traffic levels indicated that the time had come for new tonnage for the route. In the winter of 1932 the Southern Railway placed on the market two turbine steamers of 1911 vintage, *Engadine* and *Riviera*, both originally members of the South Eastern & Chatham Railway's fleet. These ships, capable of 23 knots, had served on the Boulogne and Dover route and during the First World War had seen active service as seaplane carriers.

Engadine was to be employed briefly on excursions from Tower Pier, London, but in December 1933 was sold for work in the Philippines. *Riviera* was sold to a Glasgow agent acting for Mr. H. M. S. Catherwood, a bus operator in County Antrim and County Armagh, who remained owner of the ship for only a brief time. He would appear to have been interested in operating her on an Irish Sea route. In August 1936, newspapers were to carry a drawing of a ship designed by Harland & Wolff, of Belfast, for Mr. Catherwood's proposed service between Portrush and the west coast of Scotland. The ship was to carry 1,500 passengers and a number of cars. But no more came of these plans than of his intentions for *Riviera*.

Riviera was now purchased by Burns & Laird Lines Ltd. and taken in hand at Ardrossan for an extensive overhaul, including conversion to oil fuel. On 14 and 15 June 1933, *Lairds Isle*, as she was renamed, was open to the public at the Broomielaw. The vessel had spacious accommodation for 700 saloon and 600 steerage passengers, and her facilities included a dance floor equipped with "a large electric gramophone" and two dining saloons.

On Friday, 16 June 1933, *Lairds Isle* inaugurated an accelerated daylight service, leaving Ardrossan at 0945 on the arrival of the 0830 train from Glasgow (Central), and Belfast was reached four hours later. 2¼ hours were given ashore in the city. Her season lasted usually from the beginning of June until mid-September and her winters were spent in Ardrossan Harbour.

The "New Laird", as the publicity dubbed her, sailed to Belfast daily, except Sunday, while on Sundays excursions were provided on alternate weeks to Bangor, sailing out of phase with the Stranraer–Bangor excursions. *Lairds*

Isle called at Ayr after leaving Ardrossan on her Sunday trips. Her first sailing to Bangor was on Sunday, 25 June 1933. On Sunday, 16 July 1933, the excursion was to the Giant's Causeway and Rathlin Island. On occasion, *Lairds Isle* would sail from Ardrossan after completing her Saturday trip and anchor in Rothesay Bay, and on the Sunday her excursion would start from the Bute town. From 1936, Larne was substituted for Bangor on the Sunday cruise.

Lairds Isle had no sleeping accommodation but at peak week-ends she gave a sailing during Friday night in addition to her daylight sailings. On peak days it was the practice to swing *Lairds Isle*'s lifeboats out to increase the deck space available.

THE CLYDEWAY

Burns & Laird had produced substantial competition to the Stranraer route by placing *Lairds Isle* on the summer Ardrossan service in 1933. The next move was to improve further the main overnight service between Scotland and Ireland. *Lairdscastle* and *Lairdsburn* had made a substantial contribution to the Glasgow–Belfast route, but with the high standards of *Princess Margaret* and *Princess Maud* new tonnage was required for the overnight service between Glasgow and Belfast.

Coast Lines had provided superior tonnage for the Belfast Steamship Company's Liverpool–Belfast route and now Burns & Laird were to receive two new ships. Built at Belfast by Harland & Wolff, the 3,000-ton motor ships were named *Royal Ulsterman* and *Royal Scotsman*, and after giving short inaugural cruises the ships were opened for public inspection at Belfast and Glasgow for a few days in June 1936.

On the evening of Monday, 15 June 1936, at 2200, an hour later than previously, *Royal Scotsman* left Glasgow and her sister left Belfast. The ships each had sleeping accommodation for 225 first class passengers in single, double and de luxe cabins. 110 third class passengers had overnight accommodation in two berth and large cabins.[165]

Burns & Laird launched a massive publicity campaign which involved taking whole pages in the Scottish national newspapers to advertise their "Glasgow–Belfast, the Clydeway is the Best Way". The publicity material featured drawings of the two new ships which, with scant regard to perspective, emphasised their description as "liners in miniature". *Royal Ulsterman* and *Royal Scotsman* introduced a new funnel colouring to the Burns & Laird fleet. In addition to the crimson funnel with black top, there was a pale blue band. This colour scheme was soon applied to the other Burns & Laird ships.

Lairdsburn and *Lairdscastle* were transferred to the company's Glasgow–Dublin overnight route. The introduction of the new ships on the Belfast route from Glasgow allowed the abandonment at the end of August 1936 of the overnight mail and passenger service via Ardrossan to Belfast. Two cargo-only ships were commissioned in late 1936 and combined the cargo requirements of Ayr and Ardrossan and Belfast. The ships sailed to Belfast and returned via Ayr. Passenger facilities between Ayr and Belfast were withdrawn in 1936.

With the new tonnage sailing between the south-west of Scotland and Belfast—the passenger ship *Lairds Isle*, the passenger/cargo ships *Royal Ulsterman* and *Royal Scotsman*, the cargo-only ships *Lairdscrest* and *Lairdswood*—it is not surprising to see this reflected in the Stranraer route results. The cargo figures for the "Princess" ships had increased for several years, but in 1937 the figure dropped below the previous year's result. The passenger figures continued to climb but the rate of increase was temporarily arrested. 1935 had produced a 10 per cent increase on 1934, but 1937 saw only a 3 per cent increase on 1936, and in fact the first winter of the increased competition, 1936–37, saw a drop in the passenger figures at Stranraer when compared with the corresponding period in 1935–36.

But any check in the upward trend at Stranraer was only temporary. The increased carryings were common to all Irish Sea routes. On the L M & S R Heysham–Belfast route the three new "Dukes" were so popular that they could not cope at the height of the season. In 1930, *Curraghmore*, a former Holyhead–Greenore steamer, was transferred to Heysham as spare steamer and was renamed *Duke of Abercorn*. After five years as stop-gap, a more permanent solution was arrived at in 1935 when a new ship, *Duke of York*, was commissioned at Heysham. But in January 1938 the L M & S R Board of Directors decided that their Irish Sea routes required further tonnage.

A REVOLUTIONARY SHIP

Several alterations were made to *Princess Margaret* and *Princess Maud* to increase their attractiveness. In the winter of 1937–38 improved dining facilities were installed on both ships and the younger sister was given extra seating. In October 1938 the go-ahead was given to convert the "Maud" from coal to oil fuel and the work was carried out at Dumbarton by William Denny & Bros. Ltd. in the early months of 1939. *Princess Maud* underwent trials in March and took over the mail run on Monday, 17 April 1939, from *Princess Margaret*, which was laid up. It was reckoned that the extra £2,400 cost per year in fuel for the "Maud" was justified on grounds of better steaming qualities and the absence of noise and dust in bunkering. No approval of such modification was given for *Princess Margaret*, as she was now earmarked for Heysham where the other ships were coal-burning. The pressure at Heysham was on passenger accommodation and the transfer of the "Margaret" south meant that five ships would be available. The pressure being experienced at Stranraer at the peaks was cargo and motor cars. (In contrast to the other routes there was no cargo-only ship running parallel to the main passenger ships.) The shortness of the passage between Stranraer and Larne was being nullified by the time required to load and unload these items. The schedules for the peak days required each ship to give two double runs but, as we have observed, this was rarely accomplished as printed in the time-table. In his letter of July 1937 "Indignant" blamed the chaos he experienced on the antiquated method of loading cars—individually by crane.

Car traffic continued to increase and jeopardise further the timekeeping of the steamers. In 1927, 600 cars were carried during July and August, in 1933, 2,000 cars were transported between June and September, while in 1937 over 4,000 cars made the crossing, the bulk of these being in the summer months. Nearly 5,500 were carried in 1938. This build-up was not unique to Stranraer, and on the other short sea routes—across the English Channel—different solutions had been tried.

The monopoly of the national railway companies at Dover was broken in April 1930 when Townsend Brothers Ferries Limited placed a converted

"Town"-class minesweeper, *Forde*, on the Dover–Calais route. After conversion the ferry could carry 307 passengers and 29 cars. The redesign of the ship included a stern door 9 feet wide and 6 feet long which folded down on to the quay over which cars could be driven. Unfortunately, because of difficulties at Dover, the roll-on/roll-off principle could not be used and the cars had to be transferred between ship and shore by crane.

By contrast, *Autocarrier*, the Southern Railway's reply in 1931 to this intrusion, was designed for craning only. *Autocarrier* carried 35 cars each trip between Dover and Calais. Her passenger accommodation was limited.

1936 saw the conversion of the Belgian National Railway's steamer *Ville de Liège*. This ship could carry 100 cars and 250 passengers and was placed on the Dover–Ostend route in August of 1936. The cars were loaded over special gangplanks and the upper and lower decks were linked by an incline in much the same manner as is found on the present car ferries of The Isle of Man Steam Packet Company Limited, such as *Manx Maid*. Reflecting the journey now possible over trunk roads, the ship was renamed *London-Istanbul*.

The roll-on/roll-off principles embodied in *Forde* were obviously the solution to the turn-round delays, but one problem presented to the designers of ships and terminals on the English Channel crossings was the tidal range. At Boulogne, where the tidal range was 29 feet, a link span of 215 feet was required between shore and ship if a maximum gradient of 1 in 7 is accepted. One way round this difficulty was reached in October 1936 when locked-docks were opened at Dover and at Dunkirk for three Southern Railway train ferries, *Hampton Ferry*, *Shepperton Ferry* and *Twickenham Ferry*. In these vessels the main deck, apart from a small saloon area forward, was given over to four lines for railway wagons and sleeping cars. Once the water level in the dock was adjusted the stern of the ship joined with a link span and the railway traffic was able to move on or off. The design of these ships also included a garage on the top deck for thirty cars, and these were loaded by means of a drawbridge from the shore. To give as clear a train deck as possible the two uptakes were placed at each side of the ship, thus giving two funnels athwartships. The single-reduction turbine machinery produced a service speed of 16 knots.

By contrast with the 29 feet tidal range at Boulogne, the range at Stranraer was only 9 feet and this called for a link span of 60 feet. At their meeting in January 1938 the L M & S R Board grasped the nettle and approved the building of their first cross-channel roll-on/roll-off ferry.

Expenditure of nearly £200,000 was approved to provide terminals at Stranraer and Larne for a stern-loading vehicle and passenger ferry. The order for the ship went to William Denny & Bros. Limited, and on 20 April 1939 the vessel was named *Princess Victoria*. The external appearance of the new "Victoria" was similar to that of a typical cross-channel passenger ferry of her day, but internally the new ship incorporated many novel features. The entire main deck was given over to the motor car. Apart from the engine-room casing, there was no obstruction, and 80 cars could be accommodated with a height restriction of 12 feet 6 inches. These cars were loaded through an opening in the stern which was closed by two low doors while the vessel was under way. To ease handling the cars, two 20 feet diameter turntables were situated on the car deck. A hatch forward and a small well aft gave emergency crane access to the car deck.

Unlike the pioneer *Forde* and *Autocarrier*, *Princess Victoria* was designed for carrying main passenger traffic as well as vehicles. The accommodation for the 1,400 passengers was situated entirely on the promenade deck with the exception of the ship's six staterooms (the only sleeping accommodation for passengers) on the boat deck. Buoyant seating was provided on the boat deck. Forward on the promenade deck first class passengers had a bar lounge and a dining saloon; while aft for third class passengers the same facilities were provided. The two identical dining saloons each had seating for 48 and shared a common pantry. Below the car deck were crew accommodation and stores space, and forward of the engines sheep pens were available. A simple docking bridge was built aft raised above the promenade deck and communicating with the main bridge by docking and starting telegraphs.

Another departure for the L M & S R was the engine-room: the Board had selected *Princess Victoria* to be their first diesel-propelled cross-channel vessel. One of her diesel engines was built by Sulzer Brothers, of Switzerland, and the other by Denny's under licence, and these combined to drive *Princess Victoria* at 19·93 knots when trials were conducted on 26 and 27 June 1939. The mean over six hours was 19·25 knots.

Extensive alterations were made at both Stranraer and Larne to receive the revolutionary ship. At the Irish terminal, Spencer (Melksham) Limited had difficulties to surmount in their work of installing the electrically operated moveable ramp. The main difficulty was incorporating not one but two sets of railway lines that crossed at right angles to the ramp, and these two sets each had three lines because of the two gauges then applying in Ireland. The main ramp was 70 feet long and 10 feet wide and it was counterbalanced by weights. At the seaward end, the ramp had an 11 feet long hinged flap which could be adjusted independently of the main ramp. A 4 feet section connected the hinged flap to the stern of the ship. In addition to the ramp, a parking area was provided for 38 cars and a ticket office built. A conveyer for mail and luggage was installed between the ship's berth and Larne Harbour Station.

At Stranraer, the moveable ramp was very similar to its opposite number at Larne, except that the main ramp was only 60 feet long and it lacked the final 4 feet section. It was constructed by P. & W. MacLellan Limited, of Glasgow. The pier was built out in a south-west direction at the point where it joined the long, stone approach road and so provided the situation for the ramp and also the marshalling area for cars. A small booking office was built at the car park. Provision was also made for unloading mails in platform 1 (the south platform) into a new, narrow platform situated just opposite the stern of the car ferry.[166]

Princess Victoria berthed at Gourock Pier, the headquarters of her manager, on Tuesday, 4 July, and there she was accepted by the L M & S R. The ship then gave an inaugural trip, touching Larne and Stranraer, and on Friday, 7 July 1939, took over the daylight service between Larne and Stranraer. The arrival of *Princess Victoria* allowed *Princess Margaret* to sail for assisting duties at Heysham, though the intention was that she would return north to Stranraer each winter for four or five weeks to relieve *Princess Maud* for overhaul. This was necessary, since *Princess Victoria* had sleeping accommodation for only six passengers, which rendered her unsuitable for the main mail service. This also explains the break from tradition that had always seen the newest ship sailing as the mail steamer, with the older acting as stand-by and undertaking the daylight service from Larne in summer.

J

In addition to the once-daily round trip from Larne, *Princess Victoria* gave an extra round trip on Fridays and Saturdays, leaving Stranraer at 1120 and Larne at 1450. On these days "Victoria's" usual 1008 departure from Larne was retimed to 0805. These sailings had train connections at both ends. *Princess Maud*, on Fridays and Saturdays, would appear to have operated the 1008 from Larne and returned from Stranraer at 1330 on Fridays and 1400 on Saturdays. *Princess Victoria* had arrived on the station in the midst of extra cargo, caused by a dockers' strike in Belfast. The sailings and trains were being affected, but the quicker loading of the "Victoria" lessened the delays.

Princess Victoria had been advertised for a Sunday afternoon excursion on 2 July from Larne to Stranraer, but the ship was not available until the following week, and the trip was taken by *Princess Margaret*. The 1120 sailings by the "Victoria" on Fridays and Saturdays were advertised as excursions from Stranraer with the passengers returning by the evening mail steamer. On Sunday, 13 August, she gave an afternoon trip from Larne to Stranraer, but on Wednesday, 19 July, *Princess Victoria* gave what was to be her only "proper" excursion when about 250 joined her for an afternoon cruise from Stranraer round Ailsa Craig.

CHAPTER TEN

The Second World War

IMMEDIATE changes on the Stranraer route followed the declaration of war on Sunday, 3 September 1939. The two regular ships on the route, *Princess Maud* and *Princess Victoria* were requisitioned by the Admiralty, and on 5 September the latter set off for Southampton to be followed south by the former on the 9th. *Princess Margaret* was brought back from Heysham to take up the mail run on 5 September, but for a day or so the daily round mail trip was covered by *Glen Sannox*, a turbine steamer borrowed from The Caledonian Steam Packet Company Limited. The "Margaret" was to maintain the service during most of the war with remarkably little interruption. The only lengthy break in the service was between 29 January and 3 February 1940, when for six days weather stopped the sailing.

The "Victoria" was fitted out as a minelayer and based on the Humber. Her duties took her to the Baltic and North Sea coasts, but on 21 May 1940 she ran foul of an enemy mine in the Humber and sank. Thirty-four of her crew were lost.

THE "MAUD" AND "MARGARET" GO TO WAR

The "Maud" entered service immediately at Southampton as a troop carrier operating to France. She was later transferred to Dover, still acting as a trooper, and served as a leave ship for men of the British Expeditionary Force in the early part of 1940. Later in the year she was engaged in the Dunkirk evacuation, and on her first approach to Dunkirk on 30 May, she was hit by a shell which tore a hole in the ship's side and killed four of her crew. *Princess Maud* limped back to port and after temporary repairs set out again four days later. On this occasion she made it into Dunkirk and embarked 1,200 troops and brought them over to Dover. *Princess Maud* was expected to be the last commercial ship to leave Dunkirk Harbour, but the Isle of Man steamer *Tynwald* actually earned this distinction.

After Dunkirk came St. Valery-en-Caux with the 51st Division fighting with their backs to the sea. St. Valery was a blazing furnace and visible miles out to sea. A signal received by the "Maud" ordered her to Veules des Roses, a village eight miles north-east of St. Valery. There three of the ship's boats were launched and ferried over 300 men from the shore. Others were brought to the "Maud" by coasters. *Goldfinch*, a motorship of The General Steam Navigation Company Limited, of London, transferred 500 troops to the "Maud" before she left for England. There was heavy shelling from shore batteries but the "Maud" escaped untouched.

It is recorded that the spirit of the men of the 51st Division made a lasting impression on the minds of the crew of the "Maud". At Veules, the Highlanders had to descend steep cliffs to the beach and then struggle out to the boats which carried them to the troopships lying some distance off. As one lad belonging to a bren gun team was taken on board the "Maud", bedraggled and dishevelled, his first request on reaching the deck was, "Whaur can I pit my gun up, mister?" Having brought back over a thousand from Veules des Roses, the next job for *Princess Maud* was to assist with the evacuation at St. Malo.[167]

Once the evacuation of France was complete, the ports in southern England were closed as far as cross-channel traffic was concerned, and in the summer of 1940 *Princess Maud* returned to Stranraer. From then until November 1943, she was engaged in carrying troops between Scotland and Ireland. David L. Smith records that in July 1940, *Princess Maud* took up a special schedule, leaving Larne at 0230 for Stranraer, where she connected with a troop train for Birmingham. By 1941, two troop trains left Stranraer Harbour every day, one for Cardiff and one for London, with balancing trains in the opposite direction.[168]

While engaged in this troop carrying, *Princess Maud* was attacked and machine gunned in 1941 by an enemy aircraft returning from a bombing raid on Campbeltown. One soldier was slightly wounded but the ship suffered only superficial damage.

Princess Maud was released from troop carrying when required to relieve her old sister, *Princess Margaret*, on the mail schedule. At the end of September 1940 the "Margaret" went to Belfast for three weeks overhaul, and she collided in fog with the Belfast, Mersey & Manchester Steamship Company's *Greypoint* in Belfast Lough on her return trip to Stranraer on 18 October.

The "Margaret" had developed engine trouble in December 1939 and the expedient was adopted of borrowing one of the C S P steamers then engaged on trooping duties between Stranraer and Larne. The turbine steamer *Duchess of Hamilton* took over the mail run from *Princess Margaret* on 11 December for three days. Built in 1932 for the excursion trade from Ayr, *Duchess of Hamilton* had paid a few peacetime visits to Stranraer and had moved to Stranraer for trooping in October 1939. Arrangements were made for the "Hamilton" to carry 250 passengers in addition to 400 military personnel.

At the end of September 1941 and in December 1942, *Princess Margaret* went to Holyhead for overhaul, while *Princess Maud* reappeared on the mail schedule. On 18 January 1941, the "Margaret" was leaving Larne on the evening mail run when the strong south-east wind blew her on to a ship lying at the north pier. The "Margaret" had to be withdrawn for a few days and the "Maud" took over, and on the 20th on the same run hit the same ship still lying at the north pier. These little episodes were settled at a cost to the L M & S R of £470. *Princess Maud* made other occasional war-time appearances on the mail schedule.

PLEASURE STEAMERS CARRY THE MAIL

In November 1943, *Princess Maud* was ordered to Liverpool to undergo alterations for invasion purposes. She was adapted to carry three landing craft on each side, and once this work was completed she was engaged in exercises on the South Wales coast and in Loch Fyne in preparation for D-Day.

At the beginning of 1944, *Princess Margaret* was withdrawn from the mail run and converted into a commando ship. During her absence of almost a year, *Royal Daffodil*, a motorship of the General Steam Navigation Company's fleet, was chartered by the L M & S R and her first crossing as mail steamer was on Monday, 3 January 1944. *Royal Daffodil* had been built at Dumbarton in 1939 for the summer trade across the Channel from Margate, Ramsgate and other summer resorts in the south-east corner of England. *Royal Daffodil* had been present with the "Maud" at Dunkirk. An account of the "Daffodil's" work at Dunkirk is contained in the official history of her owning company by means of extracts from the master's log.[169] Strangely the official history is silent on the vessel's heavy years of duty as a Stranraer troop ship which followed her move north after the fall of France. While on the Stranraer–Larne route her English Channel certificate for 1,392 passengers was extended to cover the crossing.

For a fortnight in July 1944, *Royal Daffodil* was off service for a quick overhaul and her place taken by *Empress Queen*, of P. & A. Campbell Limited, the Bristol Channel and South Coast steamer operators. *Empress Queen* had never seen peacetime employment, having been launched at Troon on the last day of February 1940. She was immediately taken over by the Admiralty after her trials on 4 July and employed initially on short-sea trooping. In December 1940, she was fitted out at Sheerness as an anti-aircraft ship for the Thames and given the name *Queen Eagle*. After a spell on this work she was transferred to convoy work in the North Sea and in November 1943 came under the jurisdiction of the Ministry of War Transport, who modified her accommodation for trooping, and at the end of 1943 restored her original name and placed her on the Stranraer–Larne troop run to compensate for the move south for D-Day of the other troopships from Stranraer.

During the time *Royal Daffodil* and *Empress Queen* were on the mail run in 1944, General Steam Navigation handled their own catering on board both ships. The catering profit of the L M & S R for the route dropped from £13,155 in 1943 to £194 in 1944.

A further loss of revenue arose from *Royal Daffodil's* employment on the mail run, since she carried only passengers, mail and luggage. No livestock or general cargo could be accommodated on the "Daffodil" or her relief. This loss of traffic was reflected in the financial results for the mail service. The operating profit of £156,000 in 1943 was followed by £127,000 in 1944. In 1945 the figure had risen to £186,000.

It is not always appreciated what a windfall a war or similar crisis can be to transport operators. The profit for the Stranraer service in 1939 was £16,800 with gross receipts of £98,000 and passengers carried totalled 223,000. In 1940 gross receipts of £139,000 from the 240,000 passengers produced a profit of £72,000. Thereafter the operating profit, gross receipts and passengers carried continued upwards, apart from the setback in 1944, until in 1945 504,000 passengers crossed and the gross receipts of £326,000 produced a profit of £186,000. A considerable proportion of the greatly increased profit was made possible by the nature of the traffic, since the usual seasonal peak was flattened. For example, in 1938, 50 per cent of the passenger traffic crossed over on the route in the eight weeks to 7 August, whereas in 1940 only 25 per cent of the year's travellers crossed in the corresponding period. In 1942 the figure was 16 per cent, in 1944 12 per cent. In 1945 the percentage for the eight weeks to 12 August had risen to 30 per cent.

But the increased income from the mail steamer and the benefits of the levelling of seasonal peaks did not accrue directly to the L M & S R. The major railway undertakings of Britain came under Government control from 1 September 1939 and thereafter all revenue of the railways (from all activities except road haulage) was pooled and an annual payment made to the companies by the Government. The formula employed required that of the first £43½ million of revenue, payment to the companies was based on the average net revenue for the three years 1935–37. The L M & S R received 34 per cent of this £43½ million. Any surplus over the £43½ million was split—half to the Exchequer and half to the railway companies.[170]

On the night of 5 June 1944, *Princess Maud* was part of an enormous convoy from Portland Bay for the Normandy beaches. The "Maud" brought her load of troops to Vierville and anchored off until all had disembarked by boat. By her next trip the Mulberry docks had been erected and she was able to berth alongside. The "Maud" carried over 16,000 troops of the invasion force. *Princess Margaret* sailed on D-Day with a destroyer escort, and her function that day was to assist in the destruction of heavy coastal batteries. The "Margaret" made several trips to the beaches and carried over the staff and nursing sisters of one of the first medical units to land in Normandy.

Princess Maud was the first cross-channel steamer to enter Ostend and she made several trips there. The "Maud" continued on the cross-channel routes and was kept busy once leave was started in the New Year. In September 1945, *Princess Maud* visited Guernsey on a round trip from Southampton. Very soon after this she returned to Stranraer. *Princess Margaret* arrived back at Stranraer at the end of 1944 and on Christmas Day took over the mail roster from *Royal Daffodil*. The "Margaret" remained on the mail run until the arrival of the "Maud" on Saturday, 29 September 1945. On the Monday, the younger sister took over and the "Margaret" went to Glasgow to have the grime of war removed. *Princess Margaret* returned to the mail duty on 5 November and it was now the turn of *Princess Maud* to have a spell off.

ASSISTANCE FROM THE SOUTH

In his book, David Smith gives an indication of the heavy traffic on the Stranraer route during the war. In April 1940, the 53rd Welsh Division was moved from South Wales via Stranraer to Northern Ireland. This involved the movement of over eleven thousand personnel and their baggage. Further troops were moved via Stranraer as a precaution against a possible invasion of neutral Eire by Germany. From the middle of the 1940 summer troops were also moving between Larne and Stranraer on leave. From 1 September 1939 to 31 December 1945, over four million personnel and seven hundred thousand civilians travelled over the route.[171]

Clearly, *Princess Margaret* could not cope with this traffic and even the assistance from the Caledonian turbines *Duchess of Hamilton* and *Glen Sannox* was not adequate. Mention has already been made of the return of *Princess Maud* to Stranraer in the summer of 1940 following the fall of France and the closure of the southern ports. Other ships similarly displaced from the south coast came north and, like the "Maud", were employed on trooping between Stranraer and Larne. Southern Railway ships, such as *Canterbury*, *Maid of Orleans* and *Biarritz*, came to Stranraer and utilised their large passenger accommodation and speed on the route; and the same company's cargo steamers, *Whitstable* and *Maidstone*, were also transferred to Stranraer.

Canterbury spent eighteen months at Stranraer, while the two other passenger ships were occasional visitors. The three Southern Railway train ferries, *Hampton Ferry, Shepperton Ferry* and *Twickenham Ferry*, also moved to Stranraer, the first-named arriving in September 1940 and her two sisters two months earlier. Their train decks were adapted for the conveyance of heavy military vehicles and the ferries proved indispensible on the route for the following four years. At both Larne and Stranraer they were able to use the loading ramps built for the new car ferry, *Princess Victoria*, in 1939. In 1943 the Army built an additional berth (later to be called the Continental Berth) at Larne and this included a ramp. The first call at the new berth by a troop-ship was on 22 February 1943 by *Royal Daffodil*, but being a passenger-only ship she made no use of the ramp.

The bulk of the traffic using the train ferries was able to move by road to and from the harbour at Larne. But special rail services were required on occasions, such as the conveyance of Churchill tanks from Belfast to Larne. These tanks were manufactured by Harland & Wolff and were loaded on specially strengthened 40-ton wagons for the journey to Larne Harbour. The ramps at Larne and Stranraer had to be strengthened to carry the tanks, which were despatched by rail from Stranraer Harbour. Rail transport was also employed for the carriage from Larne to Belfast and Londonderry of trailers loaded with hydrogen cylinders for the barrage balloon defences of these cities.

At the best of times, Larne Harbour Station could not be described as commodious, but during the war its platform space was further restricted by the erection of offices for the Movement Control staff and Home Office Immigration staff. A kitchen and canteen were also built within the station confines. Cattle movements through the harbour dropped off during the war and the cattle sidings were used for troop trains. Storage space for carriages was increased by adding a third rail to the narrow gauge line in the harbour area.

One of the few records we have of Stranraer during the war consists of notes made by a L M & S R official on a visit to Stranraer on 3–5 November 1942. His report gives the number of ships' calls, excluding the mail ship, for the period January to September 1942. These were: *Hampton Ferry* 67, *Twickenham Ferry* 71, *Shepperton Ferry* 75, *Maid of Orleans* 3, *Canterbury* 47, *Royal Daffodil* 119, *Princess Maud* 105. An examination of the records at Larne confirms the erratic utilisation of the ships since they depended on troop movement requirements.

The Caledonian turbine steamer *Duchess of Montrose*, an occasional pre-war excursion visitor to Stranraer, moved to Stranraer at the end of September 1939 for the trooping service to Larne. She was soon transferred by the Sea Transport Officer back to Gourock and her place at Stranraer taken by her younger sister *Duchess of Hamilton*. Probably the latter's bow rudder made her a more suitable vessel, though the "Montrose" was the better seaboat of the two. In June and July 1940 the troop movements after Dunkirk required that the "Montrose" be returned to Stranraer and both she and the "Hamilton" were employed on the crossing. With the arrival of *Royal Daffodil* and the Southern Railway passenger steamers at Stranraer, *Duchess of Montrose* and *Duchess of Hamilton* were no longer required. The "Montrose" returned to Gourock by the end of July 1940 and the "Hamilton" by October 1940. In late February 1940, *Duchess of Hamilton* was unusually overhauled at Belfast.

Royal Daffodil and *Empress Queen* have already been noted as sailing on the mail run, but both also served on the trooping schedules. The former came to Stranraer in September 1940 and remained until March 1945. In 1945, *Royal Daffodil* was transferred south, where she served as a leave ship between Calais and Dover, and Dieppe and Newhaven, until January 1947, when she was returned to her owners, General Steam Navigation Company, and went to Denny's yard, Dumbarton, for an extensive refit. Her regular programme of excursion sailings started on 19 July 1947. Another G S N passenger steamer, *Royal Sovereign*, came to Stranraer in September 1940 but left before the end of the month and was lost in December 1940 in the Bristol Channel. *Empress Queen* was based at Stranraer from the end of 1943 until 6 October 1946, on which date the last special sailing by a troopship was given between Larne and Stranraer. *Empress Queen* was taken in hand by her builders, Ailsa Shipbuilding Company, of Troon, and in June 1947 she arrived on the Bristol Channel and took up her peacetime employment.

Once the English Channel had been rendered safe for shipping, the Southern Railway ships moved south to help on the busy cross-channel routes. A ship which then came to Stranraer, in September 1945, was *St. Seiriol*, which had spent some time ferrying troops between Gourock and Inveraray for exercises. This steamer had been built in 1931 by the Fairfield Shipbuilding & Engineering Company Limited, of Govan, to the order of the Liverpool & North Wales Steamship Company Limited for their summer excursion trade from Llandudno and Liverpool. *St. Seiriol* had been engaged in the Dunkirk evacuation and had assisted *Crested Eagle*, a paddler from the same fleet as *Royal Daffodil*, when that pleasure steamer had received a direct hit. After the damage sustained by *St. Seiriol* at Dunkirk was repaired, she sailed north to the Clyde and was engaged as a trooper until transferred to Stranraer. At the end of 1945, *St. Seiriol* was de-requisitioned and taken in hand by Fairfield for rehabilitation, and on Good Friday, 19 April 1946, she gave her first postwar excursion from Liverpool to Llandudno and the Menai Straits, thus being one of the first British pleasure steamers to return to normal duty.

When *St. Seiriol* left Stranraer in early December 1945 her place was taken by *Duchess of Hamilton*. On the evening of Wednesday, 26 December 1945, while crossing from Larne with some three hundred service personnel, *Duchess of Hamilton* ran at full speed into an almost perpendicular cliff face just south of Corsewall Point. It was at first thought that the ship had struck a mine and distress signals were sent, bringing Portpatrick lifeboat out. But once the situation had been appraised the "Hamilton" went astern and, apart from a badly buckled bow, there was no damage. Many had been thrown about the ship when she struck but none was seriously injured. *Duchess of Hamilton* managed to reach Stranraer under her own power and she lay there until the following Saturday when, in the afternoon, she left for the Clyde. After a new bow had been fitted in Henderson's yard, *Duchess of Hamilton* returned to Stranraer and remained until 28 March 1946, returning north to Gourock to assist for a single day on the Clyde Coast services before going for reconditioning.

At the beginning of the war the rostering of vessels and the arrangements for special sailings were made jointly by the C S P office at Gourock and the Divisional Sea Transport Officer at Greenock. With the increase in shipping on the Stranraer–Larne route, plus the influx of a multitude of craft at Gourock, the C S P management were forced to delegate some of their authority to a local office and in 1940 Captain Hugh Montgomery was brought ashore from *Princess Maud*. Captain Montgomery was based at Stranraer Harbour and combined the duties of S T O for the Ministry of War Transport and also Marine Superintendent for the L M & S R.

THE "MILK RUN"

During the winter of 1941–42 the Ministry of War Transport and the Ministry of Food turned to the problem of increasing the milk supply to Scotland and provision was made for the transportation of milk from Northern Ireland via Stranraer. Throughout the period of the war, and for some years after, the milk in churns was carried by the mail steamer, but this supply required regular augmentation, especially during the winter. In 1941 the electric crane on *Princess Margaret* was removed to provide more space for perishable and milk traffic. During December 1941, both *Princess Margaret* and *Duchess of Hamilton* were engaged on special runs with milk between Larne and Stranraer, while in January the Ministry of War Transport chartered their *Empire Daffodil* to the L M & S R for the run. She ceased sailing in February but resumed in late October 1942 for a few weeks. After the war, *Empire Daffodil* was purchased by The General Steam Navigation Company Limited and renamed *Greenfinch*.

The next vessel to be chartered by the L M & S R for the special milk runs was *Whitstable*, of the Southern Railway. She took up service in October 1943 and remained on this duty until March 1944. This lengthy spell of duty was no doubt caused partly by the lack of suitable accommodation on *Royal Daffodil*, which acted as mail steamer during 1944. In mid-September 1944, *Scottish Co-operator*, of the Scottish Co-operative Wholesale Society Limited, was chartered for the milk sailings and remained so employed until the end of the year. *Whitstable* and *Empire Daffodil* then covered the run as best they could until a regular ship, the Southern Railway cargo ship *Maidstone*, took over until 17 March 1945. In late September 1945, the traffic was building up for the winter and another railway cargo steamer *Irwell*, from Goole, was chartered to cover the route until February 1946. For reasons unknown, *Irwell* used Belfast as the Irish port rather than Larne. This resulted in higher labour costs and harbour dues. When the service began again at the beginning of October 1946, Larne was again the Irish port from which the milk came to Scotland. The vessel used, *Hodder*, also of the L M & S R Goole fleet, was usually associated with the Hamburg route, but when she arrived at Larne on 5 October 1946 her port of departure had been Holyhead, since *Hodder* had just completed a spell on the Holyhead–Dublin (North Wall) cargo service. Each winter, for some years to come, special provisions had to be made for the milk traffic between Northern Ireland and Scotland.

Initially the milk traffic was routed via Stranraer, but when *Whitstable* took up the milk run in October 1943 it was to the nearby port of Cairnryan that she sailed. Under the pressure of war, this quiet hamlet became a busy military port. Before the outbreak of war, plans had been drawn up for an emergency port for Glasgow in the event of the city being crippled by enemy bombing. Work began on the building of a port at Cairnryan in early 1941, and on 15 May 1943 the first ship, *Fort McLoughlin*, called to land military supplies. The new port offered 1½ miles of berths and 33 feet of water at low tide. The War Department laid an extensive system of railway sidings and a line from Cairnryan connected with the L M & S R a mile east of the Stranraer Harbour Junction. Each morning a special train met the milk steamer from Larne and conveyed its cargo to Glasgow.

By 1945 the traffic through Cairnryan had dwindled sharply. After the end of the war there was a regular trade in the disposal of old ammunition, which at first was effected by loading up obsolete tonnage with the ammunition and scuttling the ships at sea. Later on, landing craft were used to carry the deadly cargo out to sea, where it was dumped. Arnott Young & Company Limited also carried out some shipbreaking at the port after the war, and the most famous ship to pass through the yard was probably the battleship *Ramillies* which arrived at Cairnryan from Portsmouth in April 1948.

The Town Council of Stranraer were advised by the War Department in August 1958 that they intended vacating their base at Cairnryan, and despite objections and consultations the move was made in April 1959. The port and equipment were sold to Mr. H. G. Pounds, of Portsmouth, who expected to revive the shipbreaking business of the port, but the degree of activity never reached the level anticipated. It was 1973 before Cairnryan really came to life again, when the European Ferries Group established a drive-on/drive-off vehicle and passenger service to Larne in direct opposition to the established route via Stranraer. European Ferries built two berths a short distance to the south-east of the shipbreaking yard.

Another source of war-time activity on land and sea and in the air at Loch Ryan was the aircraft factories and flying boat hangers of Short Brothers at Wig Bay across the loch from Cairnryan. This was the home of the famous Stranraer flying boats. After many years of indecision the factory closed in 1960.

IS YOUR

JOURNEY

REALLY

NECESSARY **?**

CHAPTER ELEVEN

Slow Return to Normality

WHEN the war in Europe ended on 8 May 1945, *Princess Margaret* was the Stranraer–Larne mail steamer. There was a slight relaxation of travel restrictions and this produced some heavy passenger traffic in the summer. Extra pressure on the route was caused by a redirection of Heysham traffic to the Stranraer route. The "Margaret" was on her own, as *Princess Maud* was still engaged on the English Channel ferry routes, and on 12 and 29 July and 5 August 1945 extra sailings had to be given between Stranraer and Larne. The "Margaret" was still dressed for war, and when the "Maud" returned to Stranraer on Saturday, 29 September, the "Margaret" left for Glasgow, where her war paint was removed. On 5 November 1945, *Princess Margaret* took over the mail run and the younger sister had an opportunity for a quick docking. She soon returned to Stranraer and the "Margaret" returned to Heysham—the base she had served briefly before the war. *Princess Maud*, with some of her war equipment removed, maintained the Larne route until the middle of February 1946, while *Princess Margaret* sailed between Heysham and Belfast, partnering *Duke of Lancaster*. *Duke of Argyll* was undergoing refit at Harland & Wolff's yard at Belfast and the other L M & S R Heysham–Belfast passenger/cargo steamers, *Duke of Rothesay* and *Duke of York*, were still retained as troop carriers on the Harwich–Hook of Holland run.

As soon as *Duke of Argyll* became available for the Heysham service, *Princess Margaret*, on 11 February 1946, sailed for Stranraer and took over the mail run. This allowed *Princess Maud* to proceed to D. & W. Henderson's yard at Glasgow where she underwent an extensive refit. It was August before the "Maud" returned to service.

POST-WAR SHORTAGE

In 1946, once again, one ship had to cope alone with the summer traffic on the Larne route, and on Saturdays in July and August additional sailings were given when the steamer returned from Larne at 1015 for Stranraer. A sailing was given at 1330 from Stranraer to Larne. These extra sailings had train connections. The additional round trip was also given on Friday, 12 July 1946, the beginning of the Glasgow Fair Holidays. On the Friday and Saturday of that week-end the "Margaret" carried over 4,300 passengers to Ireland. To prevent any overflow, a system of sailing tickets was in force for peak days.

The Burns and Laird daylight service between Ardrossan and Belfast with *Lairds Isle* recommenced after the war on 29 July 1946. *Lairds Isle* had been greatly improved during her refit: entirely new public rooms were made and the for'ard end of the promenade deck was now enclosed and provided with large windows. While the L M & S R management were no doubt glad to have another ship to spread the load of the Scottish–Irish passenger traffic there was also the reminder that the halcyon days of little competition had gone once again.

On 1 August 1946, *Princess Maud*, now restored to her peacetime condition, took over the Stranraer–Larne mail run, while *Princess Margaret* moved south again to assist *Duke of Lancaster* and *Duke of Argyll* at Heysham. It was to be September 1946 before *Duke of Rothesay* was released from her trooping duties, and December before *Duke of York* was allowed to return to Belfast for refit. So the Heysham fleet was slowly returning to normality.

But Holyhead had lost one of its ships, and in mid-September 1946 *Princess Margaret* had once more become the Stranraer ship and *Princess Maud* was transferred to Holyhead for the service to Dun Laoghaire.

Before the war the Holyhead–Dun Laoghaire mail service had been maintained by three turbine steamers: *Hibernia*, which entered service in 1920, and *Cambria* and *Scotia*, which appeared in the following year. Two ships would normally be in service with the third in reserve or off for overhaul. *Scotia* was lost at Dunkirk on 1 June 1940 and *Princess Maud* now filled the gap, by acting as assisting and relief ship to the two remaining steamers. In October 1946, *Princess Maud* had to return north to allow *Princess Margaret* off for seven weeks or so for overhaul. During the second week in December the "Margaret" returned to Stranraer and the "Maud" quickly sailed for Holyhead.

The L M & S R ordered two motorships in 1946 to replace *Hibernia* and *Cambria* at Holyhead, but it was 1949 before the two new ships, bearing the old names, entered service. In the meantime, a fuel crisis developed and the two Holyhead coal burners were laid up for part of 1947 and the oil-burning *Princess Maud* maintained single-handed the link between Holyhead and Dun Laoghaire. In addition, for most of 1947, the service via Heysham was curtailed and operated on alternate days.

Soon after *Princess Maud* became permanently based at Holyhead, improvements were made in her second-class accommodation. A docking bridge was also built above the navigation bridge.

By the summer of 1949 the new motorships *Hibernia* and *Cambria* had taken over the Holyhead service and *Princess Maud* became stand-by, assisting as required in the summer and standing in during the overhaul of the motorships. A shuffle round in 1951 resulted in *Princess Maud* visiting ports from her wartime days. Following the loss of *Prague*, of the Harwich–Hook of Holland service, *Duke of York* had been transferred thence from Heysham in 1949. The arrival of *Prague*'s replacement, *Amsterdam*, rendered *Duke of York* spare and she moved to Southampton for the summer of 1950. But the following summer *Duke of York*, with her greater sleeping accommodation, replaced *Princess Maud* as assisting ship at Holyhead and the "Maud" moved to Southampton. She remained there for a couple of quiet months, giving a Guernsey service on Friday nights from Southampton and returning from Guernsey on the Saturday. Her first arrival at Guernsey was on 14 July 1951. After this brief visit south she returned to Holyhead, and *Isle of Thanet*, based at Folkestone, undertook the extra Friday and Saturday sailings between Southampton and Guernsey in 1952.

Princess Maud remained at Holyhead as stand-by for the Holyhead, Heysham and Stranraer routes until displaced by new tonnage in 1965. Clegg & Styring summarise neatly her normal annual employment in the 1950s:

January and February relieving *Princess Margaret* at Stranraer; March and April on Holyhead–Dun Laoghaire replacing *Hibernia* and *Cambria*; May and June on Fishguard–Waterford replacing *Great Western*; July to September assisting on Holyhead–Dun Laoghaire (also occasionally Heysham–Belfast); October and November saw her being overhauled; and December was spent spare at Holyhead.[172]

1959 was the last year *Princess Maud* served Waterford, as the passenger service was withdrawn in June 1959. Thereafter cargo boats relieved on the route. During a gale in March 1950 a failure in *Princess Maud*'s steering gear while proceeding to Waterford caused her to change course for Rosslare and navigate stern first, using the bow rudder for steering. Her 136 passengers completed their journey by train.

So both "Princesses" were refitted for peace-time work but only one was allowed to remain at Stranraer. 1947 was a busy year at Stranraer with the diversion of traffic from Heysham as a result of the curtailment of the service between there and Belfast caused by the coal shortage. At Christmas 1946 and the New Year the management were taking no chances, and sailing tickets were required for sailings from Stranraer from 13 to 31 December and from Larne from 26 December 1946 to 13 January 1947. (The same procedure was adopted at Heysham.) Sailing tickets were also required over the Easter holiday period. But help was on the way, as *Princess Margaret* was soon to have a consort.

A NEW "VICTORIA"

In December 1944, the Shipping Committee (London) of the L M & S R had approved the ordering of a replacement for the lost *Princess Victoria*. This vessel was to be a virtual repeat of the 1939 "Victoria" and the Government granted a licence permitting the construction of the vessel. Five firms were invited to tender, but replies were received from only two, and the lower of these, from Wm. Denny & Bros., Dumbarton, quoted a basic price of £313,000.

Externally, the only difference between the pioneer Stranraer car ferry and her successor was the positioning and shape of certain ventilators. To all intents and purposes they were identical externally, but internally there was not only a general improvement in the third-class accommodation in both finish and size, but the car-deck did not extend for the full length of the ship. The space forward of the engine casing was given over to cabin and lounge accommodation. The new ship could provide sleeping accommodation for 54; and this included the six cabins on the bridge-deck which had been the only such accommodation on *Princess Victoria* of 1939. The new "Victoria" could carry a hundred passengers more than her 1939 sister.

The new *Princess Victoria* was named by Lady Burroughs, wife of the L M & S R chairman, on Tuesday, 27 August 1946, when the ship entered her natural element. Sea trials were carried out on 7 March 1947, and her diesel engines produced a top speed of 19·6 knots and the six hour mean was 18·9 knots. Thus she was a fraction slower than her older sister on the run. Unlike those of the 1939 "Victoria", both the Sulzer engines were built by Denny at Dumbarton.

Early on Saturday, 8 March, the new *Princess Victoria*, berthed under the command of Captain James Ferguson, at Stranraer. She was scheduled to take over from *Princess Margaret* as mail steamer on the 17th, but in the middle of the previous week Stranraer was hit by a severe snow storm which reduced the town to a state of siege. The three hundred passengers that left Larne on Wednesday, 12 March, on board *Princess Margaret* faced the full fury of the blizzard and the ship was forced to anchor off Corsewall Point when visibility dropped to zero. (Radar was not fitted to the Stranraer ships until the spring of 1949, though it is doubtful if this equipment would have been of much assistance in the thick snow.) At three in the morning of Thursday the "Margaret" made contact with the pier at Stranraer but the passengers remained on the steamer. Neither train waiting for the "Margaret" was to leave, as an earlier train had become blocked in the snow. When the food situation in the town and on the ship became acute, *Princess Margaret* proceeded to Gourock with her passengers. The mail run was abandoned until the following Tuesday, 18 March, when *Princess Victoria* took up the service. During the week-end the blockade of Stranraer was broken by a fishing boat bringing in food from Girvan and the mail followed the same route. Port-patrick's link with the outside world was its lifeboat, which again brought in mail and food.

With *Princess Victoria* maintaining the mail connection from Stranraer, *Princess Margaret* sailed to Heysham and once again took up the service on the Belfast route as an economy measure in the continuing coal shortage. She returned to Stranraer at the end of May 1947 to take over the mail run, while *Princess Victoria*, like her predecessor, was transferred to the Larne-based schedule of sailings.

The conditions prevailing at the time of *Princess Victoria*'s entry into service were such as to cause the postponement of the usual inaugural cruise for three months. On Thursday, 12 June 1947, *Princess Victoria* took invited guests from Larne and Stranraer for a cruise round Ailsa Craig.

Compared with that before the war, the daylight service was on a reduced frequency for the first two years of the new car ferry. In 1947, three sailings were given in each direction each week, round trips from Larne on Fridays and Saturdays with a single trip to Stranraer on Mondays and a single trip to Larne on Thursday. This timetable operated from 26 June to 15 September 1947. With this reduced service, sailing tickets were necessary for all passengers travelling between 5 June and 30 September. The same arrangements applied in 1948 when a similar truncated daylight programme was operated, but without the Thursday sailing, and further the service ceased at the end of August. The Monday sailing was retimed from 0955 to leave at 1100. In 1949 (and subsequent years) the daylight service returned to the pre-war pattern, with daily (except Sunday) sailings being given from 24 June until 10 September, and sailing tickets being required on only a handful of peak days.

The car carrying facilities of *Princess Victoria* were appreciated, especially in 1947 with the Heysham service remaining on a reduced frequency. During the daylight service in 1947 nearly 3,000 cars were carried compared with just over 700 the previous year.

The circumstances of 1947 ruled out any thought of excursion sailings, but on Wednesday, 25 August 1948, the "Victoria" gave her first public excursion sailing when she revived the day trip to Campbeltown, supplied for many years before the war by the Campbeltown steamer *Dalriada*. A pointer to the changed conditions can be seen in the rise from the 1939 fare of 4s. 9d. to the

1948 fare of 12*s*. 6*d*. Over a thousand were on board for what proved to be a stormy crossing. In 1949, *Princess Victoria* was billed for a sailing that was to be new ground for the Stranraer fleet, when on Sunday, 14 August, a trip from Stranraer to Rothesay was advertised. But the privilege fell to *Princess Margaret*, which took over eight hundred trippers on the excursion to Bute. This day trip was repeated in 1950 and 1951. *Princess Victoria* gave two trips in each of 1949, 1950 and 1951 from Stranraer to Ailsa Craig. In addition, during the summers following the arrival of *Princess Victoria*, day excursion fares were offered to Larne, Belfast and Portrush, sometimes daily, sometimes mid-week only. In 1952, the railway ships offered no excursion from Stranraer, but one excursion was operated when the Stranraer Travel Association chartered *King Orry*, of The Isle of Man Steam Packet Company Limited, for a day excursion on Wednesday, 27 July, to Douglas.

On Wednesday, 20 July 1949, *Princess Margaret* gave the first post-war excursion from Larne when she took about a thousand passengers for an afternoon cruise along the Antrim Coast and round Rathlin Island. This excursion was again to become a trip offered at least once each year. Some years a trip round Ailsa Craig was offered, the first post-war occasion being Monday, 2 August, 1954.

THE "MILK BOAT"

The special sailings with milk from Northern Ireland for England continued for some years after the end of hostilities. As already noted, the first winter of peacetime found *Irwell* sailing between Belfast and Cairnryan, while the following winter another railway cargo steamer, *Hodder*, operated between Larne and the Cairn. In the winter of 1947–48 the expensive expedient of transport by air was employed, but in November 1948 the sea route was once again re-opened. On Monday, 1 November 1948, *Felixstowe* made the first crossing of the winter between Larne and Cairnryan, bringing in about 20,000 gallons. Normally based at Harwich, *Felixstowe* had just finished a spell on the Channel Islands service from Weymouth. She remained on the Cairnryan route until the middle of December. In previous years military labour had handled the milk traffic at the Cairn, but with *Felixstowe* local civilian labour was engaged. However, *Felixstowe* was unequal to the task and additional milk had to be transported by air from Belfast to Liverpool.

A more satisfactory means of transport was hit upon when negotiations were completed between the Ministry of Food and the railway authorities. In May 1949, the car deck of *Princess Victoria* was strengthened to allow a load of 240 tons to be carried. Also, at this time, a spray door, which could be raised and lowered, was fitted at the stern. Following the strengthening, road tankers could be accommodated on the "Victoria" for ferrying across from Larne, thus superseding the slow business of handling thousands of individual milk churns. In July 1949, trials were started with 12-ton tankers being carried on the service sailings. At the same time trials were conducted on the Larne–Preston drive-on/drive-off service provided by Atlantic Steam Navigation Company Limited for commercial vehicles. Later we shall have cause to consider the beginnings of this service.

When the summer service ended on 10 September, *Princess Victoria* devoted her undivided attention to the milk traffic and gave two sailings each way each day. She left Larne around midnight and 0830, and on arrival at Stranraer the road tankers travelled to the town station, where the milk was loaded into special railway wagons for transporting to England. The tankers returned to the "Victoria", which sailed again at 0530 and 2000. These timings were not without their disadvantages. The main problem was presented by the 0530 departure by the "Victoria" from Stranraer while the mail boat was still occupying the outer berth at the pier. Often the mail boat had to leave the berth and lie in the loch to provide sufficient room for *Princess Victoria* to leave—these were the days before twin-rudders and lateral thrust units. The run lasted until the end of October and the schedule was repeated in the following year, 1950. In 1951 the situation was acute and the special sailings commenced on 13 August. There had also been a build-up of milk traffic during the latter part of the summer, and this had resulted in car traffic being turned away to allow space for the road tankers. For a month in 1951, then, *Princess Victoria*, in addition to her round trip between Larne and Stranraer, gave a sailing from Stranraer at 1215 and from Larne at 1515. Additional pressure on the route was caused by a strike at Heysham which diverted traffic to the short sea route. The double service continued unadvertised after the end of the season until 22 December 1951. The mail steamer was also bringing over several thousand gallons of milk in churns each day, and in 1951 over six million gallons crossed in the closing months of the year.

In 1952 the milk facilities had to be introduced in early August again, on Wednesday, 6 August, when an extra daily crossing was made. From 18 August until 13 October the "Victoria" made three round trips each day. For the rest of October 1952 she reverted to two trips and then one trip, which ceased on Saturday, 25 November.

A WARNING UNHEEDED

During all this intensive sailing over four winters the "Victoria" was not entirely accident-free. She berthed heavily at Stranraer on 20 September 1950 and damaged the ramp and dented her stern, but repairs at Stranraer quickly put her back into service. *Empire Gaelic* was leaving Larne for Preston in the late evening of Friday, 21 November 1952, when she made contact with the "Victoria" lying at her berth. Both vessels received superficial damage and the milk run to Stranraer was cancelled on the Saturday.

Two other incidents were to prove of greater significance. On the afternoon of Tuesday, 25 October 1949, *Princess Victoria* experienced heavy weather as she crossed from Larne with her load of road tankers. In the high seas running, some of the tankers broke loose from the wires lashing them to the deck and caused the ship to take on a 10° list. The "Victoria" was unable to berth at Stranraer and she lay at anchor in Loch Ryan for two hours. Milk was released from certain of the tankers to reduce the list and the deck flooded to a depth of about 9 inches. Some fuel also leaked out and concern was expressed that it required forty minutes for scuppers to clear the car deck of this fire hazard.

Princess Victoria left Stranraer at 2330 on Saturday, 24 November 1951, in good weather, but in the early hours of Sunday when running stern-first into Larne Harbour proved difficult to handle. On the second attempt the ship seemed to be setting down on the shore and her acting master, Captain

Duckels, swung her round into the strong north-west wind that had sprung up. The "Victoria" encountered a substantial sea, and waves broached her stern doors and a large quantity of water flooded the car deck. *Princess Victoria* returned to Stranraer with her cargo of empty tankers still on board. It required an hour and a half for the car deck to clear itself of water and the "Victoria" anchored in Loch Ryan at 0530 on the Sunday morning.

Applications by *Princess Victoria*'s owners for certificates that would have permitted their ship to be employed between Fishguard and Rosslare and between Harwich and the Hook of Holland were refused by the Ministry of Transport, but the vessel did have one short spell of duty away from Stranraer. Over Christmas 1948, she gave additional sailings between Holyhead and Dun Laoghaire. *Princess Victoria* was at Holyhead for overhaul when the steamer *Hibernia* (actually, to be strictly accurate, she was *Hibernia II* to free the name for the new motor ship) developed engine trouble and the Stranraer car ferry had to be brought into service for the extra sailings over the peak.

With *Princess Victoria* spending half the winter months on the special milk runs, it proved necessary for *Princess Maud* to return as relief ship on the mail run. For the first two winters of *Princess Victoria* at Stranraer, 1947–48 and 1948–49, the two Stranraer ships, "Victoria" and "Margaret", relieved one another, usually switching around Christmas. Thus it was possible at Christmas 1947 for both ships to be in service on the Larne crossing to cope with the heavy cargo and passenger traffic. A similar overlap arrangement was utilised following the return of *Princess Maud* to Stranraer at the beginning of October 1949. There was a football international at Belfast on 1 October 1949 and the three "Princesses" were engaged to cope with the traffic brought by seven special trains from Glasgow to Stranraer. On the Saturday morning *Princess Maud* left at 0230, *Princess Victoria* at 0530 and *Princess Margaret*, on the mail schedule, at 0700. The first of the returning supporters travelled back with the "Margaret" on the evening mail run.

The "Margaret" then sailed back to Larne to join the other two. *Princess Victoria* left Larne at midnight and was followed by *Princess Maud* and *Princess Margaret*. The "Victoria", employed on the milk run, returned to Larne and brought back the last batch of supporters on Sunday afternoon. On Monday, 3 October 1949, *Princess Maud* took over as mail boat for six weeks and her older sister moved to Holyhead for overhaul. *Princess Maud* was to return to Stranraer every winter up to and including 1960–61.

When *Princess Maud* took over the mail run in October 1951, *Princess Margaret* sailed to Glasgow and, in addition to her overhaul, was converted by D. & W. Henderson to burn oil fuel instead of coal. There had been complaints over the years about the "Margaret" being allowed to remain a coal-burning ship, and the modernised "Maud" was transferred to another route. In March 1952, it was a reconditioned and oil-burning, but still twenty-one year old, *Princess Margaret* that returned to the Stranraer–Larne mail route.

NATIONALISATION

The Transport Act 1947 received the Royal Assent on 6 August 1947 and had as its prime object the establishment of a British Transport Commission. The full nationalisation of the railways in Britain had been too much in the 1920s, but now the nettle was grasped and from 1 January 1948 all the major

K

railway undertakings were vested in public ownership in the British Transport Commission. Among the undertakings was the L M & S R, which had owned and operated the short sea ships since 1923.

The B T C discharged its functions through various executives, and to the Railway Executive was entrusted the shipping, as well as the undertakings explicit from its title. The trade name "British Railways" was adopted for advertising, etc. The B R house-flag which appeared in the spring of 1949 comprised a blue background with white saltire cross lined in red and in the centre a lion straddling an engine wheel.

The Caledonian Steam Packet Company Limited at Gourock had acted as managers and superintendents at Stranraer for the L M & S R throughout the years 1925 to 1947, but a change was now made following the nationalisation of the railways. A new marine management for Scotland was established at the Glasgow headquarters of the former London & North Eastern Railway in George Square. Captain Harry J. B. Perry was appointed marine superintendent for Scotland, and the assistant marine superintendent was Mr. Robert D. Kerr, formerly manager at Gourock of the C S P. Robert Kerr had taken over from Charles Bremner on his retiral in March 1946. The supervision of the Stranraer ships was by Captain Perry at George Square, and the catering and engineering superintendence continued as before from Gourock.

The involvement of both Glasgow and Gourock in the short sea route was removed when British Railways reorganised its marine affairs in 1952 by transferring to the marine office for the London Midland Region responsibility for Stranraer. This office, at Euston Station was later to receive the title "Irish Shipping Services". At Stranraer a marine agent continued to attend to routine matters.

MAIL TO BELFAST?

During the summer of 1952, rumours began to spread that a reorganisation of the Irish services was imminent which would affect the Heysham and Stranraer routes and result in the transfer of the mail boat from Larne to Belfast. Late in July, an outline of the proposals was issued. The main reason for the reorganisation was stated to be the acute congestion at Donegall Quay at Belfast, where the cargo and mail boats from Heysham berthed. The Belfast Harbour Commission was to build new berths in the Herdman Channel and an increased cargo service would operate from there to both Heysham and Stranraer. A considerable proportion of the cargo was to be moved in railway containers (wooden containers which were peculiar to British Railways and not to be confused with the later cellular I S O containers which are now so common on road, rail and sea.) So as B R could continue to claim the sole use of the shed at Donegall Quay at Belfast, it was necessary to transfer to the quay the Irish terminal of the Stranraer mail steamer. Thus both Stranraer and Heysham mail steamers would operate from Donegall Quay. The transfer from Larne to Belfast of the Stranraer steamer was considered by B R desirable on its own merits since, they claimed, 80 per cent of the ship's traffic originated at or was destined for the Ulster capital. An additional daily, all-year-round, service was to be maintained by *Princess Victoria* between Stranraer and Larne.

These proposals did not provoke much comment at Stranraer, but at

Larne it was not long before protests at the loss of the mail steamer were heard. But events overtook the scheme. Within months *Princess Victoria* was to be lost. The container service got going in only a half-hearted way with chartered tonnage, initially between Heysham and Belfast, and in 1954, as we shall see below, between Belfast and Stranraer. The new berths in the Herdman Channel were not operational until 1958. How long this elaborate scheme would have been allowed to continue before consideration was given to the withdrawal of the mail route from Stranraer is an open question. Certainly the negative attitude to the Stranraer route that the events of 1953 were to provoke from B R make it a fair guess that before long attempts would have been made to remove from Stranraer its mail boat, at least.

CHAPTER TWELVE

The loss of *Princess Victoria*

THE last day of January 1953 left its thumb print over the whole of western Europe. It was a day of hurricane force winds producing exceptionally high tides and tremendous seas. A state of emergency was declared in the Netherlands and in the northern part of Belgium with Rotterdam partially submerged and Flushing likewise almost completely under water. All round the British coast damage was widespread. The lighthouse at the end of Margate stone pier was undermined by the waves and fell into the sea. Docks were flooded. At Immingham, the lightship *Varnet* and the British Railways' cargo ship *Hebble* both capsized as water poured into the graving dock. The naval dockyard at Sheerness on the Medway also suffered serious flooding and the frigate *Berkeley Castle* capsized. The submarine *Sirdar* sank in dock.

At Ullapool on the north-west coast of Scotland, twenty-seven fishing boats were driven down Loch Broom and on to the shore. Further north, the island's steamer, *Earl Thorfinn*, had set out on one of her regular trips between Stronsay and Sanday in the Orkneys but was forced to run before the storm and fifteen hours later arrived at Aberdeen.[173]

But not all the ships at sea on 31 January 1953 were as fortunate as *Earl Thorfinn*. For the first time this century eight ships were listed on one day as missing by the Committee of Lloyd's. These ranged from the 58-ton trawler *Leopold Nera*, of Zeebrugge, to the 1,330-ton cargo steamer *Aspo*, of Stockholm. There were other ships whose loss was never in doubt, such as the 7,000-ton *Clan MacQuarrie*, driven ashore ten miles west of the Butt of Lewis while bound from Dundee to Glasgow. Among the casualties of this day was *Princess Victoria*.

31 JANUARY 1953

At 0745 on Saturday, 31, Captain James Ferguson took *Princess Victoria* away from Stranraer with 127 passengers and 49 crew on board. 44 tons of cargo had been stowed on trays in the car deck. The high winds prevented the loading of any cars and had necessitated the loading of cargo by hand—hence the late departure. As Captain Ferguson cycled down from his house overlooking the pier, he would have experienced the full force of the north-west wind, but the forecast spoke of the gale moderating to strong wind. Captain Ferguson knew the journey would be unpleasant but had no reason to expect exceptionally severe weather. As the "Victoria" sailed down the loch she ran into frequent squalls of sleet and snow. From this point on, for a reconstruction of the events subsequent to leaving the railway pier, we depend on the evidence, sometimes conflicting, of the formal investigation into the loss of the ship and the subsequent appeal by certain parties against the findings.[174]

Princess Victoria, following the course normally adopted when a strong north-west wind was blowing, ran three to four miles northward after passing

148

Milleur Buoy at the north end of the Rhinns of Galloway. Thus the seas were taken on the bow; and, on turning, the ship would, to a degree, be running with the seas as it sailed to Larne.

No one actually saw the stern doors being forced open by the sea, but the cargo man working on the car deck became aware of a quantity of water coming from the after end of the deck. On investigating, he found the stern doors open and buckled. The weight of evidence and reconstruction is that by this time *Princess Victoria* had turned and was running with a following sea. The second officer and some of the crew tried unsuccessfully to close the door. After ten or fifteen minutes, Captain Ferguson turned the ship's head into the seas and would seem to have intended navigating stern-first into the shelter of Loch Ryan, steering by means of the bow rudder. Seas were breaking over the forecastle and it proved impossible to release the pin for the bow rudder. The ship kept moving slowly out to sea, probably hoping for increased shelter from Kintyre or Arran.

Two hours after leaving Stranraer, *Princess Victoria*, at 0946, transmitted the message to Portpatrick Radio, "Hove to off mouth of Loch Ryan. Vessel not under command. Urgent assistance of tugs required". The record of radio messages tells graphically the severe weather and difficulties encountered and are reproduced as Appendix E at the end of the book. The message received by Portpatrick Radio was passed to the Marine Office at Stranraer Harbour, but the only tugs in the area were sheltering in Douglas Bay, Isle of Man, and could not put out to sea.

If *Princess Victoria*'s plight had been limited to a car deck awash with several feet of water, the chances are she would have survived the gale. The water lay on one side of the ship, giving rise to a list of 10° to starboard. Following the unsuccessful attempt to close the stern doors, the vessel was turned into the seas and this caused the 44 tons of cargo to shift, with the mail bags and parcels and the trays on which they had been placed moving to starboard, thus aggravating the list. By about 1030 a witness observed the water on the starboard side of the car deck to be about 5 feet deep. This made it impossible to open the cattle doors on the car deck, since cargo and water prevented access to the securing bolts.

The force of the water on board was increased by an extension of the area of flooding. At the forward end of the car deck on the starboard side there was a fireproof door giving access to a corridor leading to the first-class lounge. By 1030 water had found its way through the fireproof door and into the lounge and cabin accommodation. Attempts were made to bale out the lounge by hand but abandoned after about twenty minutes. It was this extension of the flooded area that proved fatal. The first S O S was broadcast at 1032 and some time within the hour following, life-jackets were issued to all passengers and crew. By the time the passengers assembled amidships on the deck over the car deck the list had increased to the extent of requiring the rigging of lifelines to allow passengers to pull themselves up towards the port side. The lifeboats were prepared for launching. Shortly after two o'clock the order was given to abandon ship. Of the six boats, only one was to be of any use.

Word was passed to the Portpatrick lifeboat crew that *Princess Victoria* was in trouble, and following the S O S from the ship at 1032 the lifeboat was launched. At 1100, *Jeanie Spiers* cleared Portpatrick Harbour and set a course for Corsewall, since *Princess Victoria* had given her position as 4 miles north-west of Corsewall Point. The method of passing information to the lifeboat was complicated. The wireless telegraph (W/T) station at Portpatrick was receiving the morse messages from *Princess Victoria* and then passed them on to the coastguard, who was responsible for guiding the lifeboat. The coast-guard's link with the coxswain on the lifeboat was via the radio telephone (R/T) station at Portpatrick. Further, the coastguard had to convert true bearings into magnetic bearings before he passed them to the lifeboat.

Unfortunately, this difficult line of communication was not always main-tained. The routine procedure was for the coxswain of *Jeanie Spiers* to call the R/T station every thirty minutes for the latest information. At 1130 the position of the "Victoria" was reported to the lifeboat as 5 miles north-west of Corse-wall. But five minutes previously the W/T station had received from the "Victoria" a position of 5 miles *west*-north-west of Corsewall. This indicated a substantial travel west and south by the ship. This position was passed to the coastguard and in turn passed by him to the R/T station and duly trans-mitted at 1134. But it was not received by the lifeboat. *Jeanie Spiers* continued to pound her way north while the "Victoria" was now drifting south. At 1203 the lifeboat was told there had been a change in the position of the ship. A message had just been received from the "Victoria" which gave her position as 5 miles west by south of Corsewall. The coastguard was perplexed, since the direction finding readings placed the ship $6\frac{1}{2}$ miles west-north-west from Portpatrick. A message was sent to the keeper of Killantringan lighthouse, north of Portpatrick asking if he could see the "Victoria". But nothing could be seen.

No further information was passed to the coxswain of the Portpatrick lifeboat until after 1315, when the coastguard transmitted the position of the "Victoria" calculated from bearings taken by Portpatrick Radio and Seaforth Radio. This position put the ship much nearer the Irish coast than had been thought and the coastguard at Portpatrick asked the Donaghadee lifeboat to put out. Some confusion was removed when a message was received at 1308 from *Princess Victoria* which indicated that her engines were now stopped. Up until this message it had been assumed *Princess Victoria* had had no power and was drifting, or had only sufficient power to remain more or less head to the sea. In fact it was estimated by a witness that the ship was making five knots.

The Portpatrick lifeboat was the first vessel to set out to the assistance of *Princess Victoria*, but because of the confusion over the position of the "Victoria" and its transmission the lifeboat was actually the last to reach the scene of the disaster.

It was a routine procedure that any message of distress is passed to the Commander-in-Chief, Plymouth, the flag officer in command of the region which includes the North Channel and the Firth of Clyde. Although the first indication of distress was received at Portpatrick at 0946, it was another forty minutes before any message was passed to a ship under Plymouth control. At 1109 the destroyer *Contest* left her moorings in Rothesay Bay and headed down Firth at her full speed of 31 knots. The heavy seas, running from 25 to 30 feet high, stove in a dinghy and two ratings were hurt. Once the shelter of Arran was left, speed had to be reduced.

The initial intention of the destroyer's commander was to attempt towing the disabled ship into Loch Ryan. The first estimate of reaching *Princess Victoria* was 1300, but with *Contest*'s reduced speed and the "Victoria's" southward movement, this was revised to 1330 and then 1415. The area where *Princess Victoria* sank was eventually reached by *Contest* at 1530.

At 1354, *Princess Victoria*'s radio officer, David Broadfoot, had tapped out the final S O S to Portpatrick Radio, "S O S estimated position now 5 miles east of Copelands entrance Belfast Lough—on beam end". Four minutes later the same position was signalled by the "Victoria" to *Contest*. Considering the appalling conditions, it is understandable that this position would appear to have been in error. As a result, six ships headed for a position nearly five miles too far south and a mile too far east.

Three ships sheltering in Belfast Lough, the trawler *Eastcotes*, the coastal tanker *Pass of Drumochter* and the cattle/cargo ship *Lairdsmoor*, heard the early distress signals being passed via the R/T by Portpatrick Radio but had taken no action, since the scene of the emergency was thought to be off the Scottish coast. Also, the impression was gained that early assistance was on the way for the "Victoria". The ships picked up the message transmitted from Portpatrick at 1323 giving a position for *Princess Victoria* and indicating that preparations were in hand to abandon the ship. The position was again in error and placed the ship farther to the east than subsequent events proved to be the case. But *Pass of Drumochter* weighed anchor and set out for the position received.

The message at 1339 from Portpatrick that *Princess Victoria* was on her beam end and could see the Irish coast was picked up by *Lairdsmoor*, and at 1414 *Lairdsmoor* followed *Pass of Drumochter* out into the squalls. When the message indicating the proximity of the "Victoria" to the Irish coast was received by *Eastcotes*, the trawler skipper immediately put out to sea.

Orchy, a coastal cargo ship of Wm. Sloan & Co., had just arrived in the shelter of Belfast Lough when the message was received and *Orchy* put back to sea. The master of *Orchy*, compensating for the considerable leeway his ship would make in its ballast condition, headed farther to the north than the others and thus at 1445 *Orchy* ran into wreckage when about 5 miles east of Mew Island. The approximate position of the disaster had been located.

Orchy now transmitted, at first incorrectly, her position and *Contest*, *Pass of Drumochter*, *Lairdsmoor*, *Eastcotes* and the two lifeboats headed for the area. Lifeboat No. 6 of the "Victoria" was found, but it proved impossible to transfer the 29 or 30 occupants because of the seas and the high sides of the coasters. *Pass of Drumochter* sheltered the lifeboat until the Donaghadee lifeboat arrived and took the men on board. Out of the 176 on board *Princess Victoria* when she left Stranraer, only 42, all men, survived.

THE FORMAL INVESTIGATION

The inquiry into the loss of *Princess Victoria* opened on 23 March 1952 in the County Court House, Belfast. The president of the court was Mr. John H. Campbell, Q.C., and he was assisted by three assessors, Captain C. V. Groves, a Younger Brother of Trinity House, Dr. A. M. McRobb, Professor of Naval Architecture at Glasgow University, and Mr. J. Shand, of the staff of the Admiralty Merchant Shipbuilding and Repair Department.

On 11 June the report of the formal inquiry was issued and stated that the loss of *Princess Victoria* was due to her unseaworthy condition arising from two circumstances:

(1) The inadequacy of the stern doors which yielded to the stress of the seas, thus permitting the influx of water into the car space.

(2) The inadequacy of clearing arrangements for the water which accumulated on the freeboard deck causing an increasing list to the starboard, culminating in the ship capsizing and foundering.

In their concluding paragraph the court remarked that "if the *Princess Victoria* had been as staunch as the men who manned her, then all would have been well and this disaster averted".

The court laid responsibility for the loss at the door of the British Transport Commission and the ship's managers in that:

(a) they failed to provide stern doors sufficiently strong to withstand the onslaught of the heavy seas which may be reasonably expected to occur from time to time in the North Channel;

(b) they failed to provide adequate freeing arrangements for seas which might enter the car space from any source;

(c) they failed to take precautionary steps after the incident of November 1951;

(d) they failed to report the November 1951 incident.

During the evidence, expressions such as "phenomenal seas", "confused seas", "dangerous seas" and "pyramidal seas" were used by witnesses to describe the conditions prevailing on 31 January 1953. The court, in its findings, pointed out that not one of the survivors had used these expressions. "The expressions themselves came from those expert witnesses who felt it their duty to put a face on the disaster. There are no exculpatory circumstances disclosed in the evidence".

The court also found fault with the management of the ship in that the two incidents of October 1949 and November 1951 were not considered of any great importance. The 1949 occurrence concerned the breaking loose of some milk tankers while *Princess Victoria* was on the milk run between Larne and Stranraer. The car deck had been flooded with milk and fuel to a depth of some inches. The attention of the management was drawn to the need for four larger scuppers for adequate drainage of the deck, but nothing was done. "The importance of the matter was not appreciated, or, if appreciated, ignored".

While attempting to enter Larne in November 1951, the stern doors of the "Victoria" had been damaged and the car deck flooded. Not only was the ship allowed to continue in service for three more round trips with temporary repairs, but the fact that it took 1½ hours for the car deck to drain of water was again allowed to pass without comment from the management. The weather at the time of the 1951 incident was severe, but not exceptional, and this should have indicated that the stern doors were not of sufficient strength to cope with weather likely to be encountered on the route.

POSTSCRIPT

The British Transport Commission and Captain Reed, manager of the ship at the time of the loss, appealed against the findings of the court, and the

judgment of the High Court of Justice in Northern Ireland was delivered on
26 November 1953. The judgment clarified the expression "managers" as used
by the lower court in its findings. The ship had had three managers from the
time of its commissioning until its loss. The first manager was Captain W. L.
Sinclair, and he managed the ship for just over a year. From 23 June 1948,
Captain Harry J. B. Perry was designated manager of *Princess Victoria*, having
been appointed marine superintendent of the Scottish Region of the B T C
at the beginning of 1948. On 1 January 1952, he handed over the managership
of the "Victoria" to Captain John D. Reed, who was based in London. In the
judgment of the High Court, the word "managers" was removed and replaced
by "manager", meaning Captain Perry who, at the time of the two significant
events of 1949 and 1951, was the officer primarily responsible to the B T C
for the seaworthiness of their ship. "He does not appear to have realised the
full implications of the exacting standard of skill and care which his office and
its responsibilities demanded of him respecting the seaworthiness of *Princess
Victoria*".

The appeal by Captain Reed was allowed and that of the B T C dismissed
in that they had not discharged their common law duty to take due care and
provide a seaworthy ship. The findings against the B T C were modified,
however, in that the High Court held there had been no breach of statutory
duties. One referred to an interpretation of design regulations and the other to
the non-reporting of the 1951 incident to the Ministry of Transport. In the
former case the High Court took the view that there had been no violation of
the regulations, and in the latter case accepted that while the damage was
material it did not affect the seaworthiness of the ship to the extent requiring
a report under the Merchant Shipping Act, 1894.

The bravery displayed during the operations on 31 January 1953 did not
go unrecognised. The radio officer on *Princess Victoria*, David Broadfoot, who
should have been travelling to Holyhead on the 31st but the previous day
turned down his promotion, was posthumously awarded the George Medal
in recognition of his selfless conduct. He must have known that by staying in
his radio cabin that he was ruling out any chance of escape for himself. William
McConnell, coxswain of the Portpatrick lifeboat, and Hugh Nelson, coxswain
of the Donaghadee lifeboat, were awarded the British Empire Medal, while
Lieut. Commander Stanley McArdle and Chief Petty Officer Wilfred Warren,
of the destroyer *Contest*, were awarded the George Medal. The masters of the
four other ships involved in rescue, Alexander Bell, of *Lairdsmoor*, David
Brewster, of *Eastcotes*, James Kelly, of *Pass of Drumochter*, and Hugh Angus,
of *Orchy*, were each created Members of the British Empire.

CHAPTER THIRTEEN

After the "Victoria"

T HE inadequacy of the escape ports on the car deck of *Princess Victoria* having been highlighted as a basic design fault, the attention of the B T C quickly turned to *Lord Warden*, a near relation of *Princess Victoria*, on the Straits of Dover services. Like the "Victoria", *Lord Warden* did not have hydraulic stern doors, and by a strange coincidence the stern doors of *Lord Warden* gave way in heavy seas only ten days after the loss of the "Victoria". Self-operating escape ports were now built into the hull of *Lord Warden* at car deck level.

On the Clyde, work was progressing on the three passenger/vehicle ferries, *Arran*, *Cowal* and *Bute*, as part of the B T C's modernisation plans for the Clyde services operated by its subsidiary, The Caledonian Steam Packet Company Limited. The design of these ships was amended to incorporate freeing ports on the car deck.

Instead of endeavouring to keep every drop of water off the car deck, the principle now was to ensure that the water which inevitably made its way on to the car deck could drain away quickly.

LOCAL MANAGEMENT

In the findings of the court of inquiry into the loss of *Princess Victoria*, mention was made of the potential dangers of remote control. If the master of a Stranraer ship wanted advice or assistance he had to communicate by telephone with the Irish Shipping Services office at Euston, London. The court was of the opinion that such an arrangement would deter a master from communicating anything other than the most serious matter to the managers outside of his daily written report. Further, the court could speak of "lack of wise superintendence of the ship". Provided there was no major incident reported to them, the managers at London saw no reason for frequent visits to the ship despite her unusual and experimental design. The court, considering the appeal by the B T C against the findings of the court of inquiry, were less severe in their criticism of the superintendence arrangements and stated that the communication and superintendence difficulties had no direct bearing on the loss of the "Victoria".

Be that as it may, the B T C now appointed a senior official to be based at Stranraer who would exercise part of the responsibility hitherto handled at a distance by Euston. In June 1953, Mr. A. L. Pepper was appointed district marine manager and in the new year a reorganisation of the harbour administration came into effect. The deputy to the district marine manager was Mr. D. M. Stewart, and in Mr. Pepper's absence he would act as district marine manager. Mr. Stewart had spent over twenty years on the Stranraer–Larne service and frequently wrote on the history of the route (see bibliography). Mr. R. Niven was appointed station master at Stranraer Harbour and was now responsible to the marine manager for outdoor commercial and operating work, while

Mr. J. Edmonds was put in charge of indoor commercial work at the harbour, which covered both goods and passenger departments. Again, Mr. Edmonds reported to Mr. Pepper, who was ultimately responsible to the Irish Shipping Services office in London.

Mr. A. L. Pepper continued in this post for nearly five years until he was promoted to a post in England. During the resulting vacancy at Stranraer, Captain B. H. Mendus, from the Fishguard–Rosslare section, acted as marine manager at Stranraer. In December 1958, Captain William Smith, a master with the C S P Clyde fleet, was appointed to the post at Stranraer. Captain Smith's previous experience with the Stranraer ships had been mixed—he had been navigating officer on board *Princess Victoria* when a mine was struck in 1940. He had then transferred to *Princess Margaret* and remained there until the end of the war. In April 1946, he joined *Duchess of Hamilton* on the Clyde as Chief Officer and prior to his move to Stranraer had command of the passenger/vehicle ferry *Arran*. When he took over as district marine manager at Stranraer he was answerable to Euston; but following the reorganisation at the end of 1960, Captain Smith reported to his old boss at Gourock, Alex. Stewart.

"HAMPTON FERRY" RETURNS NORTH

It seemed unbelievable that the "Victoria" had gone, but on the evening of Monday, 2 February 1953, it was *Princess Maud* that met a silent crowd at the railway pier. The "Maud" had brought back to Stranraer the bodies of three of the victims of the disaster: a lady passenger, a pantryman and Captain Ferguson. Captain James Ferguson was held in great esteem and his funeral on the Wednesday was reported as the largest ever seen in Stranraer. *Princess Maud* continued on the run until *Princess Margaret* returned from overhaul at Holyhead. Not long after her return to the mail route the "Margaret" took a buffeting in a storm which at times approached hurricane strength and a raft from the top deck was lost.

A single ship was adequate for the traffic for most of the year, but at certain times, and especially during the summer months, assistance was needed. Following the loss of the "Victoria", it was apparently hoped in some quarters that the B T C would purchase or charter the turbine steamer *Empress Queen* for the Larne-based roster.[175] This steamer had served for some years as a troop carrier on this route during the war and had, in fact, carried out the mail service for two weeks in 1944. *Empress Queen*'s intended trade had been no-passport trips between the south coast of England and France; but no-passport facilities were not reintroduced by the Governments of the two countries after peace had been restored. Her owners, P. & A. Campbell, tried her on different routes; but after the 1951 season spent at Torquay, *Empress Queen* was laid up at Bristol. She was not, however, to return to Loch Ryan, and on 3 April 1955, left Bristol for Greece where, as *Philippos*, she was employed as a cruise ship.

Although *Empress Queen* was available and the asking price probably was not high, the assistance required was not so much for passengers as for cars, and it fell to another war-time visitor to return to Stranraer. After refit at Cardiff, the Southern Region steamer *Hampton Ferry* arrived at Stranraer on Thursday, 18 June 1953, and on the Friday took up the Larne–Stranraer daylight service. The train ferry service between Dover and Dunkirk required only two of the trio, and while *Shepperton Ferry* and *Twickenham Ferry* operated the schedule, the spare ferry *Hampton Ferry* was able to come to Stranraer. The four tracks of rails used by the railway carriages and wagons on the English Channel crossings were covered with planking to allow the deck to be used as a car deck carrying about a hundred cars. A garage for twenty-five cars was situated on the boat deck, but as this required a high level bridge from the shore it was not used while the ferry was on the Irish Sea. Temporary seating for eighty passengers and toilet facilities were fitted in the garage space. While at Larne, her limited sleeping accommodation was not made available to the public. *Hampton Ferry*'s rather simple passenger accommodation—on her usual route her passengers remained in the sleeping cars on the train and had no occasion to use the ship's public rooms—was concentrated on the deck over the main deck, though the forward end of the main deck was given over to saloons with settee berths.[176]

It became standard practice for *Hampton Ferry* to sail north each year at the beginning of June and remain until mid-September. She took the daylight service, leaving Larne in the morning and Stranraer in the evening. Additional sailings were given at peak week-ends, and often *Hampton Ferry* would sail over from Larne on the Friday night and provide a sailing the next day around 0500 from Stranraer to Larne. In 1959 an irregular Sunday service was re-introduced from Larne to Stranraer and back by the train/car ferry.

Hampton Ferry's summers on the Irish Sea were uneventful, apart from the occasional uncomfortable crossing. There was one little bit of drama on the morning of Tuesday, 19 July 1956, however, when *Princess Margaret* passed to her a message from Portpatrick Radio that the Norwegian cargo ship *Douglas* was aground on Russell Rock, one mile from the Maidens, off the County Antrim coast. The cargo ship had five passengers on board as well as a crew of 22. *Hampton Ferry* altered course and stood by while the five passengers were brought out to her by ship's boat.

STRANRAER, SUEZ AND THE TRANSPORT FERRY SERVICE

International events put a strain on the Stranraer route in the autumn of 1956. British and French troops had invaded the Suez Canal zone in an attempt to defend European rights against what was seen as Egyptian nationalism. The only other route with drive on/drive off facilities between Britain and Ireland, that between Preston and Larne, operated by Atlantic Steam Navigation Co. Ltd., was completely denuded of its ferry fleet for the emergency. As we shall have occasion to return to this company's activities, especially at Cairnryan, it is appropriate to consider briefly its origins and routes.

The company was the brain-child of Colonel Frank Bustard, who started his shipping career with the White Star Line under Sir James Ismay and eventually became passenger traffic manager. On demobilisation in 1945, Frank Bustard turned his attention to short-haul routes and acquired on charter from the Admiralty and the Ministry of Transport three tank-landing craft and operated them between Tilbury and the Continent. The first route was to Hamburg, conveying equipment and supplies for the Allied Occupation troops in Germany. The services soon became concentrated on Rotterdam and Antwerp.

In May 1948, A S N opened their Preston–Larne service for commercial vehicles and trailers with two additional tank-landing craft, renamed *Empire Cedric* and *Empire Doric*, the first sailing being on 21 May. By 1956, the fleet based at Preston had increased to five, with the original two plus *Empire Gaelic*, *Empire Cymric* and *Empire Nordic*. These five, together with the Tilbury ships, *Empire Baltic* and *Empire Celtic*, were all chartered from the Ministry of Transport. It will be noticed that in each case the second word of the name was itself a White Star name.

In 1953, A S N was in need of capital for purposes of expansion and the Northern Ireland Government was approached with the proposition that the Ulster Transport Authority should take a controlling interest in the company by injecting new capital. The Government declined. It was left to the British Transport Commission to take up the offer, and in April 1954 the Commission purchased A S N. The A S N shares were held by the B T C for a very short time and then transferred to British Road Services Ltd., the B T C subsidiary responsible for the road haulage aspect of the Commission's operations, since A S N was seen primarily as a marine extension of road haulage. The operation of the company, therefore, remained quite separate from the shipping activities of the B T C and it retained its own distinctive colour scheme of blue funnel with broad white band and black top, and its own house-flag, a white pennant with fish-tail edged in blue. Throughout its career, A S N had used several registered trade names, since its official name implies deep-sea operations and truly reflects the original aim of the company—to provide cheap cafeteria-style ships on the North Atlantic run in the 1930s. Among the better known trade names were "Continental Line" and "The Transport Ferry Service".

In the summer of 1956 the situation in Suez slowly came to the boil, and the Ministry of Transport, making provision for any emergency that might develop, advised A S N that their seven tank-landing craft were to be requisitioned. On 17 August 1956, *Empire Doric*, *Empire Gaelic* and *Empire Cedric* arrived at Liverpool from Preston. At Birkenhead these three ferries had their decks strengthened for taking heavy-armoured vehicles. The other two ferries at Preston were newer ships and their decks did not require this attention. *Empire Cymric* was at Preston under repair, leaving one ferry, *Empire Nordic*, in service. On 28 August, these two ships sailed from Preston for Southampton, where they joined *Empire Baltic* and *Empire Celtic* from Tilbury, thus leaving both Preston and Tilbury without any drive-on/drive-off ferries. During the emergency, A S N continued to manage the vessels and in fact managed other similar craft for the Ministry of Transport.

On 5 November 1956, British and French troops made a landing in Egypt and the A S N ships by then had already set out for the Mediterranean. More than two months were to pass before any of the bow-loading craft returned to their bases, and for their Preston–Larne route A S N filled the gap as best they could by chartering five cargo ships. It was 16 January 1957 when drive-on/drive-off facilities for commercial traffic became available again, when *Empire Cedric* sailed from Preston to Larne. By the end of January, the "Cymric" and "Nordic" had also returned. *Empire Doric* was in dry-dock at Birkenhead and *Empire Gaelic* was receiving repairs in dry-dock at Naples.

While the chartered cargo ships could cope to an extent the drive-on/drive-off arrangement for lorries and containers was sorely missed and *Hampton Ferry* was allowed to extend her season at Larne past 15 September, the day on which the daylight service was scheduled to finish. There had been a great increase in the vehicular traffic using the Stranraer route, but *Hampton Ferry* was able to accommodate it on one trip each way each day. She left Larne at 0800 and left Stranraer at 1745. A case could have been made to retain *Hampton Ferry* at Stranraer until the end of the year, but she was required at Dover to meet overhaul commitments for herself and her two sisters. Her second last crossing to Larne was stormy and the night of Friday, 5 October, was spent anchored in Belfast Lough after high winds had prevented *Hampton Ferry* berthing at Larne. *Hampton Ferry* eventually arrived at Larne twelve hours late and even then only after assistance from one of Hoods' Island Magee ferry boats. *Princess Margaret* was held out of the mail berth by *Hampton Ferry* until the train ferry left on her last crossing for the year three hours late.

Figures for the 1956 summer season showed a 120 per cent increase in car traffic with 6,600 cars carried against 3,000 in 1955. These figures did not include the extra three weeks of *Hampton Ferry*'s service.

STRIKES

The 1960 season was marred by two strikes organised by the National Union of Seamen. Both *Princess Margaret* and *Hampton Ferry* tied up on strike upon their arrival at Stranraer on Tuesday, 12 July. The strike had started at Liverpool a week before and holidaymakers, fearful of being stranded in Ireland, had crowded the steamers to Stranraer during their last two days in service. The returning holidaymakers were joined by Orangemen, who had been attending a rally in Belfast, and the combination produced a situation bordering on the chaotic. After a week tied up at Stranraer the ships returned to duty, *Hampton Ferry* sailing twice on Tuesday, 19 July, at 1300 and 2145, for Larne with full complements on both occasions, and *Princess Margaret* crossing over in the afternoon. On the Wednesday, the "Margaret" gave an additional round trip and *Hampton Ferry* gave "several trips".

During the strike, an improvised ferry service brought the Portpatrick–Donaghadee route back into operation. As soon as the mail sailings ceased at Stranraer the Portpatrick fishing boat *Adoration* was pressed into service and took the letter mail over to Ireland, but she took no passengers. In all, seven fishing boats were carrying passengers over the route during the week-end of the strike. The weather was unkind and those who crossed had a very rough trip in the rain and very few would be able to enjoy this return to the historical short sea route.

On the Sunday following the strike, 24 July, a sailing was given from Stranraer to Larne to help clear the backlog, and *Princess Margaret* thus provided the first Sunday cruise from Stranraer for many years. The steamer left Stranraer at 1245 and arrived back at 2005, giving three hours in Larne. A bus tour along the Antrim Coast was operated in connection with the sailing. The excursion was repeated on 31 July. On the 24 July, *Princess Margaret* had over 700 passengers and 36 cars, while on the 31st she carried to Larne 1,200 passengers and 30 cars. *Hampton Ferry* had started operating Sunday crossings in 1959 and these were advertised as excursions from Larne. On 31 July 1960, *Hampton Ferry* arrived at Stranraer with 500 passengers and 60 cars and left again for Ireland in the evening with 800 passengers and 95 cars.

However, the sailings were soon disrupted once more by strike action. *Hampton Ferry* did not sail on Saturday, 13, or Sunday, 14 August, but with a skeleton crew did give a sailing on the Monday morning from Stranraer with cars and cargo but no passengers, and then returned with a full load of cars from Larne. Car drivers and other passengers had to travel on *Princess Margaret*. *Hampton Ferry* left Stranraer for Larne on the Tuesday afternoon and returned to Stranraer about midday on the Wednesday. On both these crossings passengers were conveyed once more since the Board of Trade had issued a modified passenger certificate allowing the ship to sail with a smaller crew.

Princess Margaret continued on the mail run, but it was soon recognised that much would be gained by replacing *Princess Margaret* by *Hampton Ferry*. Accordingly, on Monday, 22 August, *Hampton Ferry* became the mail boat and sailed on the mail schedule. This way the vehicular flow could be accommodated, though overnight passengers were put to some inconvenience since they had to sleep on the "Margaret" and transfer over to *Hampton Ferry* in the morning. Further, the catering department on *Hampton Ferry* was not functioning. On the Saturdays, *Hampton Ferry* made double runs. On Thursday, 14 September, after three weeks as the "top boat", *Hampton Ferry* sailed to Dover, *Princess Margaret* having resumed as mail boat on Monday, 11 September.

During the second strike period, *Adoration* had again been operating a regular service between Portpatrick and Donaghadee.

GARLIESTOWN AND ELSEWHERE

As mentioned above, *Princess Margaret* gave a Sunday excursion in July 1960 because of the backlog of traffic to be cleared. Since the loss of *Princess Victoria*, Stranraer had had no excursion sailings. *Hampton Ferry*, apart from giving extra sailings to Larne, had spent her weekdays at Stranraer firmly tied up at the pier and never ventured out on excursion sailings. By 1959, pressure of vehicular traffic had prompted Sunday sailings on peak week-ends by *Hampton Ferry* from Larne to Stranraer and back. These were used as excursion sailings from the Irish side. Further, *Hampton Ferry*'s departure time from Larne at 0900 made her daily sailing an attractive excursion with ample time in Galloway. In addition, *Princess Margaret* continued to give her two or three trips each year from Larne to Rathlin Island, Ailsa Craig or along the County Down coast.

But apart from a seven o'clock start in the morning, Stranraer had no excursion opportunities at all. Another feature of the Wigtownshire excursion programme disappeared at this time. In 1950, the annual sailing between Garliestown and Douglas, Isle of Man, was revived, but whereas before it had been a joint venture of the railway and the Isle of Man Steam Packet Company, it was now under charter. Buses connected from Stranraer to Garliestown for the excursion. But the trip by *Victoria* on Wednesday, 8 July 1953, leaving Garliestown at 0930, was to be the last sailing by a passenger steamer from that port. *Victoria* carried over 700 trippers for a day on the Isle of Man.

Thus ended Garliestown's career as a port for excursion ships. At one time it had ten or twelve inward and outward calls each year, giving excursions to or from such parts as the Isle of Man, Blackpool (via Fleetwood) and Stranraer. Garliestown had been considered at one time as a possible major port for the Scottish trade with the Isle of Man, and in June 1878 a weekly service commenced between Garliestown and Douglas with train connections to and from Glasgow. This service ran for at least two summers. The contemporary press complained of the lack of information available concerning the service, and this has also proved an insurmountable obstacle in determining any precise facts as to duration and vessels involved.

1952 had seen the revival of the direct excursion sailing from Stranraer to Douglas. This annual event was organised by the Stranraer Travel Association. When *Tynwald* made her morning departure on Wednesday, 28 July 1954, from the railway pier with 621 passengers, this was to be the last excursion from Stranraer by an Isle of Man steamer until 1969. Thus, until the extra Sunday sailings in July 1960 following the strike, there was no excursion offered from Stranraer. It was standard practice to provide a Sunday sailing from Stranraer at peak week-ends, but this was always advertised one way only.

In the mid 1950s, Galloway was giving itself a shake and trying to put itself back on the tourist map. In 1956, Kirkcudbright Town Council approached interested parties with a view to reviving the excursion sailings between Kirkcudbright and Douglas, the distance between the two being just over twenty miles. Nothing came of this.

At the end of the same year the Town Council of Girvan was considering a proposal to build a new harbour which would be able to accommodate Irish shipping as well as excursion steamers from the Firth of Clyde. Again, nothing came of this and Girvan had to be satisfied with its fishing fleet and occasional trips to Ailsa Craig.

With this sort of thinking going on to the east and north of Stranraer, the people of the Wigtownshire port were very aware of the silence from the B T C about any long term plans. Even the indifference displayed by the B T C in the short term was taken as indicative of a general lack of interest in the Stranraer–Larne route on the part of British Railways. Symptomatic of this attitude was a publicity leaflet which appeared in 1958 advertising the excursions by *Princess Margaret*. Unfortunately, the point of departure for these trips was given as Stranraer instead of Larne!

The subsequent attempt by British Railways to correct this error in the local press added further confusion by implying that to avail oneself of the excursion along the County Down coast one could leave Stranraer by *Hampton Ferry* and wait three hours at Larne for the "Margaret's" departure, and there was a similar delay on return to Larne before departure, again by *Hampton Ferry*, for Stranraer. One wonders if any keen traveller ever tried this impossible trip.

But the dust was not allowed to settle, and in the following winter the Town Council requested its Development Association to investigate the possibilities of excursion sailings from Stranraer. The Association decided it could not underwrite an annual charter of an Isle of Man steamer and approached British Railways to see if a through excursion fare could be made available for passengers in 1959 travelling out by the "Margaret" on the morning mail runs on the days she was scheduled to sail on afternoon excursions from Larne. This practice had been employed before and after the First World War, but the reply from British Railways summarily dismissed the request. If passengers from Stranraer wished to sail on these excursions they had to buy

Stranraer Harbour Station and Pier with *Caledonian Princess*

69

(*The Glasgow Herald*, negative K7435

70   Launch of *Caledonian Princess*

(BRITISH RAI

71   First-class lounge, *Caledonian Princess*

Caledonian Princess, in C S P (I S) colours, on trials

Caledonian Princess, right, with *Stena Nordica* and *Antrim Princess* at Stranraer

Shepperton Ferry leaving Larne

75   *Hampton Ferry* on Loch Ryan

76   *Seatern*

77   *Stena Nordica*, in Stena A/B colours, leaving Larne

Antrim Princess arriving at Stranraer

Cars leaving *Antrim Princess* at Stranraer

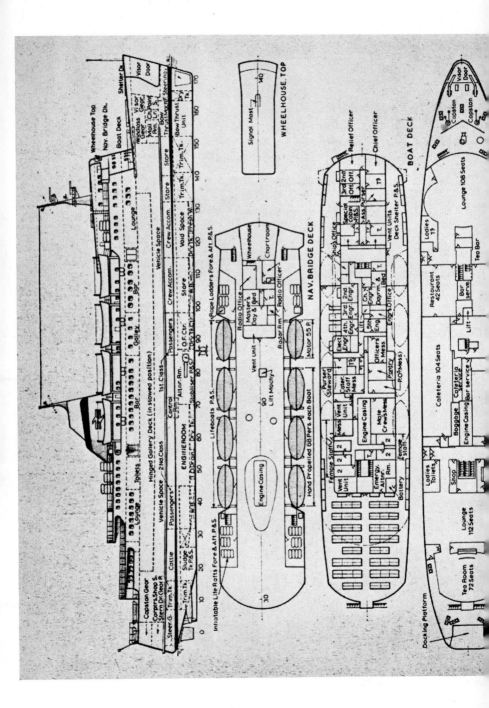

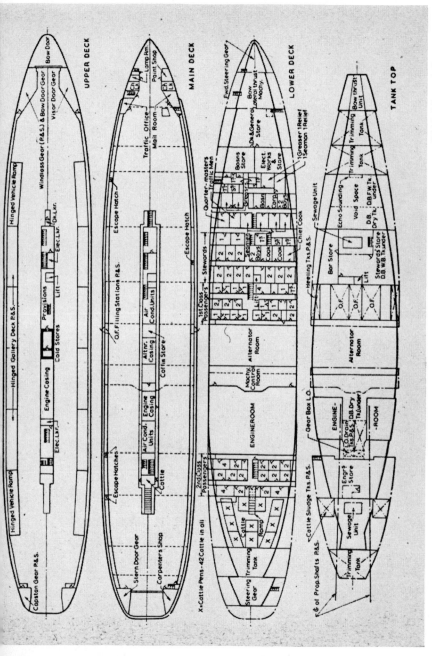

Plans of *Antrim Princess*

(*Shipbuilding and Shipping Record*)

81   Bridge house, *Antrim Princess*, with Captain T. Cree

82   Car deck of *Antrim Princess*

83   *Princess Margaret* at Bangor

(F. C. THORNLEY)

84   *Caledonian Princess* at Douglas, Isle of Man

85   *Ailsa Princess* with *Ardneil* in Ardrossan Harbour

(*The Railway Gazette*)

86   Edward J. Cotton
Manager L & S S Co/L & S S J C

(*The Galloway Advertiser and
Wigtownshire Free Press*)

87   Frederick W. Hutchinson
Stranraer Agent L & S S J C

(*The Galloway Advertiser and
Wigtownshire Free Press*)

88   William McConchie
Manager L & S S J C/L M & S R

(BRITISH RAIL)

89   John F. Sanderson
Manager B T S M (S)

90   C S P (I S) management: Captain George Sinclair (Marine Superintendent),
Alexander Stewart (General Manager), Captain William Smith (Local Manager)

91   Captain Leslie J. Unsworth
Shipping & Port Manager B T S M (S)

92   Captain Eric J. Pollock
Senior Stranraer Master

93
(*above*)
Ailsa Princess
ready for launch

94
(*left*)
First-class,
"crater" bar,
Ailsa Princess

95   *Ailsa Princess* berthing at Larne

96   *Lohengrin* off Larne

97   *Dalriada* on Loch Ryan

98   *Neckartal* off Larne

99   J. Ian Duffin

100   Captain William Close

101   *Ionic Ferry* at Cairnryan, north berth

102   *Free Enterprise III* on Loch Ryan

(TOWNSEND THORESEN CAR FERRIES LTD.;
W. RALSTON LTD., negative 57/141/F)

03   Launch of *Bardic Ferry*

(G. E. LANGMUIR)

4   *Bardic Ferry* at Larne

(AIRVIEWS (M/CR) LTD., negative 41458/2

105   Stranraer Harbour

(AEROFILMS LTD. negative A1326

106   Portpatrick Harbour

an ordinary ticket between Stranraer and Larne. In July 1959, the Town Council requested a Sunday Stranraer–Larne excursion, but this was refused as "too risky". It took the aftermath of the 1960 strike to bring about the reintroduction of the Sunday excursions from Stranraer to Larne and a limited number of Sunday sailings now became part of the summer programme.

CHRISTMAS MAIL

As already mentioned, during the summer months *Princess Margaret* had the assistance of *Hampton Ferry*, but another period of pressure on the route was Christmas, when the mail traffic built up. In 1953, *Princess Margaret* was left to cope alone with the Christmas mail, but in 1954 the B T C cargo ship *Maidstone*, a war-time visitor to Larne, was sent from Heysham to help for a few days between Larne and Stranraer. In 1955, the cargo ship *River Fisher*, which was on long term charter to B T C from James Fisher & Sons Ltd., assisted at Larne, while in 1956, *Sound Fisher*, of the same fleet, was despatched to Larne but was so delayed by stormy weather that she arrived two days late and gave only two round trips between Stranraer and Larne. Three weeks later while on a voyage from Lyness, in the Orkneys, her cargo of scrap metal shifted and *Sound Fisher* sank four miles off the Caithness coast. Her crew were rescued by trawlers and landed safely at Wick.

Much of the 1957 Christmas mail was routed via the Belfast–Stranraer container/cargo service then operating, and *Stream Fisher* and *Firth Fisher* each made a trip with mail. In subsequent years no assistance was given at Stranraer for the Christmas mail, since the bulk of the traffic was routed via new container ships operating between Heysham and Belfast.

A CONTAINER SERVICE

In the 1950s the B T C moved much of its cargo across the Irish Sea by means of chartered tonnage. In May 1955, the B T C had eleven cargo ships on charter and many of these came from the fleets of James Fisher & Sons Ltd., of Barrow-in-Furness, and its subsidiary, Seaway Coasters Ltd. The Fisher boats had black hulls with a yellow line and red boot-topping. Their funnels were yellow with black top and a black "F" on a broad white band. For some years they had been used on the Belfast–Heysham cargo service. This marked the beginning of the use of containers and these ships were adapted for their carriage.

Stranraer was added to the network in April 1954 when, on the night of Tuesday, 6 April, *Stream Fisher* arrived at Stranraer from Belfast with a cargo of containers. For the next couple of months, *Stream Fisher* sailed across to Stranraer each week. Late in May, the ship most closely associated with the Belfast–Stranraer route, *Seatern*, made her first call at Stranraer. For a few months in the summer of 1954, *Seatern* operated on a weekly Stranraer–Belfast–Heysham–Holyhead–Dublin roster. This was not typical of the rostering, and the usual pattern was for two ships to be based at Belfast and while concentrating on the service to Fleetwood (Heysham until October 1954), they also gave crossings to Stranraer.

The frequency of the Stranraer trips was variable. Some months there might be only two or three, while other months could have as many as thirteen.

L

The most frequently occurring number of crossings per month is eight—ten months out of the fifty-two during which the service operated. As well as *Seatern* and *Stream Fisher*, other units of the Fisher fleets crossed between Belfast and Stranraer.

At a meeting in London in May 1955, Mr. J. L. Harrington, Chief Officer (Marine and Administration) of the B T C, discussed the future of the cross-channel cargo boat and revealed that the B T C were considering designs of purpose-built container ships, especially for routes where train ferries were not possible. The obvious routes were those linking Ireland and Britain where the differences in the railway gauges had always ruled out train ferry operations. Less than a week later, at a luncheon in Belfast, the chairman of the London Midland Area Board of British Railways announced that, as well as the three new passenger/cargo ships then being built for the Belfast–Heysham overnight route, the fleet was to be augmented by two vessels specially designed to carry containers. A new berth was to be built at Belfast and berths at Heysham and Stranraer were to be modified for the container ships. In 1955, over 5,000 loaded containers were handled by the chartered ships through Stranraer and almost an equal number of empty containers.

The first of the purpose-built container ships, *Container Enterprise*, was launched from the Troon yard of Ailsa Shipbuilding Co. Ltd. in February 1958 and sailed on her maiden voyage from Heysham to Belfast on Monday, 21 April 1958. By this time the plans to include Stranraer in the container ships' route had been quietly dropped and the ships were to concentrate on the 125-mile passage between Heysham and Belfast in preference to a journey a third of that length between Stranraer and Belfast. The ships' design allowed sixty-eight large containers to be accommodated and little assistance was thereafter required from the chartered Fisher ships on the Heysham route.

At the beginning of May 1958, *Race Fisher*, a comparative stranger to the route, took over at Belfast from *River Fisher*, and the service to Stranraer was stepped up to a frequency of a sailing from each end every alternate day. This greatly increased service lasted less than four months. On Thursday, 14 August 1958, *Container Venturer* was launched at Troon, and by coincidence this was the day of the last arrival by *Race Fisher* at Belfast from Stranraer. Unannounced, the container service between Belfast and Stranraer was terminated. *Race Fisher* continued to give occasional sailings from Heysham to Belfast, but following the maiden voyage by *Container Venturer* from Heysham on Tuesday, 14 October 1958, *Race Fisher* appeared on the route only infrequently when assistance was required or one of the two new ships was absent for refit.

Apart from minor delays caused by weather, the only serious disruption to the Belfast–Stranraer service was brought about by a dock strike in June 1955. The service was suspended between the sailings from Belfast by *Firth Fisher* on 31 May and 20 June. To clear the backlog, six sailings were given in the remaining ten days of June: two by *Firth Fisher* and four by *Seatern*. In July 1954, possibly because of local holidays, only two crossings were made, both by *Seatern*.

An interesting development in the career of one of the regular Stranraer–Belfast cargo ships was reported in the magazine *Irish Shipping*. On 18 December 1965, *Stream Fisher* left Barrow for Italy after conversion into an atomic-fuel carrier. The alterations included the installation of a refrigeration hold to carry fifty-ton flasks of fuel and a 15 inch thick steel barrier to protect the crew. For six months of the year, *Stream Fisher* was to bring the fuel from Anzio in Italy to Barrow, while for the remainder of the year she would revert to normal tramping duties.[177]

The other regular Belfast–Stranraer cargo ship, *Seatern*, was sold in 1960 to Finnish operators.

STRANRAER TO BELFAST — BY AIR

While the British Transport Commission were considering and reconsidering a replacement for *Princess Victoria*, competition came from an unexpected quarter—the air. Stranraer came near to receiving a commercial air link with Ireland when, in 1933, Midland & Scottish Air Ferries Ltd. investigated Stranraer as a mid-way point for its intended Glasgow–Belfast service. At the end of the day, Campbeltown was selected.

From the mid-1930s, air transport had provided a measure of competition to the Stranraer route, but the L M & S R, like the other major railway and coastal shipping undertakings, had substantial interests in the main airline companies. For example, in Scottish Airways Ltd. the L M & S R had a 60 per cent financial stake, the other 40 per cent being shared equally by David MacBrayne Ltd. (thus giving the L M & S R a further 10 per cent interest through its 50 per cent holding in the capital of David MacBrayne) and the North of Scotland, Orkney & Shetland Shipping Co. Ltd.

Towards the end of the Second World War, the Minister for Civil Aviation issued a White Paper laying down the Government policy of increased co-operation in the area of civil air transport. The multiplicity of companies was to be replaced by three corporations covering Commonwealth, Foreign, and European and internal U.K. routes. Thus, British European Airways was conceived and the railway companies were to nominate four of the eleven members of the Board and their financial participation was to be up to 49 per cent of the £5 million capital.[178] Before the end of 1945, however, a general election resulted in a Socialist Government. The scheme for three separate corporations was accepted, but now the over-riding principle was state ownership. Accordingly, the Civil Aviation Act of 1946 gave birth to a nationalised British European Airways. Initially this corporation took over the internal and European air routes of the British Overseas Airways Corporation, but in 1947, B E A began to operate the services of the various aviation companies owned by the soon-to-be-nationalised railway companies.

Thus, the B T C found itself in competition with its nationalised neighbour, B E A. But the competition was muted. Operating licences were issued to private companies, but it is only in recent years that the independent airlines in Britain have been involved to any extent in internal or international scheduled flights. For many years the bulk of their traffic consisted of trooping and charter work. In 1956, for example, 65 per cent of the U.K. independent airlines' traffic came from trooping, while general charter work accounted for a further 12 per cent. Internal and international scheduled services (including vehicular air ferries) produced only 9 per cent.[179] Most travellers crossing the Irish Sea—our primary area of concern—still preferred the leisure and comfort of the sea crossing to the much shorter but more expensive journey through the clouds.

However, the threat to the Stranraer sea route in 1955 was very real, since it offered a short-hop scheduled service, not only for passengers and light freight, but also for cars. In November 1954, Silver City Airways Ltd., a member of the British Aviation Services Group (a private concern, with the Peninsular and Oriental Steam Navigation Group as its main shareholder) had applied to the Air Transport Advisory Council for a licence to operate up to twelve vehicle and passenger services each day between West Freugh (near Stranraer) and Newtonards, one of Belfast's airports.

In December 1954, there was a hint of potential supremacy of air over sea when, two days before Christmas, nearly three hundred passengers were stranded at Stranraer, since *Princess Margaret* could not sail on account of a gale. At two o'clock in the afternoon it was announced that the "Margaret" would not sail that day. One passenger, on a short holiday from Persia, hoping to spend Christmas at Carrickfergus, quickly gathered the required quota of thirty-two and chartered a plane to fly from Glasgow (Renfrew) Airport to Belfast. He would be home in Carrickfergus in time for a late tea. The following day, another five hundred joined the "Margaret" but the train from London was delayed for over two hours and the ship tied up at Larne two-and-a-half hours late.

Before the air service started, further consideration was given to the Wigtownshire base, and the war-time bomber base of Castle Kennedy was selected in preference to West Freugh. Workmen soon set about preparing the buildings at Castle Kennedy, and on 17 February 1955, the first plane for ten years landed there when a trial run was made.

The operation of the Stranraer (Castle Kennedy)–Belfast (Newtonards) service was entrusted by British Aviation Services to its subsidiary, Silver City Airways. S C A had entered the cross-channel air ferry business in 1948 when, in July, the first flight was made between Lympne, in Kent, and Le Touquet carrying cars and passengers. The Stranraer–Belfast service was officially opened on Thursday, 7 April 1955, when a party crossed over to Ireland on a Dakota and the Under-Secretary of State for Scotland crossed in a Bristol Freighter—the mainstay of the S C A fleet. As if to remind the air operators that they too were at the mercy of the weather, the party could not return to Stranraer until the Friday morning because of fog. Initially the service was to be three flights each way daily (except Sunday) with a Bristol Freighter carrying three cars which entered through the nose by means of clamshell doors. Between fifteen and forty-eight passengers could be carried, depending on the number of cars on board. On 17 June 1955, a complementary daily service was instituted by S C A between Liverpool (Woodvale) and Belfast.

The demand for the 15–20 minute crossing was greater than expected, and from 1 July 1955, the Bristol Freighter 170s were sometimes crossing fourteen times a day between Stranraer and Belfast and the 1,000th car crossed with S C A on 3 August 1955. During July alone over 500 cars and nearly 1,500 passengers used the S C A service. In 1955, 2,100 cars and 5,500 passengers were carried on the route. During the first winter, 1955–56, a single-daily service operated. The rates on the S C A flights were higher than those applying on the steamer crossing.

In the spring of 1956, Manx Airlines Ltd. (absorbed in August 1956 into the British Aviation Services Group) applied for permission to operate a service between Stranraer (Castle Kennedy) and Isle of Man (Ronaldsway), and so on 6 August, Galloway and the Isle of Man were once again linked. A Bristol Freighter 170 gave a daily round trip on the twenty-five minute journey. In 1957, the service started on 1 June and four trips a week were planned between Stranraer and the Isle of Man, with a connecting coach from Glasgow which had been tried experimentally in 1955 and now became standard practice. The coach travelling from Glasgow via Ayr and Kilmarnock connected at Castle Kennedy into flights for both Belfast and the Isle of Man.

Judging from the carryings achieved, the services linking Stranraer to Belfast and the Isle of Man were successful, but pressure on the S C A fleet was being experienced on the English Channel and the owners of the airport at Castle Kennedy were advised by S C A that they would not be resuming their services from there in the summer of 1958.

Whether the S C A operations had any effect on the Stranraer–Larne sea link is an open question. Certainly it did not precipitate any decision on building a replacement for the lost *Princess Victoria*. Perhaps the special reduced fares introduced for cars on *Hampton Ferry* in the summer of 1956 cannot even be taken as acknowledgment by the B T C of the existence of the competition from S C A.

PROMISES AND SECOND THOUGHTS

Following the loss of *Princess Victoria* in January 1953, various temporary arrangements were made: the vehicle flow was covered during the summer months by bringing the spare train ferry *Hampton Ferry* from Dover; the freight traffic was aided by the container service from Belfast employing *Seatern* and her consorts. But as time went on, the people of Stranraer and Larne began to suspect the B T C wished the two towns would quickly forget about the need for a permanent solution.

There were plenty of red herrings. In 1956, it was announced that there was to be consultation between the Ministry of Transport and the Home Office about the feasibility of constructing a tunnel between Scotland and Ireland giving connection by rail, and possibly road. The idea was not new and there had been several plans drawn up in the nineteenth century for a link under the sea bed. The consultation of 1956 got no farther than the earlier plans, but it was an interesting, if time-wasting, diversion.

There were also plenty of promises of a new ship for Stranraer, but high level officials made statements that subsequent events did not bear out. In May 1955, the chairman of the London Midland Region of the B T C said in Belfast that the Commission had arrangements well advanced for the replacement of *Princess Victoria* by another vessel of the stern-door type. In November 1955, Mr. A. L. Pepper, District Marine Manager at Stranraer, elaborated on the earlier statement when he said the replacement would be larger than the "Victoria". She would have stabilisers and also berths for two hundred passengers. Mr. Pepper went on to make what turned out to be a slight understatement when he remarked, "It will be some time before she is available for service". Yes, indeed—six years!

It did not go unnoticed that capital was being spent on areas of the B T C's activity other than Stranraer. On the Irish Sea routes alone, three new passenger/cargo ships were delivered in 1956 for the overnight Heysham–Belfast route. Two container ships were delivered in 1958 for the same route.

In 1955, Atlantic Steam Navigation Co. Ltd., then a wholly-owned subsidiary of the B T C, ordered two vehicle-carrying ferries for the Preston–Larne/Belfast routes. These ferries were to be greatly superior to the chartered tank-landing craft hitherto employed. The first of the two new ships, *Bardic Ferry*, was launched at Dumbarton by Wm. Denny & Bros. Ltd. on 5 March 1957. Unlike the "Empire" class tank-landing craft, *Bardic Ferry* had very good accommodation for 55 passengers. She was fitted with Denny–Brown stabilisers and could carry nearly a hundred vehicles compared with the sixty of the "Empire" ships. In *Bardic Ferry* the door was in the stern of the vessel (another difference when compared with the "Empire" ships where the doors were in the bow) and when lowered served as the link between ship and shore. Access to the upper deck for freight was by crane. 2 September 1957 saw *Bardic Ferry* on her first commercial crossing from Larne to Preston.

This last development was especially disturbing. It was not disputed that Belfast needed new ships for its overnight service to Heysham, since the three ships on the run were approaching their thirtieth birthday and urgently required replacing. Also, the container service with the chartered Fisher boats was still operating between Belfast and Stranraer and there had been a statement that the two new container ships would include Stranraer in their rosters just as it had been included since 1954. But funds being made available for new drive-on/drive-off tonnage before any progress had been made with a drive-on/drive-off ship for Stranraer could only mean one thing. The question of a replacement for the "Victoria" was open.

Concern was being aired during 1956 in Stranraer over certain ambiguous statements being made about the railway line between Girvan and Stranraer, and after a meeting in September with Mr. James Ness, General Manager of the Scottish Region of British Railways, the Town Council of Stranraer were no happier. The Town Council came away from their meeting with the impression, however, that the weak link in the Glasgow–Stranraer–Larne–Belfast chain was the railway on the Irish side and British Railways were considering the introduction of diesel multiple units on the Glasgow–Stranraer route.

In October, a deputation from Larne Town Council were assured that there was no question of the Belfast–Larne line closing in the foreseeable future. Mr. Ness then said (still October 1956) that no decision had been taken about the new ship, but if a suitable alternative route could be found for boat trains to Glasgow the Stranraer–Girvan line would close.

The matter became increasingly confused, but it was clear that a new ship at Stranraer could only come after a fight. It was ironic that in the year the route came under question *Hampton Ferry*'s season had to be extended into October because of traffic demands. During the normal summer months' service, the cars carried by *Hampton Ferry* had leapt from 2,500 in 1953 to 6,600 in 1956. Stranraer Town Council said that what was wanted was an all-year-round drive-on/drive-off service with fast diesel train connections between Stranraer and Glasgow. They also saw a twice-daily service as an integral part of this scheme. This provoked a strong denial in early November from Mr. Ness that there was any question of the shipping service closing and he now promised "something better than before".

This produced a rather hollow laugh at Stranraer after years of procrastination and a cartoon appeared in the local press showing a railwayman sleeping at his desk with plans of a paddle steamer with sails flapping in the breeze and the caption, "We're pressing on with the designs of the new Stranraer–Larne boat".

At the end of November 1956, when Mr. A. L. Pepper was making a presentation to two retiring members of the crew of *Princess Margaret*, he re-stated his superior's remarks and promised that an announcement of the new ship would be made before long. "If a modern vessel had been in service at present", he said, "recent statements about closing the Larne–Stranraer route would not have been made. There is nothing to beat the short sea route and I foresee a big future for it". In January 1957, the B T C announced that it had approved the provision of a new passenger and vehicle vessel for the Stranraer route. A contract was to be placed as soon as possible.

It looked as if the battle had been won. Certainly the route was popular and records were being broken each year. But after the January announcement time passed by and nothing seemed to be happening, though in August 1957 Sir Brian Robertson, chairman of the B T C, reassured the public that the new ship was at design stage.

At a meeting of Stranraer Town Council in September 1958, it came as a bombshell to hear that the keel of the ship was now not to be laid. A local carrier, in all innocence, had written to the Harbour Office at Stranraer asking about facilities for lorries between Stranraer and Larne. The reply from the harbour was to the effect that there was to be no new ship. A letter was sent to the B T C in London asking for an explanation of this latest about-face. The reply read, "Early in 1957 the Scottish Area Board announced that the British Transport Commission had approved the provision of a new passenger and vehicle carrying vessel for the Stranraer–Larne route. In view of the general financial position of the commission and recent trends in Irish traffic the economic justification for the new ship intended for this route is at present being re-examined".

A year later, almost to the day, an announcement came that a new vessel was, after all, to be built and would enter service in 1961. This was only after much lobbying within the corridors of Whitehall and the B T C. When the new vessel sailed into Loch Ryan the flag at her mainmast bore not the lion of the B T C but the lion rampant of the Caledonian Group.

CHAPTER FOURTEEN

Caledonian Steam Packet Company
(Irish Services) Limited

IT was on a cold, wet, blustery February evening in 1961 that a friend of the writer was on the pier at Stranraer to meet *Princess Margaret* on her arrival from Larne. A dozen or so passengers scurried ashore through the rain. Then Alexander Stewart, the man now responsible for the management of the Larne route, came over the gangway and, raising his hat, declared, "You know, we're going to make our fortunes here!" Not many of Alex Stewart's colleagues in the marine departments of the B T C shared his enthusiasm. After being put to the bottom of the list several times, a new ship was to be built for the Stranraer–Larne route and Alex Stewart was given the job of making a commercial success of this capital outlay. When the order for the new ship was announced, a caveat, which was to become a routine for every Stranraer ship subsequently built, was issued that unless she made a reasonable return on capital the vessel would be transferred to another route.

So great was the desire to isolate the results of the Stranraer ship that the operation of the route was transferred to a separate company—Caledonian Steam Packet Company (Irish Services) Ltd. This company was, in fact, a dormant subsidiary of the C S P. Under the name of Clyde & Campbeltown Shipping Company Ltd., it had passed from the control of David MacBrayne Ltd. to the B T C on 1 October 1949. At that date the company operated three small cargo steamers on the Firth of Clyde, but the arrival of the Caledonian car ferries caused the run down of the company and the last ship was sold in January 1958. In March 1951, the shares of the Clyde & Campbeltown Shipping Company had been transferred to the C S P.

CALEDONIAN LION RAMPANT

It was decided to use the shell of the Clyde & Campbeltown Shipping Company as the vehicle for recording the results of the Stranraer route, and in January 1960 the name was changed to the more suitable, if cumbersome, Caledonian Steam Packet Company (Irish Services) Ltd. Even before it had taken over responsibility for the Stranraer route it was decided that the company should revert to being a direct subsidiary of the B T C in case the company should earn substantial profits which could be siphoned off and set against the unprofitable C S P operations on the Clyde and Loch Lomond. On 15 November 1960, the issued share capital of C S P (I S) was transferred from C S P to B T C ownership.

A few days later, on 1 December, responsibility for the management of the Stranraer route passed to the C S P (I S). The district manager at Stranraer, Captain William Smith, now reported to Alexander Stewart, general manager and director of C S P (I S) at Gourock, and the various C S P officers and superintendents simply added Stranraer to their duties. The Caledonian house-flag, a yellow pennant with red lion rampant, was flown by the ships on the route. *Princess Margaret,* her winter relief *Princess Maud,* and her summer assistant *Hampton Ferry* were chartered by C S P (I S) from B T C.

A NEW PRINCESS

When the C S P (I S) took over at Stranraer the new ship, ordered in the autumn of 1959 by the B T C, was taking shape, and on Wednesday, 5 April 1961, at the Dumbarton yard of Wm. Denny & Bros. Ltd., *Caledonian Princess* was launched. The name reflected the new Scottish influence in the route and, while a synthetic name, retained the traditional "Princess" nomenclature and spared the Stranraer–Larne route some of the violence shown to ships' names in other areas of railway cross-channel shipping. *Caledonian Princess* was to be owned by C S P (I S) and various features pointed to her membership of the Caledonian Group of companies. In common with the Clyde car ferries, *Arran, Bute, Cowal* and *Glen Sannox, Caledonian Princess* had a white line along the hull just above the rubbing strake. In addition, the Caledonian lions appeared on her funnel and the Caley pennant was placed on her bow.

Caledonian Princess differed in many respects from the two earlier car ferries on the Larne crossing. She was larger, and this was reflected in her superior passenger accommodation. Unlike the earlier ships, *Caledonian Princess* was alone going to cover all the needs of the route. Sleeping accommodation was provided for 82 first-class passengers in one and two-berth cabins and two de luxe cabins, while 94 second-class passengers had the use of two and four-berth cabins. The first-class public rooms included a lounge beneath the bridge. Below the lounge was a bar, and below that again was a dining saloon to seat 50 people. On the same deck was a cafeteria with seating for 140 passengers from the second-class section. An attractive feature of the cafeteria was two 25 feet long murals. The balance of the second-class public accommodation consisted of a lounge on the boat deck which opened on to an open deck aft. Beneath this was a bar and forward of the bar was a lounge with seating for 312 passengers. In all, *Caledonian Princess* could carry 1,400 passengers.

The main deck was given over to the carriage of vehicles and just over a hundred cars or their equivalent could be stowed. Provision was also made on the main deck at the ship's side, port and starboard, for the stowage of motor-cycles and pushbikes. A large hatchway was fitted aft on the promenade deck and could be used for crane loading and unloading from the car deck in an emergency. A water-tight door was fitted at the after end of the car deck and this opened out and upwards. Water spray curtains were fitted on the car deck. One less desirable feature of *Caledonian Princess,* when compared with the earlier Stranraer car ferries, was that the bulk of her sleeping accommodation was situated below the car deck.

Whereas the two earlier car ferries had been fitted with diesel engines, *Caledonian Princess* was to be propelled by turbine machinery. Two water-tube boilers of Babcock & Wilcox design supplied steam to two sets of turbines and these drove the twin screws through double reduction gearing. A bow rudder was incorporated as usual, but for the first time in an Irish Sea ship a lateral bow thrust unit was fitted. Driven by an electric motor, the device had a side thrust of four tons. Further, *Caledonian Princess* was fitted with the prototype of the latest design of activated fin stabiliser. The main difference between this type of stabiliser and the earlier models lay in its method of housing. With the earlier stabilisers the fins were withdrawn by sliding athwartships into the ship's hull, whereas in the new model the fin rotated as it was withdrawn and lay in a fore and aft position, thus saving in athwartship space in the boiler room. Unlike the earlier mail steamers, the new ship had twin rudders. There was a lift from the stewards' store below the car deck to the main galley and the officers' mess.

Nothing had been spared in making the new ship the showpiece of Scottish shipping, and this was reflected in the final cost of £1,840,000—ten times the cost of *Princess Margaret*. This was paid by the B T C and treated as a loan to C S P (I S).

On trials on the Clyde on 27 September 1961, *Caledonian Princess* achieved 20·8 knots and the management at Gourock made provision for her entry into service on Monday, 2 October. The timetable of the new ship was two round trips each day, except Sunday, leaving Stranraer at 0700 and 1430 and from Larne at 1100 and 1850. All sailings had train connections with Glasgow and Belfast and the morning departure and evening arrival at Stranraer connected with London trains. The ship was given 2¼ hours for the crossing.

Trouble developed towards the end of *Caledonian Princess*'s trials and the ship had to be dry docked at Greenock and her entry into service was postponed for a week. The dry dock investigation revealed the need for an extensive repair job and *Caledonian Princess* returned to Dumbarton, where her builders had to open up one of the turbines.

It was seven weeks later, on Saturday, 25 November, that *Caledonian Princess* arrived at Stranraer. The previous day trials had been successfully completed on the Skelmorlie Mile and *Caledonian Princess* berthed at Greenock overnight. At Stranraer on the Saturday she was handed over to representatives of C S P (I S), and during early December the people of Stranraer and Larne were given an opportunity to inspect this long-awaited ship when *Caledonian Princess* had open days at each of the terminals. After years of waiting there was still apprehension about the future of the route, but the C S P (I S) denied rumours that they had plans to transfer the new ship to Ardrossan as soon as facilities were made available at the Ayrshire port.

Princess Margaret set out for the last time to Larne when she left at 0700 on the mail run on Saturday, 16 December 1961. After unloading at Larne, she returned light to Stranraer for the new ship to enter service. The first car to board *Caledonian Princess* was driven by Mr. James Ness, the chairman and managing director of C S P (I S). This was the same Mr. Ness who, with his B T C hat on, had conveyed good and bad news to Stranraer during the saga leading up to the arrival of the new "Princess". *Caledonian Princess* left at 1430 for Larne and took up the double-daily service on the Stranraer–Larne route.

TEMPORARY ARRANGEMENTS

With *Caledonian Princess* expected to enter service at the beginning of October, the charter of *Hampton Ferry* by C S P (I S) was extended beyond 9 September, the normal date for the summer daylight service to have ended. Thus there was to be no break in drive-on/drive-off facilities on the route. So from 9 September 1961, *Hampton Ferry* continued to sail but now leaving

Larne at 0900 and Stranraer at 1630. Because of overhaul commitments at Dover it was impossible for the train ferry to remain north much past the end of September, and when *Caledonian Princess* ran into trouble on her trials provisional arrangements were made to bridge what was hoped to be the few days between the departure of *Hampton Ferry* and the arrival of *Caledonian Princess.*

As the timetable for the new "Princess" called for two double trips each day, it was decided to have *Princess Margaret* attempt this roster until the new ship arrived. The "Margaret" was given a couple of days off for maintenance prior to taking up the daily double service, when on 1 and 2 October *Hampton Ferry* gave two double runs. *Hampton Ferry* then sailed for Dover on the morning of 3 October, having waited until the last possible moment. She had managed, more or less, to maintain the schedule of the double runs because she was drive-on/drive-off, but the "Margaret" did not fare so well, since the turn-rounds were quite inadequate for handling cargoes and cars on and off by cranes.

The delay in the delivery of the new ship was now seen to be weeks rather than days, and from Monday, 9 October, *Princess Margaret* returned to the usual winter sailings of 0700 from Stranraer and 1850 from Larne. On Sunday, 8 October, *Princess Margaret* had to cross light to Larne to give an afternoon return sailing to Stranraer in connection with a soccer international the previous day in Belfast. She sailed from Stranraer at 0900 on the Sunday and unloaded the balance of cargo at Larne before bringing the football supporters back to Scotland. Because of the short turn-rounds during the previous hectic week some of the cargo had crossed and re-crossed the Irish Sea several times.

Further embarrassment was caused by the non-arrival of *Caledonian Princess* at Stranraer because Bertram Mills circus had arranged to cross from Larne to Stranraer on Sunday, 8 October. After giving performances at Stranraer in June the circus had crossed to Ireland. On Sunday, 18 June, *Hampton Ferry* became a Noah's Ark and transported the animals and most of the equipment, while the next day, most of the performers travelled with the "Margaret" on the mail run. The date of the return trip, 8 October, was the same day as the football special given by *Princess Margaret*. No doubt if *Caledonian Princess* had been in service she could have accommodated both the circus and the football fans on one sailing and the balance on either crossing on the Monday, but while the "Margaret" conveyed some of the horses on the Sunday afternoon she could not hope to carry the whole circus and C S P (I S) had to charter a ship for the job. They arranged for one of the A S N Preston–Larne ferries, *Bardic Ferry*, to carry the circus on two trips, one on the Sunday and the second the following day.

With *Caledonian Princess* now in service, *Princess Margaret* lay at Stranraer as stand-by until the close of the year. The "Margaret" left Loch Ryan for the last time on Wednesday, 3 January 1962, and the following day was laid up in the Albert Harbour, Greenock, and advertised for sale. There was much speculation about the fate of *Princess Margaret*, though it was expected that the thirty-one-year-old ship would go to the breakers. Two other possibilities were the Mediterranean, where Greek shipowners had purchased much redundant British coastal passenger tonnage, or a transfer to the Southern Region of the B T C which was still being denied capital for new building pending a decision on the Channel Tunnel project. Interest in this scheme had been renewed in November 1961 when the British and French Ministers of Transport set up a working party to report on the feasibility of a Channel Tunnel or Channel Bridge.[180]

It came as a surprise when the B T C announced in April that the new owners of *Princess Margaret* were the Shun Tak Company Ltd. (very soon to be renamed the Shun Tak Shipping Co. Ltd.), of Hong Kong. The purchase price was reported as £45,000. After being prepared in the Garvel Graving Dock, Greenock, for the 10,000-mile journey out to Hong Kong via the Suez Canal, *Princess Margaret* sailed from the Custom House Quay at Greenock on Thursday, 26 April, at 1100. Passing Gibraltar on 2 May, she arrived at Port Said on 11 May for the journey through the Suez Canal. Aden was reached on 19 May, and it was the last day in May before she set out again, arriving at Karachi on 7 June. Three weeks were spent at Karachi before the voyage was taken up again. The delay at the ports was caused by repairs to boilers damaged by the use of salt water. On 28 June she sailed from Karachi and touching at Cochin, Colombo, Penang and Saigon, *Princess Margaret* reached Hong Kong on 23 July.

After an extensive refit she commenced her new career in December 1964, having received in the previous month her new name—*Macau*. The name was appropriate, as she was to run between Hong Kong and the Portuguese colony of Macau. The port of registry at this time was altered from Stranraer to Hong Kong. The original intention of renaming the ship *Princess Alexandra* was not proceeded with. As a result of the refit, *Macau* presented a changed profile: the boat deck was enclosed, the foremast rose out of the wheelhouse and the mainmast had been removed. A new funnel casing was fitted. A measure of the alterations was the increase in the gross tonnage from 2,838 to 3,670.

Typhoon "Rose" hit Hong Kong on the night of Wednesday/Thursday, 13/14 August 1971, and among the casualties was *Macau*. The vessel was holed and the boiler-room and machinery space flooded. Salvage work was completed a month later and she was towed to the Taikoo Dockyard for survey. *Macau* was then laid up pending the outcome of the insurance claim and in March 1974 was handed over to the shipbreakers.

With *Caledonian Princess* in service there was no longer the need for *Hampton Ferry* to render assistance in the summer. From her first summer, *Caledonian Princess* gave a Sunday service, initially one trip each way in July and August only. *Hampton Ferry* continued at Dover operating on the train ferry service to Dunkirk until 1969. With the arrival of new tonnage, *Hampton Ferry* was relegated to the status of cargo ship in the spring of 1969. In November, British Railways sold her and the following month she was towed from Holyhead, where she had been laid up, to Faslane on the Gareloch on the Clyde. While she was there her new owners, Claxton Ltd., of the Chandris Group, renamed her *Tre-Arddur*. Alterations were made to *Tre-Arddur* at Faslane, but it was 29 June 1971 before she was towed from Faslane to Piraeus, arriving there on 19 July. *Tre-Arddur*'s time with the Chandris Group was short, since in 1973 she was sold for breaking up and arrived under tow at Valencia on 5 July.

Another ship's sailing on Loch Ryan was also finished by the arrival of *Caledonian Princess* on the route in December 1961. About this time of year it had been normal practice for the "Margaret's" younger sister, *Princess Maud*, to return to allow the mail steamer off for six or so weeks for docking and survey.

The "Maud" also acted as stand-by steamer for the Stranraer route, and when, in March 1954, the "Margaret" had to visit dry dock for repairs to a fractured stem, the "Maud" sailed on the mail run for a week. An Ireland v. Scotland football match on 8 October 1955 required special provision on the short sea route, and *Princess Maud* came from Holyhead to augment the service. On the Friday evening she conveyed a full load over to Larne, while *Princess Margaret* took 650 on the Saturday morning mail sailing. Both ships provided return sailings from Larne on the Sunday, the "Maud" sailing early in the morning with 800 and the "Margaret" having her complement on an afternoon crossing. *Princess Maud* did not usually arrive at Stranraer until the very beginning of January, but on her second last occasion north she arrived in late December, which meant that at Christmas 1959, the "Margaret" was off at Holyhead. The passenger traffic through Holyhead was such that *Princess Margaret* had to be pressed into service to take a special sailing from Holyhead to Dun Laoghaire on Christmas Day and a return sailing from Ireland to Holyhead on New Year's Day 1960.

Princess Maud had been spare boat at Holyhead since her transfer there in the autumn of 1946 and served on various routes. She appeared on the Heysham–Belfast route as assisting ship from time to time, as in July 1958 when, on the 12th, she was damaged when in collision with *Duke of Lancaster* in Heysham Harbour, or as replacement, as on Maundy Thursday, 1965 when *Duke of Lancaster* failed. But a new ship for Holyhead–Dun Laoghaire meant the end of the "Maud's" career as a British cross-channel steamer. *Holyhead Ferry I* entered service at Holyhead in August 1965 and the "Maud" made her last sailing to Holyhead on 4 September 1965. A new colour scheme was spreading throughout the British Railways shipping fleets, but *Princess Maud* was allowed to finish her service in the old colours.

Later in the month, *Princess Maud* was sold to Lefkosia Compania, Naviera S.A., of Panama, and renamed *Venus*, her port of registry being transferred from Stranraer to Famagusta in Cyprus. On 17 September 1965, *Venus* left Holyhead for Piraeus, where she was refitted for a cruising programme, and on Wednesday, 15 June 1966, she commenced sailing on a weekly Piraeus–Limassol–Haifa–Piraeus–Brindisi–Piraeus schedule. Part of the refit for *Venus* was the fitting of side doors that allowed drive-on/drive-off facilities (no trouble with tides in her new waters). During her time in the eastern Mediterranean, Aegean and Adriatic, she was managed by Cyprus Sea Cruises (Limassol) Ltd.

Venus's days of cruising in Greek and Cyprus waters were limited, and in the summer of 1969 she was sold to the Danish shipbuilding firm of Burmeister & Wain, who renamed her *Nybø* and used her as an accommodation ship at Copenhagen for shipyard workers. After an absence of nearly twenty-five years she made a brief call at Dover in August 1969 while en route to Copenhagen. After three years at Copenhagen, *Nybø* was sold for breaking up, and on 2 January 1973 left Copenhagen in tow for Bilbao in northern Spain. Arriving at Bilbao on 13 January, *Nybø* found, by a quirk of history, the remains of another ship with Stranraer connections—the train ferry *Shepperton Ferry*.

"SHEPPERTON FERRY" AS RELIEF SHIP

Shepperton Ferry had taken over from *Princess Maud* as Stranraer relief steamer, and each year, from 1962 until 1965, had sailed north to Stranraer for three or four weeks in the early spring to allow *Caledonian Princess* off for a spell in dock. *Shepperton Ferry*'s first appearance at Stranraer came in April 1962 when, under charter to C S P (I S), she took over the double daily service from Monday, 9 April, until Tuesday, 17 April. On Sunday, 8 April, *Caledonian Princess* had sailed from Stranraer and anchored at the Tail of the Bank and in the afternoon proceeded up river to Dumbarton for her first overhaul. In subsequent years *Caledonian Princess* came off for overhaul a month or so earlier and returned to service in March.

Compared with that of *Princess Maud*, the passenger accommodation of *Shepperton Ferry* was simple and her sleeping accommodation extremely limited, but *Shepperton Ferry* had the essential quality of being able to operate as a drive-on/drive-off ferry on the route. Her speed was 4–5 knots less than that of *Caledonian Princess* and the schedule during her period on the run was advertised with eased timings with correspondingly changed train connections. Following the closure of the Denny yard at Dumbarton, *Caledonian Princess* was overhauled for some years at Greenock. On Saturday, 14 March 1964, her overhaul being completed there, she left for Stranraer and was hurriedly put on a delayed 1430 sailing from Stranraer to Larne. *Shepperton Ferry* had managed the outward run at 0700 but the strong easterly wind had caused her to remain tied up at Larne. While on the Stranraer service, *Shepperton Ferry* operated as a one-class ship charging second-class fares. Her last spell at Stranraer was 15 February to 13 March 1965.

Shepperton Ferry's duties as Stranraer relief ship were taken over in February 1966 by *Holyhead Ferry I* from Holyhead. It seems appropriate that the replacement for *Princess Maud* should have become, and now continues to be, the relief steamer on the Stranraer crossing. New tonnage at Dover rendered *Shepperton Ferry* redundant, and on 12 September 1972 she was removed from Dover to the shipbreakers' yard at Bilbao.

DR. BEECHING REPORTS

By the Transport Act of 1962 a new body, British Railways Board, took over the railway services and certain ships and harbours of the B T C as from 1 January 1963. Also established by this Act was the Transport Holding Company, and it had been hoped that all the shipping interests of the B T C might be concentrated in this statutory company and so reflect the decreasing connection between the shipping routes and the railway network. But the Act in fact divided the shipping undertakings between the Railway Board and the Holding Company. The ships owned directly by the B T C, the shares in the C S P, the C S P (I S), the Fishguard & Rosslare Railways & Harbours Company, Société Anonyme de Navigation Angleterre-Lorraine-Alsace, Société Belgo-Anglaise des Ferry-Boats S.A., were vested in the B R B, while the T H C took over the B T C's interest in Atlantic Steam Navigation, Associated Humber Lines Ltd. and David MacBrayne Ltd.

The net result of this unnatural split was that the shipping operations of the former group were supervised by a Board dominated by railway concerns, while the latter group formed a small part of a company composed mainly of road transport interests.

On Wednesday, 27 March 1963, the B R B published a stunning report of a reorganisation of the railway and associated undertakings.[181] Part of the "reshaping" envisaged in the "Beeching Report", as it came to be known, was the closure of both railway lines connecting Stranraer with the rest of the country. The line from Glasgow was to terminate at Ayr and the line from Dumfries, which provided the path for the London trains, was to be closed entirely. The B R B chairman was spared the task of closing the passenger service to Portpatrick—this had been effected in February 1950. By a coincidence the rail link between Donaghadee and Belfast was severed two months later.

Stranraer was shocked by Dr. Beeching's proposals. They had been enjoying the success and extra trade brought to their town by *Caledonian Princess*, and since 1959 the service to Glasgow had been greatly improved by the use of diesel multiple units. An eight car set which brought an excursion to Stranraer from Dundee and Glasgow on Saturday, 26 July 1958, was the first diesel train to arrive at the Harbour Station. Diesels on the public services between Glasgow and Stranraer started officially on Monday 2 November 1959, and cut twenty minutes off the journey. The evening train connection, "The Irishman" train, contained a buffet, the nearest British Railways came to replacing the restaurant car available before the Second World War. It looked as if the prevarication of the mid - 1950s about the train service to Stranraer was over, and with the arrival of *Caledonian Princess* the future of the railway was guaranteed.

But by 1962 the steamer was depending on the railway for less than half its traffic and all the indications were that this dependence would further decrease. Moreover, the trains from the south had been subject to lengthy delays which while annoying in the days of *Princess Margaret* could now cause *Caledonian Princess* to run late for the rest of the day with resulting missed connections in Belfast for Dublin and Londonderry. Some of the delays by the London train were truly monumental—three or four hours was by no means unusual. Although usually occurring in winter, delays in the summer were also experienced.

Christmas 1956 is worthy of record in this connection. On Friday, 21 December, *Princess Margaret* was delayed for five hours waiting for a special train from Birmingham which was bound for Heysham, but became so far behind schedule because of fog—it took eleven hours to reach Crewe— that it was diverted to Stranraer, since it was assumed, apparently, that a delayed sailing from Stranraer was of less consequence than a late Heysham steamer. The train eventually reached Stranraer at 1220. The next day was also difficult. The "Margaret" left at 0720 with passengers from Glasgow and Newcastle but the London train had not arrived. *Princess Margaret* arrived back at Stranraer at 1300 but the London train was still missing. At 1030 a relief train had arrived from Crewe but the London train, due at 0545, did not arrive until 1515. *Princess Margaret* set out at 1535 and did not reach Stranraer on the return journey until 2210. Christmas 1956 was extreme, but with the traffic from the south light, apart from a brief summer peak, the plan to withdraw the London train came as no surprise.

The Transport Act of 1962 laid down the procedure for the hearing of objections to projected railway closures. There were established Area Transport Users Consultative Committees, and one area was Scotland. The members of the T U C C's were appointed by the Minister of Transport and were to advise him in the light of their hearings as to the degree of hardship likely to be caused by a proposed closure.

Objections were received by the T U C C for Scotland once official notice was given of the intention to close the lines between Stranraer and Dumfries and Ayr. In the case of the Ayr line, 184 objections were received, and many of these were from Northern Ireland, and in the case of the Dumfries line, 190 objections came in and nearly half of these originated across the sea. Public hearings were held at Stranraer on 27 February 1964 to consider the Stranraer–Ayr line, and on 28 February to consider the Stranraer–Dumfries link. On both days great stress was laid on the lines being an integral part of the main routes between Belfast and Glasgow and London and not ends of branch lines. Historically, of course, this is perfectly correct, but the situation had changed since the nineteenth century—and this mainly due to the motor-car.

In preparing their report for the Minister of Transport the S T U C C were influenced by the "narrow, tortuous and, in places, precipitous nature of the road between Girvan and Stranraer". In the cases of both the Ayr line and the Dumfries line the committee were of the opinion that considerable hardship would be caused by the proposed closures and reported accordingly. They were of the opinion, however, that no material hardship would be incurred by the closing of the stations between Girvan and Stranraer and between Dumfries and Stranraer.[182.]

The Minister of Transport, after consideration of the S T U C C report, decided that the closure of the Ayr–Stranraer line could not be allowed, and he further required that the link between Stranraer and England be maintained. B R B accepted this ruling and closed, with the exception of Barrhill, all stations between Girvan and Stranraer. As from Monday, 15 June 1965, the line between Dumfries and Challoch Junction was abandoned and trains between England and Stranraer were routed via Mauchline and Ayr. This had the side benefit of providing Ayr with an overnight connection with London and this produced a little extra revenue for the train. At the time of the closure of the Dumfries line there was already in existence a local, stopping bus service between Stranraer and Dumfries, and this was now augmented by three express buses in each direction. With improvements on the London–Crewe line and in traction power, the delays in the arrival of the London train at Stranraer have been greatly reduced.

Part of the 1963 proposals of the B R B had been the closure of Glasgow (St. Enoch) Station and this was given effect on Saturday, 25 June 1966. On the following day, Glasgow (Central) became the Glasgow terminal for the Stranraer trains. Over the years further economic measures were taken on the Ayr–Stranraer section. In October 1970, the section between Dunragit and Castle Kennedy was singled having been double track since 1941, and the same economy effected between Belmont and Girvan in 1974.

PROFITS ON THE INCREASE

While the railway at Stranraer was fighting for survival the shipping side was going from strength to strength. In 1963, 46,000 vehicles and 300,000 passengers passed through Stranraer Harbour. Passenger receipts of £224,000 and vehicle receipts of £357,000 helped to produce a profit on ship's working of £370,000, nearly double the figure for 1961, the last year of *Princess Margaret* and *Hampton Ferry*. While *Caledonian Princess* was only one out of ninety-two ships owned or controlled by B R B at the end of 1963, she contributed 8 per cent of the Board's surplus from shipping, i.e. £370,000 out of £4,699,000.

The results for *Caledonian Princess* raise the old question of "What is a reasonable profit for a nationalised undertaking?" Certainly to some the C S P (I S) profit in 1963 of 48 per cent on gross earnings would appear excessive. (In 1964 it was 53 per cent, in 1965 55 per cent, and in 1966, the year of the seamen's strike, dropped to 41 per cent. These figures include net catering revenue.)

A Committee of Inquiry into shipping services to Northern Ireland, under the chairmanship of Mr. D. V. House, was appointed by the Minister of Transport in April 1962. The House Committee reported in October 1962 and their report makes interesting, if predictable, reading. Included within their terms of reference was consideration of the reasonableness of charges. The conclusion was, "We are satisfied that although occasional liner freight rates may seem high, the general level of these rates and of passenger fares on the services between Great Britain and Northern Ireland is reasonable". One wonders what they would have made of the C S P (I S) figures once *Caledonian Princess* had settled in at Stranraer.

The report is an implicit indictment of the B T C and Coast Lines, the two principal Irish Sea operators, in that *Caledonian Princess* was the only drive-on/drive-off passenger ship in service at the time of the report. Coast Lines' basic routes to Belfast, from Liverpool and Glasgow, were covered by pre-war ships, while B T C's Heysham–Belfast sailings employed three ships young in years but obsolete in design. All these ships required cars and cargo to be loaded and unloaded by cranes and none could accommodate a commercial vehicle of any description other than light vans. Apart from *Caledonian Princess*, the only other service with drive-on/drive-off facilities was on the A S N routes from Preston to Belfast and Larne. All three ships employed had very limited passenger accommodation—*Bardic Ferry* and *Ionic Ferry* carrying 55 and *Empire Nordic* carrying 33—and were primarily intended for commercial traffic.

The House Committee lamely remarked, "Some improvement in the arrangements for the carriage of accompanied cars is desirable, but we recognise that it will not be easy to provide".[183]

STOP-GAP ASSISTANCE

The upsurge in traffic clearly demonstrated the potential to be tapped. After only two summers on the route, *Caledonian Princess* was finding it impossible to cope with the traffic she had generated, and relief was sought. In March 1964, C S P (I S) announced that the cargo ship *Slieve Donard* was to be chartered from B R B for the summer and would assist *Caledonian Princess*. *Slieve Donard* was completed in 1960 by Ailsa Shipbuilding Co. Ltd. at Troon for the Holyhead–Dublin freight and cattle service. *Slieve Donard* was built as a drive-on/drive-off ship, but because of labour disputes at Dublin her stern door remained unused until her spell at Stranraer in 1964. *Slieve Donard* had no passenger certificate and passengers accompanying her load of up to sixty cars had to travel by *Caledonian Princess* and collect their cars at the other side. This led to many complaints, and it was generally admitted that *Slieve Donard* was not an ideal assisting ship. Starting on 6 July 1964, *Slieve Donard* made a daily round trip between Stranraer and Larne until 24 August. The week-end following her withdrawal from Stranraer, *Caledonian Princess* was required to make an additional sailing. This same week-end, *Slieve Donard* broke new ground when, on Saturday, 29 August, she loaded 52 containers of fresh meat and cheese at Waterford for Holyhead. This was the first Waterford–Holyhead sailing for many years.

During 1964, 56,000 cars were carried, an increase of 120 per cent over 1962. Passenger traffic was up by 50 per cent, and in the winter of 1964–65 consideration began to be given to the need to build a second ship for the Stranraer–Larne route. But the Holyhead route was to receive its first car ferry, *Holyhead Ferry I*, in the summer of 1965 and a decision was deferred until it was seen how much traffic the new ferry would draw away from Stranraer. Also an investigation was to be made to determine the prospects of finding winter employment for the second ship. However much C S P (I S) might appeal for a sister for *Caledonian Princess* the reply from B R B was always a counsel of caution because, after all, one swallow doesn't make a summer.

In the meantime, assistance was required for the 1965 summer, and on 19 January, at Larne, it was announced that C S P (I S) had arranged the charter of a commercial car carrier owned by Wallenius Lines of Bremen. The ship, *Lohengrin*, could carry up to three hundred cars but, like *Slieve Donard*, her lack of passenger certificate required all passengers to travel on *Caledonian Princess*, thus taxing passenger accommodation to the limit on busy days. Her charter lasted from 7 June to 25 September 1965, and one round trip from Stranraer was given each day. *Lohengrin* required three hours for the crossing. Her charter was completed as planned and *Lohengrin* returned to West Germany. In January 1970, *Lohengrin*, now sailing as *Zwartkops*, inaugurated South Africa's first car ferry service.

In October 1965, Alex Stewart, general manager of C S P (I S), was in Sweden investigating the possibility of chartering suitable tonnage for the Stranraer route. The decision had been taken to have a second car ferry built for the route but it could not be ready before late 1967, and in January 1966 a stop gap charter was announced. The ship was *Stena Nordica* of Stena A/B, Gothenburg.

A LUCKY CHARTER

Stena Nordica was barely a year old when her charter with C S P (I S) commenced on 28 January 1966. Built in France, she had spent the summer of 1965 trading for her owners on a service between Tilbury and Calais. *Stena Nordica* was to prove a most successful ship on the Stranraer route and she incorporated many features that were to be copied in subsequent Irish cross-channel ships. "Stena's" length was nearly 100 feet less than that of *Caledonian Princess* but her beam was almost the same. The uptakes for her two diesel engines were situated at the sides of the hull and thus allowed a clear car deck of 45 feet width compared with the car deck of *Caledonian Princess*, where the engine-room island broke up the car-deck area. The height of the car-deck, of nearly 14 feet, was in excess of that of *Caledonian Princess*. As well as a stern door, "Stena" had a bow door, and this feature especially proved a boon on the route. In the "Princess" there was no difficulty with cars having to drive up to the bow and then round and off the stern, but with commercial vehicles, especially articulated lorries, the problem of manoeuvring was considerable and often large trucks had to reverse off. Four rows of lorries or 85 cars could be accommodated on the car deck of the *Stena Nordica*, and a further 44 cars could use two removable gallery decks hinged at each side of the car deck.

The accommodation for her 935 passengers, while of simple utilitarian design, was adequate. On the boat deck were two large lounge bars, while on the deck below was a restaurant for 126 passengers and 190 could be seated in the cafeteria on the same deck. Built as a one-class ship, she traded as a two-class ship while at Stranraer, with the first-class passengers having exclusive access to the restaurant and one of the lounges. Two disadvantages with *Stena Nordica* were that she had neither sleeping accommodation for passengers nor stabilisers. Her dummy funnel (containing air conditioning plant) retained the Stena A/B colours—red funnel with white "S" (the tail of which terminated in a sea-horse) and white bands above and below the letter separating the red from a black base and top—until 1967 when the colours of British Railways appeared. Her hull colour was unique to the Stranraer route—white with bright red boot topping.

Stena Nordica arrived at Stranraer late in January 1966 and after completing berthing trials at both Larne and Stranraer, entered service on Monday, 14 February. She was based at Larne and initially gave one round trip each day (apart from Sundays). Thus the route now had three sailings in each direction each day. Extra sailings were given by "Stena" as required and from May to September she doubled her frequency. On summer Sundays, *Stena Nordica* gave a round trip from Larne. On weekdays, *Stena Nordica* left Larne at 0830 and 1530 and Stranraer at 1200 and 1900. "Stena" was able to complete the crossing in 2¼ hours, since what she may have lacked in speed was compensated for in manoeuvrability.

When *Stena Nordica* entered service on 14 February 1966, her consort was another ship new to the route. *Holyhead Ferry I*, a car ferry on the Holyhead–Dun Laoghaire route from the previous August, came to Stranraer and took over the mail roster from 14 February to 24 March 1966 while *Caledonian Princess* was off for overhaul. *Holyhead Ferry I* operated as a one-class ship at second-class fares while on the route. In 1967, *Holyhead Ferry I* returned to relieve first *Stena Nordica* and then *Caledonian Princess* for refit.

Like the previous ships chartered by C S P (I S) for the Stranraer section, *Slieve Donard* and *Lohengrin*, *Stena Nordica* brought her own crew with her with the exception of the purser's and steward's departments, who were local staff. The advantage of this came home very clearly when the National Union of Seamen's strike started on Saturday, 14 May 1966, since the only ships crossing the Irish Sea were those trading under non-British flags, i.e. Fishguard–Cork and Liverpool–Dublin routes of the British & Irish Steam Packet Group and *Stena Nordica* with her Swedish crew. For the duration of the strike *Stena Nordica* gave her double daily sailings but she could offer no catering facilities. The old short-sea route between Portpatrick and Donaghadee saw a measure of use during the strike with fishing boats carrying passengers and cargo across the Irish Sea.

For the duration of the strike *Caledonian Princess* lay at Stranraer. As soon as agreement was in sight *Caledonian Princess* sailed. She left Stranraer at 1830 on 29 June 1966, but she had jumped the gun and the dockers at Larne refused to handle her, as the official union telegram had not been received. *Caledonian Princess*, therefore, had to return to Stranraer. She re-entered service on Saturday, 2 July, and on the following day both she and her consort made two round trips in an effort to clear the traffic.

C S P (I S) SUPPRESSED

During the 1950s no one at railway headquarters had wanted to know about the Stranraer–Larne route. But Alex Stewart proved to be right in his prophecy, "We're going to make our fortunes here!" The profit of £200,000 in 1960 jumped to £370,000 in 1963 and by 1967 the figure was £616,000. Even the seamen's strike over part of 1966 only produced a slight drop, the profit for the year being £559,000. B R B in London now began taking a greater interest in this little goldmine of a route operating from an obscure Scottish loch and controlled by managers based at a small seaside resort on the Clyde coast. Iain MacArthur may be correct when he writes that in the eyes of the B R B the C S P (I S) exercised too much autonomy for its own safety.[184] Certainly in policy matters C S P (I S) had to toe the line and meet B R B requirements, but the remarkable financial results of the route meant some deference had to be shown to the C S P (I S) opinion and this had a nuisance value. Also, the B R B had little direct control over day-to-day matters.

The profits of C S P (I S) soon used up the capital tax allowances available from the cost of *Caledonian Princess* and also the tax losses inherited from the days of Clyde & Campbeltown Shipping Co. and, surprisingly, the profits for 1963 and 1964 were subject to income tax. During these years the losses of the C S P, C S P (I S)'s fellow subsidiary, had become relatively small, and after adjusting for depreciation and capital allowances the figure available as a subvention payment from C S P (I S) to C S P so as to reduce C S P (I S)'s tax liability would have been very small. Thus the C S P (I S) paid £311,000 in income tax on the profits for 1963 and 1964. In 1965 and 1966 the subvention provisions were exercised by making payments to the parent body, B R B. Why use of these provisions was not made in 1963 and 1964 is unclear.

What is clear is that the continuing existence of C S P (I S) as owner and operator of *Caledonian Princess* was a source of administrative and policy inconvenience. As from 1 January 1967, ownership of *Caledonian Princess* was vested in the B R B and control of the route passed to London. Caledonian Steam Packet Company (Irish Services) Ltd. consequently became a dormant subsidiary of B R B. Responsibility for the day-to-day administration of the route remained at Gourock as the C S P were appointed managing agents for the B R B.

A sign of the increasing interest being shown by B R B in the Stranraer route had come early in 1966. When *Caledonian Princess* returned from overhaul in the Garvel Graving Dock, Greenock, on 28 March 1966, the red Caledonian lions had disappeared from her funnel and were left on the quayside. Now the funnel was painted red with the white double arrow insignia of the B R B. When the new B R B ship colour scheme was introduced in 1965, *Caledonian Princess* had appeared in the monastral blue hull, grey masts, narrow white water line and chocolate boot-topping, and minus her extra white line above the rubbing strake, but Caledonian influence had managed to prevent the colour change extending to the funnel, and in 1965 the Caledonian ship at Stranraer shared a common colour scheme with her Caledonian colleagues on the Clyde since the Clyde steamers had adopted lions on their funnels as part of their new colour scheme. Even the chartered *Stena Nordica* was to be touched by the B R B fetish for uniformity. In January 1967, during her overhaul at Greenock, the "Stena" funnel was painted out and the B R B insignia and colours applied. The white hull was left undisturbed.

Despite the reduction in authority the yellow Caledonian pennant still flew on the ferries. But the pennant of the managing agents had a position subordinate to the blue B R B house-flag.

CHAPTER FIFTEEN

Sealink

ON 18 March 1966, a month after *Stena Nordica* took up the service between Larne and Stranraer, C S P (I S) announced that an order had been placed for another vessel for the route. The yard from which every Stranraer "Princess" had come since the 1890 *Princess Victoria*, Wm. Denny & Bros. Ltd., had closed and the order went to Hawthorn, Leslie (Shipbuilders) yard on the Tyne. The plans showed marked differences from *Caledonian Princess of* 1961 and the influence of the Swedish ferry can be detected. The new ship was to be the first in the B R B fleet with stern and bow doors, and for her prime movers the steam turbine gave way to low-slung Pielstick diesel engines which minimised obstruction in the vehicle deck area. The single funnel was placed in the centre line of the ship. On either side of the vehicle deck a gallery deck was fitted which enabled the ship to carry up to 140 cars. The vehicle deck, it was claimed, could be completely unloaded in ten minutes.

A SHIP FROM THE TYNE

A bottle of Irish whisky was broken over the bow of the ship when she was named *Antrim Princess* at her launching on Monday, 24 April 1967. *Antrim Princess* was ready for trials by 20 November, and after a delay caused by gear box trouble she attained 21·3 knots on 28 November 1967. Her French-built diesels gave her a top speed astern of 14·45 knots. *Antrim Princess* left the Tyne on 8 December and berthed at the railway pier at Stranraer two days later. On Monday 11 December, *Antrim Princess* set out for Gourock (the headquarters of her managers) to give a cruise for guests on the following day. But a failure in the oil lubricating system caused the cruise to be cancelled. *Antrim Princess* limped to Gourock and anchored off Kilcreggan while the small Caledonian motor ship *Maid of Skelmorlie* acted as tender.[185] On the 13th, *Antrim Princess* set off on a test run, but water in the fuel cut the trip short and she did not reach Stranraer until 18 December.

The public rooms of *Antrim Princess* were concentrated on two decks, contrasting with the three-deck arrangement of *Caledonian Princess*. In the new ship greater emphasis had been placed on her abilities as a commercial vehicle carrier and this necessitated a vehicle deck of considerable height for its full length. The height restriction was 14½ feet. This loss of part of the third deck for passenger facilities was reflected in her passenger capacity of 1,200, 200 less than the 1961 ship. On the boat deck, *Antrim Princess* originally had a deck bar aft and the rest of this level was given over to officers' accommodation, thus omitting the lounge of *Caledonian Princess* below the navigating bridge. On *Antrim Princess* all the principal catering and lounge areas were concentrated on the shelter or promenade deck. The ship retained the two-class structure, but this time a tea-bar was provided for second-class passengers as well as the restaurant for the first-class passengers. The former could seat 72 and the latter 42. A cafeteria on the port side also formed part of the second-class accommodation and seating was provided for 104, while on the starboard side there was placed the second-class bar. The second-class lounge had reclining seats for 112. The first-class lounge, with seating for 108, was at the forward end of the shelter deck and was fitted with an observation gallery overlooking the bow of the ship, while immediately aft of this lounge was the first-class bar. The finish in the accommodation was of a high standard but lacked the luxurious touch of *Caledonian Princess*.

The accommodation for second-class passengers was skilfully increased in December 1974 when *Antrim Princess* was at Holyhead for overhaul. The after end of the boat deck was enclosed and the large windows fitted were reminiscent of an ocean liner. The area above, on the bridge deck, was now utilised for passengers and fitted with wind deflectors which produced an ideal deck for catching the sun. Despite this increase in accommodation area the passenger certificate remained unaltered.

The original intention had been to leave *Caledonian Princess* as the principal ship on the route and base *Antrim Princess* at Larne. Because of this plan, sleeping accommodation was available for only 66 passengers and was situated, as in the 1961 ship, mostly below the car deck. But on Wednesday, 20 December 1967, *Antrim Princess* took over the mail roster and displaced *Caledonian Princess* to the secondary roster based at Larne. Just before her entry into service, *Antrim Princess* had her first "charter" when a charity reception was held on board as she lay at Stranraer on Saturday, 16 December.

"CALEY" GOES AND "STENA" STAYS

Stena Nordica, replaced by *Caledonian Princess*, lay at Larne as stand-by just in case there were any teething troubles with *Antrim Princess*. The reason for the chartering of "Stena" for the Stranraer route had been to fill in until the ship ordered in March 1966 had entered service, but now that *Antrim Princess* had arrived "Stena" was not returned to her owners but her charter extended as the B R B required every drive-on/drive-off ship they could lay their hands on. In fact it was *Caledonian Princess* that was to leave the route.

Early in 1968 the B R B established the Shipping & International Services Division, a London-based authority which took direct control of all the B R B's Irish and European shipping services. This authority took the same attitude to *Caledonian Princess* as it did to the other units in the B R B fleet and the work of the staff of the C S P at Gourock and at Stranraer was now essentially at the levels of victualling the ships and paying the crew. All matters concerning policy for the Stranraer route and the actual deployment of the vessels was now handled at London. While Gourock may have wished to overinsure on the route by having three vessels on hand, the shipping division had the task of making up for lost time in the job of supplying drive-on/drive-off tonnage for the Irish Sea routes.

Caledonian Princess now embarked on a peripatetic career. From Friday, 5 July, until Thursday, 5 September 1968, she operated on the Holyhead–Dun Laoghaire route, where she partnered the route's regular ship, *Holyhead Ferry I*. The following March, side doors were fitted to give access to the car deck, and from 20 May until 8 July and from 4 August until 11 October 1969, *Caledonian Princess* was on the Fishguard–Rosslare route, where she had as consort *Duke of Rothesay* which had been taken off the Heysham–Belfast route and converted for drive-on/drive-off side-loading work. The reason for the side-loading was the absence until July 1972 of a end-loading berth at Fishguard.

Duke of Rothesay had been transferred to the Rosslare route in 1967. In 1966, *Slieve Donard* had been employed alongside the conventional passenger/cargo steamer *St. Andrew*. As at Stranraer, *Slieve Donard* proved helpful in building up traffic to the level that justified the substantial expenditure involved in providing improved facilities on the route.

From 9 July until 3 August 1969, *Caledonian Princess* had returned to the Holyhead service, as a delay in the arrival of new tonnage on the south coast had prevented *Holyhead Ferry I*'s consort, *Dover*, from transferring north to Holyhead. On the arrival of *Dover* at Holyhead, *Caledonian Princess* returned immediately to Fishguard, where the conventional ship *St. David* had been doing her best to cover up alongside *Duke of Rothesay*.

In April 1970, while receiving her overhaul at Holyhead, a moveable gallery deck was fitted on *Caledonian Princess*'s car deck, and that summer, from early May until the middle of October, she returned to the Fishguard–Rosslare route.

Around November of each of the years 1968 to 1971 inclusive, *Caledonian Princess* returned to Stranraer to allow *Antrim Princess* to be taken in hand at Holyhead for refit and survey. *Stena Nordica* went to Greenock for overhaul when relieved by *Caledonian Princess* for short periods in January and March 1968, April 1969 and April 1970. When not required for other duties, *Caledonian Princess* took over the Larne-based roster while *Stena Nordica* was laid up in Queen's Dock, Glasgow. Such occasions were 26 April to 14 June and 18 September to 28 October 1968, 19 December 1968 to 20 February 1969 and 11 December 1969 to 6 February 1970.

Caledonian Princess also appeared on the Heysham–Belfast overnight route when required. From 16 to 23 February 1970, she helped to maintain the link between Belfast and Heysham, and at this time her consort was *Duke of Rothesay*, which had returned from the Fishguard route to relieve on the Belfast crossing. *Caledonian Princess* remained on the Heysham route until *Duke of Argyll* returned to service after conversion to a drive-on/drive-off stern-loading vessel. Her sister, *Duke of Lancaster*, was similarly treated, and from May 1970 the Heysham–Belfast route was fully drive-on/drive-off, thus completing the conversion of all the passenger routes between Britain and Ireland. The converted "Dukes" were restricted in what they could carry, since the height of the car deck was only 6 feet 6 inches, thus ruling out all commercial vehicles, except small vans. In 1970, *Caledonian Princess* spent most of October on the Belfast station, and in 1971 a few days in March and the month of October were similarly spent.

Following the final departure of *Stena Nordica* from Stranraer, *Caledonian Princess* returned to the Larne roster on Monday, 25 March 1971, and remained there until the arrival of a sister ship for *Antrim Princess*. *Caledonian Princess* sailed on the evening of 6 July 1971 to Fishguard for the summer service. Her last spell on the Stranraer–Larne route was in April 1972 when she relieved the new ship *Ailsa Princess* for her first overhaul at Holyhead. In the summer of 1972, *Caledonian Princess* found employment in new waters when, from 11 May until 20 June, she maintained the joint B R B/

S N C F Newhaven–Dieppe service. Thereafter she returned to Fishguard and settled there, apart from a spell in August 1974, until the summer of 1975 for the all-year-round vehicle and passenger service, where she was assisted by the drive-on/drive-off commercial carriers *Neckartal* and, later, *Preseli*. *Duke of Rothesay*, the pioneer car ferry at Fishguard, had been transferred to the Holyhead–Dun Laoghaire route. To add to the merry-go-round, at the end of her overhaul in 1973, *Antrim Princess* appeared for a day, 15 December, on the Holyhead–Dun Laoghaire service.

Once *Caledonian Princess* had finally bade farewell to Loch Ryan, *Holyhead Ferry I* again became the regular relief ship at Stranraer when she reappeared in November 1972 after an absence of five years. She was not an ideal relief ship. Not only was her sleeping accommodation restricted but, more important, she had no bow door and her vehicle deck, for most of its length, had a height restricting its use to cars only.

CHARTERS FOR PLEASURE AND BUSINESS

For the short time that three ships were associated with the Stranraer–Larne route there were idle moments when other activities less serious than ferrying could be entertained. *Caledonian Princess* took time off the main route on Wednesday, 26 June 1968, when she sailed under charter with an excursion party to Douglas, Isle of Man. The hour of departure from Stranraer was 0900 and the crossing to the Isle of Man took four hours. On Sunday, 4 May 1969, *Antrim Princess* had a similar charter to the Isle of Man. Usually, however, the people of Stranraer had to be content with one or two excursions each year by ships of the Isle of Man Steam Packet Company, and in recent years, on the third Sunday in July, an excursion has been given by an Isle of Man steamer from Stranraer to Douglas. (An annual excursion from Larne to Douglas has also become a regular feature.)

On Saturday, 6 September 1969, a wartime visitor returned to Stranraer and gave an excursion for the local folk. This was the Caledonian turbine steamer *Duchess of Hamilton*, which came from Ayr with a charter party and gave an afternoon cruise from Stranraer round Ailsa Craig.

Gainful employment was found for *Stena Nordica* to take up some of her spare time. On two occasions she relieved the new passenger/vehicular ferry *Lion* of the Burns & Laird fleet on the Ardrossan–Belfast daylight service. Until the arrival of *Lion* in December 1967, this route had been maintained by conventional passenger/cargo ships during the summer months only. *Lairds Isle* did not finish the 1957 season but was withdrawn on Tuesday, 6 August and *Irish Coast*, a twin-screw motor ship, took over the following day. In the press it was stated that *Lairds Isle* was to be laid up for nine months while *Irish Coast* was tried out as a possible successor. The new ship must have proved an instant success, for in October *Lairds Isle*'s sale to British Iron & Steel Corporation for scrapping at Troon was announced. In August 1956, there were plans to use *Irish Coast* as a cruise ship in 1957, sailing from Liverpool to the west of Scotland, in succession to the cruise ship *Lady Killarney*, which was to be withdrawn at the end of the 1956 season, but these plans were put aside.

Irish Coast, built in 1952 by Harland & Wolff at Belfast, became a maid-of-all-work in the Coast Lines fleet and she relieved on the Glasgow overnight routes to Belfast and Dublin and also on the Liverpool–Belfast and Fishguard–Cork routes as required. A small number of cars was carried by *Irish Coast* when she was operating the Ardrossan–Belfast daylight run and these had to be loaded by crane.

In the summer of 1965 her younger sister *Scottish Coast* switched from the Glasgow–Dublin route and took over the Ardrossan service. *Scottish Coast* had been fitted with a make-shift lift in her cargo hold and could accommodate 25 cars on the daylight crossing. In August of the same year Burns & Laird invited tenders for a drive-on/drive-off passenger/vehicular ferry for an all-the-year-round service between Ardrossan and Belfast, and on 1 December it was announced that a vessel with bow and stern doors had been ordered from Cammell Laird & Co. (Shipbuilders & Engineers) Ltd. of Birkenhead with delivery late in 1967. *Scottish Coast* battled on in the meantime. *Lion* opened the service on Wednesday, 3 January 1968, and this put the last nail in the coffin of the conventional overnight services between Glasgow and Ireland.

The alternate day passenger/cargo service to Londonderry had been abandoned after Saturday, 10 September 1966. From 2 January 1968, following the introduction of *Lion*, the frequency of the overnight service between Glasgow and Belfast was reduced to thrice-weekly, while the last sailing to Dublin from Glasgow was on Saturday, 10 February 1968, by *Irish Coast*. *Irish Coast* was sold to Greek buyers in August. The Glasgow–Belfast service was maintained by *Scottish Coast* and the two ships built in 1936 as a reply to *Princess Margaret* and *Princess Maud* were withdrawn. On Friday, 29 September 1967, *Royal Scotsman* had made her last sailing from Belfast, while *Royal Ulsterman* made her last departure from Belfast on Saturday, 30 December 1967. Both ships were sold for further service. The Glasgow–Belfast service was withdrawn with the sailing from Glasgow on the evening of Monday, 30 September 1968, but reintroduced on Friday, 20 June 1969, for the summer on a thrice-weekly frequency, and *Scottish Coast* made the last sailing from Belfast on Saturday, 30 August. This was the end of the Glasgow–Belfast service. *Scottish Coast* was laid up and later followed other Coast Line group ships when she sailed for the Mediterranean, where she traded for Greek owners.

Thus, all the Scottish passenger and much of the cargo traffic for Burns & Laird passing between Scotland and Ireland was concentrated on the Ardrossan–Belfast daylight route. The use all year round of Ardrossan Harbour by a ship of the size of *Lion* was a gamble, since the harbour approaches are made impossible under certain weather conditions and there is little room for manoeuvring within the confines of the harbour. It was not unusual for weather to interfere with *Lion*'s sailings—on her very first day, Wednesday, 3 January 1968, her departure from Ardrossan was delayed for nearly 1½ hours. And even the harbour did not always protect *Lion* from the storms: twelve days later, early on Monday, 15 January, she was torn from her moorings during a severe gale and the belting and some plating badly damaged which caused *Lion* to be withdrawn until 5 February for repairs. On occasions no attempt was made to enter Ardrossan Harbour and the vessel either sheltered off Arran or berthed at Greenock Custom House Quay where at least passengers, if not vehicles, could be landed. In the design of the C S P's drive-on/drive-off ramp at Gourock provision was made for *Lion* to call when required. Berthing trials were made at Gourock on Sunday, 19 September 1971, and the first "real" call was in the early hours of Wednesday, 20 October 1971.

During *Lion's* first overhaul, from Monday, 18 November to Saturday, 7 December 1968, the replacement ship was the Danish passenger/vehicular ferry *Travemünde*, but in 1969 this duty fell to *Stena Nordica*. On the morning of Sunday, 26 October 1969, *Stena Nordica* moved from Stranraer to Ardrossan and the following day commenced sailing to Belfast while *Lion* was at Harland & Wolff, Belfast, for refit. There was a disparity in speed between the ships, to the disadvantage of the Stranraer vessel, and "Stena" did not reach Belfast until 1530, an hour late, on her first day. Her departure from Belfast was 45 minutes late at 1715 and she reached Ardrossan 90 minutes late at 2230. Her performance on Tuesday, 28th, was of the same calibre, but on the Wednesday the weather was such that "Stena" did not attempt to enter Ardrossan Harbour until the following morning. The passenger sailing was cancelled and a cargo run was given in the afternoon with an arrival back at Ardrossan early on Thursday morning. On the Thursday and Friday the service was carried out by *Stena Nordica*, and on the evening of Friday, 31 October, "Stena" returned to Stranraer and *Lion* took over on the Saturday morning.

Despite this patchy performance, *Stena Nordica* was invited back in 1970 and relieved *Lion* from Friday, 2 October, to Saturday, 10 October. On 1 October, *Lion*, on the 1630 from Belfast, was unable to enter Ardrossan Harbour and had to spend the night off Arran and she berthed at Custom House Quay, Greenock, at midday on the 2nd. She then sailed to Ardrossan and berthed at 1900 to unload vehicles and freight and left later that evening for the shipyard at Belfast. *Stena Nordica* left Stranraer on the evening of Thursday, 1 October, but was also unable to negotiate the harbour entrance at Ardrossan and so joined *Lion* lying in the shelter of Arran. "Stena" berthed at Ardrossan at 2115 on Friday, 2nd, thus effectively cancelling the sailing on that day. The service also had to be cancelled on 6 October when the 1630 on the previous day had to be diverted because of weather to Custom House Quay, Greenock.

When it came time for *Lion's* overhaul in 1971, *Stena Nordica* had left Stranraer for home and the commercial carrier *Saaletal* operated in *Lion's* absence. *Saaletal* was later to be employed on the Stranraer route in the capacity of a relieving ship. While *Stena Nordica* was at Ardrossan in 1969 and 1970 her place on the Larne roster was taken by *Caledonian Princess*.

NEW SHORE FACILITIES

With the great increase in traffic in the 1960s and the profits being earned the shore facilities for passengers and staff were not overlooked. Prior to the arrival of *Caledonian Princess*, much strengthening had been done at Stranraer railway pier, where about 300 yards of wooden piling had been replaced by concrete piling in early 1960. Two years previously the area around the ramp had been rebuilt and wooden piles were removed to make way for steel piling. In January 1965, plans were announced for a new terminal building at Stranraer. Prior to this time, passengers had to wait in the Harbour Station with its small waiting room, while the staff were accommodated in either the station building or small, wooden huts scattered about the pier. The new building was erected at the road end of the neck connecting the pier to the shore and incorporated a waiting area, a booking office, news-stall and tea-bar. The staff of Captain William Smith, now titled Area Marine and Rail Manager following a rationalisation of duties at Stranraer, had their office accommodation in the new terminal building. A fine addition to the Stranraer–Larne facilities, it was opened on Wednesday, 17 November 1965. An extension to the terminal was commissioned on Monday, 8 July 1974. The cost of the addition was in the region of £45,000, £10,000 more than the original terminal built only eight-and-a-half years previously.

Around 1970, a store, workshop and office accommodation was built beyond the end of the platforms of the Harbour Station. This was primarily for the resident Superintendent Engineer.

The Harbour Station area at Larne had become very congested as a result of the great increase in passenger and vehicle traffic, and in the environs of the mail berth a passenger terminal was built with a waiting area, booking-office, news-stall and tea-bar. There was also accommodation for harbour staff and representatives of motoring organisations. The building was completed almost exactly two years after its counterpart at Stranraer and was opened to the public on Tuesday, 7 November 1967. The cost of £45,000 was borne jointly by the Irish Ministries of Development and Commerce and Larne Harbour Ltd. At Larne there is a main road running parallel to the line of the shore and under the old arrangement this had to be closed when a train used the Harbour Station, as a hinged platform swung round and lay across the road since the railway crossed this road on the level at a right angle. In other words, the road ran right through the middle of the station and naturally this arrangement gave rise to great inconvenience. The trains now used the platform section on the inland side of the road and thus avoided the need to close the road. A platform was rebuilt on the shore side of the road and was so designed that a three-coach diesel multiple unit could lie at the platform without obstructing the road.

Work started at Stranraer late in 1970 on replacing the car ramp. This was the ramp built in 1939 for *Princess Victoria* and which had proved such a boon during the war. The new ramp, to be able to take the wider loads that could now be accommodated on the ferries operating the route, was to be installed over the week-end 13–15 March 1971, and the bulk of the work was scheduled for the Sunday when there would be no sailings. Unfortunately, on the morning of Sunday, 14 March, a crane toppled over and the commissioning of the ramp had to be postponed for $13\frac{1}{2}$ hours. This was a busy day, since *Antrim Princess* paid an unusual visit to Belfast for docking to allow shaft repairs to be carried out. On Tuesday, 23 March, the flap of the ramp collapsed and ended up on the sea bed and *Stena Nordica* took a run from Larne to Ardrossan in the evening. On the following day, *Antrim Princess* maintained a passenger service between Stranraer and Larne, while *Stena Nordica* made two sailings between Ardrossan and Larne. The cost of the new ramp was £110,000.

GLASGOW VERSUS LONDON

The legislators at Westminster were to take nationalised transport through yet another convulsion, and in the White Paper preceding the

Transport Act of 1968 the Stranraer–Larne route received special attention. In the context of the organisation of the Scottish Transport Group, the new transport undertaking for Scotland which was to attend to Scottish bus and shipping operations, it was said that "in view of the functional relationship between the Stranraer–Larne service and other cross channel services to Ireland, the balance of advantage lies in the operation of this service continuing with the railways".[186]

There followed quite a violent debate in the press as to where control of the route should rest. Northern Ireland opinion was satisfied only partially when the lucrative route was removed from the control of the S T G, as the profits could very easily have been used to cover the substantial losses of the two shipping companies to be absorbed into the S T G, viz. David MacBrayne Ltd. and the C S P. But while glad to see the route put beyond the reach of the money-thirsty S T G shipping companies, Northern Ireland was still apprehensive about the profits of the Larne route being used by the railway headquarters in Glasgow for the subsidising of unprofitable commuter train services around the city.

Naturally, the railway chiefs at Glasgow and Gourock were not happy at the prospect of the route being completely removed from their area of control. Had they not built up the route from practically nothing in 1961 to a "goldmine" six years later? The C S P at Gourock had, from 1 January 1967, acted as managing agents of the route following the suppression of the C S P (I S) and in return for their work on behalf of B R B almost one-third of the administrative and managerial expenses of the C S P were met by the B R B.[187] Their area of responsibility at Stranraer had gradually been reduced, but the prospect of this loss of income was not attractive to the C S P. Opinion in Scotland was generally against a complete transfer of control of the Stranraer route to London; memories of the apathy and prevarication of the 1950s had not faded completely.

After much debate it was resolved that the Stranraer–Larne route would be treated as an integral part of the Shipping and International Services Division of B R B and thus responsibility and control for the route was to be in London, but, at the same time, for political reasons, it was expedient to leave the day-to-day management of the route in Scottish hands. The Scottish Region of B R B would be in charge of this aspect of the route, but following the transfer of the C S P to the S T G, the B R B had no Scottish marine department. Then, among their old files, the B R B found the Caledonian Steam Packet Company (Irish Services) Ltd., a dormant subsidiary. On 16 December 1968, the C S P (I S) Board were minuted as agreeing to change the company's name to British Transport Ship Management (Scotland) Ltd., and on 1 January 1969, the commencement date of the Transport Act 1968, B T S M (S) were appointed managers of the Stranraer–Larne ferry route. The C S P were no longer managing agents and their yellow pennant no longer flew at Stranraer.

Mr. John G. Thomson, Traffic Manager of the C S P from 1965, was appointed Manager of B T S M (S) and was joined at the B T S M (S) offices located at 87 Union Street, Glasgow, by a few of his C S P colleagues from Gourock. In 1973, John Thomson was appointed Passenger Manager for the Scottish Region, and from 15 October 1973, another railwayman, Mr. John F. Sanderson, took over management of the shipping route. Captain Leslie

J. Unsworth, who came ashore from being master of *Antrim Princess* to take over at Stranraer Harbour as Shipping and Port Manager following the sudden death of Captain William Smith, was appointed Local Manager for B T S M (S).

Part of the management agreement entered into between B R B and B T S M (S) required the principals, B R B, to pay their agents a management fee sufficient to cover the administration and maintenance costs of the managers. Certain plant and machinery was transferred to B T S M (S) from B R B and the ramp built in 1971 was treated as an asset of B T S M (S). Thus it would appear that B T S M (S) were to be responsible for the ownership and upkeep of the Stranraer terminal facilities as well as to undertake the management of the ships on the Stranraer–Larne route. Possibly, if B R B had owned the new ramp, it would not have been possible to have claimed a grant under the port modernisation scheme. B T S M (S) has never owned any ships.

One of the minor objectives behind the establishment of a separate management company for the Stranraer route was to give a sense of identity. The new company was not allowed a house-flag of its own but the initials B T S M (S) appeared on seamen's jerseys and caps and in publicity material. When visiting Stranraer in August 1971 with a friend, we were shown how seriously this was taken by one member of the staff at least. We arrived at Stranraer in the evening and decided to patronise the tea-bar in the terminal but discovered a tea-bar a bit bedraggled after a busy day and with practically no stock. One of us remarked, jokingly, "Oh, it's always the same with British Railways catering", only to receive the retort, "But, sir, we're not British Railways, we're British Transport Ship Management!" Perhaps so, but it still couldn't produce a cheese roll.

AN ADRIATIC "PRINCESS"

Before they had bowed out completely at Stranraer, the Caledonian managers had made strong representations to their principals in London concerning the need for a sister for *Antrim Princess*. In November 1968, the proposal was accepted and in July 1969 the order was placed with Cantiere Navale Breda of Venice. There was an outcry at a nationalised concern spending British taxpayers' money outside Britain, but the B R B stuck to its decision on the grounds of delivery date and price and *Ailsa Princess* was launched on Saturday, 28 November 1970. She was delivered on 22 June 1971 and began her nine-day voyage from Venice to Stranraer, arriving on 5 July and taking up service on Wednesday, 7 July 1971.[188]

In appearance almost a twin sister of *Antrim Princess*, the new "Princess" differed to an extent in the positioning of the public rooms. The immediately apparent outward difference was the funnel, which in both ships was placed well aft, but in the case of "Ailsa" the two horizontal lines of the B R B insignia were carried right round the funnel and the two "arrows" were proportionately larger. A less striking difference was that whereas the mainmast of the "Antrim" arose out of the funnel, in the case of the "Ailsa" it was separate but immediately forward of the funnel.

Accommodation for both classes of passengers (400 first and 800 second) in *Ailsa Princess* was again concentrated on the shelter deck. The first-class was situated forward and the most spectacular feature was the oval saloon bar overlooking the forecastle. The ceiling of the bar was finished in a "moon crater" effect. The first-class dining saloon was aft of the bar and could accommodate 64. The galley separated this saloon from the second-class cafeteria and served both. On the port side, divided by a moveable bulkhead, were to be found the lounges for first-class, forward, and second-class, aft. The latter had a tea-bar located at its forward end. In the two lounges the décor scheme was continuous throughout, and so in the event of the ships transferring to one-class operating there would be no clashes in colour schemes. Moving aft, 150 second-class passengers could be seated in a further lounge. In this area was the ship's shop and another tea-bar. Aft of this lounge was the second-class bar.

Antrim Princess originally had a tea-bar on the upper deck but this facility was absent from *Ailsa Princess*, where the after end of the upper deck was given over entirely to second-class seating. In the spring of 1975 the after end of the upper deck of *Ailsa Princess* was enclosed and deck space for passengers provided aft on the deck above, the bridge deck. *Antrim Princess* had been similarly altered in December 1974 during overhaul.

As in *Antrim Princess*, sleeping accommodation for passengers was provided on the new ship below the vehicle deck fore and aft of the engine space. Berths were provided for 69, and increase of three on the number for the "Antrim". Another respect in which *Ailsa Princess* differed from *Antrim Princess* was that the accommodation aft of the sleeping accommodation, which in the latter was devoted to cattle pens, was fitted out in the "Ailsa" as a sleeping lounge with reclining seats for a hundred passengers.

Ailsa Princess was fitted with a hanging deck above the vehicle deck the full width of each of the vehicle alleyways around the engine casing: that in the "Antrim" extended for only half this width. This produced an increase of capacity in the newer ship and the car capacity of *Ailsa Princess* was listed as 200 as against 160 for *Antrim Princess*. With hanging decks stowed, the height restriction on both ships was 14 feet 3 inches.

Both *Ailsa Princess* and *Antrim Princess* were driven by twin Crossley S.E.M.T.–Pielstick engines, but in the case of the "Ailsa" the engines operated, through gearing, on to controllable-pitch propellers. Each ship was equipped with a lateral bow-thrust unit.

THE GREAT UNIVERSAL STORES GROUP — SHIPOWNERS

Just to make it quite clear that *Ailsa Princess* was to be considered as part of the whole B R fleet and that Stranraer had no particular claim on the ship, "Ailsa's" port of registry was London. Like all her predecessors on the route, the port of registry for *Ailsa Princess* had originally been agreed as Stranraer and the letters could be detected on the stern where they had been burnt off to make way for "London". The "one-ness" of the fleet was reinforced when a ruling emanated from London in 1972 requiring the trade name of the Shipping and International Services Division, "Sealink", be painted on the sides of all B R ships. The veneer of independence attaching to B T S M (S) futher cracked when slowly the seamen's jerseys with "B T S M (S)" were replaced by ones with "Sealink" in blue. Gradually the company's name was pushed into the small print of publicity material and replaced by "Sealink Scotland".

The ownership of *Ailsa Princess* was to lie with B R B for only two weeks before being transferred to Carpass (Shipping) Company Ltd., a subsidiary of The Great Universal Stores Ltd. C (S) Co. was incorporated on 11 June 1971, and the issued capital was taken up 80 per cent by G U S and 20 per cent by B R B. On 24 June 1971, C (S) Co. took over ownership of *Ailsa Princess* and entered into a fifteen-year bareboat charter with B R B involving a daily hire rate in the region of £1,150. Announced in the press as costing £2¾ million the first cost of *Ailsa Princess* appeared in C (S) Co's balance sheet as £4 million.

The advantage of having *Ailsa Princess* owned by C (S) Co. was two-fold. Firstly, the tax allowances accruing from ownership of the vessel could be utilised by the G U S Group against their taxable profits, whereas B R B, with its recurring losses, had no tax liability and therefore no way of applying the tax allowances. In the accounts for the period to 31 March 1972, for C (S) Co. this tax loss (i.e. loss after deducting the allowances) was calculated as approximately £2 million and this would be made available to another G U S subsidiary for use in reducing its tax liability. Secondly, it avoided any substantial outlay of B R B funds and even though over the fifteen year charter B R B will have paid out over £6 million in hire, with interest rates at their present level this could, nevertheless, prove to be to the long-term benefit of B R B, since a pound paid tomorrow is better than a pound paid today.

But somewhere along the road, the wheel came off. On 30 April 1974, G U S sold its interest in C (S) Co. to Britravel Nominees Limited, a subsidiary of B R B. Thereafter, C (S) Co. was a wholly-owned B R B subsidiary and the advantages which prompted the creation of C (S) Co. were not to prove possible of realisation.

Once *Ailsa Princess* was well on the way towards delivery, the termination of the charter of *Stena Nordica* was taken in hand. *Stena Nordica*'s funnel was repainted in the colours of Stena A/B in stages and for a time she was sailing with a "Sealink" funnel plus a white band above and below the B R B insignia. "Stena's" charter was completed on 27 March 1971, and the following day she set out for Sweden after serving on the route for five years and a month. *Stena Nordica* was soon operating for Stena A/B between Gothenburg and Frederikshaven. Stena A/B sold *Stena Nordica* to Venezuelan owners in 1973 and she was replaced in the Stena fleet by a larger ship of the same name. The contribution of *Stena Nordica* to the route in the short term was substantial, but in the long term the experience gained by B R B in operating the Swedish ship has influenced all their cross-channel ships built in recent years.

On the departure of *Stena Nordica*, *Caledonian Princess* returned to the Larne–Stranraer route until the arrival of *Ailsa Princess*. Then she left the route which she had been instrumental in developing to such an extent that she could no longer cope with the traffic.

FREIGHT CONSIDERATIONS

Traffic had indeed built up. Not only car traffic, but also commercial traffic. This latter trade was an all-year-round traffic and the summer peaks had become an increasing embarrassment to the Stranraer management in that commercial traffic was often squeezed out by the summer car traffic. To avoid this clash of interests, the B R B had arranged the charter of a commercial carrier being built for Stena A/B. This ship, launched as *Stena Trailer*, was to replace another commercial carrier which had been chartered on a short-term basis for the Stranraer crossing.

Anticipating the departure of *Caledonian Princess* to Fishguard at the end of May 1970, B T S M (S) had negotiated the charter of *Baltic Ferry* for the Stranraer route. As her name indicates, she was a member of the A S N fleet, having been purchased by them in 1965. This former tank-landing craft was towed from Philadelphia and converted on the Tyne for A S N's work, but did little trading for them and was laid up at Barrow in 1967. *Baltic Ferry* started her daily round trip between Stranraer and Larne on Monday, 25 May 1970. She could carry 25 lorries but had no passenger certificate. While sailing under charter to B R B at Stranraer, *Baltic Ferry* retained her owners' colours with the addition of the B R B insignia on the side of the bridge. The majority of her crew were gathered by B T S M (S). *Baltic Ferry* remained on the route until the arrival of the chartered *Stena Trailer* at the end of June 1971, and then left for Barrow. In 1972, *Baltic Ferry* recrossed the Atlantic and was based at Halifax, Nova Scotia, for coastal work.

Launched as *Stena Trailer*, the name of the commercial carrier was changed to *Dalriada* on 20 June 1971. This name appropriately reflects the link the ship provided between Ireland and Scotland in that the Kingdom of Dalriada, founded in the fifth century, extended from County Antrim to Argyll. Also, by a happy coincidence, *Dalriada* was the name of a fine ship in the fleet of the Clyde & Campbeltown Shipping Company, which company had subsequently changed its name to Caledonian Steam Packet Company (Irish Services) Ltd. and then, in 1968, to British Transport Ship Management (Scotland) Ltd., the managers of the Stranraer route for B R B at the time the new *Dalriada* arrived on the service.

Dalriada was larger than *Baltic Ferry* and could accommodate 45 large lorries and 70 (unaccompanied) cars on her three decks. Thirty vehicles could be stowed on her main deck which was reached by bow and stern doors. Accommodation was available on the weather deck for a further 15 trailers, and this deck was reached from the main deck by means of a simple hydraulic lift. Forward of the machinery space and reached by a fixed ramp under a water-tight door space was available for 70 cars. Like *Baltic Ferry*, *Dalriada* had no passenger certificate but provision was made for the conveyance of up to twelve drivers and for their benefit a cafeteria was fitted. A system of shunter drivers evolved. The owner's driver would leave the lorry at the harbour and hand over the keys to the harbour office. *Dalriada*'s dock crew driver would take over and place the vehicle on the ship for the crossing, at the end of which another one of the owner's drivers collected the keys and the vehicle. *Dalriada* sailed with a B T S M (S) crew, since her charter was bareboat, but she was always under the command of a Stena A/B master. In contrast with *Stena Nordica*, the renamed *Stena Trailer* sailed in complete B R B livery from the time of her arrival at Stranraer. *Dalriada* made her inaugural trip from Stranraer on Tuesday, 24 June 1971. With a speed of 17 knots the new ship was faster than *Baltic Ferry*, and although initially giving one trip each way—out from Stranraer in the morning and back from Larne in the evening—this frequency was very soon doubled.

Plans for a second commercial carrier for the route were revealed in 1973,

N

and in November, *Neckartal* was selected as a stopgap and transferred from the Fishguard route, where she had been assisting *Caledonian Princess*. *Neckartal* was a member of the fleet of J. A. Reinbecke, of Hamburg, and while sailing for B R B continued to wear her owner's distinctive colours of grey hull with black and red funnel bearing the Reinbecke insignia. Other members of this fleet, namely *Donautal*, *Isartal* and *Saaletal*, had also been chartered to Coast Lines and B R B for services on the Irish Sea. *Saaletal* saw service at Stranraer for two weeks in March 1973, when she relieved *Dalriada* for overhaul. In 1974, however, the Shipping and International Services Division managed to find a suitable relief ship from their Dover fleet when the new train ferry *Anderida* took over from *Dalriada* for the month of March. *Anderida* had replaced *Shepperton Ferry*, the relief ship at Stranraer in the early 1960s, on the Dover–Dunkirk service, though, unlike the ship she replaced, *Anderida* had no passenger certificate.

Neckartal remained at Stranraer until November 1974, when her sister, *Isartal*, now renamed *Preseli*, took over for two months.

The new commercial carrier for the Stranraer–Larne route was *Stena Carrier*, a sister of *Dalriada* and *Anderida*. Launched in 1970 for the Stena A/B, *Stena Carrier* had been chartered by Canadian National Railways for the North Sydney (Nova Scotia)–Port-aux-Basques (Newfoundland) route, where she took over from the A S N *Cerdic Ferry*. *Cerdic Ferry* had been chartered for the summer of 1970 following the loss in a storm that spring of the Canadian National Railways ship *Patrick Morris*. In the spring of 1974, *Stena Carrier* was sold to Barclays Export and Finance Co. Ltd. and a long-term charter with B R fixed. *Stena Carrier* was renamed *Ulidia*, the latinised form of the Gaelic named for Ulster, and arrived at Dover in early July 1974. *Ulidia* then moved to Middlesbrough for docking and modifications for her new route. As with the other Stranraer ships on charter to B R, *Ailsa Princess* and *Dalriada*, *Ulidia* was painted in B R colours. Unlike *Dalriada*, *Ulidia* flew the red ensign, her port of registry being London. *Ulidia* also carried a passenger certificate for 36. Her first commercial crossing on the Stranraer route was on 16 December 1974.

HELP FROM GREAT YARMOUTH, WEYMOUTH AND HARWICH

At the time of *Ailsa Princess*'s refit in April 1975, the usual relief ship, *Holyhead Ferry I*, was committed on the Holyhead–Dun Laoghaire service and could not be made available for relief duties at Stranraer. The initial intention had been to halve the passenger service during the "Ailsa's" absence and fill the gap with a chartered commercial carrier. Thus, the West German *Roro Dania*, which had been borrowed from the U.K.–Scandinavia Express route between Great Yarmouth and Esbjerg to replace *Ulidia* and *Dalriada* in turn in March, was retained for a further month.

But the B R service between Heysham and Belfast for passengers and cars had been withdrawn from 6 April 1975, and at the eleventh hour it was decided that the full passenger service should be given between Stranraer and Larne and the Southern Region car ferry *Maid of Kent* was sent from Weymouth to join *Antrim Princess* at Stranraer. *Maid of Kent* operated on the mail roster (0700 and 1430 from Stranraer) carrying passengers only. *Maid of Kent* had sleeping berths for six, but these were not offered to passengers and intending travellers had to secure overnight accommodation ashore—a return to the pre-1898 arrangement.

But *Ailsa Princess*'s return was delayed and from 30 April to 9 May 1975 the mail roster was operated without passengers since *Maid of Kent* had to return south and no other vessel could be obtained. To complicate the Stranraer situation further, on 19 April *Dalriada*, only recently back from overhaul, had to be drydocked again at Glasgow. A substitute was found in the train ferry *Cambridge Ferry* which was brought round from Harwich. *Cambridge Ferry* arrived at Stranraer on 24 April 1975 but had to remain tied up for two days with mechanical trouble. To that date *Cambridge Ferry* was the longest vessel to have served on the Stranraer–Larne route. Thus on Tuesday, 29 April 1975, *Maid of Kent*'s last day as the mail steamer, the crossing was being maintained by five ships, *Antrim Princess* and *Ulidia*, with the visitors, *Roro Dania*, *Maid of Kent* and *Cambridge Ferry*.

INCREASED TRAFFIC

The increase in traffic through Stranraer and Larne had been quite remarkable. In the summer of 1961 there had been a thirty-year-old conventional passenger/cargo steamer, *Princess Margaret*, doing one round trip each weekday, and a train ferry, not much younger, *Hampton Ferry*, acting as a vehicle and passenger carrier, also giving one trip each way each weekday. Ten years later there were three ships, *Antrim Princess*, *Ailsa Princess* and *Dalriada*, each giving two round trips each day, plus two round trips on summer Sundays given by both "Princesses". But even this was not enough, and on Wednesdays and Fridays each of the vehicle/passenger ships gave an extra crossing on summer evenings. (This meant that in the course of the week both ships served as mail steamer.) Each year the route was now carrying more than half-a-million passengers and around 150,000 vehicles.

Indications of the build-up of commercial and seasonal traffic between Scotland and Ireland can be recognised in two other developments, one short-lived, the other more permanent.

On Friday, 8 May 1970, a new route between the two countries was opened when Western Ferries Ltd. placed one of their ships, *Sound of Islay*, on a daily service for passengers and vehicles between Campbeltown, Kintyre and Red Bay, Co. Antrim, thirty-one miles apart. In July 1970, the route had a windfall when a dock strike at Ardrossan caused lorries to be diverted to *Sound of Islay*, which operated a special overnight service between Campbeltown and Red Bay. During the first winter, a service for vehicles only was operated but thereafter it was a summer-only route. At 142 feet in length—about a third of *Ailsa Princess*—*Sound of Islay* was a small ship for the route. She was also slow. The route also earned for itself a reputation for unreliability, since the service was on occasion withdrawn without warning and seldom operated for the full duration of the advertised season. Despite these drawbacks, the Western Ferries service proved the existence of a substantial potential. The prospect of better pickings elsewhere caused *Sound of Islay* to be withdrawn and the Campbeltown–Red Bay route was abandoned after the 1973 summer.

A more lasting pointer to the increase in traffic was the introduction by Burns & Laird of a night sailing for vehicles and commercial traffic by their vessel *Lion*, sailing from Ardrossan to Larne. This service was in addition to the daylight service by *Lion* between Ardrossan and Belfast. The first sailing to Larne was given on Tuesday, 5 January 1971.

This increase in traffic was at first sight surprising when one considers that following riots in Londonderry in October 1968 the province once again slipped into sectarian strife. But while the areas around Belfast and Londonderry temporarily lost their appeal for holidaymakers, sections of the Ulster economy continued buoyant and this produced commercial movements which compensated for the drop in holiday traffic. Also, the origins of the holidaymakers altered significantly. By 1974, three-quarters were from Ireland, reversing the situation that had applied five years previously.

The "troubles" caused occasional delays in trains from Belfast, and the writer experienced a bomb scare on *Ailsa Princess* when crossing on 24 October 1973. A month previously the discovery of a quantity of gelignite in Stranraer Harbour Station caused not only delays to sailings but also the temporary re-opening of the Town Station. Strikes in Northern Ireland forced the Sealink services to be suspended on 27 and 28 March 1972, 15 to 29 May 1974, and 5 to 12 November 1974. The break in May 1974 was extended by negotiations between seamen and management over special payments for cargo handling and the passenger ships remained tied up. *Ailsa Princess* moved to Greenock on 4 June to provide more room at Stranraer. *Neckartal*, not having a B T S M (S) crew, was not affected by the extension and took up service again on 30 May, while *Dalriada* would appear to have sailed on 30 May and then tied up again until Tuesday, 4 June. It was Friday, 7 June, before *Antrim Princess* re-entered service, and on the following Sunday she was joined by *Ailsa Princess*.

NINE DEPARTURES A DAY

The basic timetable for the "Princesses" in the summer of 1975 was five departures from Stranraer and Larne each weekday. From Stranraer these were:

> 0300 (except Mondays), 0700 (mail boat), 1200, 1430, 1900, 2230 (Saturdays only).

This was not a summer-only schedule but had been introduced on an all-year-round basis in the spring of 1973. One result of this timetable was that both ships now berthed overnight at Stranraer; the 0330 from Stranraer being provided by the 2230 from Larne and the 0700 mail boat sailing by the 1850 from Larne. This meant a considerable reduction in sleeping facilities available for passengers travelling from Larne. Apart from summer Saturdays when the 2230 from Larne offered berths, the mail boat at 1850 was the only opportunity of sleeping accommodation. The Saturday-only sailing at 2230 from Stranraer resulted in the ships switching rosters and the "Princesses" spent alternate weeks on the "heavy" roster with three round trips and the "light" roster with two double trips. This frequency of service contrasted most forcibly with the other B R B routes between Britain and Ireland, where a single sailing in each direction per ship was still the order of the day.

In 1973, for the first time ever, there was a winter Sunday service for passengers and vehicles with a "Princess" making one round trip from Larne. The 1900 departure from Stranraer had a train connection from Glasgow, but the 1530 from Larne had no connection with Belfast while the evening arrival was met by a coach for Belfast. The coach service, however, was withdrawn after 5 January 1975.

In addition to the five round trips by *Ailsa Princess* and *Antrim Princess*, the commercial traffic ships, *Dalriada* and *Ulidia*, each provided two double, trips, making nine departures each day from Stranraer and Larne. The four ships on Stranraer–Larne were now sailing practically twenty-four hours a day, and this required a multiplication in crews, which meant that officers and men were no longer attached to one ship but moved from ship to ship on a shift system.

Despite the increased usage of the harbour at Stranraer, no attempt was made to supply a second ramp, but to minimise the ships' movements at the pier, a lying-off berth was provided by placing a line of dolphins parallel to the west wall of the pier, along which one of the ships could lie. These dolphins were linked to each other and to the landward end of the pier by a system of gangways. Passengers had access to the ships through the vehicle doors, but vehicles could not be loaded while the ships were berthed at the dolphins. This new berth came into use in the spring of 1973.

The need for a second ramp at Stranraer was underlined by the dis-organisation in services caused in December 1974, when *Dalriada* collided with the pier and put the ramp out of action for four days. From the afternoon of Wednesday, 4 December, to Sunday, 8 December, *Ailsa Princess* maintained a passenger and vehicular service between Larne and Ardrossan, where *Lion*'s ramp was used. On the Thursday and Friday two round trips were given, while at the week-end *Ailsa Princess* made only one round trip on each day. *Holyhead Ferry I* was relieving *Antrim Princess*, and from the Wednesday to the Saturday sailed twice daily between Stranraer and Larne with passengers and mail only. The second ship on the commercial traffic roster was *Preseli*, and from the Thursday until the following Tuesday she sailed twice daily between Larne and Cairnryan.

Mention of *Preseli* using Cairnryan as a port leads us to consideration of a remarkable development in 1973. With four first-class ships and ever-increasing traffic, it looked as if B T S M (S) could just sit back and let the profits roll in. But with very little warning, competition came to their own doorstep and could claim an even shorter sea route.

CHAPTER SIXTEEN

Townsend Thoresen Car Ferries at Cairnryan

A CRYPTIC report in the August 1970 issue of *Cruising Monthly* mentioned plans of the Atlantic Steam Navigation Company to repair "Cairnryan Pier" for use by container ships. But it was a drive-on/drive-off service for vehicles and passengers that was to come to Cairnryan when in July 1973 *Ionic Ferry* opened a service between Cairnryan and Larne. The route which had been advocated so strongly in the 1830s and 1840s during the controversy over the future of the Portpatrick–Donaghadee mail service was at last to receive its first commercial passenger and vehicular service.

This chapter, the shortest in the book, is the beginning of what promises to be one of the success stories of the Irish Sea. We have noted the origins and growth of A S N as it has formed part of the background to the Stranraer route, but now A S N is considered in its own right with Cairnryan–Larne as the third route which can claim the title of "The Short Sea Route".

EUROPEAN FERRIES

A S N, while concentrating their efforts on the mainly commercial traffic routes from Felixstowe and Preston, were no strangers to Scottish waters. When British Road Services Ltd. took over control of Anglo-Continental Container Services Ltd. in early 1960, the company's two Irish Sea routes became the responsibility of A S N. Anglo-Continental Container Services Ltd. started trading in April 1949 and in September 1956 this company had inaugurated the first exclusively container service between Ireland and Scotland, with a Dutch motor ship *Prior* sailing between Ardrossan and Larne. This unit-load route and the other Anglo-Continental service, that between Preston and Larne, were covered by chartered tonnage, latterly sailing in A S N colours.

With the dissolution of the B T C at the end of 1962 the shares in British Road Services Ltd. and its subsidiary, A S N, were allocated to the Transport Holding Company, one of the statutory companies set up under the Transport Act, 1962. The adoption of A S N by the Transport Holding Company severed the tenuous link between A S N and the bulk of British Railways shipping. By the Transport Act of 1968 the A S N moved on again, this time to become a subsidiary of the National Freight Corporation.

As part of the Conservative Government's policy of transferring back into private enterprise those parts of the nationalised undertakings which were viable, A S N and its subsidiaries, The Transport Ferry Service (Nederland) N.V. and Frank Bustard & Sons Ltd., became part of the European Ferries Group on 18 November 1971. Thus, for £5½ million, European Ferries Ltd. acquired the goodwill of several routes to Ireland and the Continent and also seven ferries.

European Ferries had made remarkable growth on its ferry routes from Dover and Southampton. In the chairman's statement accompanying the accounts to 31 March 1973, Mr. K. D. Wickenden remarks that in 1965 the company "operated one ship on one cross-channel route. We now have over thirty ships operating on twelve routes and we can claim to be a major force in the short sea shipping industry".

CAIRNRYAN REVISITED

The vessel selected to open the Cairnryan–Larne service on Monday, 10 July 1973, was *Ionic Ferry*. This ship had been launched from the yard of Wm. Denny & Bros. Ltd. at Dumbarton on 2 May 1958. *Ionic Ferry* was a sister ship to *Bardic Ferry* and replaced her on the A S N service between Preston and Larne/Belfast, making her maiden voyage from Preston to Larne on the night of Friday, 10 October 1958. *Ionic Ferry* could originally carry 95 vehicles and had two-class sleeping accommodation for 55 passengers. On the boat deck there were two lounges with officers' accommodation between. The for'ard area was reserved for first-class passengers, while second-class travellers were accommodated aft. On the deck below there were two dining saloons with a shared galley.[189]

One of the hazards of the Preston–Larne/Belfast service was the River Ribble, since its navigation is tidally restricted. Early in 1964, *Ionic Ferry* grounded in the Ribble during fog, and she had for company a ship we have already met, *Stream Fisher* which also touched bottom. At that time, *Stream Fisher* was sailing under charter to A S N.

In December 1967, a new terminal for A S N being opened at Belfast, the service to Belfast was stepped up from once to thrice weekly, and *Doric Ferry*, a slightly larger sister of *Ionic Ferry*, was transferred from the Felixstowe–Antwerp service to join *Bardic Ferry* (transferred back to Preston in 1961) and *Ionic Ferry* on the Irish Sea. As from 24 March 1973, sailings from Preston to Larne were withdrawn and concentrated on Belfast, a daily service being given with *Doric Ferry* and *Bardic Ferry*. Following the introduction of the increased Cairnryan–Larne service in July 1974, however, that to Belfast was abandoned, with *Bardic Ferry* making the last crossing on Saturday, 29 June 1974.

Initially, *Ionic Ferry* lay overnight at Larne and sailed twice daily (including Sundays) whence at 0900 and 1600, returning from Cairnryan at 1230 and 1930, but from the beginning of February 1974 the schedule was recast, with *Ionic Ferry* lying at the Scottish end overnight, leaving Cairnryan at 0800 and 1630 and Larne at 1200 and 2000. $2\frac{1}{2}$ hours were required by *Ionic Ferry* for the crossing since her speed was only 14 knots. Two extra lifeboats were fitted aft shortly after *Ionic Ferry* took up the route, and this enabled her to have a certificate for 219 passengers between Cairnryan and Larne. When built, the after end of the promenade deck had been fitted to carry about twenty containers, loaded by either quay-side crane or the ship's own. This deck had now been cleared for carrying cars, which were driven on and off by means of a long gangway. Passengers moved between ship and shore by means of the stern door ramp. Car rates were identical on the Stranraer and Cairnryan routes to Larne, and the second-class fares of the Stranraer ferries applied to the A S N service.

In March 1974, *Bardic Ferry* relieved her sister for overhaul at Glasgow, and was herself to become fully committed to the Cairnryan–Larne servce from

October 1974. Traffic levels justified a double-ship schedule during the route's second winter and *Bardic Ferry* joined *Ionic Ferry* and together they operated a timetable requiring two round trips daily from each ship. Like her younger sister before her, *Bardic Ferry* was fitted with two additional lifeboats and the upper deck aft was cleared for the carriage of cars.

FOOTHOLD SECURED

At Cairnryan, E F rehabilitated an area of the war-time port and a link span for *Ionic Ferry* was installed. Compared with Stranraer Harbour, there was ample room for expansion at Cairnryan, and within months of the opening of the route, work was in hand for the building of a second berth with link span while a large marshalling area for vehicles was cleared and levelled. The second link span at Cairnryan came into service in July 1974 and, judging from its dimensions, was built with an eye to the future.

To consolidate further the position of A S N on the Cairnryan–Larne route, E F bought out the entire share capital of the Larne Harbour Ltd. in October 1973.

The new service to Cairnryan was initially operated under the heading "Transport Ferry Service"—the trade name of A S N—but early in 1974 the title "Townsend Thoresen Car Ferries—the trade name used by E F for its south coast trade—was introduced at Cairnryan and Larne and the two names used jointly. The management of the route was based in the A S N offices at Larne Harbour.

"FREE ENTERPRISE" ASSISTANCE

New tonnage appearing on the group's Dover and Southampton routes allowed a ship faster and larger than *Ionic Ferry* to be transferred to Cairnryan, and on 1 July 1974, *Free Enterprise III* began a daily service of three round trips, based at Larne. The schedule required the newcomer to make the crossing in 1¾ hours, but this proved optimistic and an extra five or ten minutes was required on most trips. Originally, *Ionic Ferry* was intended to remain as stand-by, but in fact she continued her roster of two double sailings each day, thus producing a daily (including Sundays) frequency of five sailings from Larne and from Cairnryan. This service continued until late September 1974, when one round trip was omitted.

This was no cast-off tonnage saved from the scrap-heap by a spell serving the less-discerning people in the northern parts, for *Free Enterprise III* was barely eight years old, having been launched from the Dutch yard of Werf Gusto on 14 May 1966. She entered service that year between Dover and Zeebrugge, when she could carry 250 cars and 1,200 passengers in excellent one-class accommodation.

On the bridge deck immediately aft of the navigating bridge, *Free Enterprise III* had a non-smokers' saloon seating 86, while further aft was buoyant seating and a bridge for use when navigating stern-first. Also, on this deck, to starboard of the single red funnel with the green "TTF" insignia and black top, was a large neon sign with the name "Townsend" displayed. The boat deck contained thirteen two-berth cabins and officers' accommodation, plus some buoyant seating. The public rooms were concentrated on the promenade deck with two lounges, the forward area seating 162 and the lounge amidships seating approximately 240. The dining saloon for 120 was aft on this deck. A tea-bar and bar were integrated into the design of the for'ard lounge, while the larger lounge was served by another bar, the purser's office, a *bureau d'exchange* (closed, of course, while sailing on the Irish Sea service) and a shop with good quality goods.

The central section of the shelter deck was given over to cars which reached this level by a ramp for'ard from the main deck which was devoted entirely to vehicles. On verandah decks around the shelter deck were officers' and crew accommodation and nine single berth cabins. On the lower deck, a well-deck between the two engine rooms was utilised for additional car space. This extensive accommodation produced a gross tonnage of 4,657, which was the highest of any Irish Sea cross-channel ferry at that time.

Externally, *Free Enterprise III* was also unusual in that her hull was light green with the name "Townsend Thoresen" in white along the hull. The red underbody was continued up to the level of the rubbing strake. Her four diesel engines drove twin screws propelling the ship at over twenty knots. While operating at Larne, *Free Enterprise III* flew the flag of A S N as managers.

When *Free Enterprise III* returned south and took up duty between Dover and Calais on 21 October 1974 her place at Cairnryan was taken by *Bardic Ferry*.

The summer timetable for 1975 initially required only *Ionic Ferry* and *Bardic Ferry* on the crossing, but possibly because of a lull in the strife in Northern Ireland, the decision was taken to increase the summer schedule to six daily sailings in each direction. In May 1975, *Free Enterprise I*, an older and smaller sister of *Free Enterprise III*, came north to the Cairnryan route.

Entering service at Easter 1962 for Townsend Brothers Ferries Limited, *Free Enterprise I* had been the prototype of the series of Dover-based "Free Enterprise" ships and in design was similar to *Free Enterprise III*. Her passenger capacity was 850 compared with 1,200 of the younger ship, and the vehicle accommodation was about half. The twin funnels of *Free Enterprise I* were placed athwartships and this allowed a spacious central area for passengers with buffet and bar facilities, shops, *bureau d'exchange* and the purser's office.

Appendices

A key to abbreviations used is given on page xvi.

Appendix A

MANAGEMENT AND PERSONNEL

1 The Portpatrick–Donaghadee route, 1825–1849.

Following the Treasury Minute of 31 December 1824, the Post Office established its own packet station at Portpatrick and placed two steam packets on the route from 4 May. These steamships replaced the (latterly) three sailing packets of the Donaghadee Packet Company which had operated the service under contract for the Post Office since July 1791. From 16 January 1837, the responsibility for the operation of the mail packets passed from the Post Office to the Admiralty. The service terminated at the end of September 1849.

Superintendents: John Little, 1825–
Edward Hawes, May 1844–September 1849

Commander Hawes continued as the Government Superintendent of Portpatrick Harbour until at least 1869.

The packet station at Portpatrick had a shore staff of nine or ten in addition to the superintendent. The majority were employed in coaling the packets and in manning row boats which assisted the packets in and out of the harbour or carried the mails out to the steam packets when tidal conditions caused them to lie outside the harbour. In addition there was a carpenter and storekeeper, while later a clerk and smith were added to the establishment. A harbour master at Donaghadee was retained. The mail packets each had a crew of ten.

Ships' Commanders:

Luke Smithett	1825–1831, *Arrow.*	
E. R. Pascoe	1825–1827, *Dasher.*	
Jonathan Binny	1827–1829, *Dasher.*	
W. Henry	1829–1830, *Dasher.*	
	1831–1839, *Fury/Asp.*	
R. J. Fayrer	1831–1833, *Arrow.*	
	1833–1839, *Spitfire/Pike.*	
Leary	1839–1841, *Asp.*	
Stark	1839–1840, *Pike.*	
Parks	1840–1841, *Pike.*	
W. W. Oke	1841–1849, *Asp.*	
Day	1841–1842, *Pike.*	
Alex. Boyter	1842–1849, *Pike.*	

2. The Stranraer–Larne route, 1872 to date.

THE LARNE & STRANRAER STEAMBOAT COMPANY LIMITED, 1872–1890

The company operated the crossing from July 1872 with the seat of management situated at York Road, Belfast, in the office of the Belfast & Northern Counties Railway.

Incorporated on 23 December 1871 under the Companies Act, 1862.
Capital: Authorised £20,000 in £10 shares; Issued £19,250.
  Portpatrick Railway took up £10,000.
  Individual Irish shareholders took up £9,250.
  Unallocated £750.
Chairmen: Randolph, 9th Earl of Galloway, 1872–1873.
  Allan, 10th Earl of Galloway, 1873–1890.

Secretary: Charles Stewart, 1871—8 April 1889. Also Secretary, B & N C R.
Pro tem Secretary: W. R. Gill, May 1889–February 1890. Also Secretary, B & N C R.
Manager: Edward J. Cotton, 1872–1890. Also Manager, B & N C R.
Stranraer Agents: William Grafton, 1873–1885. Also Traffic Manager, P R & W R.
 William Cunning, 1885–1890. Also Traffic Manager, P & W J C.
Supervision of hulls and machinery:
 R. M. Beath, 1872–1873, Consultant Engineer.
 Alex McGibbon, 1873–1876. Also Marine Superintendent, Glasgow & Londonderry Steam Packet Company.
 Messrs. G. & J. Weir, 1877–1885, Ships Engineers at Glasgow.
 Admiral Dent, 1885–1890. Also Marine Superintendent L & N W R.

The ships had black hulls, red underbodies without white line, funnels were red with black top. The house-flag was a red pennant with a white, angled square containing the red hand of Ulster.

By the Portpatrick & Wigtownshire Railways (Sale and Transfer) Act, 1885 the railways of the title were sold and transferred to the L & N W R, M R, C R and G & S W R. With this went the 1,000 £10 shares owned by the P R in The Larne & Stranraer Steamboat Company Limited. Vesting date was 1 August 1885. By Section 19 of the Act a Joint Committee was incorporated for the management of the railways, the Portpatrick & Wig-townshire Joint Committee.

The shareholders of the P R and the W R received, in the former case, a holding of 3½ per cent Portpatrick & Wigtownshire Guaranteed Stock equal to their original P R stock, while in the latter case the exchange was one unit of 3½ per cent Guaranteed Stock for two W R shares. The stock was guaranteed by the four companies comprising the P & W J C. Each of the constituent companies appointed two directors to the P & W J C.

The L & S S Co. Board meeting on 15 April 1887 created a Managing Committee consisting of eight directors, four of whom were appointed by the P & W J C and four by the Irish shareholders.

By a scheme of arrangement in 1889 the shareholders of the L & S S Co. were paid off at the rate of 62½p in the £ and the company wound up. Until a new company with greater resources was created, the Larne & Stranraer Steamship Joint Committee was formed. Because of legal difficulties en-countered in the attempt to form the new company, the L & S S J C lasted until the railway "grouping" in 1923.

THE LARNE & STRANRAER STEAMSHIP JOINT COMMITTEE, 1890–1922

Formed by agreement in 1893. Signed on behalf of the P & W J C, L & N W R, M R, C R, G & S W R and B & N C R. The agreement was held to have commenced on 1 January 1890.

Capital: £100,498·20p.

L & N W R	£19,747·05
M R	19,747·05
C R	19,747·05
G & S W R	19,747·05
B & N C R	21,510·00

The L & S S J C had six members: four representatives from the P & W J C and two from the B & N C R. Following the takeover by the M R of the B & N C R in July 1903, the successor body to the latter, the Northern

Counties Committee, continued to appoint two representatives to the L & S S J C, but they had no voting rights.

Chairmen:

Miles MacInnes	L & N W R	1890–1899
Sir Ernest Paget	M R	1900
Hugh Brown	C R	1901
Patrick Caird	G & S W R	1902
John Young	B & N C R/N C C	1903
Miles MacInnes	L & N W R	1904
Sir Ernest Paget	M R	1905
Hugh Brown	C R	1906*
Patrick Caird	G & S W R	1907
Miles MacInnes	L & N W R	1908
Sir Ernest Paget	M R	1909
Sir Charles Bene Renshaw	C R	1910
Patrick Caird	G & S W R	1911
Charles Cropper	L & N W R	1912
G. Murray Smith	M R	1913
Sir Charles Bene Renshaw	C R	1914
Sir James Bell	G & S W R	1915
Charles Cropper	L & N W R	1916
G. Murray Smith	M R	1917
Henry Allan	C R	1918
Sir James Bell	G & S W R	1919
Charles Cropper	L & N W R	1920
Charles Booth	M R	1921
Henry Allan	C R	1922

Secretaries: John Thomson, 1890–December 1906. Also Secretary, P & W J C.
     F. W. Hutchinson, January 1907–December 1913. Also Manager and Secretary P & W J C and Stranraer Agent L & S S J C.
     William McConchie, January 1914 – 1923. Also Manager L & S S J C and Manager and Secretary P & W J C.
Managers: Edward J. Cotton, 1890–July 1899. Also Manager, B & N C R.
     James Cowie, 1899–1904. Also Manager, B & N C R.
     Baptist Gamble, 1904–1905.
     William McConchie, April 1905–(December 1924). At Belfast until 1913, then transferred to Stranraer.
Stranraer Agents: William Cunning, 1890–December 1894. Also Traffic Manager, P & W J C.
     F. W. Hutchinson, January 1895–December 1913. Also Traffic Manager, P & W J C.
Traffic Agent, Belfast: W. Murray Reid, December 1913–
Shore Superintendents: John P. Cumming, January 1906–1922.
     William Fraser, 1922–(1923). Also Marine Superintendent, G & S W R, Greenock.

The Marine Superintendent of the L & N W R continued to be available for advice after the appointment of Captain Cumming.

The duties of Catering Superintendent were included within the position of Shore Superintendent created on the appointment of Captain Cumming. Captain George Campbell had managed the catering on his own account from 1872 until the end of September 1897. From 1 May 1887, he paid an annual fee to the L & S S Co. and latterly the L & S S J C. In October 1897, the B & N C R took over the catering for a year and a fee of £500 paid to the

* Deceased 5 October 1906

L & S S J C. The L & S S J C thereafter undertook the catering but retained the B & N C R as superintendents and a fee of 5% on gross receipts paid them for this duty. This arrangement continued until the appointment of Captain Cumming in January 1906.

The ships' funnels were buff and the old L & S S Co. pennant flown.

By the Railways Act, 1921 all four companies comprising the P & W J C (and therefore the B & N C R also) were absorbed into the London Midland & Scottish Railway with effect from 1 January 1923.

THE LONDON MIDLAND & SCOTTISH RAILWAY, 1923–1947

Ultimate responsibility for the Stranraer service was now vested in the L M & S R Shipping Committee at Euston, London, while management of the route was delegated to the Steam Vessels Sub-Committee of the Scottish Local Committee.

On 31 December 1924, the railway office at Stranraer was closed and the Manager, William McConchie, retired. It would appear that during 1923 and 1924 the superintendence of the technical aspects of the ships' operating remained with the former G & S W R office at Princes Pier, Greenock. In 1925, the L M & S R Marine Superintendent (Scotland), Charles Bremner, was appointed Manager of the Stranraer–Larne route and technical superintendence undertaken from his offices at Gourock Pier. The superintendence of the catering on board the ships was by the L M & S R (N C C) until 1931, but was then transferred to Charles Bremner's office at Gourock. From June 1937 the Heysham shipping office of the L M & S R assumed responsibility for the technical supervision of the Stranraer steamers.

At Stranraer, following the closure of the railway office, day-to-day matters at the harbour and on the steamers were handled by the Harbour Stationmaster, who was appointed steamboat agent.

During the Second World War a Marine Superintendent was based at Stranraer.

Chairmen of the Steam Vessels Sub-Committee:
    Sir Alexander Gracie, May 1923–January 1930.
    Charles Ker (acting), February 1930–March 1930.
    David Cooper (acting), April 1930–May 1930.
    Sir H. Arthur Rose, June 1930–April 1937.
    Charles Ker (acting), May 1937–July 1937.
    David Cooper (acting), September 1937–September 1938.
    Sir Robert B. Greig, October 1938–October 1940.
    A. Murray Stephen, November 1940–December 1947.
Managers: William McConchie, 1923–December 1924.
    Charles A. Bremner, 1925–March 1946. Also L M & S R Marine Superintendent (Scotland).
    Robert D. Kerr, April 1946–December 1947. Also L M & S R Marine Superintendent (Scotland).
Technical Supervisors: William J. Fraser, 1923–1924, at Princes Pier.
    Captain Vamish, June 1937–1940, at Heysham.
Steamboat Agents: J. Hope Smith, January 1925–September 1933.
    Hugh Irons, October 1933–December 1939.
    David Valentine, January 1940–December 1940.
Marine Superintendent: Captain Hugh Montgomery, M.B.E., 1940–1946.

In 1923 and 1924 the yellow funnels of the two Stranraer steamers had black tops and a red band added, but from 1925 the red band was dropped. The L M & S R house-flag was flown—red with a white St. George's cross, and the L M & S R crest, containing rose, thistle and harp, in the centre.

THE BRITISH TRANSPORT COMMISSION, 1948–1960

By the Transport Act, 1947 the railways of Britain, including the L M & S R, were grouped into a statutory, nationalised body—the British Transport Commission. The Scottish headquarters for shipping affairs moved from Gourock to the Railway Executive (Scottish Region) offices in George Square, Glasgow, where the Marine Superintendent (Scottish Region) was based. From 1 January 1948 the overall management of the Stranraer service rested with the Marine Superintendent, Glasgow, while the technical and catering affairs were still handled by the Gourock office. This arrangement existed until the end of 1951.

Manager: Captain Harry J. Perry, January 1948–December 1951. Also Marine Superintendent, Railway Executive (Scottish Region).

From 1 January 1952, Irish Shipping Services, the renamed London Midland Region Marine Department at Euston, became responsible for, *inter alia*, the Stranraer–Larne route. Following the loss of *Princess Victoria* a local Marine Manager was appointed.

Manager: Captain John D. Reed, January 1952–(1964). Also Manager, Irish Shipping Services.
Local Agent: David M. Stewart   –December 1953. Thereafter Deputy to the District Marine Manager until 1960.
District Marine Manager: A. L. Pepper, June 1953–April 1958.
                            Captain B. H. Mendus, June 1958–November 1958.
                            Temporarily transferred from Fishguard.
                            Captain William Smith, December 1958–(1968).

THE CALEDONIAN STEAM PACKET COMPANY (IRISH SERVICES) LIMITED, 1960–1966

Part of the decision to build *Caledonian Princess* was the re-establishment of a management team in Scotland to be responsible for the marketing, operations and superintendence of the Stranraer–Larne service. The London-based Irish Shipping Services passed these tasks to the C S P office at Gourock under the general managership of Alexander Stewart. B T C London advanced the money for the new ship and remained ultimately in control, but the decision to devolve responsibility produced a high degree of autonomy. A dormant subsidiary of the C S P, the Clyde & Campbeltown Shipping Co. Ltd., was renamed and revived to operate and superintend the route from 1 December 1960.

The C & C S Co. was registered on 19 August 1915 as Clyde Cargo Steamers Ltd. and operated a small fleet of cargo steamers from Glasgow to various Clyde ports. In 1935 the company became a subsidiary of David MacBrayne Ltd. and in March merged with the Campbeltown & Glasgow Steam Packet Co. Ltd. On 31 March 1937, the name of Clyde Cargo Steamers Ltd. was changed to Clyde & Campbeltown Shipping Co. Ltd. On 1 October 1949, the financial responsibility for the remaining C & C S Co. services passed from David MacBrayne Ltd. to the B T C, though the formal transfer of the capital of C & C S Co. did not pass to the C S P, a B T C subsidiary, until March 1951. The last ship owned by C & C S Co. was sold in January 1958 and the company ceased to trade. On 20 January 1960, the name of the company was changed to Caledonian Steam Packet Company (Irish Services) Ltd., and on 15 November 1960 the company's capital was transferred from the C S P to the B T C, making the C S P (I S) a direct subsidiary of the B T C. At the date of transfer from the C S P to B T C the authorised capital of C S P (I S) was £30,000 in shares of £1, all of which was issued. *Caledonian Princess* was owned by C S P (I S) from her entry into service until 31 December 1966. C S P (I S) ceased to act as owners and managers of the Stranraer–Larne service on 31 December 1966.

Chairmen: James Ness, December 1959–March 1964. Also General Manager, B R (Scotland).
    William G. Thorpe, March 1964–(July 1967). Also General Manager B R (Scotland).

General Manager: Alexander Stewart, December 1959–December 1966. Also General Manager C S P.

Secretaries: H. M. Hunter, December 1959–June 1962. Also Secretary, C S P.
    John A. Gunn, June 1962–February 1966. Also Secretary, C S P.
    David P. Knighton, February 1966–(June 1968). Also Secretary, C S P.

Local Managers: Captain William Smith (December 1958)–July 1968. Appointed Area Marine and Rail Manager from August 1965.
    Captain Eric Pollock, July–November 1968. Acting

Shipping and Port Manager: Captain Leslie J. Unsworth, M.B.E., December 1968–

Caledonian Princess carried the standard C S P colour scheme, except that a large, red Caledonian lion rampant was placed on each side of the funnel. *Caledonian Princess* and the ships chartered by C S P (I S) flew the pennant of the Caledonian Group of companies—a red lion rampant on a yellow pennant. In the opening months of 1965 a new colour scheme was adopted for the cross-channel and estuarial fleets of the B R B and this change extended, in part, to the B R B subsidiaries, C S P (I S) and C S P. In place of black hulls with red underbodies there appeared blue hulls with red underbodies and chocolate boot-topping. The white line over the rubbing strake on the vehicular ferries disappeared, while the ventilators and masts became grey. The funnel of *Caledonian Princess* was not immediately altered, but in the spring of 1966 the lions were removed and the funnel repainted red with the white B R insignia. The Stena A/B funnel of the chartered *Stena Nordica* gave way, in January 1967, to a standard B R funnel, though otherwise the ship retained the colour scheme of her Swedish owners.

THE BRITISH RAILWAYS BOARD, THE SHIPPING & INTERNATIONAL SERVICES DIVISION, AND THE CALEDONIAN STEAM PACKET COMPANY LIMITED, 1967–1968

On 1 January 1967, the ownership of *Caledonian Princess* passed from C S P (I S) to B R B and the Board took a greater direct interest in the route. The C S P were engaged by B R B as managing agents and at the Stranraer terminal both the B R house-flag—a blue flag with pearl grey insignia—and the C S P pennant flew side by side. From 1 January 1967, C S P (I S) became a dormant subsidiary of B R B.

From the beginning of 1968 the supervision of the B R B's Irish and European shipping operations was undertaken by the newly-created Shipping & International Services Division of the B R B. The Division had its headquarters in Liverpool Street, London. The C S P were still retained as managing agents until 31 December 1968. The termination of the use of the Gourock company as managing agents was caused by the Transport Act, 1968 which severed the link between the C S P and the B R B when the former company was transferred to the Scottish Transport Group, a new statutory body created by the Act. Of the B R B's shipping interests in Scotland, the Stranraer route was alone to remain owned by the B R B, and to attend to the

o

management of the route a small B R B shipping department had to be set up in Scotland.

THE BRITISH RAILWAYS BOARD, THE SHIPPING & INTERNATIONAL SERVICES DIVISION, AND BRITISH TRANSPORT SHIP MANAGEMENT (SCOTLAND) LIMITED, 1969–

The management of the route on behalf of B R B was entrusted to British Transport Ship Management (Scotland) Ltd. from 1 January 1969. General oversight of the route and policy matters still remained with the London-based Shipping & International Services Division. B T S M (S) was a renamed C S P (I S) and had its registered office in Glasgow, at Buchanan House, 58 Buchanan Street. The Manager had his staff at 87 Union Street. The Harbour Office at Stranraer became a B T S M (S) office.

B T S M (S) owned no ships, but on its appointment as agents for the Stranraer service had transferred to it from B R B certain plant, machinery, stocks and debtors. Also the capital expenditure in 1971 and 1972 on a new ramp and foundations was borne by B T S M (S). An annual management fee is paid by B R B to B T S M (S) at a figure which varies and is calculated to cover exactly the revenue expenditure by the agent each year.

Chairmen: Gordon W. Stewart (July 1967)–June 1971. General Manager, B R (Scotland).

Alexander Philip, July 1971–April 1974. General Manager, B R (Scotland).

David J. Cobbett, May 1974–   General Manager, B R (Scotland).

Secretaries: Samuel K. Thomson January 1969–

Managers: John Thomson, January 1969–October 1973.

John F. Sanderson, October 1973–

Shipping and Port Manager: Captain Leslie J. Unsworth, M.B.E. (December 1968)–

Engineer Superintendent: B. Lambert, January 1969–

The duties of Marine and Catering Superintendents were contained within the department of Captain Unsworth, the Shipping and Port Manager.

The ships, which were either owned by B R B or on long-term charter to B R B, sailed in the colours of B R B and flew that body's house-flag. Late in 1972 the trade name of the Shipping & International Services Division, "Sealink", was painted in white on the ships' sides.

Ships' Masters: George Campbell   1872–1876, *Princess Louise*
1876–1890, *Princess Beatrice*
1890–1892, *Princess Victoria*
1892–1898, *Princess May*

John Cumming   1892–1897, *Princess Victoria*
1897–1902, *Princess May*
1902–1903, *Princess Beatrice*
1904–1905, *Princess Maud*

John McCracken   1897–1899, *Princess Victoria*
H. McNeill   1899–1903, *Princess Victoria*
1903–1905, *Princess May*
1906–1910, *Princess Maud*

William McCalmont   1903–1905, *Princess Victoria*
1906–1907, *Princess May*
1907–1910, *Princess Victoria*
1910–1912, *Princess Maud*
1912–1921, *Princess Victoria*

Ships' Masters: Andrew Hamilton

1910–1912, *Princess May*
1912–1921, *Princess Maud*
1921–1931, *Princess Victoria*
1931–1933, *Princess Margaret*
1934   , *Princess Maud*

John Munro

1922–1931, *Princess Maud*
1931–1933, *Princess Victoria*
1933–1934, *Princess Margaret*
1934–1936, *Princess Maud*

Hugh Montgomery

1934–1936, *Princess Margaret*
1936–1940, *Princess Maud*

James M. Ferguson

1936–1939, *Princess Margaret*
1939   , *Princess Victoria*
1940–1943, *Princess Maud*
1943–1946, *Princess Margaret*
1946   , *Princess Maud*
1947–1953, *Princess Victoria*

Samuel S. Iles

1940–1943, *Princess Margaret*
1943–1946, *Princess Maud*
1946–1958, *Princess Margaret*

John F. Hey

1958–1961, *Princess Margaret*
1961–1963, *Caledonian Princess*

Leslie J. Unsworth

1964–1967, *Caledonian Princess*
1967–1968, *Antrim Princess*

Eric C. Pollock

1967–1968, *Caledonian Princess*
1968–1971, *Antrim Princess*
1971–   , *Ailsa Princess*

Robert L. Bathgate

1968–1971, *Caledonian Princess*
1971–   , *Antrim Princess*

Thomas Cree   1969–
David McHarg   1970–
D. Cameron   1970–
Ian Thomson   1970–   Masters are no longer
Robin Livingstone   1970–   attached to one ship
D. Bark   1971–
D. Brown   1974–
H. McConnell   1974–

Stena A/B
Masters:

Sven Alm   1966–1968, *Stena Nordica*
Inger Blom   1968–1971, *Stena Nordica*
1971–   , *Dalriada*
Erik Hammerstrom   1971–1974, *Dalriada*
Rhinebecke   1974–   , *Dalriada*

3.   The Cairnryan–Larne route 1973 to date.

ATLANTIC STEAM NAVIGATION COMPANY LIMITED AND TOWNSEND THORESEN CAR FERRIES LIMITED

From its opening on 10 July 1973, the service between Larne and Cairnryan for passengers and vehicles was managed by Atlantic Steam Navigation Co. Ltd., a member of the European Ferries Group of companies. Initially the service operated under the A S N trade name "Transport Ferry Service", but from early 1974 it was considered as an integral part of the Townsend Thoresen activities of European Ferries Ltd. and the trade name "Townsend

Thoresen Ferries" adopted for most publicity. The ships engaged on the route have flown the house-flag of A S N, either as owner or manager.

The name, Atlantic Steam Navigation, suggests a deep-sea rather than cross-channel sphere of operation, and the former was in fact the original intention for the company. A S N was formed in 1936 for the purpose of providing cheap trans-Atlantic travel. The fares were to cover the passage only and the catering would be on a cafeteria system with passengers paying as they ate. The company, for various reasons, remained dormant, however, until after the Second World War, when two tank-landing craft (L.S.T.) were taken on charter from the Ministry of Transport and converted for a freight route between Tilbury and Hamburg. The service opened in September 1946. Hamburg dropped from the schedule in 1955 but a service to Antwerp was inaugurated and later the ships' duties extended to include Rotterdam, Europort and Zeebrugge. Felixstowe was adopted by A S N in 1965 and gradually replaced Tilbury as the east coast port until 1968 when Tilbury ceased receiving A S N ships.

The Preston–Larne service of A S N opened on 21 May 1948 and Belfast included from 1950. Again the route was supplied by bow-loading converted tank-landing craft on charter. The passenger/vehicular sailings between Preston and Larne ceased in 1973 and between Preston and Belfast in June 1974.

A S N has had several parents, natural and adoptive. A private company until 1954, in April of that year it became a subsidiary of the British Transport Commission and in 1963 passed to the Transport Holding Company. The National Freight Corporation was the parent from 1969 until 18 November 1971 when A S N became a wholly-owned subsidiary of European Ferries Ltd.

Ionic Ferry and *Bardic Ferry* sailed in the colours of A S N: red underbody, black hull with white line just below the white superstructure. The funnel was blue with a white band and black top.

Townsend Thoresen Car Ferries Ltd. was formed in 1968 following an amalgamation of the interests of Townsend Car Ferries Ltd. and Otto Thoresen Shipping Company A/S. The latter, a Norwegian concern, commenced operation of vehicle/passenger ferries between Southampton and Cherbourg and Le Havre in May 1964, while the former can trace its origins at Dover back to 1930. Following an issue of shares in 1956, Townsend Brothers Ferries Ltd. (as it was then named) became a subsidiary of George Nott Industries Ltd., this latter company changing its name to European Ferries Ltd. in 1968.

Free Enterprise III, although nominally owned by the European Ferries subsidiary, Stanhope Steamship Co. Ltd., sailed in the standard Townsend Thoresen colours—red underbody, green hull with "Townsend Thoresen" in white. The dark red funnel with black top bore the "TTF" symbol in green.

Manager:	Ian Duffin, 1973–	. A S N Manager at Larne since 1948.
Ships' Masters:	William Close	1973–1975, *Ionic Ferry*
		1975– , *Free Enterprise I*
	Charles Hughey	1974– , *Free Enterprise III*
		1974– , *Bardic Ferry*
	A. Ogilvie	1975– , *Ionic Ferry*

Appendix B

1. The Portpatrick–Donaghadee route.

Downshire	c. 1790–c. 1825. Royal Mail Packet.
Hillsborough	c. 1790–c. 1825. Royal Mail Packet.
Palmer	c. 1790–c. 1825. Royal Mail Packet.
Westmoreland	c. 1790–c. 1825. Royal Mail Packet.

One of the above sailing vessels was lost c. 1824.

Arrow	4 May 1825–1833. Royal Mail Packet.
Dasher	4 May 1825–19 December 1830. Royal Mail Packet.
Fury/Asp	1831–August 1849. Royal Mail Packet.
Spitfire/Pike	1833–August 1849. Royal Mail Packet
Dolphin	11 July–October 1868.
Reliance	1870–3 September 1870.
Aber	18 August–29 August 1871.
Avalon	7 June–12 July 1873.
Terrible	29 June–August 1891.
"Three motor boats"	23 May 1921–1921.

2. The Stranraer–Belfast route.

  (i) Stranraer Steam Shipping Company, 1835–1846.
  Glasgow & Stranraer Steam Packet Company, 1846–1864.
  Matthew Langlands & Sons, 1864–1873.

Lochryan	27 June 1835–1843.
Maid of Galloway	August 1836–1844.
Albion	May 1844–April 1860.
Briton	1847–1855. Occasional crossings.
Caledonia	1856–1862. Occasional crossings.
Albion	November 1860–April 1865. August 1869–June 1873.
Scotia	March–October 1861. Occasional crossings before and after.
Briton	July–September 1862.
Staffa	April–August 1865.
Albion	August 1865–June 1873.

  (ii) Caledonian Railway in conjunction with the Portpatrick Railway.

Fannie	1 December 1865–1867.
Alice	6 February 1866–30 January 1868.

  (iii) British Transport Commission—cargo only.

Stream Fisher	7 April 1954–August 1954. May 1956–February 1958.
Seatern	27 May 1954–March 1958.
Firth Fisher	1954–1958. Occasional crossings.
River Fisher	1954–1958. Occasional crossings.
Lough Fisher	1956–1957. Occasional crossings.
Race Fisher	May 1958–17 August 1958. Occasional crossings before.

3. The Stranraer–Larne route.

    (i) Ships regularly employed on the route.

Briton	1 October 1862–31 December 1863.
Princess Louise	1 July 1872–30 April 1890.
Princess Beatrice	4 February 1876–1904.
Princess Victoria	1 May 1890–1909.
Princess May	9 May 1892–June 1914.
Princess Maud	1 June 1904–9 June 1931.
Princess Victoria	29 April 1912–11 October 1914.
	22 April 1920–17 September 1933.
	On war service October 1914–December 1919.
Princess Margaret	1 April 1931–7 July 1939.
	5 September 1939–1 January 1944. Note 1.
	25 December 1944–16 December 1961.
Princess Maud	1 March 1934–2 September 1939. Note 2.
	1 October 1945–18 September 1946.
Princess Victoria	7 July 1939–2 September 1939.
	On war service from September. Lost 21 May 1940.
Princess Victoria	18 March 1947–31 January 1953. Lost at sea.
Hampton Ferry	19 June 1953–2 October 1961. Summer only, usually mid-June to mid-September.
Caledonian Princess	16 December 1961–6 July 1971. Note 3.
Stena Nordica	14 February 1966–27 March 1971.
Antrim Princess	20 December 1967–
Dalriada	24 June 1971– Commercial traffic only.
Ailsa Princess	7 July 1971–
Ulidia	16 December 1974– Commercial traffic only.

Notes: 1. Based at Heysham, July, August 1939. Transferred to Heysham, December 1945–February 1946, August–September 1946, April, May 1947. On war service 1944.
2. On war service September 1939–September 1945. Transferred to Holyhead in September 1946. See also Appendix B, 3 (ii) and (iii).
3. Transferred to Holyhead, 5 July–5 September 1968 and 9 July–3 August 1969; to Fishguard, 20 May–8 July 1969, 4 August–11 October 1969, May–September 1970, 12 December 1970–January 1971 (based at Fishguard from July 1971); to Heysham 16–23 February 1970, 12 October–15 November 1970, March 1971. See also Appendix B, 3 (ii).

(ii) Ships employed as relief vessels or in emergency or temporarily.

		Owners
Garland	6–27 December 1872	Glasgow & Londonderry
	1–20 December 1873	S. P. Co.
	30 Nov. 1875–2 Feb. 1876	
	9–15 February 1876	
Albion	23, 25, 27 April,	M. Langlands & Sons
	21 September 1874	
	8 February 1875	
Midland	17–30 October 1875	Ardrossan Shipping Co.
Elm	26 January 1889	Alex. A. Laird & Co.
Mona	4 June 1891	Ayr Shipping Co.

		Owners
Armagh	5, 6 June 1891	Barrow S. N. Co.
Duchess of Argyll	10–17 June 1911	C S P
Galtee More	3–29 May 1915	L & N W R
	6–25 March 1916	
	9–23 October 1916	
	12–24 March 1917	
	1–12 October 1917	
	27 May–14 June 1918	
	14–25 April 1918	
	31 March–9 April 1919	
	27 Oct.–8 Nov. 1919	
Glen Sannox	? 4 September 1939	C S P
Duchess of Hamilton	11–13 December 1939	C S P
Princess Maud	27 Sept.–19 Oct. 1940	L M & S R, B T C
	20–24 January 1941	
	13–21 June 1941	
	29 Sept.–Oct. 1941	
	18 Dec. 1942–6 Jan. 1943	
	28 Jan.–13 March 1943	
	27 June–13 July 1943	
	28 Oct.–10 Dec. 1946	
	3 Oct.–Nov. 1949	
	October–November 1950	
	October–December 1951	
	2– February 1953	
	January–February 1954	
	22–27 March 1954	
	3 Jan.–12 Feb. 1955	
	9 Jan–11 Feb. 1956	
	January–February 1957	
	January–February 1958	
	5 Jan.–14 Feb. 1959	
	Dec. 1959–13 Feb. 1960	
	23 Jan.–7 March 1961.	
	See also Appendix B, 3 (i)	
Royal Daffodil	3 Jan.–24 Dec. 1944	G S N
Empress Queen	10–25 July 1944	P. & A. Campbell Ltd.
Maidstone	17–22 Dec. 1954 (mail)	B T C
River Fisher	17–21 Dec. 1955 (mail)	James Fisher & Sons Ltd.
Sound Fisher	20, 21 Dec. 1956 (mail)	James Fisher & Sons Ltd.
Bardic Ferry	8, 9 October 1961	A S N
Shepperton Ferry	9–17 April 1962	B T C, B R B
	2–19 March 1963	
	24 Feb.–14 March 1964	
	15 Feb.–13 March 1965	
Holyhead Ferry I	14 Feb.–26 Mar. 1966	B R B
	9–20 January 1967	
	6–26 March 1967	
	25 Nov.–16 Dec. 1972	
	16 April–5 May 1973	
	19 Nov.–13 Dec. 1973	
	18 March–11 April 1974	
	28 Nov.–19 Dec. 1974	

Owners

Slieve Donard	6 July–24 Aug. 1964 (vehicles only)	B R B
Lohengrin	6 June–24 Sept. 1965 (vehicles only)	Wallenius Lines
Baltic Ferry	25 May 1970–23 June 1971 (commercial traffic)	A S N
Caledonian Princess	1–25 November 1971 April 1972 See also Appendix B, 3(i)	B R B
Saaletal	Mar. 1973 (two weeks) (commercial traffic)	Partenreederei m.s.*Thule* (J. A. Reinbecke, Hamburg)
Neckartal	29 Nov. 1973–28 Oct. 1974 (commercial traffic)	Transbaltica Trailer Schiffahrtsges mbH & Co. (J. A. Reinbecke, Hamburg)
Anderida	3–15 March 1974 (commercial traffic)	C (S) Co. on long-term charter to B R B
Preseli	16 Nov.–17 Dec. 1974 (commercial traffic)	Rollonoff Shipping Ltd.
Roro Dania	3 Mar.–2 May 1975	M.s. Namomark Edwin Heyer, Schiffahrts KG (Christian F. Ahrenkiel)
Maid of Kent	1–29 April 1975	B R B
Cambridge Ferry	24 April–8 May 1975	B R B

(iii) Ships engaged on Government service as troopships—September 1939–October 1946.

Owners

Glen Sannox	September 1939	C S P
Duchess of Montrose	September 1939 June–July 1940	C S P
Duchess of Hamilton	Oct. 1939–Oct. 1940 July–September 1945 December 1945 February–March 1946	C S P
Princess Maud	July 1940–Nov. 1943	L M & S R
Shepperton Ferry	July 1940–June 1944	S R
Twickenham Ferry	July–December 1940 Mar. 1941–Jan. 1944	S R / A L A
Hampton Ferry	Sept. 1940–April 1944	S R
Royal Sovereign	September 1940	G S N
Royal Daffodil	Sept. 1940–Jan. 1944 January–March 1945	G S N
Maid of Orleans	Oct. 1940–Jan. 1941 January 1942 January–February 1943	S R
Biarritz	December 1940 April–June 1941	S R S R
Canterbury	Dec. 1940–April 1942	S R

		Owners
Empress Queen	Dec. 1943–6 Oct. 1946	P. & A. Campbell Ltd.
St. Seiriol	Sept.–Nov. 1945	Liverpool & North Wales S. S. Co. Ltd.

4. The Cairnryan–Larne route.
    (i) Ships regularly employed on the route.

Ionic Ferry	10 July 1973–
Free Enterprise III	1 July–19 Oct. 1974
Bardic Ferry	19 Oct. 1974–
Free Enterprise I	25 May 1975–

    (ii) Ship employed as relief vessel.

Bardic Ferry	7–25 March 1974

5. Special Milk Service between Northern Ireland and Scotland.

	Note		*Owners*
Princess Margaret	1	7–21 December 1941	L M & S R
Duchess of Hamilton	1	7–21 December 1941	C S P
Empire Daffodil	1	January 1942	M o W T
	1	22 October–12 December 1942	
	2	19, 21, 22 January 1945	
Whitstable	2	1 Nov. 1943–15 March 1944	S R
	2	1–14 January 1945	
Scottish Co-operator	2	1 October–30 December 1944	S C W S
Maidstone	2	23 January–17 March 1945	S R
Irwell	3	30 Sept. 1945–15 Feb. 1946	L M & S R
Hodder	2	5 October 1946–February 1947	L M & S R
Felixstowe	2	1 November–mid-December 1948	B T C
Princess Victoria	1	August–October 1949	B T C
		8 September–20 October 1950	
		13 August–22 December 1951	
		6 August–25 November 1952	

Notes:
   The routes on which the various ships were employed—
   1. Larne–Stranraer.
   2. Larne–Cairnryan.
   3. Belfast–Cairnryan.

6. Ships' Details.
    Aber
       Hull: 116′ 4″ × 21′ 1″ × 10′ 11″, wood, built at Sunderland.
       Engine: Paddle.
       Launched 1867.

    Ailsa Princess
       Hull: 369′ 5″ × 57′ 3″ × 12′ 0″, steel, Cantiere Navale Breda, Venice.
          Bow and stern doors.
       Engines: 2 Vee oil 4 SA, each 16-cy., 400 × 600 mm, Pielstick/Crossley
          Premier Engines Ltd.
          Twin controllable-pitch propellers, bow thrust unit.
       Launched 28 November 1970, entered service 7 July 1971.

    Albion
       Hull: 145′ 0″ × 21′ 3″ × 10′ 7″, iron, Tod & McGregor, Partick.
       Engine: Paddle, Tod & McGregor, Partick.
       Launched 1844, entered service 28 April 1844.

Albion
> Hull: 165' 0" ×24' 2" ×11' 8", iron, Tod & McGregor, Partick.
> Engine: S 2-cy., 46" ×60", paddle, Tod & McGregor, Partick.
> Launched 18 October 1860, entered service 15 November 1860.

Albion
> Hull: 160' 6" ×20' 2" ×10' 5", iron, Tod & McGregor, Partick.
> Engine: S 2-cy., single screw, Tod & McGregor, Partick.
> Launched 1865, entered service 8 August 1865.

Alice
> Formerly *Sirius* '63.
> Hull: 231' 6" ×26' 2" ×13' 4", iron, Caird & Co., Greenock.
> Engine: S O 2-cy. 60" and 72", paddle, Caird & Co., Greenock.
> Launched 18 June 1859, completed August 1859.

Anderida
> Hull: 347' 9" × 52' 7" ×16' 2½", steel, Trosvik Verksted A/S, Brevik.
> Bow, side and stern doors.
> Engines: 2 oil, 4 SA, each 8-cy., 250 ×300 mm, and 2 oil 4 SA, each 9-cy.,
> 250 ×300 mm, one of each geared to each shaft, Normo Gruppen
> A/S, Bergen.
> Twin controllable-pitch propellers, bow thrust unit.
> Launched 1971, entered service 28 August 1972.

Antrim Princess
> Hull: 369' 6" ×57' 1" ×12' 0", steel, Hawthorn Leslie (Shipbuilders) Ltd.,
> Newcastle.
> Bow and stern doors.
> Engines: 2 Vee oil, 4 SA, each 16-cy., 400 ×460 mm, geared, twin screw,
> Ateliers & Chantiers de Nantes (Bretagne–Loire).
> Bow thrust unit.
> Launched 24 April 1967, entered service 20 December 1967.

Armagh
> Formerly *Talbot* '70.
> Hull: 263' 6" ×27' 0" ×12' 0", iron, Henderson & Co., Renfrew.
> Engine: D 2-cy., 44" and 60", paddle, Henderson & Co., Renfrew.
> Launched 1860.

Arrow
> Later *Ariel* '37.
> Hull: 100' 0" ×17' 3" ×5' 11", wood, William Evans, Rotherhithe.
> Engines: 2 side-lever engines each of 20 h.p., 26½" ×30", paddle, Boulton
> & Watt, Soho.
> Launched 1821, entered service 25 January 1822.

Asp—see *Fury*

Baltic Ferry
> Formerly *Pima County* '65, *LST* 1081; later *Sable Ferry* '72.
> Hull: 327' 9" × 50' 2" ×   , steel, American Bridge Co., Ambridge,
> Mass.
> Bow ramp.
> Engines: 2 oil, 2 SA, each 12-cy., 8½" ×10", twin screw, General Motors
> Corp., Cleveland, Ohio.
> Launched January 1945.

Bardic Ferry
   Hull: 339' 4" × 54' 11" × 12' 11¾", steel, Wm. Denny & Bros. Ltd.,
      Dumbarton.
      Stern door.
   Engines: 2 oil, 2 SA, each 10-cy., 360 × 600 mm, twin screw, Sulzer/Wm.
      Denny & Bros. Ltd., Dumbarton.
      Bow thrust unit.
   Launched 5 March 1957, entered service 2 September 1957.

Biarritz
   Hull: 341' 2" × 42' 1" × 12' 7½", steel, Wm. Denny & Bros., Ltd.,
      Dumbarton.
   Engines: 4 steam turbines geared to twin screws, Denny & Co., Ltd.,
      Dumbarton.
   Launched 7 December 1914, entered Government service March 1915
   and commercial service 1921.

Briton
   Hull: 144' 0" × 20' 0" × 8' 7", iron, Tod & McGregor, Partick.
   Engine: Paddle.
   Completed and entered service 1847.

Briton
   Hull: 175' 6" × 24' 0" × 11' 6", iron, Tod & McGregor, Partick.
   Engine: S 2-cy., 46" and 60", paddle, Tod & McGregor, Partick.
   Launched 2 June 1862, entered service July 1862.

Caledonia
   Hull: 162' 9" × 18' 8" × 9' 5", iron, Tod & McGregor, Partick.
   Engine: Paddle.
   Launched 12 February 1856, entered service 4 March 1856.

Caledonian Princess
   Hull: 353' 0" × 57' 2" × 12' 0", steel, Wm. Denny & Bros., Ltd.,
      Dumbarton.
      Stern door and, from 1969, side doors.
   Engines: 2 steam turbines geared to twin screws, Wm. Denny & Bros.
      Ltd., Dumbarton.
      Bow thrust unit.
   Launched 5 April 1961, entered service 16 December 1961.

Cambridge Ferry
   Hull: 403' 0" × 61' 4" × 12' 0¾", steel, Hawthorn Leslie (Shipbuilders)
      Ltd., Newcastle.
   Engines: 2 oil 4 SA each 7-cy., 15" × 20" geared to twin controllable-pitch
      propellers, Mirrlees National Ltd., Stockport.
   Launched 1 November 1963, entered service 2 January 1964.

Canterbury
   Hull: 341' 6" × 50' 6" × 12' 10", steel, Wm. Denny & Bros. Ltd.,
      Dumbarton.
   Engines: 4 steam turbines geared to twin screws, Wm. Denny & Bros.
      Ltd., Dumbarton.
   Launched 13 December 1928, entered service 15 May 1929.

Dalriada
Formerly *Stena Trailer* '71.
Hull: 347' 9" × 52' 7" × 16' 2½", steel, Brodrene Lothe A/S, Haugesund.
Bow, side and stern doors.
Engines: 2 oil, 4 SA, each 8-cy., 250 × 300 mm, and 2 oil 4 SA, each 9 cy., 250 × 300 mm, one of each geared to each shaft, Normo Gruppen A/S, Bergen.
Twin controllable pitch propellers, bow thrust.
Launched 27 February 1971. Swedish registry.

Dasher
Hull: 100' 0" × 17' 3" × 5' 11", wood, Wm. Paterson, Rotherhithe.
Engines: 2 side-lever engines, each of 20 h.p., 26½" × 30", paddle, Boulton & Watt, Soho.
Launched 13 September 1821, entered service 17 October 1821.

Dolphin
Formerly *Islay* '68.
Hull: 172' 0" × 21' 10" × 10' 10", iron, Tod & McGregor, Partick.
Engine: Paddle, 145 h.p.
Launched 1849, entered service October 1849.

Downshire
Hull: 40' 0" (keel), 52' 0" (deck) × 17' 6" × 9' 0" (depth of hold), wood, Marmaduke Stalkartt, Rotherhithe.
Launched *c.* 1790.

Duchess of Argyll
Hull: 250' 0" × 30' 1" × 10' 1", steel, Wm. Denny & Bros. Ltd., Dumbarton.
Engines: 3 steam turbines, triple screw, Denny & Co., Dumbarton.
Launched 10 March 1906, entered service May 1906.

Duchess of Hamilton
Hull: 272' 3" × 32' 3" × 7' 2", steel, Harland & Wolff Ltd., Govan.
Engines: 3 steam turbines, triple screw, Harland & Wolff Ltd., Belfast.
Launched 5 May 1932, entered service 29 June 1932.

Duchess of Montrose
Hull: 273' 0" × 32' 3" × 7' 2", steel, Wm. Denny & Bros. Ltd., Dumbarton.
Engines: 3 steam turbines, triple screw, Wm. Denny & Bros. Ltd., Dumbarton.
Launched 10 May 1930, entered service 1 July 1930.

Dumbarton Castle
Hull: 87' 0" × 16' 6" × 7' 9", wood, James Lang, Dumbarton.
Engines: 2 paddle, Wm. Watson.
Launched 13 February 1815, entered service May 1815.

Elm
Later *Gaurarapes* '10.
Hull: 182' 2" × 27' 7" × 12' 10", steel, A. & J. Inglis, Partick.
Engine: C 2-cy., 23" and 46" × 24", single screw, A. &. J. Inglis, Partick.
Launched June 1884.

Empire Daffodil
Formerly *Caribe II* '40; later *Greenfinch* '46, *Moira* '66, *Star of Medina* '66.
Hull: 180' 4" × 27' 10" × 7' 7", steel, Gebr. van Diepen N.V., Waterhuizen.

Engine: 1 oil, 7-cy., 4 SA, $11'' \times 17\frac{11}{16}''$, single screw, Klockner-Humboldt-Deutz A.G., Koln-Deutz.
Completed 1940.

Empress Queen
Formerly H.M.S. *Queen Eagle* '43, *Empress Queen* '40; later *Philippos* '55.
Hull: 269' 5" × 37' 6" × 12' 0", steel, Ailsa Shipbuilding Co. Ltd., Troon.
Engines: 4 steam turbines geared to twin screws, Harland & Wolff Ltd., Belfast.
Launched 29 February 1940, entered Government service 4 July 1940 and commercial service June 1947.

Fannie
Formerly *Orion* '63 .
Hull: 231' 6" × 26' 2" × 13' 4", iron, Caird & Co., Greenock.
Engine: O, 2-cy., 60" and 66", paddle, Caird & Co., Greenock.
Launched 14 June 1859, completed August 1859.

Felixstowe
Formerly *Colchester* '46, *Felixstowe* '41; later *Kylemore* '51.
Hull: 215' 1" × 33' 2" × 14' 0", steel, Hawthorns & Co. Ltd., Leith.
Engine: T, 3-cy., 21", 33" and 54" × 36", single screw, Hawthorns & Co. Ltd., Leith.
Launched November 1918, entered service 1919.

Firth Fisher
Formerly *Turkis* '54; later *Agioi Anargyroi III* '71.
Hull: 219' 7" × 32' 7" × 13' 7¼", steel, Goole Shipbuilding & Repairing Co. Ltd., Goole.
Engine: 1 oil, 4 SA, 6-cy., 350 × 535 mm, single screw, British Oil Engines (Export) Ltd., Stockport.
Launched 24 October 1949, completed January 1950.

Free Enterprise I
Formerly *Free Enterprise* '64.
Hull: 316' 6" × 53' 9" × 13' 4¾", steel, N.V. Werf "Gusto", Schiedam.
Stern door.
Engines: 2 oil, 4 SA, each 12-cy., 450 × 660 mm, J. & K. Smit's Mach., Kinderdijk.
Twin controllable-pitch propellers, bow thrust unit.
Launched 2 February 1962, entered service 22 April 1962.

Free Enterprise III
Hull: 385' 6" × 62' 7" × 13' 3¾", steel, N.V. Werf "Gusto", Schiedam.
Bow and stern doors.
Engines: 4 oil, 4 SA, 2 × 12-cy., and 2 × 6-cy., 450 × 660 mm, J. & K. Smit's Mach., Kinderdijk.
Twin controllable-pitch propellers, bow thrust unit.
Launched 14 May 1966, entered service August 1966.

Fury/Asp ('39).
Hull: 94' 0" × 16' 2" × 5' 11", wood, M. Graham, Harwich.
Engines: 2 side-lever engines of 20 h.p. each, 26¾" × 30", paddle. In 1833 cylinders of greater diameter were fitted and the engine rating increased to 30 h.p. Boulton & Watt, Soho.
Launched and entered service 1824.

Galtee More
Hull: 276′ 1″ ×35′ 1″ ×14′ 2″, steel, Wm. Denny & Bros. Ltd.,
    Dumbarton.
Engines: T, 8-cy., (2) 19″, (2) 29″ and (4) 31½″ ×30″, twin screw, Denny &
    Co., Dumbarton.
Launched 24 May 1898.

Garland
Formerly *Bridgewater* '68, *City of Petersburg*
Hull: 228′ 6″ ×25′ 2″ ×13″ 6″, iron, Caird & Co., Greenock.
Engine: O, 2-cy., 58″ and 66″, paddle, Caird & Co., Greenock.
Launched 1863.

Glen Sannox
Hull: 249′ 11″ ×30′ 1″ ×10′ 1″, steel, Wm. Denny & Bros. Ltd.,
    Dumbarton.
Engines: 3 steam turbines, triple screw, Wm. Denny & Bros. Ltd.,
    Dumbarton.
Launched 24 February 1925, entered service May 1925.

Hampton Ferry
Formerly H.M.S. *Hampton* '40, *Hampton Ferry* '39; later *Tre-Arddur* '69.
Hull: 360′ 0″ ×60′ 8″ ×13′ 6″, steel, Swan, Hunter & Wigham Richardson,
    Newcastle.
    Stern door.
Engines: 4 steam turbines geared to twin screws, Parsons Marine Steam
    Turbines Ltd., Wallsend.
Launched 30 July 1934, completed November 1934, entered service
    October 1936.

Highland Chieftain
Formerly *Duke of Wellington* '20.
Hull: 81′ 0″ ×14′ 10″ ×7′ 5″, wood, Denny & Co., Dumbarton.
Engine: Paddle, D. McArthur & Co., Dumbarton.
Launched 1817.

Hillsborough
Hull: 40′ 0″ (keel), 52′ 0″ (deck) ×17′ 6″ ×9′ 0″ (depth of hold), wood,
    Marmaduke Stalkartt, Rotherhithe.
Launched *c.* 1790.

Hodder
Hull: 240′ 2″ ×34′ 1″ ×15′ 5″, steel, Wm. Dobson & Co. Ltd.,Newcastle.
Engine: T, 3-cy., 22″, 36″ and 61″ ×39″, single screw, Wallsend Slipway
    Co. Ltd.
Launched January 1910, entered service February 1910.

Holyhead Ferry I
Hull: 369′ 0″ ×57′ 2″ ×12′ 9″, steel, Hawthorn Leslie (Shipbuilders) Ltd.,
    Newcastle.
    Stern door.
Engines: 2 steam turbines geared to twin screws, Hawthorn Leslie
    (Engineers) Ltd., Newcastle. Bow thrust unit.
Launched 17 February 1965, entered service 19 July 1965.

Ionic Ferry
Hull: 338' 0" × 55' 2" × 12' 11¾", steel, Wm. Denny & Bros. Ltd.,
Dumbarton.
Stern door.
Engines: 2 oil, 2 SA, each 10-cy., 360 × 600 mm, twin screw, Sulzer/Wm.
Denny & Bros. Ltd., Dumbarton. Bow thrust unit.
Launched 2 May 1958, entered service 10 October 1958.

Irwell
Hull: 255' 0" × 36' 1" × 15' 5", steel, Swan, Hunter & Wigham Richardson
Ltd., Newcastle.
Engine: T, 3-cy., 23", 38" and 62" × 42", single screw, Swan, Hunter &
Wigham Richardson Ltd., Newcastle.
Launched May 1906, entered service June 1906.

Lochryan
Hull: 106' 6" × 16' 3" ×   , wood, James Lang, Dumbarton.
Lengthened to 125' 0" in 1839.
Engines: 2, Paddle.
Launched August 1830, entered service 16 September 1830.

Lohengrin
Later *Zwartkops* '69.
Hull: 272' 11" × 42' 4" × 11' 9¾", steel, Fr. Lurssen.
Bow and stern doors.
Engine: 1 oil, 4 SA, 8-cy., 400 × 580 mm, single screw, Klockner-Humboldt-
Deutz, Cologne.
Completed 1964. West German registry.

Lough Fisher
Formerly *Slaney* '55.
Hull: 219' 6" × 32' 8" × 13' 5½", steel, Clelands (Successors) Ltd., Wallsend.
Engine: 1 oil, 4 SA, 6-cy., 350 × 535 mm, single screw, Mirrless, Bickerton
& Day Ltd., Stockport.
Launched 6 December 1949, completed February 1950.

Maid of Galloway
Hull: 116' 6" × 17' 4" × 11' 6" (depth of hold), wood, built Glasgow.
Engine: Paddle.
Launched 1836, entered service August 1836.

Maid of Kent
Hull: 373' 0" × 60' 3" × 13' 0", steel, Wm. Denny & Bros. Ltd., Dum-
barton.
Stern door.
Engines: 2 steam turbines geared to twin screws, Wm. Denny & Bros.
Ltd., Dumbarton.
Bow thrust unit.
Launched 28 November 1958, entered service 28 May 1959.

Maid of Orleans
Hull: 341' 2" × 42' 1" × 12' 7½", steel, Wm. Denny & Bros. Ltd.,
Dumbarton.
Engines: 4 steam turbines geared to twin screws, Denny & Co.,
Dumbarton.
Launched 4 March 1918.

Maidstone
   Hull: 220' 9" × 33' 7" × 12' 9¼", steel, D. & W. Henderson & Co. Ltd.,
      Glasgow.
   Engines: T, each 6-cy., 15", 25" and 41" × 24", twin screw, D. & W.
      Henderson & Co. Ltd., Glasgow.
   Launched 16 March 1926.

Midland
   Later *Vertumnus* '82.
   Hull: 200' 1" × 26' 2" × 12' 8", iron, Wm. Simons & Co., Renfrew.
   Engine: C, 2-cy., 30" and 52" × 36", single screw, Wm. Simons & Co.,
      Renfrew.
   Launched 1873.

Mona
   Formerly *Margaret* '89.
   Hull: 160' 0" × 24' 2" × 14' 0", iron, Barrow Shipbuilding Co. Ltd.,
      Barrow.
   Engine: C, 2-cy., 23" and 46" × 24", single screw, Barrow Shipbuilding Co.
      Ltd., Barrow.
   Launched 1878.

Neckartal
   Hull: 318' 3" × 57' 10" × 13' 7", steel, Krogerwerft G m b H, Rendsburg.
      Stern door.
   Engines: 2 oil, 2 SA, each 9-cy., 320 × 450 mm, twin screw, Atlas-Mak,
      Masch, Kiel.
   Launched 19 December 1969, completed April 1970. West German
      registry.

Palmer
   Hull: 40' 0" (keel), 52' 0" (deck) × 17' 6" × 9' 0" (depth of hold), wood,
      Marmaduke Stalkartt, Rotherhithe.
   Launched *c.* 1790.

Pike—see *Spitfire*

Preseli
   Formerly *Antwerpen* '74, *Isartal* '73.
   Hull: 318' 3" × 52' 0" × 13' 7½", steel, Krogerwerft G m b H, Rendsburg.
      Stern door.
   Engines: 2 oil, 2 SA, each 9-cy., 320 × 450 mm, twin screw, Atlas-Mak,
      Masch, Kiel.
   Launched 17 July 1970, completed October 1970.

Princess Beatrice
   Hull: 234' 6" × 24' 0" × 12' 6", iron, Harland & Wolff, Belfast.
   Engine: (1) D, 2-cy., 54" × 60", paddle, Harland & Wolff, Belfast.
          (2) C D, 2-cy., 39" and 71" × 60", paddle, David Rowan & Co.,
              Glasgow N E '83.
   Launched 4 November 1875, entered service 4 February 1876.

Princess Louise
   Later *Islay* '91.
   Hull: 211' 4" × 24' 1" × 12' 4", iron, Tod & McGregor, Partick.
   Engine: Steeple, 2-cy., 54" × 60", paddle, Tod & McGregor, Partick.
   Launched 7 May 1872, entered service 27 June 1872.

Princess Margaret
Later *Macau* '64.
Hull: 325' 2" ×47' 1" ×11' 8", steel, Wm. Denny & Bros. Ltd.,
Dumbarton.
Engines: 4 steam turbines geared to twin screw, Wm. Denny & Bros.
Ltd., Dumbarton.
Launched 21 January 1931, entered service 1 April 1931.

Princess Maud
Hull: 300' 6" ×40' 1" ×15' 8", steel, Wm. Denny & Bros. Ltd.,
Dumbarton.
Engines: 3 steam turbines, triple screw, Parsons Marine Steam Turbine
Co. Ltd., Newcastle.
Launched 20 February 1904, entered service 1 June 1904.

Princess Maud
Later *Venus* '65, *Nybø* '69.
Hull: 330' 0" ×49' 1" ×11' 6¼", steel, Wm. Denny & Bros. Ltd., Dum-
barton.
Engines: 4 steam turbines geared to twin screws, Wm. Denny & Bros.
Ltd., Dumbarton.
Launched 19 December 1933, entered service 1 March 1934.

Princess May
Hull: 280' 6" ×35' 6" ×13' 5", steel, Wm. Denny & Bros. Ltd., Dumbarton.
Engine: C D, 2-cy., 51" and 90" ×66", paddle, Denny & Co., Dumbarton.
Launched 18 February 1892, entered service 9 May 1892.

Princess Victoria
Hull: 280' 6" ×35' 6" ×13' 4", steel, Wm. Denny & Bros. Ltd.,
Dumbarton.
Engine: C D, 2-cy., 51" and 96" ×66", paddle, Denny & Co., Dumbarton.
Launched 23 January 1890, entered service 1 May 1890.

Princess Victoria
Hull: 300' 6" ×40' 2" ×15' 8, steel, Wm. Denny & Bros. Ltd.,
Dumbarton.
Engines: 3 steam turbines, triple screw, Denny & Co., Dumbarton.
Launched 22 February 1912, entered service 29 April 1912

Princess Victoria
Hull: 309' 10" ×48' 1" ×13' 0", steel, Wm. Denny & Bros. Ltd.,
Dumbarton.
Stern door.
Engines: 2 oil, 2 SCSA, each 7-cy., 18⅞" ×27$\frac{9}{16}$", twin screw, Wm. Denny
& Bros. Ltd., Dumbarton, and Sulzer Bros. Ltd., Winterthur.
Launched 20 April 1939, entered service 7 July 1939.

Princess Victoria
Hull: 309' 10" ×48' 1" ×13' 0", steel, Wm. Denny & Bros. Ltd.,
Dumbarton.
Stern door.
Engines: 2 oil, 2 SCSA, 7-cy., 18⅞" ×27$\frac{9}{16}$", twin screw, Wm. Denny &
Bros. Ltd., Dumbarton.
Launched 27 August 1946, entered service 18 March 1947.

P

Race Fisher
  Formerly *Empire Jill* '46; later *Faradad* '68.
  Hull: 192′ 7″ ×30′ 4″ ×13′ 6″, steel, S. P. Austin & Son Ltd., Sunderland.
  Engine: 1 oil, 2 SA, 5-cy., 340 ×570 mm, single screw, British Auxiliaries
       Ltd., Glasgow.
  Completed April 1942.

Reliance
  Hull: 101′ 1″ ×18′ 7″ ×9′ 7″, wood, built at North Shields.
  Engine: Paddle, 56 n.h.p.
  Launched 1869.

River Fisher
  Formerly *Empire Jack* '46, launched as *River Fisher*; later *Owenduv* '67.
  Hull: 192′ 0″ ×30′ 4″ ×13′ 6″, steel, Vickers-Armstrong Ltd., Barrow.
  Engine: 1 oil, 2 SA, 6-cy., 340 ×570 mm, single screw, British Auxiliaries
       Ltd., Glasgow.
  Completed December 1941.

Roro Dania
  Formerly *Nanomark* '74.
  Hull: 347′ 7″ ×49′ 11″ ×10′8¾″, steel, Ankerløkken Verft Glommen A/S,
       Fredriksted.
  Engines: 2 Vee oil, 4 SA, each 12-cy., 250 ×300 mm, Nydquist & Holm
       A/B, Trollhatten.
       Twin controllable-pitch propellers.
  Launched 12 June 1972. West German registry.

Royal Daffodil
  Hull: 313′ 0″ ×50′ 2″ ×8′ 9″, steel, Wm. Denny & Bros. Ltd., Dumbarton.
  Engines: 2 oil, 2 SA, each 12-cy., 14 3/16″ ×23⅝″, twin screw, Wm. Denny &
       Bros. Ltd., Dumbarton.
  Launched 24 January 1939, entered service 27 May 1939.

Royal Sovereign
  Hull: 269′ 7″ ×47′ 0″ ×9′ 1″, steel, Wm. Denny & Bros. Ltd., Dumbarton.
  Engines: 2 oil, 2 SA, each 12-cy., 14 3/16″ ×23⅝″, twin screw, Sulzer Bros.
       Ltd., Winterthur.
  Launched 28 May 1937, entered service 14 July 1937.

Saaletal
  Formerly *Thule* '71; later *Cotentin* '74.
  Hull: 317′ 7″ ×51′ 11″ ×13′ 7⅜″, steel, Reckmers Werft, Bremerhaven.
       Stern door.
  Engines: 2 oil, 2 SA, each 9-cy., 320 ×450 mm, twin screw, Atlas-Mak
       Masch, Kiel.
       Bow thrust unit.
  Launched 9 August 1969, completed October 1969. West German
       registry.

St. Seiriol
  Hull: 279′ 0″ ×37′ 1″ ×9′ 0″, steel, Fairfield Co. Ltd., Glasgow.
  Engines: 4 steam turbines geared to twin screws, Fairfield Co. Ltd.,
       Glasgow.
  Launched 5 March 1931, entered service 23 May 1931.

Scotia
   Hull: 141′ 3″ ×17′ 5″ ×8′ 7″, iron, Tod & McGregor, Partick.
   Engine: Paddle, Tod & McGregor, Partick.
   Launched 1845, completed August 1845.

Scottish Co-operator
   Later *Edinburgh Merchant* '50, *Annika* '59.
   Hull: 209′ 11″ ×30′ 1″ ×9′ 0″, steel, NV Industrielle Maats, De Noord
      Alblasserdam.
   Engine: 1 oil, 2 SA, 6-cy., 13⅜″ ×22⅟₁₆″, single screw, Atlas-Diesel A/B,
      Stockholm.
   Launched October 1938, completed January 1939.

Seatern
   Formerly *Kyle Fisher* '49; later *Marina* '60.
   Hull: 171′ 7″ ×28′ 7″ ×12′ 8¼″, steel, De Haan & Oerlemans Scheepsbwf,
      Heusden.
   Engine: 1 oil, 2 SA, 4-cy., 340 ×570 mm, single screw, British Polar
      Engines Ltd., Glasgow.
   Launched 6 March 1939, completed May 1939.

Shepperton Ferry
   Formerly H.M.S. *Shepperton* '40, *Shepperton Ferry* '39.
   Hull: 360′ 0″ ×60′ 8″ ×13′ 6″, steel, Swan, Hunter & Wigham Richardson,
      Newcastle.
   Stern door.
   Engines: 4 steam turbines geared to twin screws, Parsons Marine Steam
      Turbines Ltd., Newcastle.
   Launched 23 October 1934, completed March 1935, entered service
   October 1936.

Slieve Donard
   Hull: 310′ 3″ ×47′ 3″ ×13′ 0½″, steel, Ailsa Shipbuilding Co. Ltd., Troon.
      Side and stern doors.
   Engines: 2 oil, 2 SA, each 8-cy., 340 ×570 mm, twin screw, British Polar
      Engines Ltd., Glasgow.
   Launched 1 October 1959, completed January 1960.

Sound Fisher
   Formerly *Benveg* '51, *Polperro* '50.
   Hull: 226′ 0″ ×34′ 2″ ×14′ 2″, steel, Charles Hill & Sons Ltd., Bristol.
   Engine: 1 oil, 2 SA, 6-cy., 340 ×570 mm, single screw, British Polar
      Engines Ltd., Glasgow.
   Launched 1949, completed April 1949.

Spitfire/Pike ('39)
   Hull: 94′ 0″ ×16′ 2″ ×5′ 11″, wood, M. Graham, Harwich.
   Engines: 2 side-lever engines, each 26¾″ ×30″, paddle, Boulton & Watt,
      Soho. In 1834, larger cylinders were fitted that increased the
      engine rating by 50 per cent.
   Launched 1824.

Staffa
   Hull: 153′ 0″ ×23′ 1″ ×11′ 2″, iron, J. & G. Thomson, Clydebank.
   Engine: S, 2-cy., single screw, J. & G. Thomson, Clydebank.
   Launched 1863.

Stena Nordica
Later *Santa Ana* '74.
Hull: 236′ 4″ × 50′ 0″ × 12′ 9″, steel, Ateliers & Chantiers de la Seine Maritime Le Trait.
Bow, side and stern doors.
Engines: 2 oil, 4 SA, each 12-cy., 400 × 500 mm, Klockner-Humboldt-Deutz, Cologne.
Twin controllable-pitch propellers, bow thrust unit.
Launched 15 May 1965, entered service 3 July 1965. Swedish registry.

Stream Fisher
Formerly *Empire Judy* '46; later *Ramaida* '69.
Hull: 192′ 7″ × 30′ 4″ × 13′ 6″, steel, S. P. Austin & Son Ltd., Sunderland.
Engine: 1 oil, 2 SA, 5-cy., 340 × 570 mm, single screw, British Auxiliaries Ltd., Glasgow.
Completed June 1943.

Terrible
Hull: 129′ 8″ × 19′ 4″ × 10′ 7″, iron, built at Low Walker.
Engine: Paddle.
Launched 1869.

Twickenham Ferry
Hull: 366′ 0″ × 60′ 8″ × 13′ 6¼″, steel, Swan, Hunter & Wigham Richardson, Newcastle.
Stern door.
Engines: 4 steam turbines geared to twin screws, Parsons Marine Steam Turbines Ltd., Newcastle.
Launched 15 March 1934, completed July 1934, entered service October 1936. French registry.

Ulidia
Formerly *Stena Carrier* '74.
Hull: 347′ 5″ × 52′ 7″ × 16′ 2½″, steel, Kristiansands M/V A/S.
Bow, side and stern doors.
Engines: 2 oil, 2 SA, each 8-cy., 250 × 300 mm, and 2 oil, 4 SA each, 9-cy., 250 × 300 mm, one of each geared to each shaft, Normo Gruppen A/S, Bergen.
Twin controllable-pitch propellers, bow thrust unit.
Launched 1970.

Westmoreland
Hull: 40′ 0″ (keel), 52′ 0″ (deck) × 17′ 6″ × 9′ 0″ (depth of hold), wood, Marmaduke Stalkartt, Rotherhithe.
Launched *c.* 1790.

Whitstable
Hull: 229′ 6″ × 33′ 7″ × 12′ 9¼″, steel, D. & W. Henderson & Co. Ltd., Glasgow.
Engine: T, 6-cy., 15″, 25″ and 41″ × 24″, single screw, D. & W. Henderson & Co. Ltd., Glasgow.
Launched 26 June 1925.

Appendix C

STATISTICS

1. Passengers travelling by the mail packets via Portpatrick and Donaghadee, 1825–1838.

	To Donaghadee		To Portpatrick	
	Cabin	Steerage	Cabin	Steerage
1825*	569	6,152	595	3,481
1826	556	6,580	557	5,385
1827	447	6,961	450	5,178
1828	536	6,712	539	4,903
1829	459	6,570	483	4,868
1830	522	7,069	554	5,871
1831	520	6,686	500	5,942
1832	554	5,399	430	3,849
1833	427	4,348	435	3,847
1834	470	5,171	483	4,593
1835	429	4,525	397	4,249
1836	543	3,566	519	4,059
1837	531	3,443	455	4,103
1838 to 1 Aug.	222	1,670	213	2,683

*Probably from 4 May.

Sources: 1825–1831 Parl. Papers 1831–32 (716), XVII, p. 373.
1832–1838 The New Statistical Account of Scotland, volume IV, p. 154.

2. Passengers travelling by the Stranraer and Larne route 1925–1946.

1925	108,219	1932	145,786	1940	239,930
1926	96,223	1933	138,952	1941	333,665
1927	125,400	1934	168,810	1942	346,866
1928	128,136	1935	181,475	1943	377,091
1929	134,038	1936	193,291	1944	472,345
1930	130,339	1937	199,626	1945	504,655
1931	137,200	1938	219,341	1946	334,790
		1939	223,083		

Source: Minutes of the Steam Vessels Sub-Committee of the Scottish Committee of the L M & S R.

3. Passengers travelling by the Stranraer and Larne route for the four years
    1933, 1938, 1943 and 1946, demonstrating seasonal peaks.

Four	1933		1938		1943		1946	
weeks to	Per cent	Carried	Per cent	Carried	Per cent	Carried	Per cent	Carried
30 Jan.	2·2	3,103	2·1	4,806	7·2	27,294	9·2	30,598
26 Feb.	0·8	1,401	1·4	3,055	6·5	24,819	6·4	21,276
26 Mar.	1·2	1,641	1·5	3,304	6·6	25,035	6·9	23,016
23 April	2·6	3,685	2·0	4,416	7·1	26,817	6·6	21,952
21 May	2·7	3,734	2·6	5,660	7·1	26,665	6·1	20,572
18 June	8·8	12,169	7·4	15,858	6·9	25,919	7·9	26,338
10 July	20·2	27,943	21·2	46,540	8·3	31,201	10·3	34,640
13 Aug.	26·4	36,576	26·9	59,006	8·9	32,330	14·6	48,720
5 Sept.	20·0	27,794	18·9	41,466	8·9	33,690	10·3	34,425
8 Oct.	8·2	11,409	8·1	17,822	8·4	31,482	6·3	21,156
5 Nov.	2·3	3,184	4·6	10,164	8·1	30,438	5·8	19,283
3 Dec.	1·8	2,537	1·5	3,338	7·9	29,624	4·6	15,563
31 Dec.	2·8	3,776	1·8	3,906	8·4	31,777	5·0	16,803
	100·0		100·0		100·0		100·0	

Note: The dates do not correspond exactly from year to year but the
      periods covered do.
Source: Minutes of the Steam Vessels Sub-Committee of the Scottish
        Committee of the L M & S R.

4. Detailed return of passengers, livestock and freight carried between Stran-
    raer and Larne by *Princess Louise* in May, June and July 1874.

Week ending	Passengers		Horses	Cattle	Sheep	Pigs	Boxes of fish	Tons of goods
	Cabin	Steerage						
2 May	91	149	79	246	50	0	65	70
9 May	89	213	37	431	0	14	62	72
16 May	86	206	37	331	0	9	79	66
23 May	92	229	14	604	150	0	96	85
30 May	78	210	17	479	133	0	77	67
6 June	92	240	134	519	0	65	87	52
13 June	122	205	16	581	0	22	110	56
20 June	185	261	47	212	88	11	84	64
27 June	175	218	71	123	0	5	111	61
4 July	143	204	41	974	0	8	123	69
11 July	150	327	20	220	0	0	127	70
18 July	165	303	20	172	0	0	134	70
25 July	251	353	70	268	0	0	172	82
	1,719	3,118	603	5,160	421	134	1,327	884

Source: Report from Captain George Campbell in *The Galloway Advertiser
        and Wigtownshire Free Press* of Thursday, 30 July 1874.

5. Details of wages paid.
    (i)   At Portpatrick in December 1837 to officers and crew of *Fury* and
          Spitfire.

Commander	£250 per ann.	Mate	£58·50 per ann.
Engineer	£109·20 per ann.	Steward	£34·12½ per ann.
Firemen (2)	£50·70 each per ann.	Seamen (4)	£34·12½ each per ann.

Source: Parl. Papers 1837–38 (203), XLV, p. 595.

(ii) At Stranraer in December 1886 to officers and crew of *Princess Beatrice*
      and *Princess Louise*.

Ship in service:

Master	£5·00 per week.	Mate	£2·50 per week.
Engineer	£3·15 per week.	Engineer	£2·25 per week.
Carpenter	£1·60 per week.	Seamen (7)	£1·25 each per week.
Firemen (6)	£1·25 each per week.	Fireman (1)	£1·10 per week.
Steward (1)	£1·20 per week.	Steward (1)	£0·75 per week.
Stewardess (1)	£0·50 per week.	Cook (1)	£1·00 per week.
Boy (1)	£0·50 per week.		

Ship laid up:

Watchman	£1·25 per week.	Fireman	£1·25 per week.

Source: Memorandum of 2 December 1886 accompanying L & S S Co's
Accounts for the half year to 30 June 1886.

6. Financial results of the Stranraer–Larne route for the years 1888, 1905,
    1935 and 1965.

	1888	1905	1935	1965
Revenue—				
Passengers	£4,559	£11,900	£38,011	£279,039
Freight	2,942	4,583	22,989	221,748
Mails	1,088	7,000	8,866	64,523
Accompanied Vehicles	—	*	*	552,118
Livestock	3,353	1,980	6,214	*
	£11,942	£25,463	£76,080	£1,117,428
Expenditure—				
Ships' Operating Expenses		17,673	31,755	193,552
Maintenance of Ships		3,214	7,790	46,585
Depreciation	Not	7,645	11,713	73,894
Other Traffic Expenses	disclosed	*	7,595	127,264
General		4,802	3,097	69,936
		33,334	61,950	511,231
Surplus/(Loss)		(7,871)	14,130	606,197
Catering Net Revenue	50†	354	1,623	10,142
Surplus/(Loss) on Ships' Operating	£(7,517)	£15,753	£616,339	

* Not shown separately.   †Cabin rent.

Sources: 1888   Minutes of the 19th Ordinary General Meeting of the
                L & S S Co.
         1905   Abstract of Receipts and Expenditure for the Ten Years
                ending 31 December 1909. Scottish Record Office reference
                BR/LSS/4/4.
         1935   Minutes of the Steam Vessels Sub-Committee of the
                Scottish Local Committee of the L M & S R.
         1965   Accounts of C S P (IS) for the year ended 31 December 1965.

Appendix D

AIRCRAFT

Particulars of aircraft used by Silver City Airways Ltd. on the Stranraer (Castle Kennedy)–Belfast (Newtonards) route 1955–1957.

Silver City Airways was taken over in 1962 by British United Airways Ltd. and became part of British United Airways Ferries Ltd. British United Airways Ltd. was in turn absorbed in the British Caledonian Airways Group in 1970.

DAKOTA (DC 3)

First prototype flew on 18 December 1935.

Capacity: 30–32 passengers.

Power: 2 1,200 h.p. Pratt & Whitney Twin-Wasp R-1830-92 piston radial motors.

Weights: Maximum all-up 28,000 lb., empty 16,840 lb., wing loading 28·3 lb. per sq. in.

Dimensions: Span 95′ × length 64′ × height 16′ 11″.

Performance: Economic cruising (with 6,340 lb. payload) 143 m.p.h. at 8,000′ for still air range of 340 miles.

BRISTOL 170

First prototype flew on 2 December 1945.

Capacity: 3 motor cars of 14′ length and 20 passengers or 48 passengers. Cars entered by nose which had clamshell doors which hinged outward.

Power: 2 2,000 h.p. Bristol Hercules 734 piston radial motors.

Weights: Maximum all-up 44,000 lb., empty 29,465 lb., wing loading 29·5 lb. per sq. in.

Dimensions: Span 108′ × length 73′ 8″ × height 21′ 6″.

Performance: Economic cruising (with 8,000 lb. payload) 164 m.p.h. at 5,000′ for still air range of 1,270 miles.

Appendix E

LOG OF MESSAGES BETWEEN *PRINCESS VICTORIA* AND SHORE AND SHIPS ON 31 JANUARY 1953

Reproduced by kind permission of Charles Birchall & Sons Ltd., from *Report of the Ministry of Transport Inquiry into the Loss of the Motorship* Princess Victoria *and the Findings of the Court.*

0806.   *Princess Victoria* to GPK (Portpatrick Radio) — I am now leaving Stranraer bound Larne.

0946.   *Princess Victoria* to GPK — X.X.X. (urgency signal) — Hove to off mouth of Loch Ryan. Vessel not under command. Urgent assistance of tug required.

1031.   Alarm signal re SOS. GMZN (*Princess Victoria*'s call sign).

1032-34 *Princess Victoria* to SOS. — *Princess Victoria* four miles north-west of Corsewall. Car deck flooded. Heavy list to starboard. Require immediate assistance. Ship not under command.

1034.   GPK to *Princess Victoria* — R. SOS.

1035.   GPK to CQ (all ships) — Alarm signal.

1043.   GPK to *Princess Victoria* — The destroyer *Contest* proceeding from Rothesay to your assistance. Estimated time of arrival 1400.

1054.   *Princess Victoria* to GPK — SOS.

1054.   *Princess Victoria* to SOS. — We require immediate assistance now.

1100.   *Princess Victoria* to SOS. — *Princess Victoria* GMZN four miles north-west of Corsewall. Require immediate assistance.

1114.   GPK to *Princess Victoria* — I have a message for you. Portpatrick lifeboat launched to your assistance.

1125.   *Princess Victoria* to GPK — SOS. Position approximately five miles W.N.W. from Corsewall.

1135.   *Princess Victoria* to SOS. — *Princess Victoria* GMZN. Position approximately five miles W.N.W. from Corsewall. Car deck flooded. Very heavy list to starboard. Ship not under command. Require immediate assistance.

1143.   Destroyer *Contest* to *Princess Victoria* — Am proceeding to your assistance with all dispatch. ETA (estimated time of arrival) 1300. Request details of extent of flooding and list.
Have you power? If so, voltage a.c. or d.c.?

1157.   *Princess Victoria* to *Contest* — 35 deg. list to starboard. Approximately 200 tons water and cargo in car deck. Power 220 volts d.c. 123 passengers, 60 crew. Position approx. five miles W. by S. of Corsewall. Master GMZN.

1211.   *Princess Victoria* to *Contest* — Have started radar. Will try to get bearing.

1217.   GPK to CQ — SOS. Following received from British ship *Princess Victoria* at 1034 G.M.T. Begins: SOS. Position five miles W. by S. of Corsewall. Bearing from Portpatrick 282 deg. Bearing from Malin Head Radio 112·5 deg.

1232.   *Princess Victoria* to *Contest* and GPK — Approx. position 280 deg., seven miles from Killingtringan. Position grave but list not appreciably worsening.

233

1243.   *Contest* to *Princess Victoria* — Regret will not reach you until 1330. Are you in any danger of sinking? If not, intend to pass tow on arrival and proceed to shelter of Loch Ryan for trying to send over a pump.

1246.   GPK to *Princess Victoria* — What is your approx. distance off Scottish shore, ref. your radar?

1247.   *Princess Victoria* to GPK — Sorry, radar no use. Too much list.

1252.   *Princess Victoria* to GPK — Position critical. Starboard engine-room flooded.

1252.   GPK to CQ — SOS. Following received from British ship *Princess Victoria* at 1252. Begins: SOS. Position critical. Starboard engine-room flooded. Bearing from Portpatrick Radio 264 deg. Bearing from Seaforth Radio 312 deg.

1307.   *Princess Victoria* to *Contest* — SOS.

1308.   *Princess Victoria* to CQ — SOS. Now stopped. Ship on her beam end. Snap bearing 260–262.

1315.   *Princess Victoria* to GPK — We are preparing to abandon ship.

1321.   *Princess Victoria* to *Contest* — Can you see us?

1326.   *Contest* to *Princess Victoria* — Cannot see you yet.

1330.   *Contest* to *Princess Victoria* — My ETA is now 1415. Can you hold out until then?

1335.   *Princess Victoria* to GPK — SOS. Endeavouring to hold on but ship on beam end. Can see Irish coast. Shall fire rocket if you wish.

1339.   *Contest* to *Princess Victoria* — Good luck. Am coming as fast as I can. Please fire a rocket.

1347.   *Princess Victoria* to SOS. (GPK) — Captain says he can see . . . lighthouse . . .opeltnd . . . off entrance Belfast Lough. Sorry for Morse.

1347.   GPK to *Princess Victoria* — Is it Copeland?

1347.   *Princess Victoria* to GPK — Yes.

1347.   GPK to *Princess Victoria* — Can you get a bearing?

1349.   *Princess Victoria* to GPK — Sorry, can't see it for squall.

1354.   *Princess Victoria* to GPK — SOS. Estimated position now five miles east of Copelands, entrance to Belfast Lough.

1354.   *Princess Victoria* to GPK — Sorry for Morse, OM (old man). On beam end.

1354.   GPK to *Princess Victoria* — R. Do not let that worry you, OM.

1358.   *Princess Victoria* to *Contest* — SOS. Estimated position now five miles east of Copelands, entrance to Belfast Lough.

1359.   GPK to CQ — Bearing *Princess Victoria* at 1356, 250 deg. Class B ($\pm$ 5 deg.).

1431.   *Pass of Drumochter* (oil tanker) to m.v. *Lairdsmoor* (cargo vessel) — Have you seen anything on your radar screen?

1432.   *Lairdsmoor* to "Drumochter" — Something on the screen; maybe it's him.

1433.   *Lairdsmoor* to "Drumochter" — Something big east. Picked up ship on port bow.

1435.   Aircraft GAJNE to GPK — Looking for *Princess Victoria*. Are you in touch with her?

1435.   GPK to GAJNE — Yes. Last known position was five miles east of Copelands, entrance Belfast Lough.

1435.   Portpatrick radio to "Drumochter" — Give me your position.

1436.   "Drumochter" to Portpatrick — Checking my position. Can see something on port bow, five miles.

1436½.   "Drumochter" to Portpatrick — Copeland 2½ miles due south but ship we see is a destroyer.

1437½. "Drumochter" to Portpatrick — Ask *Princess Victoria* to fire rockets.

1439. GPK to *Princess Victoria* — Nil heard. Please, if possible, fire rockets, fire rockets.

1442. *Orchy* (cargo ship) to Portpatrick — Have you any later position of *Princess Victoria*. Cannot see anything on radar.

1445. Portpatrick to *Orchy* — No news. What range are you using?

1446. *Orchy* to Portpatrick — Three miles range.

1449. *Orchy* to Portpatrick — Have come across oil and wreckage and life-jackets approximately five miles east of Mew Island.

1450. *Orchy* to Portpatrick — We see people on the rafts.

1453. GPK to aircraft GAJNE — Infs. coming in on R.T. Wreckage and oil in position five miles east of Copelands lighthouse.

1453. *Orchy* to Portpatrick — People on rafts waving.
Portpatrick to *Orchy* — Do your best.

1454. Portpatrick to all ships — All ships make for the position of *Orchy*.

1455. "Drumochter" to Portpatrick — We are one mile off *Orchy* and proceeding at full speed.

1455½. "Drumochter" to Donaghadee lifeboat — Now three miles north-east of Mew Island.

1456. Donaghadee lifeboat to "Drumochter" — Blow your horn to let destroyer know where you are.

1458. *Orchy* to Donaghadee lifeboat — Come to me. I am among people and bodies.

1459. Portpatrick to *Orchy* — Come on the air with your position.

1501. *Orchy* to Portpatrick. Five miles east of Copeland and drifting quickly.

1503. *Orchy* to "Drumochter" — There are a lot of people here but they cannot get hold of the line.

1505. "Drumochter" to *Orchy* — We are very low in the water, so we may be able to do something.

1507. *Orchy* to Portpatrick — Position hopeless. Cannot lower lifeboats but doing our best.

1508. Portpatrick to *Orchy* — O.K. Keep your chin up.

1509. Portpatrick lifeboat to Portpatrick — Ask big ships to guide us to position.

1511. Donaghadee lifeboat to "Drumochter" — Four miles east of Mew Island.

1512. "Drumochter" to Portpatrick — Coming up to lifeboat full of people.

1513. *Lairdsmoor* to "Drumochter" — Coming up to you with lines, etc.

1514. *Orchy* to all ships — All lifeboats please come to me.

1515. "Drumochter" to *Orchy* — We are coming up to two lifeboats.

1515½. Portpatrick to "Drumochter" — Can you give me your exact position?
"Drumochter" to Portpatrick and Donaghadee lifeboats — We are 4½ miles north-east of Mew Island.

1517. "Drumochter" to Donaghadee lifeboat — If you see a ship with a black funnel and white bands go to her.

1520. Portpatrick lifeboat to Portpatrick — See three steamers; am going straight for them.

1521. Portpatrick to Portpatrick lifeboat — Some boats in vicinity fire rockets. If they cannot do that, start blowing whistles.

1522. "Drumochter" to Portpatrick — Two lifeboats, one with one in it and one nearly full.

1523. "Drumochter" to all lifeboats — If you can pick anyone up, you can put them on us, as our decks are low.

1525. "Drumochter" to Portpatrick — I am trying to get near lifeboats.

1525¼.   *Orchy* to Donaghadee lifeboat — Can you see us? Are you in the vicinity? Please come to us.
1526.   "Drumochter" to *Orchy* — Have you got anyone?
1527.   *Orchy* to "Drumochter" — The position is hopeless. The ship will not do anything for us.
1527½.   "Drumochter" to *Orchy* — We cannot get alongside lifeboat, but the chief is going to pour fuel oil over the side and we will do our best, as I have a brother-in-law there.
1530.   Portpatrick to trawler *Eastcotes* — They are picking up survivors four miles north-east of Mew Island.
1531.   Unknown transmitter — There is a hell of a sea. Can hear an aircraft overhead.
1532.   *Lairdsmoor* to Portpatrick — In the vicinity of *Orchy* and wreckage, but no people.
1534.   Portpatrick to Portpatrick lifeboat — How are you getting on?
1534¼.   Portpatrick lifeboat to Portpatrick — Heading for tanker, but very heavy seas and cannot see very much.
1538.   *Orchy* to *Lairdsmoor* — Are you getting me?
1539.   *Lairdsmoor* to Donaghadee lifeboat — There is wreckage here but no people.
1539.   *Orchy* to Donaghadee lifeboat — There are people between me and *Lairdsmoor*. Can you come to us?
1540.   *Orchy* to "Drumochter" — Donaghadee lifeboat is coming to us now. He will be able to do better than we can, as our light ship is high and the position was hopeless.
1545.   *Lairdsmoor* to Portpatrick — Position five miles north-east of Copeland but only see wreckage. See numerous rafts but no one on them.
1547.   Portpatrick lifeboat to Portpatrick — See boats but no living people.
1547½.   Portpatrick to Portpatrick lifeboat — Proceed to *Orchy*. There are lifeboats with people on them.
1548.   Portpatrick lifeboat to Portpatrick. Proceeding with all speed.
1551.   Donaghadee lifeboat to "Drumochter" — Come over to us, as we cannot do anything.
1552.   Donaghadee lifeboat to "Drumochter" — We are coming to you.
1553.   *Orchy* to Donaghadee lifeboat — Come over between us and the destroyer. There are people on raft.
1554.   *Orchy* to Portpatrick — Can see the Portpatrick lifeboat.
1556.   "Drumochter" to *Orchy* — The Donaghadee lifeboat is alongside one of the lifeboats and will transfer them to us.
1559.   "Drumochter" to Donaghadee lifeboat — There is another lifeboat off us with one in it. We will go up to windward and make lee for you. Will you follow us?
1559½.   Donaghadee lifeboat to "Drumochter" — Yes, we will follow.
1603.   "Drumochter" to *Lairdsmoor* — The Donaghadee lifeboat is picking up one boat and is taking the other man out of the other boat. We have poured oil out and it doesn't seem to be much good.
1607.   "Drumochter" to Donaghadee lifeboat — The other boat is on our beam. We are making a lee for you. Come up close to us, and if you wish to put them on board, you can.
1609.   Portpatrick lifeboat to "Drumochter" — Can you direct me to any more people?
1610.   "Drumochter" to Portpatrick lifeboat — There is wreckage between me and the *Orchy* but I don't think there is anyone in it.
1613.   Donaghadee lifeboat to "Drumochter" — Can you see any more people?

1614.   "Drumochter" to Donaghadee lifeboat — The *Orchy* says there is a lifeboat to windward of me. Can you see if there is anyone in it?

1618.   Portpatrick lifeboat to all ships — Can you direct me to anything?

1618½.   *Orchy* to Portpatrick lifeboat — Cannot see anything. Fear it is all over, but if we do see anything we will direct you.

1623.   *Lairdsmoor* to Portpatrick lifeboat — There is a ship's lifeboat abeam of me now.

1624.   Donaghadee lifeboat to *Lairdsmoor* — That is an empty lifeboat.

1624½.   *Lairdsmoor* to Donaghadee lifeboat — There's a flashing light on the water. Don't know if it is a lifeboat or what it is.

1630.   Portpatrick to Donaghadee lifeboat — How many survivors have you?

1630½.   Donaghadee lifeboat to Portpatrick — Cannot count them but should say about 40.

1633.   "Drumochter" to *Orchy* — I am going through a lot of lifeboats but no sign of life.

1634.   *Orchy* to "Drumochter" — No sign of life here, but we will cruise around for a little while longer. I am afraid nothing can last in this.

1635.   *Lairdsmoor* to "Drumochter" — We can see nothing, either. Nothing whatever can live in that.

1636.   "Drumochter" to Donaghadee lifeboat — We cannot see anything only lifeboats and lifejackets but will cruise around until dark.

1637.   "Drumochter" to Donaghadee lifeboat — Can you find out if any more lifeboats were launched? It is funny that there were no women among the survivors.

1640.   *Lairdsmoor* to "Drumochter" — I have cattle on board and they are getting great abuse, so at 1700 we shall have to make for shelter so that they may be fed.

1645.   "Drumochter" to Portpatrick lifeboat — Aircraft has dropped flares ahead of us, so we are going up to see what it is and we will direct you.

1649.   "Drumochter" to Donaghadee lifeboat — If you can take them (survivors) into Donaghadee you had better do so, as it would be difficult to transfer them and something might happen.

1651.   "Drumochter" to Donaghadee lifeboat — We have just passed through a lot of wreckage and lifeboats but no sign of life. I expect that is what the aircraft saw.

At 1750 "Drumochter" told Portpatrick that she had been through the wreckage again and had seen no sign of life, and at 1734 *Orchy* radioed "Can do nothing more. Am going back to Belfast Lough".

Appendix F

EXCURSIONS ASSOCIATED WITH STRANRAER – LARNE ROUTE

This listing is prepared from newspaper advertisements, press reports and sailing bills and may, therefore, not be complete. It will be appreciated that certain sailings while advertised as excursions were primarily extra crossings for peak traffic.

Date	Time Out	Back	Destination	Steamer	Remarks
FROM LARNE					
1872					
Thursday 27 & Friday, 28 June			Stranraer	Princess Louise	To view warships
Saturday, 29 June			Belfast Lough	Princess Louise	
1876					
Saturday, 22 July			Stranraer	Princess Louise	
1876–1889					
One Tues. in July except 1883			Stranraer	Princess Louise	Stranraer Cattle Show Day
1878					
Saturday 13, 20 & 27 July			Stranraer	Princess Louise	Special train to Castle Kennedy
1895					
Sat. 6, 13, 20 & 27 July, 3, 10, 17, 24 & 31 Aug.			Antrim Coast		
1896					
Saturday 4, 11, 18 & 25 July, 1, 8, 15, 22 & 29 August	1400 1400		Antrim Coast		
1897					
Monday, 2 August	1400	1600	Antrim Coast	Princess Victoria	
1898					
Friday 15 & Saturday, 16 July	1115	1600	Bangor Bay	Princess May	Bangor Regatta
1899					

Date			Route	Ship	Notes
Saturday, 14 July	1200		Antrim Coast and Rathlin Island	*Princess Maud*	
Monday, 6 August	1145		Antrim Coast and Rathlin Island	*Princess Maud*	Atlantic Fleet in bay
Saturday, 11 August			Bangor Bay	*Princess Maud*	
Saturday, 8 September	1145		Antrim Coast and Rathlin Island	*Princess Maud*	
1907					
Friday, 12 July	1215	1630	Antrim Coast and Rathlin Island	*Princess Maud*	
Saturday, 13 July	1400	1740	Isle of Sanda	*Princess Maud*	
Monday, 15 July	1215	1630	Antrim Coast and Rathlin Island	*Princess Maud*	Warships in bay
Saturday, 27 July	1415	1800	Isle of Sanda	*Princess Maud*	
Saturday, 3 August	1415	1645	Bangor Bay	*Princess Maud*	
Monday, 5 August	1215	1630	Antrim Coast and Rathlin Island	*Princess Maud*	
1908					
Monday, 3 August	1215	1630	Antrim Coast and Rathlin Island	*Princess Maud*	
1909					
Mon. 12, Sat. 17, Wed. 21 July & Mon., 2 August	1215	1630	Antrim Coast and Rathlin Island	*Princess Maud*	
1910					
Tuesday, 12 July, Monday 1 & Saturday 27 Aug.	1215	1630	Antrim Coast and Rathlin Island	*Princess Maud*	
1911					
Saturday, 10 June	a.m.	2200	Stranraer	*Duchess of Argyll*	In place of *Princess May*
Thur., 22 June, Wed., 12 July & Mon., 7 Aug.	1230	1630	Antrim Coast and Rathlin Island	*Princess Maud*	
1912					
Friday, 12 July	1100		Ailsa Craig and Loch Ryan	*Princess Maud*	Called at Stranraer
Sat., 13 July & Mon., 5 Aug.	1215	1615	Antrim Coast and Rathlin Island	*Princess Maud*	
1913					
Sat., 12 July & Mon., 4 Aug.	1215	1615	Antrim Coast and Rathlin Island	*Princess Maud*	
1914					
Mon., 13 July & Mon., 3 Aug.	1215	1615	Antrim Coast and Rathlin Island	*Princess Maud*	
1922					
Friday, 14 July	0945		Stranraer	*Princess Victoria*	No daylight service in 1922
Monday, 7 August	2030		Stranraer	*Princess Victoria*	
1924					
Mon., 14 July & Mon., 4 Aug.	1215	1615	Antrim Coast and Rathlin Island	*Princess Victoria*	

Date	Out	Back	Destination	Steamer	Remarks
1925					
Tues., 14 July & Mon., 3 Aug.	1225	1630	Antrim Coast and Rathlin Island	Princess Victoria	First Sunday cruise
1926					
Sunday, 25 July	1225	1630	Antrim Coast and Rathlin Island	Princess Victoria	
Sunday, 1 August			Stranraer	Princess Victoria	
Monday, 2 August	1045	1630	Campbeltown	Princess Victoria	1¼ hours ashore
1927					
Sunday, 3 July			Stranraer	Princess Maud	
Wednesday, 13 July	1045	1630	Campbeltown	Princess Victoria	1¼ hours ashore
Fri., 15 & Sat., 16 July	1400	2145	Stranraer		
Sunday, 31 July	1100	2100	Campbeltown	Princess Victoria	1¼ hours ashore
Monday, 1 August	1045	1630	Stranraer	Princess Victoria	
Sunday, 21 August			Stranraer	Princess Victoria	
1928					
Saturday, 25 February	0025 / 0715		Stranraer	Princess Victoria / Princess Maud	Football match at Glasgow. Returning early Sunday
Sunday, 8 July	1110	1630	Stranraer	Princess Maud	
Monday, 16 July	1215	2100	Antrim Coast and Rathlin Island	Princess Maud	
Sunday, 22 July	1110	1630	Stranraer	Princess Maud	
Monday, 6 August	1215	2100	Antrim Coast and Rathlin Island	Princess Maud	
1929					
Sunday, 7 July	1415	2105	Stranraer	Princess Maud	
Monday, 15 July	1215	1630	Antrim Coast and Rathlin Island	Princess Maud	
Sunday, 21 July	1415	2105	Stranraer	Princess Maud	
1930					
Thursday, 3 July	1300	2145	Stranraer	Princess Victoria	
Every Fri., 11 July – 29 Aug.	1450	2145	Stranraer	Princess Victoria	
Mon., 14 July & Mon., 4 Aug.	1220	1630	Antrim Coast and Rathlin Island	Princess Victoria	
1931					
Sunday, 12 July	1100	2000	Bangor and Stranraer	Princess Victoria	Bangor – 1200; 1900
Tues., 14 July & Mon., 3 Aug.	1220	1630	Antrim Coast and Rathlin Island	Princess Margaret	Bangor – 1200; 1900
Sunday, 9 August	1100	2000	Bangor and Stranraer	Princess Victoria	Bangor – 1200; 1900
1932					
Sunday, 24 July	1100	2000	Bangor and Stranraer	Princess Victoria	Bangor – 1200; 1900
[line cut off at foot of page]	1?20	1630	Antrim Coast and Rathlin Island	Princess Margaret	

Date	Dep.	Arr.	Destination	Vessel	Notes
Monday, 7 August	1220	1630	Antrim Coast and Rathlin Island	*Princess Victoria*	Bangor – 1200; 1900
Q Sunday, 27 August	1100	2000	Bangor and Stranraer	*Princess Margaret* *Princess Victoria*	Bangor – 1200; 1900
1934					
Monday, 16 July	1220	1630	Ailsa Craig	*Princess Maud*	
Sunday, 22 July	1100	2000	Bangor and Stranraer	*Princess Margaret*	Bangor – 1200; 1900
Monday, 6 August	1220	1630	Antrim Coast and Rathlin Island	*Princess Maud*	
Sunday, 12 August	1100	2000	Stranraer	*Princess Maud*	
Sunday, 19 August	1100	2000	Bangor and Stranraer	*Princess Margaret*	Bangor – 1200; 1900
1935					
Sunday, 14 July	1100	2000	Bangor and Stranraer	*Princess Margaret*	Bangor – 1200; 1900
Monday, 5 August	1230	1630	Antrim Coast and Rathlin Island	*Princess Maud*	
Sunday, 18 August	1100	2000	Bangor and Stranraer	*Princess Margaret*	Bangor – 1200; 1900
1936					
Sunday, 12 & 26 July	1150	2025	Stranraer	*Princess Margaret*	Crossing on Sun., 16 Aug., cancelled
1937					
Sun., 11 July & Sun., 15 Aug.	1150	2030	Stranraer	*Princess Margaret*	
1938					
Sun., 10 July & Sun., 14 Aug.	1415	2035	Stranraer	*Princess Margaret*	
1939					
Sunday, 2 July	1415	2035	Stranraer	*Princess Maud*	
Monday, 7 August	1230	1630	Antrim Coast and Rathlin Island	*Princess Victoria*	
Sunday, 13 August	1415	2035	Stranraer		
1949					
Wed., 20 July, Mon., 1 Aug., & Wed., 24 Aug.	1200	1630	Antrim Coast and Rathlin Island	*Princess Margaret*	First post-war cruise
1950					
Wed., 19 July, & Mon., 7 Aug.	1200	1630	Antrim Coast and Rathlin Island	*Princess Margaret*	
1951					
Mon., 6 Aug., & Wed., 22 Aug.	1200	1630	Antrim Coast and Rathlin Island	*Princess Margaret*	
1952					
Monday, 4 August	1200	1630	Antrim Coast and Rathlin Island	*Princess Margaret*	
1953					
Monday, 3 August	1200	1630	Antrim Coast and Rathlin Island	*Princess Margaret*	

Date	Time Out	Back	Destination	Steamer	Remarks
1954					
Wednesday, 14 July	1200	1630	Antrim Coast and Rathlin Island	Princess Margaret	
Monday, 2 August	1200	1630	Ailsa Craig	Princess Margaret	
1955					
Saturday, 27 August	1200	1630	Antrim Coast and Rathlin Island	Princess Margaret	
1956					
Thursday, 12 July	1200	1630	Antrim Coast and Rathlin Island	Princess Margaret	
Wednesday, 18 July	1200	1630	Ailsa Craig	Princess Margaret	
Monday, 6 August	1200	1630	County Down Coast	Princess Margaret	
1957					
Tuesday, 16 July	1200	1630	County Down Coast	Princess Margaret	
Monday, 5 August	1200	1630	Antrim Coast and Rathlin Island	Princess Margaret	
1958					
Wednesday, 16 July	1200	1630	Antrim Coast and Rathlin Island	Princess Margaret	
Monday, 4 August	1200	1630	County Down Coast	Princess Margaret	
1959					
Wednesday, 15 July	1200	1630	County Down Coast	Princess Margaret	
Monday, 3 August	1200	1630	Antrim Coast and Rathlin Island	Princess Margaret	
1960					
Sunday, 24 & 31 July			Stranraer	Hampton Ferry	
Monday, 1 August	1200	1630	Antrim Coast and Rathlin Island	Princess Margaret	
1961					
Monday, 7 August	1200	1630	Antrim Coast and Rathlin Island	Princess Margaret	
FROM STRANRAER					
1872					
Saturday, 29 June	0800	1900	Larne (for Belfast and Belfast Lough)	Princess Louise	
1888					
Tuesday, 17 July	1330	1530	Loch Ryan and Ayrshire Coast	Princess Louise	Stranraer Cattle Show
1889					
Tuesday, 16 July	1330		Loch Ryan and Ayrshire Coast	Princess Louise	Stranraer Cattle Show
1890					
Tuesday, 15 July			Loch Ryan and Ayrshire Coast	Princess Beatrice	Stranraer Cattle Show
1893					

Date			Destination	Ship	Notes
1895					
Every Sat. in July and August	1315	1615	Ayrshire Coast and Ailsa Craig	*Princess Victoria*	Stranraer Cattle Show
Thursday, 1 August	1315	1615	Ayrshire Coast and Ailsa Craig	*Princess Victoria*	Stranraer Fast Day
1896					
Every Sat. in July and August	1315	1615	Ayrshire Coast and Ailsa Craig		Stranraer Cattle Show
Tuesday, 14 July	1315	1615	Ayrshire Coast and Ailsa Craig		
Thursday, 30 July	1315	1615	Ayrshire Coast and Ailsa Craig		Stranraer Fast Day
1897					
Every Sat. in July and Aug. &	1315	1615	Ayrshire Coast and Ailsa Craig	*Princess May*	Stranraer Cattle Show
Friday, 16 July	1315	1615	Ayrshire Coast and Ailsa Craig		Stranraer Fast Day
Friday, 23 July	1315	1615	Ayrshire Coast and Ailsa Craig		Dumfries Holiday
Thursday, 29 July	1315	1615	Ayrshire Coast and Ailsa Craig		Ship failed on cruise
Thursday, 19 August	1500	1800	Ayrshire Coast and Ailsa Craig		
Saturday, 25 September	1430		Ayrshire Coast and Ailsa Craig	*Princess May*	
1898					
Every Sat. in July and Aug., except Saturday, 20 August	1315	1615	Ayrshire Coast and Ailsa Craig	*Princess May*	Stranraer Cattle Show
Friday, 22 July	1315	1615	Ayrshire Coast and Ailsa Craig	*Princess May*	
Wednesday, 17 August	1430	1730	Ayrshire Coast and Ailsa Craig	*Princess May*	
1899					
Wednesday, 5 & 19 July, 2, 16 & 30 August	1315	1615	Ayrshire Coast and Ailsa Craig	*Princess May*	Stranraer Cattle Show
Sat., 15 & 29 July, 12 & 26 Aug.,	1500	1800	Ayrshire Coast and Ailsa Craig	*Princess May*	
Friday, 21 July	1415	1715	Ayrshire Coast and Ailsa Craig		
1900					
Wed., 4 & 18 July, 15 & 29 Aug.,	1500	1800	Ayrshire Coast and Ailsa Craig	*Princess May*	Stranraer Cattle Show
Sat. 14 & 28 July, 11 & 25 Aug.	1415	1715	Ailsa Craig	*Princess May*	Stranraer Fast Day
Tuesday, 24 July	1500	1800	Ailsa Craig	*Princess May*	
Thursday, 2 August					
1901					
Saturday, 13 July	1500	1800	Ailsa Craig	*Princess Victoria*	
Wednesday, 17 July	1415		Off Portpatrick		
Friday, 19 July	1415		Off Portpatrick		Stranraer Cattle Show
Thurs., 1 & Sat., 10 Aug.	1415		Off Portpatrick		
Wednesday, 14 August	1500	1800	Ailsa Craig	*Princess May*	
Sat. 24 & Wed. 28 August	1415		Off Portpattick		

Date	Time Out	Back	Destination	Steamer	Remarks
1902					
Thurs., 26 June, and 31 July,	1500	1800	Off Portpatrick	Princess May	Stranraer Cattle Show
Sat., 19 July, and 23 August	1415	1700	Off Portpatrick		Cruise on Saturday, 12 July, cancelled on account of rain
Friday, 18 July					
Wed., 23 July, 13 & 27 Aug.	1500	1800	Ayrshire Coast and Ailsa Craig		
1903					
Saturday, 18 July	1400	1700	Ayrshire Coast and Ailsa Craig	Princess May	Stranraer Cattle Show
Saturday, 5 September	1245	1545	Ayrshire Coast and Ailsa Craig	Princess May	
1904					
Friday, 15 July	1400	1700	Ayrshire Coast and Ailsa Craig		Stranraer Cattle Show
Saturday, 20 August			Ailsa Craig		
Wednesday, 31 August			Off Portpatrick		
1905					
Saturday 3 June, and 15 July	1400	1700	Ayrshire Coast and Ailsa Craig	Princess May	
Thursday, 3 August	1500	1800	Off Portpatrick		
Wednesday, 16 August	1530	1830	Ayrshire Coast and Ailsa Craig	Princess May	
Saturday, 26 August	1500	1800	Off Portpatrick		
1906					
Friday, 13 July	1330	2148	Larne (for Belfast)		
Saturday, 14 July	0600	2148	Rathlin Island, via Larne		Out and back by mail steamer
Saturday, 14 July	1330	2148	Larne (for Belfast)		
Saturday, 14 July	1400	1700	Ailsa Craig		
Wednesday, 18 July	0930		Larne (for Belfast)		
Wednesday, 18 July	1400		Off Portpatrick		
Saturday, 28 July	1400	1700	Ailsa Craig		
Thursday, 2 August	1530		Wigtownshire Coast		
Monday, 6 August	0600	2148	Rathlin Island, via Larne	Princess Maud	Out and back by mail steamer
Saturday, 11 August	0600	2148	Bangor Bay, via Larne	Princess Maud	To view Atlantic Fleet, out and back by mail steamer
Saturday, 25 August	1400	1700	Ailsa Craig		
Saturday, 1 September	1530		Wigtownshire Coast		
Saturday, 8 September	0600	2148	Rathlin Island, via Larne		Out and back by mail steamer
1907					
Wednesday, 26 June	1500	1800	Ailsa Craig	Princess Victoria	

Date	Destination	Time	Time	Vessel	Notes
Monday, 15 July	Rathlin Island via Larne	0825	2025	Princess Maud	
Thursday, 18 July	Mull of Kintyre and Round Sanda	1400			
Saturday, 27 July	Larne (for Belfast)	1005	2025		
Thursday, 1 August	Ailsa Craig	1500	1800		
Monday, 5 August	Rathlin Island, via Larne	0600	2148		Out and back by mail steamer
Saturday, 10 August	Mull of Kintyre and Round Sanda	1400			
Wednesday, 14 August	Larne (for Belfast)	1005	2025		
Saturday, 24 and 31 August	Rathlin Island, via Larne	0600	2148		Out and back by mail steamer
Saturday, 31 August	Ailsa Craig	1500	1800		
1908					
Saturday, 27 June	Ailsa Craig	1530	1830	Princess Victoria	
Saturday, 4 July	Off Girvan	1530	1830	Princess Victoria	
Saturday, 11 July	Mull of Kintyre and Round Sanda	1400	1800	Princess Victoria	Stranraer Cattle Show
Friday, 17 July	Ailsa Craig	1400	1700		
Saturday, 18 July	Mull of Kintyre and Round Sanda	1400	1800		
Monday, 20 July	Ailsa Craig	1400	1700		
Tuesday, 21 July	Campbeltown	0920	1830	Princess May	
Thursday, 30 July	Mull of Kintyre and Round Sanda	1400	1800		
Monday, 3 August	Rathlin Island, via Larne	0600	2148	Princess Victoria	Out and back by mail steamer
Wednesday, 5 August	Wigtownshire Coast	1530		Princess May	
Saturday, 15 August	Mull of Kintyre and Round Sanda	1400	1800	Princess May	
Wednesday, 19 August	Ayrshire Coast	1530	1830		
1909					
Saturday, 19 June	Ailsa Craig	1530	1830	Princess Victoria	
Wednesday, 30 June	Portlogan Bay	1400	1800		
Saturday, 10 July	Heads of Ayr	1400	1800		
Monday, 12 July	Rathlin Island, via Larne	0600	2148	Princess Maud	Out and back by mail steamer
Friday, 16 July	Larne (for Belfast)	1330	2149		
Friday, 16 July	Ailsa Craig	1400	1700		
Saturday, 17 July	Rathlin Island, via Larne	0600	2148	Princess Maud	Stranraer Cattle Show / Out and back by mail steamer
Saturday, 17 July	Larne (for Belfast)	1300	2148		
Monday, 19 July	Portlogan Bay	1400	1800		
Tuesday, 20 July	Campbeltown	0925	1830		
Tuesday, 20 July	Ballantrae Bay	1930	2130		Cancelled by weather
Wednesday, 21 July	Rathlin Island, via Larne	0925	2025 or 2148		Optional time at Larne
Thursday, 29 July	Culzean Bay	1400	1800		
Monday, 2 August	Rathlin Island, via Larne	0600	2148	Princess Maud	Out and back by mail steamer

Date	Time Out	Back	Destination	Steamer	Remarks
1909—continued.					
Saturday, 14 August	1400	1800	Portlogan Bay		
Wednesday, 18 August	1530	1830	Ailsa Craig		
Saturday, 28 August	1400	1800	Culzean Bay		
1910					
Wednesday, 29 June	1400	1800	Mull of Galloway	*Princess Maud*	Out and back by mail steamer
Tuesday, 12 July	0600	2148	Rathlin Island, via Larne	*Princess Maud*	Stranraer Cattle Show
Friday, 15 July	1330	2148	Ailsa Craig		
Friday, 15 July	1400	1700	Larne (for Belfast)		
Saturday, 16 July	1330	2148	Larne (for Belfast)	*Princess Maud*	
Wednesday, 20 July	1400	1700	Portlogan Bay		
Monday, 1 August	0600	2148	Rathlin Island, via Larne	*Princess Maud*	Out and back by mail boat
Thursday, 4 August	1400	1700	Culzean Bay		
Wednesday, 17 August	1500	1800	Off Portpatrick		
Saturday, 27 August	0600	2148	Rathlin Island, via Larne	*Princess Maud*	Out and back by mail steamer
1911					
Saturday, 10 June	1500	1800	Ailsa Craig	*Duchess of Argyll*	In place of *Princess May*
Thursday, 22 June	0600	2148	Rathlin Island, via Larne	*Princess Maud*	Coronation Holiday – out and back by mail steamer
Thursday, 22 June	1400	1800	Portlogan Bay		Coronation Holiday
Wednesday, 12 July	0600	2148	Rathlin Island, via Larne	*Princess Maud*	Out and back by mail steamer
Fri. 14 and Sat. 15 July	1325	2148	Larne (for Belfast)		
Saturday, 15 July	1400	1800	Culzean Bay		
Tuesday, 18 July	1400	1700	Ailsa Craig	*Princess May*	Stranraer Cattle Show
Thursday, 3 August	1500	1800	Off Portpatrick	*Princess Maud*	
Monday, 7 August	0600	2148	Rathlin Island, via Larne	*Princess May*	Out and back by mail steamer
Wednesday, 16 August	1400	1800	Portlogan Bay		
1912					
Sat. 1, 8, 15, 22 and 29 June	1315	2148	Larne (for Belfast)	*Princess Victoria*	N.B.—Evening cruise
Sat. 1, 8, 15 and 22 June	1933	2400	Larne (non-landing)	*Princess May*	
Wednesday, 26 June	1900	2230	Ailsa Craig	*Princess May*	
Friday, 12 July	0600	1530	Ailsa Craig, via Larne		Out by mail steamer
Saturday, 13 July	0600	1830	Rathlin Island, via Larne		Out by mail steamer
Tuesday, 16 July	1400	1700	Ailsa Craig	*Princess Maud*	Stranraer Cattle Show
Thursday, 1 August	1300	1830	County Down Panoramic Cruise — Bangor Bay, Belfast Lough, …		Optional time at Larne, with connection to Belfast, returning by mail steamer

Date			Destination	Ship	Notes
...day, ?? August		2148	Larne (for Belfast)	*Princess Victoria*	
Wednesday, 21 August	1330	2148	Larne (for Belfast)	*Princess Victoria*	
Wednesday, 11 September	1330		Culzean Bay	*Princess Maud*	
1913					
Saturday, 7, 14 and 21 June	1933	2400	Larne (non-landing)	*Princess May*	N.B.—Evening cruise
Wednesday, 18 June	1930	2230	Ailsa Craig	*Princess May*	
Saturday, 12 July	0600	2148	Rathlin Island, via Larne	*Princess Maud*	Out and back by mail steamer
Tuesday, 22 July	1400	1700	Ailsa Craig	*Princess Maud*	Stranraer Cattle Show
Thursday, 31 July	1300	1830	County Down Panoramic Cruise		Optional time at Larne, with connection to Belfast, returning by mail steamer
Monday, 4 August	0600	2148	Rathlin Island, via Larne	*Princess Maud*	Out and back by mail steamer
1914					
Wednesday, 20 May	0930	2025	Larne (for Belfast)	*Princess May*	
Saturday, 13 and 20 June	1935	2400	Larne (non-landing)	*Princess May*	N.B.—Evening cruise
Wednesday, 17 June	1830	2200	Ailsa Craig	*Princess Maud*	Stranraer Merchants' Assocn.
Wednesday, 24 June	0800		Larne (for Portrush)	*Princess Victoria*	Out and back by mail steamer
Monday, 13 July	0600	2148	Rathlin Island, via Larne	*Princess Maud*	
Wednesday, 22 July	1320	1820	Larne (for Belfast)		
Friday, 24 July	1400	1700	Ailsa Craig		
Thursday, 30 July	1300	1830	County Down Coast Cruise	*Princess Maud*	Postponed from 21 July because of fog. Optional time at Larne, with connection to Belfast, returning by mail steamer
Tuesday, 17 August	1430	1830	Portlogan Bay		
1922					
Saturday, 15 July	1415	1715	Ailsa Craig	*Princess Maud*	
1923					
Thursday, 12 July	1415	1715	Ailsa Craig	*Princess Maud*	
1924					
Tuesday, 22 July	1415	1715	Ailsa Craig	*Princess Maud*	Postponed from 10 July—Stranraer Cattle Show—because of fog
Saturday, 16 August	1415	1715	Ailsa Craig	*Princess Maud*	
1925					
Tuesday, 21 July	1415	1715	Ailsa Craig	*Princess Maud*	
Saturday, 15 August	1415	1715	Ailsa Craig	*Princess Maud*	Stranraer Cattle Show

Date	Time Out	Time Back	Destination	Steamer	Remarks
1926					
Monday, 2 August	1415	1715	Ailsa Craig	*Princess Maud*	
1927					
Tuesday, 31 May	1055	1800	Larne (for Belfast)	*Princess Maud*	First Sunday cruise
Sunday, 19 June	1345	1800	Portlogan Bay	*Princess Victoria*	
Sunday, 17 July	1345	1800	Portlogan Bay	*Princess Victoria*	
Tuesday, 19 July	1415	1715	Ailsa Craig		Stranraer Cattle Show
Thursday, 4 August			Wigtownshire Coast	*Princess Maud*	Stranraer Fast Day
Sunday, 21 August	1400	1830	Ailsa Craig	*Princess Victoria*	
1928					
Sunday, 1 July	1415	1745	Ailsa Craig	*Princess Victoria*	
Sunday, 22 July	1330	1945	Larne		
Thursday, 2 August	1415		Off Portpatrick		
Sunday, 5 August	1330		Bangor	*Princess Victoria*	
Saturday, 18 August	1415	1745	Ailsa Craig		
1929					
Tuesday, 16 July	1415	1745	Ailsa Craig	*Princess Victoria*	Stranraer Cattle Show
Sun. 21 July, 4 and 18 Aug.	1330	2000	Bangor	*Princess Maud*	
Saturday, 10 August	1415		Off Portpatrick	*Princess Maud*	
Wednesday, 21 August	1415		Ailsa Craig		
1930					
Saturday, 31 May	1215	2148	Larne (for Belfast)	*Princess Victoria*	
Sunday, 15 June, 20 July, 3 and 17 August	1330	2000	Bangor		
Thursday, 3 July	1330	2148	Larne (for Belfast)	*Princess Victoria*	
Sunday, 6 July	1330	1945	Larne	*Princess Maud*	
Tues., 22 July, and Sat., 6 Aug.	1415	1715	Ailsa Craig		Ulster Road Race Day
Saturday, 23 August	0540		Larne		Special sailing on 24 August, arriving Stranraer 1600
1931					
Saturday, 21 February	0330		Larne (for Belfast)		Football Special. Return to Stranraer morning of 22 Feb.
Sun. 7 and 21 June, 5 and 19 July, 2 and 16 August	1315	2015	Bangor.	*Princess Margaret*	
Fri. 17, 24 and 31 Sat. 18 July,					

Date			Destination	Ship	Notes
10 and 24 July, 7 and 21 Aug.	1315	2015	Bangor	*Princess Victoria* on 26 June, *Princess Margaret* on other days *Princess Victoria*	Stranraer Cattle Show. Football Special. Return to Stranraer morning of 18 Sept.
Tuesday, 19 July	1415	1715	Ailsa Craig		
Saturday, 17 September	a.m.		Larne (for Belfast)		
1933					
Wednesday, 31 May	1400	2105	Larne	*Princess Victoria*	
Sun. 4 and 18 June, 2, 16 and 30 July, 13 and 27 Aug. & 10 Sept.	1315	2015	Bangor	*Princess Margaret*	
Every Saturday in July and August and Friday, 14 July	1330	2105	Larne (for Belfast)		
Tuesday, 18 July	1415	1730	Ailsa Craig	*Princess Victoria*	Stranraer Cattle Show
1934					
Sun. 3 and 17 June, 1, 15 and 22 July, 5 & 19 Aug., 2 & 16 Sept.	1315	2015	Bangor	*Princess Maud*	
Sat., 9 June and every Fri and Sat. 6 July–1 September	1330	2105	Larne (for Belfast)		
Saturday, 20 October	0310		Larne (for Belfast)		Football Special. Return to Stranraer morning of 21 Oct.
1935					
Friday, 31 May	1400	2105	Larne (for Belfast)	*Princess Margaret*	
Sun. 16 and 30 June, 14 and 28 July, 4 & 18 Aug., 1 & 15 Sept.	1315	2015	Bangor		
Every Friday and Saturday, 5 July–14 September	1330	2105	Larne (for Belfast)		
Tuesday, 16 July	1415	1715	Ailsa Craig	*Princess Margaret*	Stranraer Cattle Show
1936					
Saturday, 30 May	1400	2110	Larne (for Belfast)	*Princess Margaret*	
Sun., 14, 21 & 28 June, 12 & 19 July, 2, 16 & 30 Aug. & 13 Sept.	1315	2015	Larne via Bangor Bay		
Every Fri. and Sat., 10 July–12 Sept. & Mon., 27 July	1330	2110	Larne (for Belfast)		
Saturday, 31 October	a.m.		Larne (for Belfast)		Football Special. Return to Stranraer morning of 1 Nov.

Date	Time Out	Time Back	Destination	Steamer	Remarks
1937					
Saturday, 15 May	1400	2105	Larne (for Belfast)	Princess Margaret	
Sun. 13 and 27 June, 11 July, 8 and 22 Aug. and 5 Sept.	1315	2015	Larne		
Every Fri., 2 July–10 Sept. and Saturday, 3 July	1330	2105	Larne (for Belfast)		
Every Sat, 10 July–11 Sept.	1400	2105	Larne (for Belfast)		
Wednesday, 21 July	1415	1730	Ailsa Craig	Princess Margaret	Stranraer Cattle Show
1938					
Sun., 12 & 26 June, 10 & 24 July, 7 & 21 Aug. & 4 Sept.	1315	2015	Larne		
Every Fri., 1 July–9 Sept. and Saturday, 2 July	1330	2110	Larne (for Belfast)		
Every Sat., 9 July–10 Sept.	1400	2110	Larne (for Belfast)		
Wednesday, 20 July	1415	1700	Ailsa Craig	Princess Margaret	Stranraer Cattle Show
1939					
Wednesday, 31 May	1400	2110	Larne	Princess Margaret	
Sun. 11 & 25 June, 9 & 23 July, 6 & 20 August	1315	2015	Larne		Advertised for 3 Sept. also
Every Fri. & Sat., 14 July–2 September	1120 & 1400	2110	Larne (for Belfast)		Advertised until 9 Sept.
Wednesday, 19 July	1415	1700	Ailsa Craig	Princess Victoria	Stranraer Cattle Show
1948					
Wednesday, 25 August	1000	2045	Campbeltown	Princess Victoria	Stranraer & District Indep. Retail Traders' Assocn.
1949					
Wed., 6 July and 3 August	1400	1630	Ailsa Craig	Princess Victoria	Stranraer & District Indep. Retail Traders' Assocn.
Sunday, 14 August	0930		Rothesay	Princess Margaret	
Saturday, 1 October	0230		Larne (for Belfast)	Princess Maud	Football Specials. Return to Stranraer on morning of 2 Oct.
Saturday, 1 October	0530		Larne (for Belfast)	Princess Victoria	
1950					
	1100	1620	Ailsa Craig	Princess Victoria	

Date			Rothesay Ailsa Craig	Princess Margaret Princess Victoria	
..., 4 June	0730	2000			
Wed., 4 July and 1 August	1400	1630			
1955 Friday, 8 October	p.m.		Larne (for Belfast)	Princess Margaret and Princess Maud	Football Specials. Return to Stranraer on 10 Oct.
1960 Sunday, 24 and 31 July	1245	2005	Larne	Princess Margaret	
1961 Sunday, 30 July Saturday, 7 October	1300 0700		Larne Larne (for Belfast)	Princess Margaret Princess Margaret	Football Special. Return to Stranraer on 8 Oct. at 1730
1963 Saturday, 12 October	0700		Larne (for Belfast)	Caledonian Princess	Football Special. Return to Stranraer on 13 Oct. at 1730
1968 Wednesday, 26 June	0900		Douglas, Isle of Man (No. 2 Berth, Victoria Pier)	Caledonian Princess	Galloway Traders' Assocn.
1969 Sunday, 4 May	0900		Douglas, Isle of Man (No. 1 Berth, Victoria Pier)	Antrim Princess	Galloway Traders' Assocn.

Notes

[1] The original letter from Hamilton is in the National Library of Scotland, reference State 123. Section 27, (vi) 33.1.1.

[2] The warrant is quoted in full in John Stevenson, *Two Centuries of Life in County Down 1600-1800* (Belfast: McGaw, Stevenson and Orr Ltd., 1920), pp 247–252.

[3] Register of the Privy Council of Scotland, series 1, volume X, p 463.

[4] RPC, series 1, volume XIII, p 429.

[5] RPC, series 2, volume I, p 621f.

[6] RPC, series 2, volume I, p 626.

[7] RPC, series 2, volume II, p 321.

[8] W. Harris, *The Antient* [sic] *and Present State of the County of Down* (Dublin: Edward Exshaw, 1744), p 65.

[9] Hume Brown, ed *Early Travellers in Scotland* (Edinburgh: David Douglas, 1891), p 158.

[10] RPC, series 2, volume VII, p xxvi.

[11] ibid, p 229.

[12] ibid, p 327.

[13] ibid, p 279.

[14] The relation between Scottish money and sterling in the seventeenth century was £12 Scots = £1 sterling.

[15] RPC, series 3, volume I, p 263.

[16] ibid, p 309f.

[17] RPC, series 3, volume II, p 387.

[18] RPC, series 3, volume V, p 285f.

[19] RPC, series 3, volume IX, p 173f.

[20] ibid, p 381.

[21] The old style calendar (i.e., pre-1752) was eleven days behind the new style. This explains the commemoration of the battle now on 12 July.

[22] J. C. Beckett, *The Making of Modern Ireland 1603-1923* (London: Faber & Faber, 1966), p 145.

[23] RPC, series 3, Volume XIII, p 448.

[24] RPC, series 3, volume XIV, p 58.

[25] Stevenson, *Two Centuries of Life in County Down*, p 271.

[26] RPC, series 3, volume XVI, p 341.

[27] Great Britain, *The Acts of the Parliament of Scotland* (1822), IX, 417f.

[28] The original is in the Scottish Record Office, reference GD 72, number 632.

[29] *The Statistical Account of Scotland*, volume I, number 3, Parish of Portpatrick (Edinburgh: William Creech, 1791), p 40.

[30] *The Journal of the Rev. John Wesley, A.M.*, Nehemiah Curnock, ed, volume V (London: Charles H. Kelly), p 113.

[31] ibid, p 139.

[32] Not Stranraer as stated by Robert Haire, *Wesley's One-and-Twenty Visits to Ireland* (London: The Epworth Press, 1947), p 93.

[33] *The Journal of the Rev. John Wesley*, Curnock, ed, volume V, p 224.

[34] *Boswell in Search of a Wife*, Frank Brody, ed, The Yale Edition of the Private Papers of James Boswell (London: William Heineman Ltd., 1957), p 211.

[35] *Reports of the late John Smeaton, F.R.S.* (London: Longman, Hurst, Rees, Orme & Brown, 1812), volume III, pp 60–67.

[36] ibid, pp 68–70.

[37] Ian Donnachie, *The Industrial Archaeology of Galloway* (Newton Abbot: David & Charles (Publishers) Ltd., 1971), p 76.

[38] Twenty-Second Report of the Commissioners of Revenue Inquiry, *Parl Papers* 1830 (647), XIV, p 402.

[39] Report from committee appointed to examine into Mr. Telford's Report and

Survey Relative to Communication between England and Ireland by the North [sic]-West of Scotland, *Parl Papers* 1809 (269), III, p 49.

[40] *The Statistical Account of Scotland*, volume I, p 43.

[41] I. F. MacLeod, *Shipping in Dumfries and Galloway in 1820*, Scottish Local History Texts, number 1 (Glasgow: 1973), p 10

[42] *Parl Papers* 1809 (269), III, p 49.

[43] ibid, p 38.

[44] At that time called Portnessock.

[45] RPC, series 3, volume VII, p 345.

[46] *The Statistical Account of Scotland*, p 153.

[47] Quoted in *Parl Papers* 1809 (269), III, p 19.

[48] ibid, pp 15–52.

[49] Donnachie, *The Industrial Archaeology of Galloway*, p 238.

[50] *The New Statistical Account of Scotland*, volume IV, Wigtown (Edinburgh: William Blackwood & Sons, 1845), p 201.

[51] *Parl Papers* 1809 (269), III, p 45.

[52] ibid, p 4.

[53] *Autobiography of Sir John Rennie, F.R.S.* (London: E. & F. N. Spon, 1875), p 17.

[54] Report on the Harbours at Donaghadee and Portpatrick, *Parl Papers* 1820 (252), IX.

[55] Letter from Charles Barr to the *Liverpool Evening Express* of 15 August 1931 reproduced in *Sea Breezes*, volume XLI, number 263 (November, 1967), p 811.
George Dodd relates (*An Historical and Explanatory Dissertation on Steam Engines and Steam Packets*, London 1818, p 259) how the ship that was to be the second steamship on the Thames, *Thames* was caught in a gale on 20 May 1815 off Portpatrick while en route from the Clyde. She was unable to enter Portpatrick Harbour, and the frontispiece to the book depicts *Thames* riding out the gale outside Portpatrick Harbour.

[56] The plans and description of Donaghadee Harbour are from Sir John Rennie, *The Theory, Formation and Construction of British and Foreign Harbours*, volume II (London: John Weale, 1854), p 189f.

[57] The plans and description of Portpatrick Harbour are also found in Rennie, *The Theory, Formation and Construction of British and Foreign Harbours*, p. 187f.

[58] John McDiarmid, *Sketches from Nature* (London: Oliver & Boyd, 1830), p 165f.

[59] *The Glasgow Herald*, 19 April, 1824.

[60] In 1821, *Lightning* was renamed *Royal Sovereign* after conveying King George IV from Dun Laoghaire and it was from this date that Dun Laoghaire was renamed Kingstown. This ship should not be confused with the Dover mail packet *Sovereign*.

[61] Select Committee on Post Office Communication, *Parl Papers* 1842 (373), IX, p 366.

[62] Select Committee on Glasgow and Portpatrick Roads, *Parl Papers* 1823 (486), V, 1824 (428), VII. The road between Carlisle and Portpatrick had been examined earlier by the Committee upon the Roads between Carlisle and Portpatrick, *Parl Papers* 1810–11 (119), III.

[63] *Parl Papers* 1824 (428), VII, p 16.

[64] *Parl Papers* 1842 (373), IX, p 576.

[65] The Treasury Minute is quoted in *Parl Papers* 1830 (647), XIV, p 238.

[66] *Parl Papers* 1823 (486), V, p 48.

[67] J. H. Lucking, *The Great Western at Weymouth* (Newton Abbot: David & Charles (Publishers) Ltd., 1971), p 28.

[68] Select Committee on Navy, Army and Ordnance Estimates, *Parl Papers* HL 1847–48 (551), XXI, p 873.

[69] Select Committee on Post Communication with Ireland, *Parl Papers* 1831–32 (716), XVII, p 384f.

[70] *Parl Papers* 1830 (647), XIV.

[71] *Parl Papers* 1831–32 (716), XVII.

[72] ibid, pp 239, 220, 373.

[73] ibid, p 373.
Parl Papers 1830 (647), XIV, p 541.

[74] *Parl Papers* 1830 (647), XIV, pp 292, 544.

[75] *Parl Papers* 1831–32 (716), XVII, pp 373, 331.
Parl Papers 1823 (486), V, pp 58f.

[76] *Parl Papers* 1831–32 (716), XVII, pp 203, 355.

[77] ibid, pp 204, 350.
[78] E. R. R. Green, *The Industrial Archaeology of County Down* (Belfast: HMSO, 1963), p 77.
[79] *Parl Papers* 1831–32 (716), XVII, p 326.
[80] Philip Bagwell, "The Post Office Steam Packets, 1821–36, and the Development of Shipping on the Irish Sea", *Maritime History*, volume I, number 1 (April 1971), p 18.
[81] *Parl Papers* 1830 (647), XIV, p 494.
   Parl Papers 1831–32 (716), XVII, p 373.
[82] *Parl Papers* 1831–32 (716), XVII, p 381.
[83] *The Glasgow Herald*, 1 June 1832.
[84] *Parl Papers* 1831–32 (716), XVII, p 381.
[85] Sixth Report of the Commission appointed to inquire into the Management of the Post Office Department, *Parl Papers* 1836 (51), XXVII, p 217.
[86] Return showing rates and fares charged on board the Packets at Liverpool, &c. *Parl Papers* 1837–38 (203), XLV.
[87] *Parl Papers* 1831–32 (716), XVII, p 4.
[88] ibid, p 4.
[89] *Parl Papers* 1836 (51), XXVIII, p 355.
[90] Rennie, *The Theory, Formation and Construction of British and Foreign Harbours*, p 195f.
[91] 19 February 1836.
[92] *Parl Papers* 1836 (51), XXVIII, p 428.
[93] *The Belfast News-Letter*, 20 November 1835, 6 May 1836, 10 May 1836.
[94] *Parl Papers* 1842 (373), IX, pp 350f, 395, 576f.
[95] Reproduced in Portpatrick and Donaghadee Harbours, *Parl Papers* 1859 (session 1) (104), XXV, pp 1–5.
[96] Quoted in Herbert Joyce, *The History of the Post Office from its Establishment down to 1836* (London: Richard Bentley & Son, 1893), p 428.
[97] J. Howard Robinson, *Britain's Post Office* (London: Oxford University Press, 1953), p 121.
[98] David Quayle, "Isle of Man Steamer Service 1819–1831", *Journal of the Manx Museum*, volume VII, number 87 (1971), p 186.
[99] Lucking, *The Great Western at Weymouth*, pp 19, 229.
[100] *Parl Papers* 1836 (51), XXVIII, pp 242, 244, 19.
[101] ibid, p 4.
[102] Ann Parry, *Parry of the Arctic* (London: Chatto & Windus, 1963), p 191.
[103] *Parl Papers* 1847–48 (551), XXI (Part I), q 3571.
[104] Official sources do not reveal the precise date, but the change is reported in *The Belfast News-letter* of 22 January 1839.
[105] Bagwell, "The Post Office Steam Packets", *Maritime History*, p 22.
[106] *The Galloway Advertiser and Wigtownshire Free Press*, 23 October 1845.
[107] Reproduced in Portpatrick Harbour, *Parl Papers* 1884, LXXI, 441.
[108] *Parl Papers* 1847–48 (551), XXI (Part I), qq 3570, 1086.
[109] Edwin Hodder, *Sir George Burns, Bart.* (London: Hodder & Stoughton, 1892), p 196.
[110] *Parl Papers* 1836 (51), XXVIII, p 363.
[111] The correspondence and contract between the Post Office and G. and J. Burns is reproduced in *Parl Papers* HL 1849 (207), XXV.
[112] Memorandum and Returns comparing the present mail service between Greenock and Belfast with the late service between Port Patrick and Donaghadee, *Parl Papers* HL 1850 (37), XX.
[113] "The Scottish and Irish Mail Service", *The West of Scotland Magazine and Review* Glasgow: Thomas Murray & Son, January 1857), p 319.
[114] Based on information kindly supplied by Mr. G. A. Osbon, of the National Maritime Museum, Greenwich, from his research into Admiralty paddle craft.
[115] Reports of the Board of Trade Inspector, 8 August 1851, number 696.
[116] *The New Statistical Account of Scotland*, p 153.
[117] D. B. McNeill, *Irish Passenger Steamship Service*, volume I (Newton Abbot: David & Charles (Publishers) Ltd., 1969), p 94.
[118] James Williamson, *The Clyde Passenger Steamer* (Glasgow: James MacLehose & Sons, 1904), p 28.

[119] *The Glasgow Herald*, 30 November, 3 December 1827.
[120] C. L. D. Duckworth and G. E. Langmuir, *West Highland Steamers*, third edition (Prescot, Merseyside: T. Stephenson & Sons Ltd., 1967), p 10.
   Ian McCrorie, "The Last of the Castle Steamers", *Clyde Steamers*, number 6 (Glasgow: Clyde River Steamer Club, 1970), p 11.
   The reports of 20 November 1829 and 15 November 1830 in *The Glasgow Herald* can be interpreted as indicating the ship was a total loss.
[121] Duckworth and Langmuir, *West Highland Steamers*, p 42.
[122] Beckett, *The Making of Modern Ireland*, pp 341–44.
[123] *The Galloway Advertiser and Wigtownshire Free Press*, 5 August 1858.
[124] op. cit. (Newton Abbot: David & Charles (Publishers) Ltd., 1969).
[125] Various plans are to be seen in the Scottish Records Office, ref RHP 2733, 2946, 16470–74, 16724.
[126] The agreement is in the Scottish Records Office, ref BR/CAL/4/67, p 225.
[127] Copies of the Treasury minutes, reports and correspondence are contained in Portpatrick and Donaghadee Harbours, *Parl Papers* 1859 (session 1) (104), XXV.
[128] ibid, pp 15f.
[129] The correspondence concerning the Admiralty land and the position of the booking office is contained in Portpatrick Harbour, *Parl Papers* 1866 (263), LXVI.
[130] Portpatrick and Donaghadee Harbours, *Parl Papers* 1867–68 (356), LXIII, p 4.
[131] Reproduced as Plate V in Pictorial Supplement III of "Blockade Runners", *The American Neptune* (Salem, Mass.: 1961).
[132] Francis B. C. Bradlee, "Blockade Running During the Civil War", *The Essex Institute Historical Collection*, volume LX (Salem, Mass.: The Essex Institute, 1924), pp 157–60.
[133] ibid, volume LXI (1925), p 402.
[134] Minutes of Evidence, Select Committee on Railway Bills, on Portpatrick Railway (Capital, Deviations, &c.), 1864, qu 203.
[135] Frank Burtt, *Cross-Channel and Coastal Paddle Steamers* (London: Richard Tilling, 1934), pp 190f.
   Marcus W. Price, "Ships that Tested the Blockade of the Carolina Ports, 1861–1865". *The American Neptune*, volume VIII, number 3, July 1948, pp 228f.
   The Times, 24 December 1864.
   The Glasgow Herald, 24 May 1865.
[136] Caledonian Railway Agreement Book, Agreement No. 1. Scottish Record Office reference BR/CAL/4/67.
[137] ibid, Agreement No. 23.
[138] R. A. Williams, *The London & South Western Railway*, volume 2 (Newton Abbot: David & Charles (Holdings) Ltd., 1973), p 286.
   C. L. D. Duckworth and G. E. Langmuir, *Railway and Other Steamers*, second edition (Prescot, Merseyside: T. Stephenson & Sons Ltd., 1968), p 165.
[139] The correspondence between the Treasury, the Belfast & County Down Railway and the Portpatrick Railway is contained in *Parl Papers* 1867–68 (356), LXIII.
[140] A copy of this prospectus is among the Glasgow & South Western Railway papers in the Scottish Record Office, reference BR/GSW/4.
[141] *pace* Duckworth and Langmuir, *West Highland Steamers*, third edition, p 9, an examination of ships' registers has shown that the *Dolphin* at Portpatrick was not the ship of that name built in 1844. *Dolphin* of 1844 went blockade running and was eventually wrecked in 1874.
[142] Grahame E. Farr, *West Country Passenger Steamers*, second edition (Prescot, Merseyside: T. Stephenson & Sons Ltd., 1967), p 220.
[143] Joseph Tatlow, *Fifty Years of Railway Life in England, Scotland and Ireland* (London: The Railway Gazette, 1920), pp 97f.
[144] Marcus W. Price, "Ships that Tested the Blockade of the Caroline Ports 1861–1865", *The American Neptune*, volume VIII, number 3 (July 1948), pp 229, 233, 236.
[145] *Irish Shipping*, volume IV, number 2 (1966), p 18.
[146] Smith, *The Little Railways of South-West Scotland*.
[147] The decree is lodged with the Scottish Records Office, ref BR/CAL/8/69.
[148] The timetable for 1883 between Ballymena, Ballyclare and Stranraer via Larne is reproduced in Edward M. Patterson, *The Ballymena Lines* (Newton Abbot: David & Charles (Publishers) Ltd., 1968), p 169.
[149] Instructions given to the civil engineer of the Belfast & Northern Counties Rail-

way, quoted in J. R. L. Currie, *The Northern Counties Railway*, volume I (Newton Abbot: David & Charles (Publishers) Ltd., 1973), p 149.

[150] Smith, *The Little Railways of South-West Scotland*, p 80.

[151] op. cit., p 154. The traders' meeting is reported in *The Cornish Evening Tidings*, 10 December 1908.

[152] Smith, *The Little Railways of South-West Scotland*, p 164.

[153] For details of excursions from Stranraer by non-railway steamers see F. G. MacHaffie, "From Bonnie Loch Ryan to Dark Loch Goil", *Clyde Steamers*, number 10 (1974), pp 15–19.

[154] Larne and Stranraer Mail Service, *Parl Papers* 1895 (471), LXXX.

[155] For the ferocity and extent of this gale see R. N. W. Smith, "Notes and News Series", number 5, 1901 (Glasgow: Clyde River Steamer Club).

[156] The correspondence concerning the chartering of *Princess Victoria* and her transfer to the Dover–Dunkirk service is lodged with the Public Record Office, London, ref. MT23 361 X/K1015.

[157] The indices are: June 1920 June 1922 June 1933
Basic weekly rates of wages, all manual workers,
    June 1956 = 100   53·6   38·8   34·4
Cost of Living Index, July 1914 = 100   250   180   136
(Source: *British Labour Statistics, Historical Abstract 1886–1968*. Department of Employment and Productivity. London: Her Majesty's Stationery Office, 1971. Tables 13 and 89.)

[158] Plans of the cabin accommodation of *Lairdscastle* are given in D. B. McNeill, *Irish Passenger Steamship Services*, volume II (Newton Abbot: David & Charles (Publishers) Ltd., 1971), p 54.

[159] G. Grimshaw, "From Mambeg . . . to Moville", *Clyde Steamers*, number 9, 1973, p 29.

[160] Smith, *The Little Railways of South-West Scotland*, p 182.

[161] Joseph Tatlow tells of the negotiations prior to the opening of the route in *Fifty Years of Railway Life in England, Scotland and Ireland*, pp 112f.

[162] W. Paul Clegg, "Short Sea Survey", *Sea Breezes*, volume XLV, number 302, February 1971, p 107.

[163] The arrival at Belfast is illustrated in A. W. H. Pearsall, *North Irish Channel Services* (Belfast: Belfast Museum and Art Gallery, 1962), plate III (a).

[164] 338 H.C. Deb., 5s., 13 July 1938, col. 1326f.

[165] Plans of the cabin accommodation of *Royal Scotsman* and *Royal Ulsterman* are given in McNeill, *Irish Passenger Steamship Services*, volume I, p 18.

[166] Detailed plans of both terminals appear in *Shipbuilding and Shipping Record*, 17 August 1939, pp 202ff.

[167] This reconstruction of the war service of *Princess Maud* is based on an account in *The Galloway Advertiser and Wigtownshire Free Press*, 1 November 1945.

[168] Smith, *The Little Railways of South-West Scotland*, p 186.

[169] H. E. Hancock, *Semper Fidelis* (London: The General Steam Navigation Company Ltd., 1949), pp 33ff.

[170] Government Control of Railways. Cmnd. 6168, February 1940.

[171] *The Operating Department in War-time 1939–1945* (Belfast: London Midland & Scottish Railway Northern Counties Committee, 1946), p 51.

[172] W. Paul Clegg and John S. Styring, *British Nationalised Shipping* (Newton Abbot: David & Charles Ltd., 1969), pp 147f.

[173] *Earl Thorfinn*'s journey is described in Alastair and Anne Cormack, *Days of Orkney Steam* (Kirkwall: Kirkwall Press, 1971), p 105.

[174] *Reports of the Court of Formal Investigation into the Circumstances Attending the Loss of the British Motor Ship* Princess Victoria, 11 June 1953, number 7980; and *Report of the Ministry of Transport Inquiry into the Loss of the Motor Ship* Princess Victoria *and the Findings of the Court* (Liverpool: Charles Birchall & Sons Ltd., 1953); and the *Appeals of the British Transport Commission and John Dudley Reed against the Decision of the Court holding a Formal Investigation into the loss of the British Motor Ship* Princess Victoria, 26 November 1953, number 7980a.

[175] E. C. B. Thornton, *South Coast Pleasure Steamers*, second edition (Prescot, Merseyside: T. Stephenson & Sons Ltd., 1969), p 123.

[176] The train deck of *Hampton Ferry* is illustrated in Fig. 98 of Rixon Bucknall, *Boat Trains and Channel Packets* (London: Vincent Stuart Ltd., 1957).

R

[177] *Irish Shipping*, volume 3, number 1, 1965, p 52.
[178] *British Air Transport*, cmnd. 6605, March 1945.
[179] Gerald H. Freeman, "Whither the British Independents?" *The Shipping World*, 9 January 1957, p 60.
[180] *Proposals for a Fixed Channel Link*, cmnd. 2137, July 1963.
[181] *The Reshaping of British Railways* (London: H M S O, 1963).
[182] *Annual Report of the Transport Users Consultative Committee for Scotland for the Year ended 31 December 1964*, cmnd. 168, 1965, pp 7–9.
[183] *Shipping Services to Northern Ireland* (London: H M S O, 1963).
[184] Iain C. MacArthur, *The Caledonian Steam Packet Company Limited* (Glasgow: Clyde River Steamer Club, 1971), p 164.
[185] ibid. Illustration 111 records the occasion.
[186] *Public Transport and Traffic* (London: H M S O, 1968), p 15.
[187] MacArthur, *The Caledonian Steam Packet Company Limited*, p 165.
[188] A photograph of *Ailsa Princess* at Gibraltar while on her delivery voyage is on page 37 of illustrations of C. L. D. Duckworth and G. E. Langmuir, *Clyde River and Other Steamers*, third edition (Glasgow: Brown, Son & Ferguson Ltd., 1972).
[189] Plans, illustrations and a description of *Bardic Ferry*, *Ionic Ferry*'s sister are given in *The Shipping World*, 16 October 1957, pp 334–337.

Bibliography

BOOKS AND ARTICLES

Abernethy, John S. *James Abernethy, C.E., F.R.S.E.* London: Abbott, Jones & Co. Ltd., 1897.

Austen, Brian. "Dover Post Office Packet Services 1633–1837", *Transport History*. Volume 5, number 1, March 1972, pp. 29–53.

Bagwell, Philip. "The Post Office Steam Packets, 1821–1836, and the Development of Shipping on the Irish Sea", *Maritime History*. Volume 1, number 1, April 1972, pp. 4–28.

Beckett, J. C. *The Making of Modern Ireland, 1603–1923.* London: Faber & Faber, 1966.

Boucher, Cyril T. G. *John Rennie, 1761–1821.* Manchester: Manchester University Press, 1963.

Boyd, John S. "Rise and Fall of Even Shorter Route—Portpatrick–Donaghadee Mail Service. Three Centuries of History", *Wigtownshire Free Press*, 18 October 1962.

Boyd, John S. *The Royal and Ancient Burgh of Stranraer 1617–1967.* Stranraer: Wigtownshire Free Press, 1967.

Bradlee, Francis B. C. "Blockade Running during the Civil War", *The Essex Institute Historical Collection.* Volume LX. Salem, Mass.: The Essex Institute, 1924, pp. 157–160.

Clegg, W. P. and J. S. Styring. *British Nationalised Shipping.* Newton Abbot: David & Charles (Publishers) Ltd., 1969.

Clegg, W. P. and J. S. Styring. *Steamers of British Railways.* Prescot: T. Stephenson & Sons Ltd., 1962.

Corrie, John M. *The Dumfries Post Office 1642–1910.* Dumfries: The Council of the Dumfriesshire and Galloway Natural History and Antiquarian Society, 1912.

Cunningham, R. R. *Portpatrick Through the Ages.* Portpatrick: 1974.

Currie, J. R. L. *The Northern Counties Railway.* Volume 1 1845–1903; volume 2 1903–1972. Newton Abbot: David & Charles (Publishers) Ltd., 1973, 1974.

Donnachie, Ian. *The Industrial Archaeology of Galloway.* Newton Abbot: David & Charles (Publishers) Ltd., 1971.

Duckworth, C. L. D. and G. E. Langmuir. *Clyde and Other Coastal Steamers.* Glasgow: Brown, Son & Ferguson Ltd., 1939.

Duckworth, C. L. D. and G. E. Langmuir. *Clyde River and Other Steamers.* Third edition. Glasgow: Brown, Son & Ferguson Ltd., 1972.

Duckworth, C. L. D. and G. E. Langmuir. *Railway and Other Steamers.* Second edition. Prescot: T. Stephenson & Sons Ltd., 1968.

Duckworth, C. L. D. and G. E. Langmuir. *West Coast Steamers.* Third edition. Prescot: T. Stephenson & Sons Ltd., 1966.

Duckworth, C. L. D. and G. E. Langmuir. *West Highland Steamers.* Third edition. Prescot: T. Stephenson & Sons Ltd., 1967.

Farr, Grahame. *West Country Passenger Steamers.* Second edition. Prescot: T. Stephenson & Sons Ltd., 1967.

Green, E. R. R. *The Industrial Archaeology of County Down.* Belfast: H.M.S.O., 1963.

Haldane, A. R. B. *Three Centuries of Scottish Posts, An Historical Survey to 1836.* Edinburgh: Edinburgh University Press, 1971.

THE SHORT SEA ROUTE

Harrington, J. L. "Development of Vehicle Ferry Services", *The Institute of Transport Journal*. November 1966, pp. 13–19.

Harris, W. *The Antient and Present State of the County of Down*. Dublin: Edward Exshaw, 1744.

Hodder, Edwin. *Sir George Burns, Bart., His Times and Friends*. London: Hodder & Stoughton, 1892.

Journal of the Rev. John Wesley, A.M. Ed. Nehemiah Curnock. London: Charles H. Kelly, n.d.

Joyce, Herbert. *The History of the Post Office from its Establishment down to 1836*. London: Richard Bentley & Son, 1893.

Kerr, J. Lennox. *The Great Storm*. London: George G. Harrap & Co. Ltd., 1954.

Lang, T. B. *An Historical Summary of the Post Office in Scotland*. Edinburgh: General Post Office, 1856.

de Latocnaye. *A Frenchman's Walk through Ireland 1796–7*. Trans. John Stevenson. Belfast and Dublin: McCaw, Stevenson & Orr Ltd., and Hodges, Figgis & Co. Ltd., 1917.

Lyon, D. J. *Catalogue of Denny Material at the National Maritime Museum, Greenwich*. London: H.M.S.O., about to be published.

MacArthur, I. C. *The Caledonian Steam Packet Company Limited*. Glasgow: Clyde River Steamer Club.

MacHaffie, F. G. "From Bonnie Loch Ryan to Dark Loch Goil", *Clyde Steamers*. Number 10. Glasgow: Clyde River Steamer Club, 1974, pp. 15–19.

MacHaffie, F. G. "Stranraer for Ireland 1862–1922", *Clyde Steamers*. Number 8. Glasgow: Clyde River Steamer Club, 1972, pp. 19–35.

MacHaffie, F. G. and I. C. MacArthur. "Portpatrick–Donaghadee. The Real Short Sea Route", *Clyde Steamers*. Number 7. Glasgow: Clyde River Steamer Club, 1971, pp. 23–27.

Macleod, I. F. *Shipping in Dumfries and Galloway*. Glasgow: Scottish Local History Texts, 1973.

McNeill, D. B. *Irish Passenger Steamship Services*. Volume 1, North of Ireland,; volume 2, South of Ireland. Newton Abbot: David & Charles (Publishers) Ltd., 1969, 1971.

Marmion, Anthony. *The Ancient and Modern History of the Maritime Ports of Ireland*. Holborn: Anthony Marmion, 1855.

Montgomerie, William. *The Montgomery Manuscripts, 1603–1706*. Ed. George Hill. Belfast: James Cleeland and Thomas Dargan, 1869.

The New Statistical Account of Scotland. Edinburgh: William Blackwood & Sons, 1845.

Norway, Arthur H. *History of the Post Office Packet Service Between the Years 1793–1815*. London: Macmillan & Co., 1895.

The Operating Department in War Time 1939–1945. Belfast: London Midland & Scottish Railway Northern Counties Committee, 1946.

Patterson, E. M. *The Belfast & County Down Railway*. Lingfield, Surrey: The Oakwood Press, 1958.

Patterson, E. M. *The Ballymena Lines*. Newton Abbot: David & Charles (Publishers) Ltd., 1968.

Pearsall, A. W. H. *North Irish Channel Services*. Belfast: Belfast Museum and Art Gallery, 1962.

Price, Marcus W. "Ships that Tested the Blockade of the Carolina Ports 1861–1865". *The American Neptune*. Volume VIII, number 3. Salem, Mass.: The American Neptune Incorporated, 1948, pp. 196–241.

Rennie, John. *Autobiography*. London: E. & F. N. Spon, 1875.

Rennie, John. *The Theory, Formation and Construction of British and Foreign Harbours*. 2 volumes. London: John Weale, 1854.

Report of the Ministry of Transport Inquiry into the Loss of the Motorship Princess Victoria *and the Findings of the Court.* Liverpool: Journal of Commerce and Shipping Telegraph Ltd., 1953.

Reports of the late John Smeaton, F.R.S. 3 volumes. London: Longman, Hurst, Rees, Orme, and Brown, 1812.

Robinson, J. Howard. *Britain's Post Office.* London: Oxford University Press, 1953.

Robinson, J. Howard. *The British Post Office: A History.* Princeton, N. J.: Princeton University Press, 1948.

Robinson, J. Howard. *Carrying British Mail Overseas.* London: George Allen & Unwin Ltd., 1964.

"The Scottish and Irish Mails". *The West of Scotland Magazine and Review.* Glasgow: Thomas Murray & Son, January 1857, pp. 313–320.

"The Short Sea Route via Stranraer and Larne". *Sea Breezes.* Volume 39, number 234. Liverpool: The Journal of Commerce and Shipping Telegraph Ltd., June 1965.

Smith, David L. *The Little Railways of South-West Scotland.* Newton Abbot: David & Charles (Publishers) Ltd., 1969.

The Statistical Account of Scotland. Edinburgh: William Creech, 1791.

Stevenson, John. *Two Centuries of Life in Down 1600–1800.* Belfast: McCaw, Stevenson & Orr Ltd., 1920.

Stewart, David M. "Stranraer and Larne". *L M S Railway Magazine.* Volume IV, number 11, November 1927, pp. 364–366.

Stewart, David M. "Stranraer–Larne; the Short Sea Route to Ireland". *British Railways Magazine.* Volume 1, number 6, June 1948, pp. 128–129.

Stewart, David M. "Stranraer". *British Railways Magazine.* Volume 7, number 3, March 1956, pp. 50–52.

Watson, Edward. *The Royal Mail to Ireland.* London: Edward Arnold, 1917.

Williamson, James. *The Clyde Passenger Steamer.* Glasgow: James MacLehose & Sons, 1904.

NEWSPAPERS AND PERIODICALS

Annual Review (Clyde River Steamer Club).
Belfast News-Letter.
Clyde Bill of Entry and Shipping List.
Cruising Monthly (Coastal Cruising Association).
Downpatrick Recorder.
Dumfries and Galloway Courier.
East Antrim Times (until 1962 *The Larne Times*, until 1936 *The Larne Times and Weekly Telegraph*).
Glasgow Herald.
Greenock Telegraph and Clyde Commercial Telegraph.
Irish Shipping (World Ship Society, Belfast Branch).
Journal of Commerce and Shipping Telegraph.
Lloyd's List.
Marine News (World Ship Society).
Newry Commercial Telegraph.
Newtonards Chronicle.
Sea Breezes.
Ship Ahoy (World Ship Society, South Wales Branch).
Shipbuilding and Shipping Record.
Wigtownshire Free Press (until 1962 *The Galloway Advertiser and Wigtownshire Free Press*).

GOVERNMENT RECORDS, PAPERS AND REPORTS

The Register of the Privy Council of Scotland. Series I, 1545–1624; Series II, 1625–1660; Series III, 1661–1691.

Parl Papers 1809 (269), III. *Report of the Committee appointed to examine into Mr. Telford's Report and Survey relative to communication between England and Ireland by the North-West of Scotland.*

Parl Papers 1810–11 (119), III. *Report of the Committee on the road between Carlisle and Portpatrick.*

Parl Papers 1820 (252), IX. *Report on the Harbours at Donaghadee and Portpatrick.*

Parl Papers 1821 (556), XVI. *Donaghadee and Portpatrick Harbours.*

Parl Papers 1823 (486), V. *Report of the Select Committee on Glasgow and Portpatrick Roads.*

Parl Papers 1824 (428), VII. *Report of the Select Committee on Glasgow and Portpatrick Roads.*

Parl Papers 1829 (90), XVII. *A Return of the number of ships now building at any port of Great Britain, calculated to be navigated by steam.*

Parl Papers 1830 (647), XIV. *Twenty-Second Report of the Commissioners of Revenue Inquiry.*

Parl Papers 1831-32 (716), XVII. *Report of the Select Committee on Post Communication with Ireland.*

Parl Papers 1834 (156), XLIX. *Post Office Steam Packets.*

Parl Papers 1836 (51), XXVII. *Sixth Report of the Commission appointed to inquire into management of the Post Office.*

Parl Papers 1837–1838 (203), XLV. *Return showing rates and fares charged on board the packets at Liverpool, &c.*

Parl Papers 1841 (321), XXVI. *Amount charged against the public for the Portpatrick–Donaghadee Mail Packet.*

Parl Papers 1842 (373), IX. *Report of the Select Committee on Post Office Communication.*

Parl Papers 1842 (150), XXXIX. *Return relating to Mail Steam Packets.*

Parl Papers 1842 (558), XXXIX. *Returns relating to the Post Office.*

Parl Papers 1844 (207), XLV. *Returns relative to the Post Office.*

Parl Papers 1846 (467), XLV. *Returns relating to the Post Office.*

Parl Papers 1847–48 (207), XXI, HL. *Returns of all sums voted on account of the Mail Packet Service in each of the 10 years 1838–1847.*

Parl Papers 1847–48 (551), XXI, HL. *Minutes of Select Committee on Navy, Army and Ordnance Estimates.*

Parl Papers 1847–48 (332), LX. *Return showing total expense incurred for packet service in year 1847.*

Parl Papers 1847–48 (421), LX. *Expense incurred by the Admiralty for the packet service.*

Parl Papers 1847–48 (582), LXII. *Account of the revenue for the General Post Office for the year ending 1 January 1847.*

Parl Papers 1849 (207–II), XXV, HL. *Correspondence regarding the conveyance of mails from Greenock to Belfast.*

Parl Papers 1850 (37), XX, HL. *Memorandum and Return comparing the present mail service between Greenock and Belfast and the late service between Port Patrick and Donaghadee.*

Parl Papers 1851 (310), LII. *Return of steam vessels registered on or before 1 January 1851.*

Parl Papers 1852–1853 (1005), XCV. *Report of the Committee on contract packets.*

Parl Papers 1857 (Session 2) (57), XXXIX. *Return of steam vessels registered on or before 1 January 1857.*

Parl. Papers 1859 (Session 1) (104), XXV. *Portpatrick and Donaghadee Harbours.*
Parl Papers 1860 (123), LXII. *Portpatrick and Donaghadee Harbours, &c.*
Parl Papers 1860 (159), LXII. *Portpatrick Harbour.*
Parl Papers 1866 (166), LXVI. *Portpatrick and Donaghadee Harbours, &c.*
Parl Papers 1866 (263), LXVI. *Portpatrick Harbour.*
Parl Papers 1867–68 (356), LXIII. *Portpatrick and Donaghadee Harbours.*
Parl Papers 1884 (441), LXXI. *Portpatrick Harbour.*
Parl Papers 1895 (471), LXXX. *Larne and Stranraer mail service.*
Parl Papers 1903 (325), LXIII. *Report from the Harbour Authorities, &c., of the United Kingdom.*
Shipping Services to Ireland (The "House Report"), 1963.
The Reshaping of British Railways (The "Beeching Report"), 1963.
Annual Report of the Transport Users Consultative Commitee for Scotland for the year ended 31 December 1964. 1965.
Public Transport and Traffic (Cmnd. 3481), 1967.

COMPANY RECORDS, ETC.

British Transport Ship Management (Scotland) Limited—Annual Reports, Accounts and Returns.
*Caledonian Railway—Minutes, Joint and Other Arrangements File.
The Caledonian Steam Packet Company Limited—Annual Reports, Accounts and Returns.
Caledonian Steam Packet Company (Irish Services) Limited—Annual Reports, Accounts and Returns.
Carpass (Shipping) Company Limited—Annual Reports, Accounts and Returns.
European Ferries Limited—Annual Reports, Accounts and Returns.
*The Larne and Stranraer Steamboat Company Limited—Minutes, Cash Book and Share Register.
*Larne and Stranraer Steamship Joint Committee—Minutes.
*London Midland & Scottish Railway, Scottish Committee—Minutes.
*Portpatrick Railway—Minutes.
*Portpatrick & Caledonian Railways Joint Committee—Minutes.
*Portpatrick & Girvan Junction Railway Committee—Minutes.
*Portpatrick & Wigtownshire Joint Committee—Minutes, Officers' Minutes.
    *Records lodged with the Scottish Record Office (West Register House), Edinburgh.

MISCELLANEOUS

Glasgow Harbour Report Book (Glasgow City Archives).
Lloyd's Register of Shipping.
Mercantile Navy List.
Portpatrick Packet Station—Copy Letter Book, 1844–47 (County Library, Stranraer).
Records of the Clyde River Steamer Club, Glasgow.
Shipping Records of Larne Harbour Limited.
The Wotherspoon Collection (Mitchell Library, Glasgow).

Index

Figures in bold indicate references to illustrations

Ayr & Maybole Junction Railway   ...... 46.
Ayr Steam Shipping Co.   .... 75, 91, 95, 215.
Ayrshire & Galloway Railway   ...... 29.
Ayrshire & Wigtownshire Railway ...... 77, 87.

Babcock & Wilcox   .... 169.
Ballantrae – Belfast   .... 42.
Ballymena & Larne Railway ...... 77, 98.
Bangor – Ardrossan   .... 12, 122, 125.
       – Ayr .... 122, 126.
       – Belfast 61, 62
       – Peel .... 121, 122.
       – Portlogan   .... 9, 12, 13, 14, 121.
       – Portpatrick   .... 12, 122.
       – Stranraer   .... 120, 121, 125.
       – Workington   .... 12.
Bangor Harbour   .... 12, 13, 14.
Barclay Curle & Co.   .... 71, 73, 78.
Barclay, J. Norman   .... 69.
Barker, Samuel   .... 55, 57.
Barrow – Belfast   .... 76, 91, 99.
       – Isle of Man .... 99.
Barrow Steam Navigation Co.   ...... 64, 76, 91, 93, 99, 215.
Beath, R. M. .... 66, 205.
Beeching Report   .... 175.
Beeching, Richard   .... 175.
Belfast – Ardrossan 30, 39, 61, 74, 75, 82, 90, 91, 101, 111, 112,
                                            115, 117, 124, 125, 126, 139, 185, 186, 187, 196.
       – Ayr .... 40, 75, 91, 126.
       – Ballantrae   .... 42.
       – Bangor   .... 61, 62.
       – Barrow   .... 76, 91, 99.
       – Cairnryan   .... 25, 41, 137, 143, 217.
       – Fleetwood   .... 76, 91, 109, 161.
       – Girvan   .... 74, 160.
       – Glasgow 7, 17, 18, 19, 24, 32, 35, 74, 75, 90, 91, 112,
                                            115, 117, 124, 126, 177, 186.
       – Gourock   .... 82.
       – Greenock   .. .   . 18, 28, 30, 31, 72, 74, 75, 82, 87.
       – Heysham 99, 101, 113, 114, 115, 119, 120, 124, 127, 129,
                                            139, 140, 142, 144, 146, 147, 161, 162, 165,
                                            166, 173, 177, 184, 194.
       – Isle of Man .... 36.
       – Liverpool   .... 32, 36, 76, 91, 111, 115, 123, 126, 177, 186.
       – Londonderry   .... 61.
       – Port Carlisle .... 36.
       – Preston   .... 166, 177, 199, 212.
       – Stranraer 26, 31, 35, 36, 38, 39, 49, 50, 52, 53, 54, 55, 56,
                                            57, 59, 61, 62, 69, 70, 72, 146, 161, 162, 163,
                                            165, 166, 213; **13, 18.**
       – Whitehaven   .... 36.
       – Workington .... 12.
Belfast & Co. Down Railway 40, 41, 42, 48, 52, 53, 55, 58, 59, 60, 61, 62,
                                            121.
Belfast & Northern Counties Railway 46, 50, 51, 64, 65, 67, 77, 80, 81, 83, 84, 90, **97,**
                                            98, 99, 204, 205, 206, 207.
Belfast Harbour Commissioners   ...... 41, 123, 146.
Belfast, Holywood & Bangor Railway 55.
Belfast, Mersey & Manchester
    Steamship Co.   .... 132.
Belfast News-Letter   .... 8, 51, 91.

Fairfield Shipbuilding & Engineering
  Co. Ltd. .... 136, 226.
Fairlie – Campbeltown .... 64.
Farr, Grahame E. .... 63, 86.
Felixstowe – Antwerp .... 199, 212.
Ferguson, James M. .... 141, 148, 149, 155, 211; **66.**
Fishguard – Cork .... 179, 186.
      – Rosslare .... 145, 155, 183, 184, 185, 194.
      – Waterford .... 141.
Fishguard & Rosslare Railways &
  Harbours Co. Ltd. .... 174.
Fitzwilliam, William .... 9.
Fleetwood – Belfast .... 76, 91, 109, 161.
Fort William – Glasgow .... 33.
Frank Bustard & Sons Ltd. ...... 198.
Fraser, Trenholm & Co. .... 50.
Frederikshaven – Gothenburg ...... 192.
Freeling, Francis .... 26.
Freeling, George .... 19, 28.
Fullerton, William .... 5.

Galloway Advertiser & *Wigtownshire*
  Free Press .... 29, 36, 42, 46, 63, 113.
Galloway, Earl of .... 80, 204.
Galloway, Liverpool & Lancashire
  Steam Navigation Co. .... 37.
Galloway Steam Navigation Co. ...... 36.
G. & J. Burns 24, 30, 31, 32, 46, 68, 72, 75, 81, 82, 87, 90,
    101, 106, 111, 112, 115, 117, 122.
G. & J. Weir .... 66, 80, 205.
Garlies, Lord .... 60.
Garliestown – Douglas .... 94, 159, 160.
      – Liverpool .... 36, 37, 70, 94.
Gell, W. R. .... 84, 205.
General Steam Navigation Co. (Ltd.) 37, 70, 131, 132, 133, 136, 137, 215, 216.
George VI, King .... 123.
Giles, Francis .... 14.
Gillespie, James .... 35.
Girvan – Belfast .... 74, 160.
Girvan & Portpatrick Junction Railway 74, 76, 77, 78, 81, 87.
Girvan Steam Packet Co. .... 88.
Girvan Town Council .... 160.
Glasgow – Arran .... 26.
      – Arrochar .... 34.
      – Ayr .... 33.
      – Belfast 7, 17, 18, 19, 24, 32, 35, 74, 75, 90, 91, 112,
    115, 117, 124, 177, 186.
      – Campbeltown .... 26, 35, 88, 101, 102.
      – Dublin .... 17, 111, 126, 186.
      – Fort William .... 33.
      – Inveraray .... 17.
      – Islay .... 34, 60, 72, 86.
      – Isle of Man .... 17.
      – Larne .... 26, 75.
      – Liverpool .... 17, 35.
      – Londonderry .... 17, 35, 124, 186.
      – Manchester .... 91.
      – Newry .... 35.
      – Oban .... 26, 34.
      – Stranraer 17, 33, 34, 35, 36, 38, 49, 50, 53, 60, 70, 71,
    88, 96, 101, 102.
Glasgow & Belfast Union Railway ...... 29, 73, 74.

S

278   THE SHORT SEA ROUTE

Ships' Index

Figures in bold indicate references to illustrations